A Critical History
of
English Literature

VOLUME III

DAVID DAICHES

A Critical History
of
English Literature

SECOND EDITION

IN FOUR VOLUMES

VOLUME III

LONDON · SECKER & WARBURG

First published in England 1960 by
Martin Secker & Warburg Limited
54 Poland Street, London W1V 3DF

Reprinted 1960, 1961, 1963, 1968

Copyright © 1960 by
THE RONALD PRESS COMPANY

Second edition, revised with minor corrections, 1969

Reprinted 1971, 1972, 1975, 1979

New matter Copyright © 1969
by David Daiches

SBN 436 12110 7 (cloth)
436 12106 9 (paper)

Printed and bound in Great Britain by
Morrison & Gibb Ltd, London and Edinburgh

Contents

VOLUME III

A Critical History
of
English Literature

VOLUME III

CHAPTER FIFTEEN

The Restoration

THE PURITAN EXPERIMENT in government did not long survive
Cromwell's death in 1658; less than two years later—in May, 1660—
Charles II returned from exile amid popular acclamation. "The
shouting and joy expressed by all is past imagination," recorded the
diarist Samuel Pepys, and though, as one of those who went over to
Holland to escort the King back, he cannot be considered a wholly
impartial witness, there can be no doubt that a majority of the nation
was weary both of the rigors of Puritan rule and of the instability in
government that followed Cromwell's death. There remained, as
time was to show, a strong Puritan core in England, but for the moment monarchist sentiment was in the ascendant, and the Cavaliers
came back to enjoy an Indian summer until the bad judgment of
Charles' brother and successor, James II, alienated finally the great
Protestant heart of the country and so brought about the "Glorious
Revolution" of 1688 and the accession of a king and queen not by
divine right but on Parliament's terms. There was a strong tradition-
alist element in England which had never reconciled itself to the
execution of Charles I and to the various forms which Cromwell's
rule took, and this was true even of many who were on the Puritan
side in the conflict. The popular welcome given to Charles on his
return was largely due to the general belief that continuity and legality had now been re-established without loss of any of the real
gains for Protestant freedom and variety won in the fight against
royal absolutism and episcopal dictatorship in the 1640's. This view
proved to be unduly optimistic; if it had been well-founded, the revolution of 1688 would have been unnecessary.

The reaction against Puritan manners and morals was inevitable.
It was all the more violent because many of the returned Cavaliers
had spent their exile in France and become expert in French wit and
French gallantry, and because the King himself, an indolent sensual-
ist possessed of both wit and cunning, encouraged an atmosphere of

C.H.E.L. III.—B

hedonistic liveliness at Court. Charles set the tone for the Court
Wits, and the Court Wits set the tone if not for all the literature of
the period at least for a certain segment of it, notably dramatic
comedy. They were themselves often poets or dramatists. They
wrote, however, not as professional men of letters but as gentlemen
amateurs writing for their own amusement. John Wilmot, Earl of
Rochester (1647–80), a wit and a rake of the first rank, was a skilled
practitioner of the witty and polished verses, often erotic (and not
infrequently pornographic) and sometimes satiric, which represented
the courtly literary fashion of the time. Of the major Court Wits—
and they represented a definite group, who flourished from about
1665 to 1680—George Villiers, Duke of Buckingham; Charles Sack-
ville, Lord Buckhurst; Sir Charles Sedley; John Sheffield, Earl of
Mulgrave; Sir Carr Scrope; and Rochester himself, the most poetically gifted of the wits who were noblemen, were all amateur versifiers or poets and many were also patrons of humbler writers. Sir
George Etherege and William Wycherley, two of the most important
Restoration dramatists, were also members of the Court circle of wits
and wrote to amuse themselves.

The amoral wit and stylized hedonism which represented the
ideals (in both life and letters) professed by the Restoration wits had
no real roots in the larger and deeper patterns of life at the time.
The mood and tone which we think of as Restoration, and which is
reflected so brilliantly in the best Restoration comedy, was confined
to London, and in London only to courtly and fashionable circles.
There was no provincial culture in England which corresponded to
it. More than at any previous time in the history of English literature,
the most characteristic Restoration literature was metropolitan.
Nothing is more striking among the sentiments expressed by wits in
Restoration plays than the universal praise of London and detesta-
tion of the country. In Etherege's *The Man of Mode,* the supreme
test of Dorimant's love for Harriet is his willingness to follow her into
the country, even after Harriet has summed up all the disadvantages
of country living in a speech that epitomizes the attitude of these
writers to life outside London:

> To a great rambling lone house, that looks as it were not inhabited, the fam-
> ily's so small; there you'll find my mother, an old lame aunt, and my self, Sir,
> perched up on chairs at a distance in a large parlour; sitting moping like three
> or four melancholy birds in a spacious volery—does not this stagger your
> resolution?

In Restoration comedy generally, people from the country are consistently ridiculed for their uncouthness and lack of sophistication.

Husbands from the country could go so far as to resent their wives' amours with city gentlemen (as in Wycherley's *The Country Wife*)— a vulgar trait which showed no proper understanding of the Restoration attitude toward sex. That attitude is basic to the tone of Restoration high society, and it is most clearly revealed in the most characteristic literary product of that society—Restoration comedy. The influence of the returned King and his circle of Court Wits on the literature of the period is thus most strikingly and immediately apparent in the theater.

The Puritan government had stopped the performance of plays in September, 1642, and though there were occasional surreptitious performances at the various theaters after the passing of the ordinance of suppression, and though Sir William Davenant received permission to give some private dramatic performances (and perhaps also some more public performances) in the late 1650's, on the whole it can be said that the English theater did not exist between 1642 and 1660. With the restoration of King Charles came the restoration of the theater. But it was a different theater, playing to a different kind of audience, from that which had called forth the plays of Shakespeare. The modern theater, with its picture-frame stage, its actresses taking female parts, its moveable scenery designed to create a visual image of the locale of each scene, its artificial light, was developed during this period. This was partly because of the influence of France, where so many of Charles' hangers-on had spent their exile, and partly because the Restoration theater took over and developed the traditions of the *private* rather than the public Elizabethan and Jacobean theater, which had in some degree managed to survive the prohibition of public dramatic performances. The audience for Restoration drama was also more restricted both geographically and socially than it had been before the closing of the theaters. There was no dramatic activity of any consequence outside London, and the two theaters within the metropolis catered to wits and gallants who went to the play as much for the purpose of engaging in amorous intrigue or of displaying their own dress and manners as of seeing and enjoying a dramatic performance. The playhouse was regarded by the respectable citizens of London as a center of vice and exhibitionism, and they accordingly avoided it, while the dramatists in their turn took every opportunity of ridiculing the middle-class virtues and as often as not presented the citizenry as made up of foolish and jealous husbands whose wives were fair game for seduction by court gallants.

Restoration drama was thus a class drama to a degree that no earlier English drama—not even the "citizen comedy" of the Elizabethans—had been. It represented the stylization of a deliberately cultivated upper-class *ethos*. There is no need to maintain, with Charles Lamb, that the amoral world of Restoration comedy was a pure dream world with no relation to the life of the time. It had a very precise relation to the life of the time, being based on the attitude of the Court Wits of the 1660's. It would be truer to say that it was a wish-fulfilment world rather than a dream world, for a man like Etherege created in a character like Dorimant in *The Man of Mode* an ideal rake and wit of the kind that he and his friends would have liked to be in all their behavior. On the other hand, it was a class drama drawn from and appealing to a tiny minority of the public of the time. That it lasted beyond the Restoration period into the first decade of the eighteenth century, by which time the Court Wits and their ideal of social behavior had largely disappeared from the social scene, results from the fact that Restoration Comedy, though it arose out of the manners and ideals of a specific class, took on a life of its own after that class declined, preserving in a highly stylized art form what no longer existed in any appreciable degree in the life of the nation. The most perfect of Restoration comedies, Congreve's *The Way of the World,* was first produced in 1700, fifteen years after the death of Charles II.

The break with the Elizabethan and Jacobean theater was not as sharp or as complete as it has sometimes been taken to be. Although the Restoration developed the picture-frame stage that became standard throughout the following two-and-a-half centuries, Restoration theaters preserved a projection to the front of the proscenium onto which the actors and actresses could come to achieve a more intimate relationship with the audience than was possible in the later theater, a kind of relationship which was normal in the Elizabethan playhouse. And though elaborate scenic machinery was often introduced, giving visual localization to specific scenes, examples can still be found, as late as 1690, of the more fluid kind of moving from scene to scene that we associate with the Elizabethan stage. The Restoration theater was in fact a halfway house between the Elizabethan theater and that of the nineteenth or early twentieth century.

In terms of dramatic influence, the Elizabethan strain was much stronger. On Restoration comedy, Ben Jonson was the strongest influence, and though Jonson's comedy of humours was both more moral in tone and purpose and more cunningly worked out in patterns of imagery as well as in plot than the Restoration comedy of manners, the Restoration dramatists derived the basis of their comedy from Jonson's tone and manner. They refined, localized, aerated, and sometimes dandified his kind of comedy, but what they learned from him remained fundamental. There are anticipations of Restoration wit, of the typical Restoration wit-combat between the sexes and of the attack on marriage, scattered throughout Elizabethan and Jacobean comedy, and Professor Dobrée has quoted some interesting parallels between Massinger and Marston on the one hand and Congreve on the other. But these are less fundamental. Fletcher is a more clearly discernible influence; Beaumont and Fletcher remained highly popular on the Restoration stage, and influenced both tragedy and comedy in the period. It was Fletcher who began the process of aerating Jonson with a more flippant kind of wit and a less moral tone. The comedies of Molière were well known and often translated and adapted in the last forty years of the seventeenth century. But, though plots and situations in Molière had their influence and French wit and clarity were admired and imitated, the tone of Molière's plays remained essentially different from that of any Restoration dramatist. Restoration comedy was often more particularized in reference and more localized in topography than Molière's, and it lacked entirely Molière's handling of large moral issues and his underlying concern with such serious general questions as the relation between convention and morality. Restoration writers admired and imitated French wit and much in French life, but they had none of Molière's fundamental generosity of spirit. Though there was Spanish influence too—the plays of Calderon were well known and sometimes translated or adapted—and though the comic element in the Italian *commedia dell'arte* appears to have provided a note of farce in some later Restoration comedies, the heredity of Restoration comedy was essentially English.

The first accomplished practitioner of the Restoration comedy of manners was Sir George Etherege (1634/5–91), though other dramatists had produced plays exhibiting some characteristics of this kind of drama before Etherege's first play, *The Comical Revenge, or, Love in a Tub,* was performed in 1664. This combined a comic plot dealing with gallants, tricksters, fools, bullies, and ladies of varying degrees of wit and honesty with a "heroic" subplot presenting in rhymed couplets the convolutions of conflicting loves and loyalties in the breasts of fantastically high-minded protagonists. The combination is not successful, and the two worlds neither come together nor in any significant way comment on each other. Etherege was never a great plot-weaver, but at his best he manipulates the action through a variety of rapidly changing situations so as to provide occasion for the kind of wit-combats and studies in competitive sophistication that the age loved. His next play, *She Would if She Could,* performed in 1668, is a more consistently polished performance. The "two hon-

est gentlemen of the town," who represent male wit and sophistication in the play, speak a dynamic prose of remarkable poise and elegance, and the two young ladies with whom they are involved in the
usual Restoration battle between male lust and female prudence
have great vivacity and charm. There are also country knights, of
course ridiculed, a lustful wife who reverses the major action by pursuing a gallant with desperate cunning, and a variety of comic or
foolish characters. The plot is sufficient to bring the characters together in the kinds of situation where they reveal their dispositions
and their patterns of living in dialogue that never flags. It is all done
with a certain bright coldness, a lack of full implication in the life
depicted. But it is not heartless, still less brutal, and the conclusion
establishes a satisfactory *modus vivendi* between wit and virtue.

The Man of Mode, or, Sir Fopling Flutter, produced in 1676, is
Etherege's last and most brilliant comedy. The play is more purely
amoral than the two previous, and the treatment by Dorimant, the
hero, of his various women (except for Harriet, who is his match in
both wit and poise, and who can make her own terms) would be
brutal if related to any other world than one in which the relation
between the sexes was purely a matter of finding the best accommodation between lust and self-interest. The wit-combats between
Dorimant and Harriet develop a tradition which goes back at least
to Shakespeare's Beatrice and Benedick, adding that new note of
bargaining which serves to remove it in large measure (but never
quite wholly) from the life of real passion. It is this note of witty bargaining between two people of the opposite sex who are powerfully
attracted to each other physically but who want to retain as much
freedom of movement as they can for as long as possible—thus
achieving an adjustment both between desire and prudence and between surrender and freedom—that achieves its most consummate
expression in the dialogue between Millamant and Mirabell in Congreve's *The Way of the World*.

William Wycherley (1640–1716) produced his four comedies between 1671 and 1676; by far the most interesting of them are the
last two, *The Country Wife* and *The Plain Dealer*. These show a
very different spirit from that of Etherege, the easy courtier who was
part of the life he created in his plays. Though Wycherley was, for
a short period before his decline into debt and other misfortunes, a
Court Wit, it is clear from his plays that he never completely accepted the standards of the Restoration. There is a savagery in his
plays, a brutal insistence on the unscrupulous selfishness and obsessive animality of all men and women, on the cruel dishonesties implied in the ordinary courtesies of social life, that is worlds apart

from the amoral cheerfulness of Etherege or Congreve. The element of Jonsonian "humour" can be seen in Wycherley to a greater degree than in other writers of comedies in the Restoration period; such a character as the Widow Blackacre in *The Plain Dealer* is a caricature of the litigious amateur of law who is "gulled" in the end in a somewhat Jonsonian manner, and the moral feeling in that play is sometimes reminiscent of that in *Volpone*. But Jonson was satirizing deviations from a commonly accepted norm, whereas *The Plain Dealer* (which was probably written before *The Country Wife*, but revised before performance and, later, publication as the last of his plays) conveys a sense of general outrage before human nature and society as a whole. The play is a strange mixture of savage indignation and Restoration wit. The principal character is Manly, an honest misanthrope disgusted with the hypocrisies and dishonesties of ordinary social behavior who insists on speaking his mind (which means indulging in abuse) before all comers. He is obviously suggested by the Alceste of Molière's *Misanthrope,* but not only is he particularized as a sailor who "chose a Sea-life only to avoid the World," but his motives as well as the situations in which he becomes involved reveal no clear-cut issue between moral idealism and worldly compromise, as Molière's play does, but only a universal moral squalor which the hero rails at not in order to achieve improvement but out of a masochistic compulsion. The contrast between public pretension and private reality, in Etherege as in Congreve the source of so much delicate and witty maneuvering and bargaining to enable reputation to coexist with self-indulgence, is in *The Plain Dealer* the universal perfidy that underlies all human relationships. The following speech of Manly's sums up much of the play:

Not but I know that generally no man can be a great enemy but under the name of friend; and if you are a cuckold, it is your friend only that makes you so, for your enemy is not admitted to your house: if you are cheated in your fortune, 'tis your friend that does it, for your enemy is not made your trustee: if your honour or good name be injured, 'tis your friend that does it still, because your enemy is not believed against you. . . .

But the play contains more than exposures of the selfishness and lust underlying the surface of all social pretension. There are some witty satires of fops, coxcombs, and eccentrics, and there is, too, a suggestion of Fletcher in the character of Fidelia, who is in love with Manly and disguises herself as a boy to serve him. This oddly sentimental plot is only sketched in, though it provides the basis for some of the most important parts of the action. The real interest of the plot, however, lies in the relation between Manly and his ex-mistress Olivia, who is exposed with brutal exaggeration as cruel, lustful, and dishonest, deceiving equally her friends, her enemies, and her husband, yet in her public conversation maintaining an affected prudery that disgusts by its patent exaggeration.

The Country Wife is a more coherent and polished play, whose outward form at least is nearer to the general pattern of Restoration comedy. But, for all its wit and liveliness, there is a brutality beneath the surface which seems to indicate a tone of moral disgust almost Swiftian in its intensity. The main plot concerns the successful device of Mr. Horner to enable him to enjoy the favours of outwardly respectable and virtuous ladies with the consent of their husbands: he proclaims himself a eunuch, but convinces each of the ladies in turn of his real situation. The tensions between outward respectability and secret lustfulness and promiscuity are not here mere wit-combats, as they are in large measure in Etherege and Congreve; they reveal themselves in grim exposures of the selfishness and lust that lie behind professed virtue and honour. The play's name derives from another strand in the plot: Mr. Pinchwife has married a country girl and, bringing her to London, he tries, in his jealousy, to keep her from contact with the gallants of the town. But Mr. Horner manages to get Mrs. Pinchwife too and to win if not her love (for there is no love in the play) her physical desire. The jealous husband is of course ridiculed and gulled; cuckoldry is his deserved fate; but this does not make the behavior of his wife in any degree acceptable. Mrs. Pinchwife has neither wit nor principle; she begins by being a simpleton and ends by becoming a nasty animal. The play ends with Horner triumphant, husbands deluded or silenced, and lust and deception rampant. This is not the amoral comedy of Etherege; for all the wit and invention (as in the brilliant and well-known scene where the ladies compete for Mr. Horner's china, one of the most skillful, and nasty, pieces of *double entendre* in English literature), there is a strain of moral outrage running through the play.

Wycherley's prose is rapid and colloquial, but it has overtones of the extravagance of Jonson's *Volpone* or *The Alchemist,* as well as bouts of violence and exaggeration, that give it a note of its own. Strength and movement rather than polish are its characteristics, and there are elements of parody and of "humour" writing in all four plays.

John Dryden, who knew so well how to adapt himself to the varying modes of his time, produced comedies of manners too. His early comedies were modeled on the Spanish comedies of intrigue, sometimes with serious or melodramatic scenes in rhyming couplets in addition to Jonsonian humors and love-disputes and wit-combats. Spanish intrigue and heroics, Jonsonian humor, Fletcherian sentimentality. Restoration wit and immorality (and in Dryden it is immorality rather than amorality, because it does not spring from a native easiness of outlook but from a determination to be smutty if smut is in fashion)—it is a strange and hardly a successful dramatic mixture. *The Wild Gallant, The Rival Ladies, Secret Love,* and *Sir Martin Mar-all* (the last deriving from Molière's *L'etourdi*) all have some elements of the Restoration comedy of manners, but, though the latter two of these plays have some fine comic scenes, none has the unity of tone or the lightness of touch of the best of Etherege or Congreve. Dryden's most successful essay in the Restoration comedy of manners is his *Marriage à la Mode,* first produced in 1672. Here the main plot, presented in a deft and witty prose, explores with brilliant humor the implications of the Restoration attitude to sex, marriage, honor, virtue, and society, in a situation where *A*'s wife is *B*'s mistress and *B*'s fiancée is *A*'s mistress—although, by continuous cunning contrivance, everyone is left technically virtuous and the conclusion is an agreement on the part of all four to respect conventional morality because in the circumstances it is the most practical solution. The play is set in Sicily, because of the requirements of the otiose heroic action which is stuck onto (one can hardly say blended with) the comedy in rhetorical blank verse varied with some rhymed couplets. There is social satire as well as the true Restoration wit-combat in the comic plot, yet even here we have the feeling that the attitude of the Court Wits to love and marriage is achieved by hard work instead of springing effortlessly from the dramatist's view of life.

Dryden's career as a writer of comedies is a relatively unimportant part of his career as a poet and man of letters; his friend Congreve (1670–1729), as Dryden well knew, was the real master of this mode. In the verses "To My Dear Friend Mr. Congreve, on his Comedy call'd the Double Dealer," Dryden expressed his unbounded admiration for Congreve as a comic dramatist:

> Well then, the promised hour is come at last;
> The present age of wit obscures the past:
> Strong were our sires, and as they fought they writ,
> Conqu'ring with force of arms, and dint of wit;
> Theirs was the giant race, before the flood.
> And thus, when Charles returned, our empire stood.
> Like Janus he the stubborn soil manured,
> With rules of husbandry the rankness cured;
> Tamed us to manners, when the stage was rude,
> And boist'rous English wit with art indued.
> Our age was cultivated thus at length,

But what we gained in skill we lost in strength.
Our builders were with want of genius cursed;
The second temple was not like the first:
Till you, the best Vitruvius, come at length,
Our beauties equal, but excel our strength.
Firm Doric pillars found your solid base,
The fair Corinthian crowns the higher space:
Thus all below is strength, and all above is grace.
In easy dialogue is Fletcher's praise;
He moved the mind, but had not power to raise.
Great Jonson did by strength of judgment please,
Yet, doubling Fletcher's force, he wants his ease.
In diff'ring talents both adorned their age;
One for the study, t'other for the stage:
But both to Congreve justly shall submit,
One matched in judgment, both o'ermatched in wit.
In him all beauties of this age we see,
Etherege his courtship, Southerne's purity,
The satire, wit and strength of manly Wycherley. . . .

These verses are important as giving a clear picture of how Dryden's age looked at the literary achievement of Shakespeare and Fletcher in comparison with that of their own. They also show Dryden's critical soundness in picking out Congreve as the greatest writer of the species of comedy first developed in the early years of the Restoration.

Not all Congreve's comedies are, however, in the true Restoration mode. *The Old Bachelor,* first produced in 1693, combines farce, satire, and Jonsonian humors in an atmosphere that often seems as much Elizabethan as Restoration. The characteristic Restoration attitude to marriage is given a new dimension in the dilemma of Heartwell, the old bachelor, trapped by his lust into a supposed marriage, and Fondlewife, the jealous bourgeois husband of a young and modern wife. The prose dialogue is brisk and witty, and helps to provide a unity of tone that the plot, with its separate strands and levels, cannot give.

Love for Love, produced in 1695, is in many respects more reminiscent of the Jonsonian comedy of humors than the Restoration comedy of manners; the devices of an impoverished gallant to avoid his creditors and restore his fortunes as well as to win the love of his mistress, the war between the generations represented by the conflict between Valentine and his unloving father, type characters such as the bluff sailor, the credulous astrologer, the witty and resourceful servant, the awkward country girl, the boastful beau—all this suggests not only Jonson but at times also Plautus. The element of satire

in the play is not, however, truly Jonsonian: the exposure of sophisticated manners in the scene where Mr. Tattle teaches Prue, the country girl, the importance of saying one thing and doing another brings
into the open the contrast between public reputation and private
behavior which is implicit in so many of the Restoration wit-combats.
Love for Love is the most satirical of all Congreve's plays: in the
prologue Congreve deliberately stated his intention of lashing the
age:

> Since the Plain Dealer's scenes of manly rage,
> Not one has dared to lash this crying age.
> This time the poet owns the bold essay, . . .

The Way of the World, produced in 1700, was Congreve's last and
finest comedy. The plot contains many of the standard situations of
Restoration comedy—the witty pair of lovers, the amorous widow,
the would-be wit, the squire from the country (who is, however, less
mocked for his rusticity than admired for his openness and honesty),
intrigues and adulteries and all the usual tensions between desire and
reputation. But in the handling of this material, in the perfect balance and control of the prose dialogue and the levels of meaning
developed in individual scenes, Congreve develops a tone that is
radically different from that found in Etherege or Wycherley. The
tone is half amused, half sad. Amid all the perfection of the dialogue,
especially the brilliant bouts between the hero and the heroine, Mira-
bel and Millamant, there are overtones of a partly rueful, partly
compassionate awareness of the ambiguities and ironies of life, of
youth and age, of love and marriage, of vanity and affection. Thus,
though from one point of view *The Way of the World* represents the
fine flower of Restoration comedy, blooming a generation and more
after the society which first bred it had passed away or at least radically changed, if we look at the play more closely we see something
very different from either the hedonist ease of Etherege or the brutal
wit of Wycherley—a mellower and profounder comedy in which hero
and heroine, perfectly aware of each other's faults and willing to
keep up the usual social games in order to save them from the embarrassment of confrontation with each other's naked emotions, reveal in their mutual conversation something of the complexity and
sadness of all human relationships.

Sir John Vanbrugh's comedies (*The Relapse*, 1696, *The Provoked
Wife*, 1697, and the unfinished *Journey to London*) show the Restoration comic mode breaking down. Not only does he lack the wit and
poise of his contemporary Congreve, but his imagination does not
inhabit the world of amoral conflict between reputation and desire,

the world in which the conflict between the sexes is a witty game played for its own sake, which is the true world of Restoration comedy. *The Relapse* treats a husband's adultery as an act of sexual passion forced on him against his better judgment and against his genuine love for his wife. The real comedy of this play lies in the subplot, where a younger brother gulls his elder brother (an interesting character, both foppish and calculating) and carries off the heiress designed for the elder. *The Provoked Wife* has some strong scenes, especially those where Sir John and Lady Brute reveal their mutual antipathy, but this very strength is more Elizabethan than Restoration. Vanbrugh harks back in some respects to Elizabethan and Jacobean comedy and in others looks forward to the sentimental comedy of the eighteenth century. He did his best to write in the fashion, but he had neither the literary genius nor the required view of sex and society.

With George Farquhar (1678–1707) English comedy moves still further away from the Restoration ideal, though not always in the direction of the genteel, sentimental comedy that was coming into fashion. In some respects Farquhar, too, writes comedy like an Elizabethan, with a gaiety and relish for the humor and color of life very different from the witty stylization of Congreve's dialogue and action. There is irony, humor, and vitality in the dialogue at its best; Farquhar both mocks and enjoys human passions, follies, hypocrisies, and stratagems, but even his bitterest mockery (as in the few passages on the relation between reputation and money in *The Beaux' Stratagem*, 1707, his last and best play) has an air of enjoyment about it. Farquhar is perhaps the least literary of the writers of comedies of any significance between 1660 and 1707; a kind heart, a moral sense, a satirical wit, a love of vitality however it manifested itself, and a relish of the social scene—this unusual combination of qualities produced some inconsistencies and some oddities in his plays and prevented him from working out an art form as perfect as that achieved by Congreve; but it often enabled him to write with vigor and liveliness.

Restoration comedy thus begins with Etherege and reaches its consummation in Congreve. Jeremy Collier's *Short View of the Immorality and Profaneness of the English Stage*, which appeared in 1698, did not immediately kill this kind of comedy of manners, but it reflected an approach to both life and letters far different from the amoral attitude of the Restoration Court Wits which was the basis of the world of Restoration comedy. There were, of course, many other practitioners of the comedy of manners during the period, as well as writers who combined this genre with the comedy of intrigue, with farce, or with varying degrees of sentimentalism. Colley Cibber was already developing a more sentimental bourgeois comedy in the 1690's. (Vanbrugh's *The Relapse* was written as an ironic sequel to Cibber's *Love's Last Shift; or The Fool in Fashion*, 1696.) Among minor Restoration dramatists who employed the Restoration mode of comedy in greater or less degree might be mentioned Sir Charles Sedley, Thomas Shadwell, John Crowne, Thomas D'Urfey, and the irrepressible Mrs. Aphra Behn, some of whose plays combine the influence of Spanish comedy of intrigue with pure farce.

Restoration comedy reflects the ideal social world of the Court Wits of the reign of Charles II; its relation to the spirit of the age is thus easily discernible, even though the literary form, once established, developed a momentum of its own which carried it considerably beyond the limits of the age and the class that produced it. Restoration tragedy never achieved the literary perfection of the best Restoration comedy, nor is it related to the social life of the time in such a direct way. The heroic tragedy, often but by no means always written in rhymed couplets and almost always dealing in a high rhetorical manner with the conflict between love and honor or love and duty, is a characteristic phenomenon of the 1660's and 1670's. The world of high passion, of grandiose declamation, of valiant heroes and beautiful heroines torn between conflicting emotions, is as far removed as could be from the actual world of Restoration England. The heroic play demands heroic characters—not tragic heroes with fatal flaws, not confused idealists like Brutus or trapped sensibilities like Hamlet's, but daring and passionate lovers who do everything with an air and when they are trapped in the irreconcilable conflict between their passion as lovers and their honor as friends or subjects or rulers vent their agony in strong declamatory set speeches or highly stylized meditations on life and death before meeting their spectacular end. The writers of Restoration tragedy learned from Corneille to add admiration to the Aristotelian effects of pity and fear; their heroes were admirable as well as unfortunate, and they were as a rule admirable for two qualities, passion and valor. It is almost as though the heroic virtues, denied any place in the world of the Court Wits, found exaggerated expression in the drama to compensate for their exclusion from the real world. For this drama, like the comedy of the period, was an upper-class drama: the same witty gentlemen went to see Dryden's *Aureng-Zebe* as went to see Etherege's *Man of Mode*, produced the following year. Yet in Etherege's play the audience wanted to recognize themselves, in Dryden's to be thrilled by a world which every theatrical and rhetorical device helped to make utterly remote from their own.

The Restoration was an unheroic age, and perhaps that is why its conception of heroism was so artificial and inflated. Most of its heroic tragedies seem preposterous to the modern reader—and indeed sometimes, for all their popularity, seemed preposterous to contemporaries, as Buckingham's ridicule of the species in *The Rehearsal* (1671) so clearly shows. As far as the use of the rhymed couplet in drama goes, Davenant brought it first onto the stage, and its use was encouraged by the example of the French. The romantic plays of Beaumont and Fletcher suggested some of the themes and attitudes; the heroic world of Davenant's *Gondibert* (the preface to which has an interesting discussion and defense of the heroic poem) also contributed its influence. But the fact is that the concept of heroism in literature and the proper way of writing "heroic" plays and poems had for some time been exercising literary (and philosophical, for Hobbes contributed to the argument) minds in both England and France. The development of the heroic couplet provided a medium that could combine rhetoric with polish, precisely what was required in presenting heroes whose passions were both tremendous and conventional. There is for the most part little psychological subtlety in these plays; emotions are predictable; but the dramatist is always seeking for new and surprising ways of expressing them.

One of the most important critical documents on the heroic play is the *Essay on Heroic Plays* which Dryden wrote as a preface to *The Conquest of Granada*. Here he defends extravagance of action by asserting that "an heroic poet is not tied to a bare representation of what is true, or exceeding probable; but . . . he might let himself loose to visionary objects, and to the representation of such things, as depending not on sense, and therefore not to be comprehended by knowledge, may give him a freer scope for imagination." But miraculous action is not what differentiates Restoration from Jacobean tragedy. It is less extravagance of the events than the predictable extravagance of the sentiments that requires defense. And with this, Restoration dramatic criticism, with its interest in the dramatic "unities," in structure, in diction, and in the most proper verse form for drama, is little concerned.

Sir Robert Howard and Dryden himself first popularized the heroic tragedy, and Dryden was its most successful practitioner. George Cartwright, with his play *The Heroic Lovers*, published in 1661, pioneered the species, and Roger Boyle, Earl of Orrery, was another early heroic dramatist, who used English historical material and a conception of the dramatic moment derived from Corneille in his tragedies. But Dryden, who took up the heroic play quite deliberately because he saw it was proving popular, developed the species to its limit. Between *The Indian Queen*, acted in 1664, and *Cleomenes*

(1692) he produced a large number of heroic tragedies which for structural neatness and complexity (two qualities not easy to combine) and brilliance of rhetorical craftsmanship stand out among all the others of their kind. *The Indian Emperor,* acted in 1665, a spectacular and ingeniously wrought drama, is sometimes preposterous in both its passions and its situations; *Tyrannic Love, or, The Royal Martyr* (1669) is studded with high declamatory speeches which from now on are the hallmark of the heroic play; *The Conquest of Granada* (1670) and *Aureng-Zebe* (1675), though they too deal in what are by now the standard passions and conflicts, do so with such richness of plot and varied craftsmanship in verse style that the result, though oddly baroque in some respects, is impressive. Though there is much extravagant ranting in Dryden's heroic plays, and though his heroic situations often tremble on the brink of the absurd and sometimes fall over, the plays are put together with cunning, showing, it might perhaps be said, a first-rate craftsman working in a dubious mode. The lyrics which stud the plays have charm and variety.

Nathaniel Lee (ca. 1653–92) was the most successful writer of this kind of play after Dryden, but his plays show less artistic control and greater verbal violence. In Lee the Restoration heroic rant reaches a frenzied climax; sometimes he seems to be moving in a world of words merely, words which have no relation to any situation or any action. The passions of his heroes and heroines flare up on the slightest occasions and vent themselves in the most extraordinary whirling language. Though there are echoes of Jacobean dramatists, we are really far removed here from the Elizabethan or Jacobean attitude to poetic drama. Lee's swirling images are not intended to build up a picture of a human situation or to explore human consciousness; they exist in their own right, to represent passion in a general sense. The result is that this is a highly artificial kind of drama, with no real relation to life at all, and the more passionate the language the more aloof and unreal the characters and their behavior become.

No other writer of heroic tragedies—and they include such minor figures as John Crowne, Thomas Southerne (who wrote in blank verse and mingled the sentimental and the moral with the heroic), Elkanah Settle, Thomas D'Urfey—contributed any work of real litary significance. Otway's *Don Carlos, Prince of Spain* (1676) is a lively and craftsmanlike example of the species, but Otway's greatest success was in a somewhat different kind of tragedy.

There were other forces working in Restoration tragedy besides those already discussed. Elizabethan and Jacobean elements entered,

in various ways, into a number of Restoration tragedies and sometimes gave them a tone and feeling very unlike that of the characteristic heroic play. Dryden's *All for Love* (1677) is a rewriting of
Shakespeare's *Antony and Cleopatra* with the whole theme narrowed
down and concentrated on the conflict between love and honor. In
structure it is neatly contrived (preserving, as did so many Restoration tragedies, the unities of time and place) and the great poetic
reverberations of Shakespeare's highly charged blank verse are
exchanged for a rhetorical and sometimes sentimental blank verse
of considerable dramatic power but much less psychological subtlety
and poetic suggestiveness. *All for Love* shares with most heroic
plays the simplification of psychology in the interests of emotional
conflict, but Dryden described it as written in imitation of Shakespeare's style and it does have a Shakespearean dimension in spite
of the over-ingeniously devised crises and conflicts, the drastic simplification of the theme, and the forcing of all the characters into the
scheme provided by the basic conflict between Egypt (love) and
Rome (honor). It is without doubt Dryden's finest play and probably
the finest Restoration tragedy.

Elizabethan in another way are the later tragedies of Thomas
Otway (1652–85). *The Orphan* (1680) is pathetic rather than tragic;
the blank verse is decidedly Fletcherian, and there are also echoes
of Webster and others. But Otway's masterpiece is *Venice Preserved*
(1682), also written in blank verse. It is not a heroic tragedy, though
it has elements in common with that species of play. The conflict
between love and honor is here complicated both morally and
psychologically (and sometimes confused by contemporary political
allusions), and though there are traces of that overstylization of
emotion that we find in all Restoration tragedy, a note of true and
deep passion sounds in much of the dialogue in a way and to a
degree reminiscent of the greatest Elizabethan tragedies. The blank
verse is more rhetorical and less poetically complex than Shakespeare's, but more disciplined than Marlowe's, and wholly lacking
in the haunting poetic morbidities of Webster; it is dramatic verse,
and the passionate speeches never degenerate into the ranting monologues so dear to Restoration writers of tragedy. Though *Venice
Preserved* lacks the dimensions of Shakespearean drama, it is a
powerful and genuinely tragic work, well imagined, well expressed,
and well organized, one of the very few real tragedies of its age.

Congreve's *The Mourning Bride*, acted in 1697, has obvious echoes
of Ford and Webster and is written in a blank verse characterized
by both weight and flexibility. It is a curious sort of horror play, at
the same time heroic, sentimental, and sensational. The tragedies of

Nicholas Rowe (1674–1718) modulate heroic action to a more domestic plane, and the sentimentality that results is not the Fletcherian stylization of passion but that bourgeois sentimentality which is
based on generalized moral ideas rather than on indulged emotion.
In tuning down the heroic passions of Restoration tragedy to a lower
key Rowe was able to add nothing to compensate for the loss of
"admiration." The result is sometimes prettiness, sometimes pathos,
but rarely dramatic excitement and never true tragic feeling. Rowe's
importance—apart from his claim as the first editor of Shakespeare—
is historical: his plays mark the belated transition from Restoration
drama to the moral and sentimental drama of the Augustans.

The development of Restoration drama, especially comedy, illustrates very clearly the rise and decline of a deliberately induced
pseudo-courtly ideal in England, or at least in London. How far
removed it was from the true courtly ideal of the Elizabethans can
be seen at once by contrasting the knightly code of Spenser or
Sidney with the Restoration notion of the gallant. The Restoration
view was short-lived and it did not represent any really wide or deep
current in English life. Much more significant, though not so immediately and simply attributable to the restoration of Charles II,
was the new attitude to poetry which developed in the latter part
of the seventeenth century and which was to determine the course
of English poetry for over a hundred years. This attitude with its
emphasis on urbanity, decorum, elegance, and "sweetness of
numbers" does not represent a total revolution in English taste. There
was a classical element in Elizabethan literature and criticism, an
emphasis on order and control and fitness, which we find most
notably in Ben Jonson but also intermittently in much sixteenth-
and seventeenth-century writing. After the Restoration this current,
which hitherto had been a minor one in English literature (even if
we consider, as we should, that Milton was much influenced by it—
but he diverted it into his own channels), became swollen by other
streams to become for a long period a dominant strain in English
literary theory and practice. A major influence was that of France,
which by the middle of the seventeenth century had become a major
(if not *the* major) cultural influence in Europe. Returning Royalist
exiles brought back with them an admiration for everything French,
and French influence can be found in philosophy, literature, the theater, and the social behavior of the wits. In France the neoclassic tradition in criticism developed more fully and logically than it ever did
in England, and Rapin's *Réflexions sur la poétique* (1672) together
with Boileau's *L'Art Poétique* (1674) represented for English as well

as for French critics the culmination of generations of European critical thought. "Good sense," "reason," "nature," terms that were to be taken up again and again by English critics in the late seventeenth and in the eighteenth centuries, derive from these sources. Nevertheless, the trend of English literature after the Restoration was not toward a French neoclassicism; rather it was toward an ideal of elegance and wit—the wit being not metaphysical wit but the kind of wit defined by Addison in the sixty-second *Spectator:*

For Wit lying most in the Assemblage of Ideas, and putting those together with quickness and variety, wherein can be found any resemblance or congruity, thereby to make up pleasant pictures and agreeable visions in the fancy; Judgment, on the contrary, lies quite on the other side, in separating carefully one from another ideas wherein can be found the least difference, thereby to avoid being misled by similitude, and by affinity to take one thing for another. This is a way of proceeding quite contrary to metaphor and allusion; wherein, for the most part, lies that entertainment and pleasantry of wit which strikes so lively on the fancy, and is therefore so acceptable to all people.

The separation of wit and judgment, which had been made by Locke and accepted by Davenant and Dryden, provides an important clue to one significant difference between metaphysical poetry and the "new" poetry which came to the fore in the latter part of the seventeenth century. In Dryden's *Essay of Dramatic Poesie,* Eugenius claims that the older writers "can produce nothing so courtly writ, or which expresses so much the conversation of a gentleman, as Sir John Suckling; nothing so even, sweet, and flowing as Mr. Waller; nothing so majestic, so correct, as Sir John Denham; nothing so elevated, so copious, and full of spirit as Mr. Cowley; . . . " And all who participated in the dialogue "were thus far of Eugenius his opinion, that the sweetness of English verse was never understood or practised by our fathers." Beside this we might put Dryden's remark in his preface to *Annus Mirabilis:* "The composition of all poems is or ought to be of wit; and wit in the poet . . . is no other than the faculty of imagination in the writer; which, like a nimble spaniel, beats over and ranges through the field of memory, till it springs the quarry it hunted after: or, without metaphor, which searches over all the memory for the species or ideas of those things which it designs to represent."

Elegance and wit (in the sense Dryden gives to the word) thus become the criteria of good verse, and poets of the period congratulated each other on the "reform of our numbers" by such men as Sir John Denham (1615–69) and Edmund Waller (1606–87), neither of whom was in any sense a great poet but each of whom was influential in establishing the new poetic ideal. Waller, whose long life spanned four reigns and the period of the Commonwealth, shows clearly how the new style descended from Jonson through the Cavalier poets; the traditions of Jonsonian neatness and force, of Cavalier ease and grace, and of metaphysical passionate thought came together often in the mid-seventeenth century, though the last element became increasingly either fantastic or unduly mild or merely decorative. Waller's lines "On a Girdle" conclude:

> A narrow compass, and yet there
> Dwelt all that's good and all that's fair;
> Give me but what this riband bound
> Take all the rest the sun goes round!

Here the wit is very mild indeed, yet there is a faint echo of Donne's passionate ingenuity in love-compliment. Waller's best known poem, "Go, lovely rose," is in the best tradition of Cavalier song, while his poem "Of the Last Verses in the Book," written in the heroic couplet verse which is soon to become the dominant English verse form, illustrates the trend toward epigram in verse expression which was to culminate in Pope, as well as the modulation of metaphysical wit into something more in conformity with Dryden's and Addison's definitions:

> The soul's dark cottage, battered and decayed,
> Lets in new light through chinks that time has made;
> Stronger by weakness, wiser, men become
> As they draw near to their eternal home;
> Leaving the old, both worlds at once they view,
> That stand upon the threshold of the new.

Denham's most influential work is his descriptive poem, "Cooper's Hill," which Dryden called "an exact pattern of good writing." A discursive poem in heroic couplets, "Cooper's Hill" combines description of a landscape with historical and moral reflections and in doing so founded a species of descriptive poem which is found in Pope (in his "Windsor Forest") and which underwent various modifications (as in John Dyer's "Grongar Hill") throughout the eighteenth century to become eventually one of the ancestors of the poetry of natural description linked with meditation which culminates in Wordsworth's "Tintern Abbey." Dr. Johnson called the species founded by Denham "local poetry, of which the fundamental subject is some particular landscape, to be poetically described, with the addition of such embellishments as may be supplied by historical retrospection, or incidental meditation."

Both Dryden and Johnson agreed in singling out for praise in "Cooper's Hill" the following four lines:

> O could I flow like thee, and make thy stream
> My great example, as it is my theme!
> Though deep, yet clear, though gentle, yet not dull,
> Strong without rage, without o'erflowing full.

Johnson's comment makes clear the principles underlying praise of Denham from the Restoration until Johnson's own day: " . . . so much meaning is comprised in so few words; the particulars of resemblance are so perspicaciously collected, and every mode of excellence separated from its adjacent fault by so nice a line of limitation; the different parts of the sentence are so accurately adjusted; and the flow of the last couplet is so smooth and sweet; that the passage, however celebrated, has not been praised above its merit." Smoothness and sweetness, as opposed to ruggedness and violence, represented the ideals of the new poets of the Restoration and later, in matters of versification at least.

There were other influences at work on the literary language of the age besides the ambition to imitate ideal gentlemanly conversation. The Royal Society—in unofficial existence since 1645, more formally founded in 1660, and receiving its charter incorporating it as the Royal Society in 1662—had for its primary purpose the carrying out of practical scientific experiments; its various committees were concerned with mathematics, astronomy, optics, chemistry, agriculture, among other subjects, and it was concerned also with such matters as trade, geography, shipbuilding, architecture, hydraulics, and history. The Society's *Philosophical Transactions* first began to appear in 1665, with the object of making public the "undertakings, studies and labours of the ingenious in many considerable parts of the world." The Society demanded from its members "a close, naked, natural way of speaking; positive expressions, clear senses, a native easiness, bringing as near the mathematical plainness as they can, and preferring the language of artisans, countrymen and merchants before that of wits or scholars." This would seem a far cry from the "conversation of a gentleman" that Dryden hailed in the poetic diction of Suckling, yet in fact the demand for gentlemanly ease coming from the Court and the demand for clear and natural speech coming from the scientists often worked toward the same end—the raising of clarity above suggestiveness and the elimination from both poetry and prose of those allusive complexities which in different ways characterized both the poetry of the metaphysicals and the prose of the great pre-Restoration preachers and thinkers. Nobody could now discuss scientific or philosophic topics in the

style of Sir Thomas Browne, and Bishop Sprat's *History of the
Royal Society* (1667) both exemplified and recommended a plainer
prose style which is seen, in different ways, in Cowley's essays, in
the miscellaneous writings of George Savile, Marquis of Halifax
(1633–95), in the sermons of Archbishop Tillotson (1630–94), and in
Dryden's essays. Scientist, Cavalier, citizen, and professional writer
met in the Royal Society, in whose proceedings Charles II took an
interest and whose members included not only Robert Boyle and
Isaac Newton but also John Dryden, John Evelyn, and Samuel Pepys.
And the fact that its history was written by a bishop illustrates the
part the Anglican clergy were now playing in the intellectual life of
the country: the difference between the style of Jeremy Taylor and
Bishop Sprat, like that between the sermons of Lancelot Andrewes
and those of John Tillotson, is as significant as the difference in
content and attitude.

All this is symptomatic of an important change in the intellectual
climate of the seventeenth century. Religious and political extremism
had produced civil war followed by a Puritan Commonwealth which
was in turn followed by the Restoration and a swaggering Cavalier
reaction. But the real temper of the country, disciplined by Puritan-
ism, chastened by events, educated in the consequences of fanaticism, was sober, pragmatic, and anti-Utopian. The great empirical
philosopher John Locke (1632–1704) spoke, if not for his own generation, then for the generations immediately succeeding him. Though a
strong Puritan core remained in the country throughout the late
seventeenth and eighteenth centuries, more and more educated
people came to interpret Christianity in a vague and general way as
meaning that a First Cause had originally set the world going and
had arranged the machinery in such a manner as to make sure that
things turned out for the best. More and more, Newtonian physics
came to be accepted as the final "explanation" of the physical universe—proof that there was a divine order after all, but one to be
explained by the mathematician and physicist rather than inter-
preted through the mysteries of religion, for religion, to the Deist of
this age, was not mysterious, as the title of John Toland's book,
Christianity Not Mysterious (1696), clearly proclaimed. And more
and more the epistemology of Locke, with its basis in sensation, came
to be regarded as the most sensible account of the relation between
man's mind and the external world. The universe appeared to be
reasonable, and it was up to man to be so too. For Donne the new
philosophy had called all in doubt; for the gentleman of the late
seventeenth century and for some time afterward the newer philosophy brought assurance back again. This assurance may not have

gone very deep; the logical conclusions of the premises on which it rested led, as David Hume was to show, to skepticism; but it proved sufficient foundation for the English Augustan Age.

John Dryden (1631–1700) is the great poet of his age, who built on the "reform of our numbers" achieved by (or attributed to) Waller and Denham to perfect a poetic style, both eloquent and flexible, cogent and conversational, that is not only remarkable in itself but also one of the landmarks in the history of English poetry. To Dr. Johnson, looking back in the late 1700's, Dryden was the founder of the "new versification," and from his time "it is apparent that English poetry has had no tendency to relapse to its former savageness." "There was," Johnson remarked, ". . . before the time of Dryden no poetical diction, no system of words at once refined from the grossness of domestic use, and free from the harshness of terms appropriated to particular arts." Language neither vulgar nor technical was what the Restoration as well as the eighteenth-century poet looked for; the fact that Johnson praised Dryden in terms that Dryden would have understood and largely acquiesced in is itself evidence of the importance and influence of his poetry. Dryden did not, however, demonstrate from the beginning that ease and control in the handling of the heroic couplet that was to characterize so much of his best writing. His youthful poem on the death of Lord Hastings is both clumsy in versification and absurdly mannered in its handling of poetic conceits. His "Heroic Stanzas on the Death of Oliver Cromwell" (1659) is written in quatrains with alternating rhyme, a form of verse he got from Sir William Davenant's *Gondibert* (1651). Though it has some ringing lines, it is for the most part a strained and tedious poem. Always prone to support established authority, out of a genuine philosophical, almost Hobbesian, fear of disorder and of popular irresponsibility, Dryden welcomed the restoration of Charles II with "Astraea Redux," a poem in heroic couplets in which such poetic devices as similes and metaphors are shaken out over the verses as from a pepper pot. More interesting is his account of the "wonderful year," 1666, and its chief events, a four days' naval battle with the Dutch and the Great Fire of London. He called the poem *Annus Mirabilis;* it is an ambitious historical piece in 304 quatrains. "I have called my poem historical, not epic," he wrote in his introductory account of the work, "though both the actions and actors are as much heroic as any poem can contain. But since the action is not properly one, nor that accomplished in the last successes, I have judged it too bold a title for a few stanzas. . . ." The verse form, "stanzas of four in alternate rhyme," as Dryden described it, he considered "more noble and of greater dignity both for the sound and number than any other verse in use amongst us; . . . ." Davenant's *Gondibert*, a romantic epic (or epical romance) written in the same stanza, had precipitated much discussion of the nature and scope of heroic poetry and of the verse form most appropriate to it. But though the critics agreed on the pre-eminent place of heroic or epic poetry (this was the standard neoclassic position) and the poets kept paying lip service to the idea of the epic, no epic poetry of any interest or value was produced. The Restoration and Augustan periods of English culture were fundamentally unheroic; not the heroic but the mock-heroic was their chosen province. It was the neoclassic theory of "kinds," which put the epic at the top of the hierarchy of poetic kinds, that led so many poets of the late seventeenth and of the eighteenth century to sigh after the epic; their real genius was for a more intimate, social poetry, dealing knowingly with contemporary events and personalities. Hence they had to invent the mock-heroic in order to be able both to have their cake and eat it—to work within the neoclassic theory of kinds and yet to employ a tone and style appropriate to their situation and genius.

Though Dryden was eventually to emerge as England's great speaking voice in poetry, the master of verse argument, it took him time to discover where his true genius lay, and for long he strained toward a rhetorical "wit poetry" in which grandiloquence and ingenious conceits were conscientiously but far from organically employed. *Annus Mirabilis*, like so many of Dryden's earlier poems, shows this fault. In many of the quatrains the first two lines give the description and the last two add a simile to make the stanza more "poetic," e.g.,

> On high-raised decks the haughty Belgians ride,
>   Beneath whose shade our humble frigates go;
> Such port the elephant bears, and so defied
>   By the rhinoceros, her unequal foe.

> His fiery cannon did their passage guide,
>   And following smoke obscured them from the foe;
> Thus Israel, safe from the Egyptian's pride,
>   By flaming pillars and by clouds did go.

The appended comparisons show a somewhat mechanical determination to be poetic. When Dryden strove after "wit writing" he was liable to fall into absurdity or at least into frigidity. When he strove after high eloquence, as in so many of his heroic plays, he was often absurd, though sometimes impressively rhetorical. The paradox in which he was involved was one he shared with his age, which at the same time cultivated artificial heroics and demanded that poetry should reflect the ease and flexibility of a gentleman's conversation.

Later, Dryden found his proper kind of wit in his satirical verse; but in this earlier stage of his career he was at the mercy of any bright idea for garnishing his verses that ingenuity, imitation, or luck might suggest to him. Nevertheless, there is some vigorous writing in *Annus Mirabilis* and many stanzas have an impressive directness and cogency.

For some twenty years after the Restoration, Dryden's main output consisted of plays, together with panegyrics, prefaces, prologues, and epilogues. His plays have been discussed earlier; what is interesting to note here is his recantation of the "heroic" phase of his literary career which he put into the preface to *Troilus and Cressida* (1679): "To speak justly of this whole matter, 'tis neither height of thought that is discommended, nor pathetic vehemence, nor any nobleness of expression in its proper place; but 'tis a false measure of all these, something which is like them, and is not them; 'tis the Bristol stone, which appears like a diamond; 'tis an extravagant thought, instead of a sublime one; 'tis roaring madness, instead of vehemence; and a sound of words, instead of sense." This exposure of the style of the heroic play preceded (and one is tempted to think necessarily preceded) his turning to those great satirical narrative poems in which he first revealed his full stature as a poet.

Dryden first approached his true style as a panegyrist. He was a master of the verse compliment, and could combine suppleness with gravity in a way that complimentary verse requires. One can watch him polishing his skill in this form of verse. "To My Honoured Friend Sir Robert Howard, on his Excellent Poems," written in 1660, moves rather stiffly and the classical allusions sound somewhat forced, but "To My Honoured Friend Dr. Charleton," written a year or two later, has a new assurance; it shows that ability to *discuss* in verse that Dryden was to develop so remarkably:

> The longest tyranny that ever swayed
> Was that wherein our ancestors betrayed
> Their free-born reason to the Stagirite,
> And made his torch their universal light.
> So truth, while only one supplied the state,
> Grew scarce and dear, and yet sophisticate; . . .

This is the opening, and it shows the poem moving rapidly and easily into discussion. "To the Lady Castlemaine" (1663) shows his ability to use the couplet to strike out the ringing complimentary phrase:

> But those great actions others do by chance
> Are, like your beauty, your inheritance.

Dryden is here writing in a tradition of verse compliment that goes
back to Jonson in English poetry. In addressing particular people
on particular occasions he was peculiarly at home. Dr. Johnson
remarked that "in an occasional performance no height of excellence
can be expected from any mind, however fertile in itself, and however stored with acquisitions" and went on to complain that "the
occasional poet is circumscribed by the narrowness of his subject."
This is an interesting revelation of the gap between Johnson's and
Dryden's mind—indeed, the gap between their ages (for all the
similarities). In fact, Dryden's occasional poetry is among his very
best; he had the ability to lend the occasion dignity without losing
intimacy. Much of his complimentary verse is occasional, in the
sense that it was addressed to a friend on a specific occasion. One
of his last poems of this kind is one of his best, "To my Dear
Friend Mr. Congreve, on his Comedy Called the Double Dealer,"
which is quoted on page 545. The controlled Horatian assurance of
"To My Honoured Kinsman, John Driden," written in 1699, the
year before his death, shows that he was improving in his handling
of this kind of verse to the last. One must read all of its 209 lines
and receive the cumulative impact of the flexible yet carefully woven
verse to recognize its true quality, but the conclusion may give some
idea of the way in which Dryden can work up to a quiet climax:

> O true descendant of a patriot line,
> Who, while thou sharest their lustre, lendst them thine,
> Vouchsafe this picture of thy soul to see;
> 'Tis so far good as it resembles thee.
> The beauties to the original I owe,
> Which when I miss, my own defects I show.
> Nor think the kindred Muses thy disgrace;
> A poet is not born in every race.
> Two of a house few ages can afford,
> One to perform, another to record.
> Praiseworthy actions are by thee embraced;
> And 'tis my praise to make thy praises last.
> For even when death dissolves our human frame,
> The soul returns to Heaven from whence it came,
> Earth keeps the body, verse preserves the fame.

Dryden's elegies are less numerous than his poems of compliment
to the living, but among them is one of his finest occasional pieces,
the poem "To the Memory of Mr. Oldham." Here for once Dryden
almost transcends the necessary limits of his kind of good verse to
achieve a note of sadness, of *desiderium*, that is more often associated with the Victorian poets, yet the control, the dignity, the

adroit use of classical illusion, the total direction of the poem toward its subject rather than inward in self-pity toward the grieving poet, remove it far from the Victorian elegiac mode. John Oldham died at the age of twenty-nine, and the poem is a lament for an untimely death:

> Farewell, too little and too lately known,
> Whom I began to think and call my own:
> For sure our souls were near allied, and thine
> Cast in the same poetic mould with mine.
> One common note on either lyre did strike,
> And knaves and fools we both abhorred alike.
> To the same goal did both our studies drive:
> The last set out the soonest did arrive.
> Thus Nisus fell upon the slippery place,
> Whilst his young friend performed and won the race.
> O early ripe! to thy abundant store
> What could advancing age have added more?
> It might (what nature never gives the young)
> Have taught the numbers of thy native tongue.
> But satire needs not those, and wit will shine
> Through the harsh cadence of a rugged line.
> A noble error, and but seldom made,
> When poets are by too much force betrayed.
> Thy generous fruits, though gathered ere their prime,
> Still showed a quickness; and maturing time
> But mellows what we write to the dull sweets of rhyme.
> Once more, hail and farewell; farewell, thou young,
> But ah too short, Marcellus of our tongue!
> Thy brows with ivy, and with laurels bound;
> But fate and gloomy night encompass thee around.

Dryden had a tendency to overwork the alexandrine, used as a third rhyming line, but here the two alexandrines are used to slow down and swell out the verse with great effectiveness.

It was in his prologues and epilogues to plays that Dryden first achieved that combination of familiarity and dignity that distinguishes so much of his best verse. This was the kind of occasional poetry which he found peculiarly congenial, and he used the couplet here with complete assurance. He could be ironical, critical, apologetic, humorous, indecent, or topical in a variety of ways, and he chose the most suitable actor or actress to speak each type. These verses show Dryden operating in the midst of a society which he knew, and the tone of social knowingness which is characteristic of this phase of his writing now becomes important in English poetry for the first time and remains so well into the eighteenth century.

Dryden's greatest achievement was his satirical and argumentative verse. *Absalom and Achitophel* (Part I, 1681) was a contribution to debate on public affairs in the form of verse satire. Dryden had been Poet Laureate and Historiographer Royal since 1670, but even apart from the fact that he had an official position his reason and instincts were all on the side of legitimism and settled government, so that the Whig agitation to exclude from succession to the throne Charles II's heir and brother James on the grounds that he was a Roman Catholic and to encourage Charles's illegitimate son the Duke of Monmouth to assert his claims found Dryden on the Tory side, supporting legality and the true succession. Protestant Whig agitation in favor of the exclusion of James, Duke of York, from the succession was led by the Earl of Shaftesbury and the Duke of Buckingham (the latter of whom had in 1671, in his mocking play *The Rehearsal*, ridiculed the extravagances of heroic drama and satirized Dryden as "Mr. Bayes"). Dryden took the biblical story of the rebellion of Absalom against his father King David (2 Samuel, 15–18) and applied it to the contemporary situation, with Charles as King David, Shaftesbury as Achitophel (Absalom's chief adviser until in the end his advice was rejected and he hanged himself), Monmouth as Absalom, and Buckingham as Zimri (a name Dryden took from 1 Kings, 16, where Zimri figures as the slayer of King Elah of Israel and a man who "did evil in the sight of the Lord" and "made Israel to sin"). There is a certain ironic humor in the parallels themselves, and the development of the story in biblical terms but with a strict eye on contemporary events and characters in England gave Dryden abundant scope for the exercise of his gift for innuendo and suggestion, which was not confined to attacks on his enemies. The very comparison of Charles with King David allows some sly digs at the Merry Monarch's life. The poem opens:

> In pious times, ere priestcraft did begin,
> Before polygamy was made a sin,
> When man on many multiplied his kind,
> Ere one to one was cursedly confined,
> When nature prompted and no law denied
> Promiscuous use of concubine and bride,
> Then Israel's monarch after Heaven's own heart
> His vigorous warmth did variously impart
> To wives and slaves, and, wide as his command,
> Scattered his Maker's image through the land.

From the first lines one can see the poet relishing the exercise of his powers. The satire is not a savage black-and-white affair; the tone is more often amused than outraged, and if the villains are on the side of evil they nevertheless have interesting and even admirable qualities as men. Consider the famous portrait of Shaftesbury as Achitophel:

> Of these the false Achitophel was first,
> A name to all succeeding ages curst:
> For close designs and crooked counsels fit,
> Sagacious, bold, and turbulent of wit,
> Restless, unfixed in principles and place,
> In power unpleased, impatient of disgrace;
> A fiery soul, which working out its way,
> Fretted the pigmy body to decay
> And o'er informed the tenement of clay.
> A daring pilot in extremity,
> Pleased with the danger, when the waves went high
> He sought the storms; but, for a calm unfit,
> Would steer too nigh the sands to boast his wit.
> Great wits are sure to madness near allied
> And thin partitions do their bounds divide;
> Else, why should he, with wealth and honour blest,
> Refuse his age the needful hours of rest?
> Punish a body which he could not please,
> Bankrupt of life, yet prodigal of ease?
> And all to leave what with his toil he won
> To that unfeathered two-legged thing, a son,
> Got, while his soul did huddled notions try,
> And born a shapeless lump, like anarchy.
> In friendship false, implacable in hate,
> Resolved to ruin or to rule the state;
> To compass this the triple bond he broke,
> The pillars of the public safety shook,
> And fitted Israel for a foreign yoke;
> Then, seized with fear, yet still affecting fame,
> Usurped a patriot's all-atoning name.
> So easy still it proves in factious times
> With public zeal to cancel private crimes.

It is a picture of a complex and tortured character, and though the attack on Shaftesbury's son is a needless piece of cruelty, on the whole the impression is one of twisted brilliance, of genius gone wrong, of *corruptio optimi*, rather than of simple evil or of little nastiness. The verse is admirably controlled; after a line or two of balanced phrases, Dryden will ram the point home or sum it up in a line which runs straight on without a pause:

Resolved to ruin or to rule the state.

With public zeal to cancel private crimes.

The antithesis in these lines is emphasized through the lack of pause.
Dryden rounded out his picture of Shaftesbury by adding in the
second edition of the poem praise of his capacity as a judge:

Yet fame deserved no enemy can grudge;
The statesman we abhor, but praise the judge.
In Israel's courts ne'er sat an Abbethdin
With more discerning eyes or hands more clean,
Unbribed, unsought, the wretched to redress,
Swift of despatch and easy of access.
Oh! had he been content to serve the crown
With virtues only proper to the gown,
Or had the rankness of the soil been freed,
From cockle that oppressed the noble seed,
David for him his tuneful harp had strung
And Heaven had wanted one immortal song.

This is almost in the vein of Dryden's panegyrics, yet the rising emotion in the line "Oh! had he been content . . ." gives a sense of
virtue wasted and distorted which is an essential part of the total
picture. Another feature of Dryden's set portraits in this poem is his
occasional deliberate expansion of the context from the particular to
the general. "That unfeathered two-legged thing, a son," is as much
a comment on the vanity of human desires to found a family as it is
an attack on Shaftesbury's son, and the lines

So easy still it proves in factious times
With public zeal to cancel private crimes

suddenly relate Shaftesbury's crimes to a basic fact about the relation between public and private morality.

There is a touch of Milton's Satan in Achitophel, and when Dryden
puts into his mouth a brilliantly plausible speech in which he persuades Absalom to rebellion we are reminded of the temptation of
Eve. Yet there are significant differences. Dryden's persuasive verse
moves from point to point with sharp, arresting remarks—

How long wilt thou the general joy detain,
Starve and defraud the people of thy reign?

And nobler is a limited command,
Giv'n by the love of all your native land,
Than a successive title, long and dark,
Drawn from the mouldy rolls of Noah's ark.

The rhetoric of Milton's Satan is more richly woven and more variously cadenced; in Dryden's verse the couplet plays an important part in carrying the rhetorical force of the argument, and the rhymes can convey anything from exaltation to contempt: consider the rhyming of "detain" and "reign" in the first quotation given above and the contemptuous matching of "long and dark" with "the mouldy rolls of Noah's ark."

Dryden's portrait of the Duke of Buckingham as Zimri (his belated reply to Buckingham's portrait of himself as Mr. Bayes in *The Rehearsal*) is much briefer than that of Shaftesbury, but no less complex and balanced:

> In the first rank of these did Zimri stand,
> A man so various that he seemed to be
> Not one, but all mankind's epitome:
> Stiff in opinions, always in the wrong,
> Was everything by starts and nothing long;
> But in the course of one revolving moon
> Was chymist, fiddler, statesman, and buffoon; . . .

The description of Monmouth (as Absalom) courting the people is done with a characteristic mixture of admiration for the virtuosity displayed and contempt for the actual deed; the contempt is displayed in the rhymes and in the run of the verse: there is nothing in the words themselves to indicate it:

> Surrounded thus with friends of every sort
> Deluded Absalom forsakes the court;
> Impatient of high hopes, urged with renown,
> And fired with near possession of a crown.
> The admiring crowd are dazzled with surprise
> And on his goodly person feed their eyes.
> His joy concealed, he sets himself to show,
> On each side bowing popularly low,
> His looks, his gestures, and his words he frames
> And with familiar ease repeats their names.
> Thus formed by nature, furnished out with arts,
> He glides unfelt into their secret hearts.
> Then, with a kind compassionating look,
> And sighs, bespeaking pity ere he spoke,
> Few words he said, but easy those and fit,
> More slow than Hybla-drops and far more sweet.

The arguments on both sides are presented with equal cogency, and one gets some real insight into the nature of the political debate that was going on in the late 1670's and early 1680's from this poem.

Dryden's genius for verse argument led him to give each side the full benefit of his expression. It is, indeed, in the balance between his own portraits of the different characters and the characters' speeches that the true substance of the poem lies. The narrative is rudimentary; it is the speeches and the portraits, both standing out in their own right and reacting on each other, that make the poem.

Absalom and Achitophel appeared about a week before Shaftesbury was tried on a charge of high treason, and it caused tremendous excitement. Shaftesbury was acquitted, and to celebrate the victory the Whigs struck a medal. This gave Dryden another opportunity, and in 1682 he published *The Medal*, a more single-minded and more savage attack on Shaftesbury, where the couplets lash and sting:

> Bartering his venal wit for sums of gold,
> He cast himself into the saint-like mould;
> Groaned, sighed, and prayed, while godliness was gain,
> The loudest bag-pipe of the squeaking train.
> But, as 'tis hard to cheat a juggler's eyes,
> His open lewdness he could ne'er disguise.
>
> But thou, the pander of the people's hearts,
> (O crooked soul and serpentine in arts!)
> Whose blandishments a loyal land have whored,
> And broke the bonds she plighted to her lord,
> What curses on thy blasted name will fall,
> Which age to age their legacy shall call,
> For all must curse the woes that must descend on all!
> Religion thou hast none: thy mercury
> Has passed through every sect, or theirs through thee.
> But what thou givest, that venom still remains,
> And the poxed nation feels thee in their brains.

This is savage stuff, but it is skillfully done.

The Medal was answered by Thomas Shadwell's *Medal of John Bayes,* a coarse and brutal work beside which Dryden's attack on Shaftesbury was politeness itself, and Dryden took his revenge on Shadwell in the finest of his shorter satirical poems, *Mac Flecknoe* (1682). Dryden did not reply in kind; *Mac Flecknoe* is a genial poem, in which Shadwell is treated with humorous contempt. Indeed, it is this combination of geniality with witty contempt that gives the poem its special flavor. Richard Flecknoe was an Irish priest who mistakenly considered himself a poet. Andrew Marvell had visited Flecknoe in Rome and written a mocking poem about him, "Flecknoe, an English Priest at Rome." Flecknoe was dead by the time Dryden wrote his poem, but his name remained as a symbol of bad poetry. The theme of *Mac Flecknoe* is the choice of Shadwell by Flecknoe as his heir (Mac Flecknoe, i.e., son of Flecknoe) and successor to the kingdom of nonsense and dullness in prose and verse. Flecknoe's announcement of Shadwell's pre-eminent fitness to succeed to the throne of the empire of dullness and "all the realms of Nonsense" well illustrates the tone of laughing abuse which dominates the poem:

> . . . Cried: " 'Tis resolved; for Nature pleads, that he
> Should only rule, who most resembles me.
> Shadwell alone my perfect image bears,
> Mature in dullness from his tender years:
> Shadwell alone of all my sons is he
> Who stands confirmed in full stupidity.
> The rest to some faint meaning make pretense,
> But Shadwell never deviates into sense.
> Some beams of wit on other souls may fall,
> Strike thro', and make a lucid interval;
> But Shadwell's genuine night admits no ray,
> His rising fogs prevail upon the day. . . ."

The humorous shock of such lines as "Who stand confirmed in full stupidity," "But Shadwell never deviates into sense," where the form of a compliment is found unexpectedly to bear the content of an insult, represents one of the most successful devices employed in the poem. It is a device which depends on the heroic couplet and could not have been developed without it.

Part II of *Absalom and Achitophel,* of which Dryden only wrote 200 of the 1140 lines (the bulk being by Nahum Tate) is less interesting than Part I and on the whole more simply abusive. Shadwell reappears here as Og, and is portrayed by Dryden with calculated disgust:

> Now stop your noses, readers, all and some,
> For here's a tun of midnight work to come,
> Og from a treason-tavern rolling home.
> Round as a globe, and liquored every chink,
> Goodly and great he sails behind his link. . . .
> The midwife laid her hand on his thick skull,
> With this prophetic blessing—*Be thou dull;*
> Drink, swear, and roar, forbear no lewd delight
> Fit for thy bulk, do anything but write.

The third and fourth of these lines show a certain cunning in associating grossness and treason (the combination "treason-tavern," though simple enough, is in context very effective), but the whole tone is coarser than that of the first part of *Absalom and Achitophel* and of *Mac Flecknoe*. Further on, Dryden has some good fun with Shadwell's double crimes of treason and dullness:

> To die for faction is a common evil,
> But to be hanged for nonsense is the devil.
> Hadst thou the glories of thy King exprest,
> Thy praises had been satires at the best;
> But thou in clumsy verse, unlicked, unpointed,
> Hast shamefully defied the Lord's annointed:
> I will not rake the dunghill of thy crimes,
> For who would read thy life that reads thy rhymes?
> But of King David's foes be this the doom,
> May all be like the young man Absalom;
> And for my foes may this their blessing be,
> To talk like Doeg and to write like thee.

Doeg is Elkanah Settle, another bad poet and playwright who feuded with Dryden. There is a rollicking note in Dryden's treatment of Doeg and Og; they are presented as figures of comical grossness, objects of mirth and amazement as well as of contempt, but never of hate.

Dryden's satirical character sketches in *Absalom and Achitophel* and elsewhere owed much to the Theophrastian tradition of character writing, which, as it developed throughout the seventeenth century, grew ever more interested in particular cases as distinct from general types. His own view of what he was doing was expressed in "A Discourse concerning the Original and Progress of Satire" which he prefaced to his verse translation of Juvenal in 1693. "How easy is it to call rogue and villain, and that wittily! But how hard to make a man appear a fool, a blockhead, or a knave, without using any of those opprobrious terms! . . . there is still a vast difference betwixt the slovenly butchering of a man, and the fineness of a stroke that separates the head from the body, and leaves it standing in its place. . . . The character of Zimri in my *Absalom* is, in my opinion, worth the whole poem: it is not bloody, but it is ridiculous enough: and he for whom it was intended was too witty to resent it as an injury. If I had railed, I might have suffered for it justly: but I managed my own work more happily, perhaps more dexterously. I avoided the mention of great crimes, and applied myself to the representing of blind sides and little extravagances; to which the wittier a man is, he is generally the more obnoxious. It succeeded as I wished; the jest went round, and he was laughed at in his turn, who began the frolic."

With *Religio Laici*, published late in 1682, Dryden established himself as the master of verse argument. This poem of 456 lines in heroic couplets is a discourse on religion, in which the fallibility of human reason, the necessity of a revealed religion, the uncertainty of tradition, and the advisability of staying within the Church of England are discussed in adroitly modulated couplets. Dryden's position here, as so often, was to embrace faith through skepticism of knowing certainty by any other way. "We have indeed," he wrote toward the end of his life, "the highest probabilities for our revealed religion; arguments which will preponderate with a reasonable man, upon a long and careful disquisition; but I have always been of opinion, that we can demonstrate nothing, because the subject-matter is not capable of demonstration. It is the particular grace of God that any man believes the mysteries of our faith; which I think a conclusive argument against the doctrine of persecution in any Church." *Religio Laici* opens with a statement of the inadequacy of reason, expressed in couplets as effectively varied in movement as Dryden ever wrote:

> Dim as the borrowed beams of moon and stars
> To lonely, weary, wandering travellers
> Is Reason to the soul: and as on high
> Those rolling fires discover but the sky,
> Not light us here, so Reason's glimmering ray
> Was lent, not to assure our doubtful way,
> But guide us upward to a better day.

How skillfully Dryden suggests the give and take of argument between reasonable people is illustrated by this characteristic passage:

> Oh but, says one, Tradition set aside,
> Where can we hope for an unerring guide?
> For since the original Scripture has been lost,
> All copies disagreeing, maimed the most,
> Or Christian faith can have no certain ground
> Or truth in Church tradition must be found.
>
> Such an omniscient Church we wish indeed;
> 'Twere worth both Testaments, and cast in the Creed;
> But if this mother be a guide so sure
> As can all doubts resolve, all truth secure,
> Then her infallibility as well
> Where copies are corrupt or lame can tell;
> Restore lost canon with as little pains,
> As truly explicate what still remains;
> Which yet no Council dare pretend to do,
> Unless, like Esdras, they could write it new;
> Strange confidence, still to interpret true,

Yet not be sure that all they have explained
Is in the blest original contained.
More safe and much more modest 'tis to say,
God would not leave mankind without a way: . . .

The argument is neither profound nor wholly logical, but its tone
is one of sweet reasonableness and the accents of conversation are
conveyed with the formal neatness of the rhymed couplet. We do
not feel that here is a man who has labored to put a prose argument
into verse, but rather that here is a man who most readily gives form
to his ideas by submitting them to the discipline of verse. The limits
of Dryden's logic are from skepticism to authority—the former leads
to a search for the latter. It is not therefore surprising that Dryden
joined the Church of Rome in 1686. But for the moment he was content to bow to the authority of the Church of England:

And after hearing what our Church can say,
If still our reason runs another way,
That private reason 'tis more just to curb
Than by disputes the public peace disturb.
For points obscure are of small use to learn:
But common quiet is mankind's concern.

Dryden's conversion to Roman Catholicism has often been regarded as mere self-interest, since James II, a Catholic king, had
ascended the throne on the death of Charles II in 1685. But in fact
his combination of distrust of reason and desire for ecclesiastical authority and order would in any case have led him in this direction.
Further, Dryden reaped no personal advantage from his conversion,
and when, in 1688, James was repudiated by the people and William
of Orange and his wife Mary (James' daughter) brought in to restore
the Protestant succession and guarantee it in future, Dryden had
to give up his position as Poet Laureate and as Historiographer Royal;
he stuck to his new religion in a period of strong anti-Catholic feeling, and spent the last eleven years of his life in relative poverty. Yet
Dryden was always anticlerical, and his temperament was not truly
religious: it was his basic skepticism that led him to religion.

Dryden's second poem of religious discussion, written to defend
the Roman Catholic position, is more argumentative than *Religio
Laici*. *The Hind and the Panther* (1687) was a contribution to a
debate that was raging throughout the nation. "The nation is in too
high a ferment for me to expect either fair war or even so much as
fair quarter from a reader of the opposite party," wrote Dryden at the
beginning of his prefatory address to the reader. Yet Dryden's tone
remains quietly reasonable, in spite of a few violent passages. The

poem is in the somewhat unexpected form of a beast fable, the hind
being the Roman Catholic Church, and the panther, the best of the
beasts of prey, the Church of England. Other religions and sects are
represented by other animals, e.g., the Bear represents the Independ-
ents, the Wolf the Presbyterians, the Hare the Quakers, the Ape the
Freethinkers. Though Dryden expends considerable ingenuity in
translating the religious situation into animal terms, fable soon gives
way to argument. Part I is largely a statement of Dryden's own present position as a Catholic in the midst of disruptive sectaries:

> What weight of ancient witness can prevail,
> If private reason hold the public scale?
> But, gracious God, how well dost thou provide
> For erring judgments an unerring guide!

After developing a number of arguments in favor of submitting
imperfect reason to faith, he concludes:

> Rest then, my soul, from endless anguish freed:
> Nor sciences thy guide, nor sense thy creed.
> Faith is the best insurer of thy bliss;
> The bank above must fail before the venture miss.

(The alexandrine here, with its commercial image, sounds an odd
note, but one not uncharacteristic of Dryden's religious discourse.)
He goes on to attack "the insatiate Wolf" (the Presbyterians) and
other wild beasts who are laying Britain waste. He then comes to
the Panther:

> The Panther, sure the noblest next the Hind,
> And fairest creature of the spotted kind;
> Oh, could her inborn stains be washed away,
> She were too good to be a beast of prey!

A lengthy discussion of the imperfections and disadvantages of the
Anglican position follows. The first part concludes with the Panther
walking pensively in the forest at evening, while the Hind, recently
encouraged by the Lion (King James II), comes out of hiding and
is fawned on by the other animals. There follows a conversation
between the Hind and the Panther, which occupies Book II. The
tone in which Dryden tells, at the close of Book I, of the preliminary
conversation between the two animals reveals the ease with which
he could move half-humorous verse with strong colloquial overtones
to more serious matters:

> For when the herd sufficed did late repair
> To ferny heaths and to their forest lair
> She made a mannerly excuse to stay,

Proff'ring the Hind to wait her half the way;
That, since the sky was clear, an hour of talk,
Might help her to beguile the tedious walk.
With much good-will the motion was embraced,
To chat awhile on their adventures passed;
Nor had the grateful Hind so soon forgot
Her friend and fellow-sufferer in the Plot.
Yet wondering how of late she grew estranged,
Her forehead clouded and her count'nance changed,
She thought this hour th' occasion would present
To learn her secret cause of discontent,
Which well she hoped might be with ease redressed
Consid'ring her a well-bred civil beast
And more a gentlewoman than the rest.
After some common talk what rumours ran,
The lady of the spotted muff began.

This is almost Chaucerian in its amused account of animals as humans.

Part II is almost pure argument, and nowhere does Dryden show with such assurance his mastery of discussion in verse. The argument is often more ingenious and more detailed than that in *Religio Laici*, though it is not—and in a poem of this kind could scarcely be expected to be—more profound. Though the points adduced on either side may seem irrelevant or tedious to the modern reader, the adroit march of the couplets, flexible, responding neatly and happily to each turn of thought, will continue to excite his admiration. It is a remarkable technical performance.

At the end of Part II the Panther is given hospitality in the Hind's humble home. Part III opens with a brief apology by Dryden for using the beast fable; he cites Aesop and Spenser as precedents. Then the argument between the Hind and the Panther continues, with descriptive interludes describing the psychological effect of different points on one animal or the other. The fable element returns, particularly in the Panther's story of the swallows and the martin, which refers to the situation of the English Catholics at the time. Many of the detailed points made by the animals refer to contemporary history and are not easily grasped by the modern reader. But again the skill with which the verse argument is conducted can be continuously recognized. At the end the Hind tells the Panther an elaborate fable full of oblique references to the political situation of the time and designed to warn the Panther of the dangers of her position. The Panther remains unconvinced, and both retire to rest.

The position maintained by Dryden through the Hind's argument was, as Professor Bredvold has conclusively demonstrated, that of the moderate English Catholics, who were far from happy about King James' zeal for promoting their cause, for they feared an inevitable anti-Catholic reaction when James' protection would be withdrawn at his death. Though critics have made much of Dryden's change of religion and professed to find no real conviction in any of his expressions of religious views, there can be no doubt that in *The Hind and the Panther* Dryden gave expression more elaborately and in greater detail than anywhere else to his considered opinions on religion and politics. Again we find a basic skepticism underlying his faith and providing the reason for it. The point of view that emerges is shrewd, pragmatic, chastened, and conservative in an almost Burkean sense.

In the latter part of his career Dryden produced a large number of translations, including Virgil's *Aeneid* and Pastorals, parts of the *Iliad*, parts of Lucretius and of Ovid's Epistles and *Metamorphoses*, and tales from Boccaccio and Chaucer. These were published in various miscellanies and collections of poems between 1684 and 1711. His translations are very uneven. As a professional handler of the heroic couplet, he could turn out without any great effort large quantities of verse which was often embellished with pasted-on rhetorical figures and exhibitions of "wit." This is especially true of his *Virgil*, though it has passages of strength and vigor. Like so many poets of the period, Dryden had his views of what was appropriate to the epic, in terms of diction and style, and discussed the matter in his Epistle Dedicatory to his *Aeneid*: "The French have set up purity for the standard of their language; and a masculine vigour as that of ours. Like their tongue is the genius of their poets, light and trifling in comparison of the English [this was a common English view at the time]; more proper for sonnets, madrigals, and elegies, than heroic poetry. The turn on thoughts and words is their chief talent; but the Epic Poem is too stately to receive those little ornaments. The painters draw their nymphs in thin and airy habits; but the weight of gold and of embroideries is reserved for queens and goddesses. . . ." But Dryden had a fondness for those "little ornaments" and tried them many times in his *Aeneid*:

> With court informers' haunts and royal spies,
> Things done relates, not done she feigns, and mingles truth with lies.

Sometimes Dryden imposes a false dignity on his originals by substituting high-sounding generalizations for clearly realized particulars. His *Fables*, published in 1700, the year of his death, contain his renderings from Chaucer and Boccaccio, and this includes some of his most vigorous narrative, though even here his tendency to heighten the language, to give a rhetorical gloss to simple statement, is often in evidence. Mark Van Doren has pointed out that for one word in Chaucer, "huntyng," Dryden has (in his "Palamon and Arcite," Chaucer's Knight's Tale) four lines of generalized elaboration:

> A sylvan scene with various greens was drawn,
> Shades on the sides, and in the midst a lawn;
> The silver Cynthia, with her nymphs around,
> Pursued the flying deer, the woods with horns resound.

This is the kind of generalized nature scene that the Augustan poets were to go in for; it is not necessarily bad, but it is not always appropriate.

Dryden's embellishments of his original did not always take the form of substituting elaborate generalizations for simple particulars. Sometimes he added effective particulars, as occasionally in his rendering of Chaucer's Nun's Priest's Tale:

> The cattle in her homestead were three sows,
> An ewe called Mally, and three brinded cows.
> Her parlour window stuck with herbs around
> Of savoury smell; and rushes strewed the ground.
> A maple dresser in her hall she had, . . .

Sometimes the particulars are less happy. Chaucer's Wife of Bath's Tale opens

> In th'olde dayes of the Kyng Arthour,
> Of which that Britons speken greet honour,
> Al was this land fulfild of feyerye.
> The elf-queene, with hir joly compaignye,
> Daunced ful ofte in many a grene mede.

This becomes in Dryden:

> In days of old, when Arthur filled the throne,
> Whose acts and fame to foreign lands were blown,
> The king of elves and little fairy queen
> Gambolled on heaths, and danced on every green;
> And where the jolly troop had led the round,
> The grass unbidden rose, and marked the ground.
> Nor darkling did they dance; the silver light
> Of Phoebe served to guide their steps aright,
> And, with their tripping pleased, prolonged the night.
> Her beams they followed, where at full she played,
> Nor longer than she shed her horns they stayed,
> From thence with airy flight to foreign lands conveyed.

> Above the rest our Britain held they dear,
> More solemnly they kept their sabbaths here,
> And made more spacious rings, and revelled half the year.

In his translations Dryden is most often the rhetorical rather than the familiar poet. His masterly combination of the formal and the familiar which we find in so much of his satirical and his argumentative verse represented the resolution of a paradox which in other areas continued to bedevil him, as it did his age. As a rhetorical poet, Dryden has strength and vigor, though he can be verbose and repetitious. But the strength and vigor turn easily to brassiness. The voice is often that of a man shouting, and sonority often gives way to shrillness. Yet among the vast quantities of verse he wrote in this manner, it is not difficult to pick out passages of weight and dignity.

Dryden's lyrical poetry shows him in quite a different aspect. Restoration song was for the most part marked by stronger dance-rhythms than the more delicate Elizabethan and Caroline song-lyrics, and the poet was more ready to follow the lead of the music or to try to imitate musical effects by verbal devices. In the numerous songs scattered throughout his plays Dryden employed a variety of styles and meters, from the swinging dactylic—

> After the pangs of a desperate lover,
> When day and night I have sighed all in vain,
> Ah what a pleasure it is to discover
> In her eyes pity, who causes my pain!

to the simple ballad measure:

> You charmed me not with that fair face
>   Though it was all divine:
> To be another's is the grace
>   That makes me wish you mine.

Occasionally an early song has more delicacy and complexity of movement:

> Ah fading joy, how quickly thou art past!
>   Yet we thy ruin haste:
> As if the cares of human life were few,
>   We seek out new,
> And follow Fate that does too fast pursue.

But speed and strength are commoner characteristics:

> Whilst Alexis lay prest
>   In her arms he loved best,
> With his hands round her neck,

> And his head on her breast,
> He found the fierce pleasure too hasty to stay,
> And his soul in the tempest just flying away.

Pastoral characters such as Amyntas, Damon, Phyllis, Celimena, Alexis, abound in these songs, many of which have that combination of neoclassic artifice and contemporary vulgarity which was to mark a kind of English lyric poetry well into the eighteenth century. Some of the songs are wittily indecent, others express a crude hedonistic view in a simple rhythmic pattern:

> Why should a foolish marriage vow
>   Which long ago was made,
> Oblige us to each other now
>   When passion is decayed?
> We loved and we loved as long as we could,
>   Till our love was loved out in us both:
> But our marriage is dead when the pleasure is fled:
>   'Twas pleasure first made it an oath.

The great majority are love songs, spoken either by the man or by the woman; sometimes grief or anguish is expressed, often melodramatically, at the loved one's infidelity or betrayal, as in this song where Dryden uses a stanza form to which Keats was to give very different employment in his lyric "In a drear-nighted December":

> Farewell, ungrateful traitor,
>   Farewell, my perjured swain,
> Let never injured creature
>   Believe a man again.
> The pleasure of possessing
> Surpasses all expressing,
> But 'tis too short a blessing,
>   And Love too long a pain.

Many of Dryden's songs employ a dactylic or an anapestic lilt (as in the second four lines of "Why should a foolish marriage vow"); the majority of them have a rhythmical gusto though they lack all lyrical complexity and subtlety. He wrote several operas ("an odd medley of poetry and music wherein the poet and the musician, equally confined one by the other, take a world of pain to compose a wretched performance," as St. Evremond not ineptly described that sort of opera), where the attempt to imitate or follow the musical line is not often successful. They include *The State of Innocence*, a vigorously rhetorical rewriting of Milton's *Paradise Lost*. Of all the pieces he wrote for stage representation with music, *The Secular*

Masque, written for a benefit performance at the Theatre Royal only a few weeks before his death, contains the only lines that really haunt the imagination. This masque celebrates the end of the seventeenth century and welcomes the eighteenth. Momus, pointing successively (in the second, third, and fourth lines) to Diana, Mars, and Venus, announces the failure of the past and a hope for the future:

> All, all of a piece throughout:
>   Thy chase had a beast in view;
> Thy wars brought nothing about;
>   Thy lovers were all untrue.
> 'Tis well an old age is out,
>   And time to begin a new.

It was one of Dryden's last utterances, a curiously elegiac one for so robust a poet.

Dryden's attempts to imitate the effects of music in language reach their height in his two songs for St. Cecilia's Day, the first called simply "A Song for St. Cecilia's Day" (1687) and the second, "Alexander's Feast; or, The Power of Music" (1697). Poems in praise of music for St. Cecilia's day had become the fashion in the seventeenth century, and Dryden was following a common custom. His two odes, however, display a virtuosity like nothing else of their kind. They were intended to be "Pindaric" in structure—and to Dryden as to so many of his contemporaries the Pindaric Ode was a model of deliberate wildness, where the meter and stanza form were continually changed to fit shifts in the thought and emotion. Cowley's Pindaric Odes are among his worst pieces—formless and extravagant verbiage. Congreve realized that there was a true pattern in Pindar's odes and pointed out their strophic structure (which had earlier been recognized and imitated by Ben Jonson among others). Dryden, without adopting the true strophic pattern, realized that the Pindaric Ode could not be a mere excuse for every kind of verbal license. ". . . the ear must preside, and direct the judgment to the choice of numbers," he wrote in his Preface to a collection of miscellaneous poems entitled *Sylvae* (1685): "without the nicety of this, the harmony of Pindaric verse can never be complete; the cadence of one line must be a rule to that of the next; and the sound of the former must slide gently into that which follows, without leaping from one extreme to another." "Alexander's Feast" shows the effects of different kinds of music on Alexander the Great and enables Dryden to run the gamut of moods from the military to the tender. It is a fine *bravura* piece, full of exhibitionist virtuosity:

'Twas at the royal feast for Persia won
   By Philip's warlike son:
   Aloft in awful state
   The godlike hero sate
   On his imperial throne;
  His valiant peers were placed around;
Their brows with roses and with myrtles bound:
  (So should desert in arms be crowned.)
The lovely Thais by his side,
Sate like a blooming Eastern bride,
In flower of youth and beauty's pride.
   Happy, happy, happy pair!
     None but the brave,
     None but the brave,
  None but the brave deserves the fair.

Later on the musician turns to praise of Bacchus, and the verse changes to the lilt of a drinking song:

   Bacchus' blessings are a treasure,
   Drinking is the soldier's pleasure;
     Rich the treasure,
     Sweet the pleasure,
   Sweet is pleasure after pain.

One would have to go through the whole poem to demonstrate the different kinds of shading and the modulations from one key and one mode to another. It is fine verbal fireworks, but in the last analysis rather cheap stuff. The rhetorical quality in the earlier St. Cecilia song, though not as elaborately contrived, is in parts at least more impressive, as in the resounding opening:

   From harmony, from heavenly harmony
   This universal frame began; . . .

The attempt later in the poem to imitate by metrical changes the varying tones of the trumpet, the "soft complaining flute," the "sharp violins," and the human voice is clever, but something of a mere verbal trick.

Dryden's finest achievement in his Pindaric manner is neither of his musical odes but his ode "To the Pious Memory of the Accomplished Young Lady, Mrs. Anne Killigrew" (1686). In spite of several barren patches this poem has true rhetorical splendor, combining sure metrical control with a sense of having been forced out of the poet by the strength of his emotion.

O gracious God! how far have we
Profaned the heavenly gift of Poesy!
Made prostitute and profligate the Muse,
Debased to each obscene and impious use,
Whose harmony was first ordained above,
For tongues of angels and for hymns of love!
O wretched we! why were we hurried down
    This lubric and adulterate age,
    (Nay, added fat pollutions of our own,)
    To increase the steaming ordures of the stage?
What can we say to excuse our second fall?
Let this thy Vestal, Heaven, atone for all:
Her Arethusian stream remains unsoiled,
Unmixed with foreign filth and undefiled;
Her wit was more than man, her innocence a child!

Dryden's place as a prose writer and a critic is at least as important as his position as a poet. "Dryden may be properly considered as the father of English criticism," wrote Dr. Johnson with perfect justice. As a practicing poet who was interested in his craft, he punctuated his poetic career with frequent essays discussing questions of technique, structure, characterization, diction, and literary taste and fashion. In the great debate between those who claimed that the finest writers of Greece and Rome transcended any possible modern achievement and those who believed, on the other hand, that literature, like the other arts and sciences, could progress beyond anything attainable by the ancient world—the debate between the Ancients and the Moderns—Dryden took no extreme position, but on the whole argued moderately and tolerantly on the side of the Moderns. He was more interested in a work's being good of its kind than in its conformity to any preconceived theories about good art. His own changing tastes and interests helped to make him responsive to different kinds of literary skill and of artistic conventions, thus giving him that primary qualification of the good literary critic—the ability to read the work under consideration with full and sympathetic understanding.

Dryden's first important critical work was his *Essay of Dramatic Poesie* (1668), a dialogue on the nature of poetic drama and the respective merits of classical, modern French, Elizabethan, and Restoration plays, in which everyone agrees to define a play as "a just and lively image of human nature, representing its passions and humours, and the changes of fortune to which it is subject, for the delight and instruction of mankind." The very fact that Dryden cast this essay into dialogue form, where different people, each representing a different point of view, were allowed their full say, is evidence of his tolerant and inquiring mind. The characters, who have classical names, represent real people, and Dryden himself is introduced as Neander. Crites begins by trying to prove that the Ancients were superior to the Moderns, in that they kept to the so-called Aristotelian unities of time, place, and action and also had better style; Eugenius urges the superiority of the Moderns on a variety of grounds, including the threadbare plots of classical tragedy and the superior "regularity" of modern drama. Lisideius then champions neoclassic French drama and attacks the English Elizabethan and Jacobean drama for its irregularity, improbability, and general lack of artistry. Neander (Dryden) defends the English against the French: liveliness is better than cold formality. He praises the "variety and copiousness" of the English plays as opposed to "the barrenness of the French plots" and defends "variety, if well ordered." Dryden includes in this essay a careful examination of Jonson's play, *Epicoene, or the Silent Woman*, one of the first detailed pieces of practical criticism in English.

Much of Dryden's critical prose is found in his dedications and prefaces. *A Defence of an Essay of Dramatic Poesie* was included in the second edition of his play, *The Indian Emperor* (1668). His preface to *An Evening's Love* discussed comedy, farce, and tragedy. His essay *Of Heroic Plays* was prefixed to *The Conquest of Granada* (1672), and his essay *On the Dramatic Poetry of the Last Age* appeared the same year with the second part of the same play. *An Apology for Heroic Poetry and Poetic Licence* was prefixed to *The State of Innocence* (1677). The preface to *All for Love* (1678) discussed the nature of tragedy and his own intentions in writing the play. His essay on *The Grounds of Criticism in Tragedy* was the preface to *Troilus and Cressida* (1679). His preface to a volume of translations from Ovid in 1680 discussed Ovid and the art of translation. And so it went, each new literary venture provoking new reflections on the theory and practice of his art. If he was at his best as an "occasional" poet, he was also at his best as an occasional critic, discussing questions as they arose from the point of view of a practitioner. His favorite role is that of the professional writer discussing his craft.

Dryden's prose style combines the elegance of good conversation with the regulated flow of art. His sentences are never artificially balanced, but consist of clauses cunningly varied in size and shape. Consider the placing of the pauses and the nature of the *flow* in the following:

No man is capable of translating poetry who, besides a genius to that art, is not a master both of his author's language, and of his own; nor must we understand the language only of the poet, but his particular turn of thoughts and expressions, which are the characters that distinguish, and, as it were, individuate him from all other writers. When we come thus far, 'tis time to look into ourselves, to conform our genius to his, to give his thought either the same turn, if our tongue will bear it, or, if not, to vary the dress, not to alter or destroy the substance. The like care must be taken of the more outward garments, the words. (Preface to his translation of Ovid's *Epistles*.)

That which distinguishes Theocritus from all other poets, both Greek and Latin, and which raises him even above Virgil in his *Eclogues*, is the inimitable tenderness of his passions, and the natural expression of them in words so becoming of a pastoral. A simplicity shines through all he writes: he shows his art and learning by disguising both. His shepherds never rise above their country education in their complaints of love: there is the same difference betwixt him and Virgil as there is betwixt Tasso's *Aminta* and the *Pastor Fido* of Guarini. (Preface to *Sylvae*.)

The advantages which rhyme has over blank verse are so many that it were lost time to name them. Sir Philip Sidney, in his *Defence of Poesy*, gives us one, which, in my opinion, is not the least considerable; I mean the help it brings to memory, which rhyme so knits up, by the affinity of sounds, that, by remembering the last word in one line, we often call to mind both the verses. Then, in the quickness of reparties (which in discoursive scenes fall very often), it has so particular a grace, and is so aptly suited to them, that the sudden smartness of the answer, and the sweetness of the rhyme, set off the beauty of each other. But that benefit which I consider most in it, because I have not seldom found it, is, that it bounds and circumscribes the fancy. (Epistle Dedicatory of *The Rival Ladies*.)

As Dryden grew older and his criticism became more relaxed and discursive, his prose style grew a trifle more prolix, with a tendency to increase the number of qualifying or parenthetical clauses. Yet even here the control of the prose rhythm is clear:

'Tis with a poet, as with a man who designs to build, and is very exact, as he supposes, in casting up the cost beforehand; but generally speaking he is mistaken in his account, and reckons short of the expense he first intended. He alters his mind as the work proceeds, and will have this or that convenience more, of which he had not thought when he began. So has it happened to me; I have built a house where I intended but a lodge; yet with better success than a certain nobleman, who, beginning with a dog-kennel, never lived to finish the palace he had contrived. (Preface to *Fables Ancient and Modern, translated into Verse from Homer, Ovid, Boccace and Chaucer*, 1700.)

The preface to the *Fables* is Dryden's last and most relaxed piece of critical writing, where the old poet moves from subject to subject with the ease of an experienced talker drawing on rich and wide experience. He talks of the authors he has been translating—Homer, Virgil, Ovid, Chaucer, Boccaccio. There is an illuminating comparison between Homer and Virgil, and another between Ovid and Chaucer, but the high point is the long account of Chaucer which

occupies the whole of the second part of the essay. Historical and biographical facts are here mingled with more strictly critical observations, but the central aim—to give the reader a sense of Chaucer's literary character and achievement—is never lost sight of, and Dryden
succeeds admirably in projecting into the reader's mind his own feeling for Chaucer as well as providing an objective account of his qualities. This is practical criticism really working; it is not written for the
specialist or the fellow critic; the language is free from jargon, the
movement from literature to life and back again is made effortlessly;
a variety of tools are used to build up a picture of both the man and
his work, and of the effect of his work on the reader; and the tone
is continuously relaxed and almost colloquial. In spite of some
inevitable historical errors and misunderstandings, the essay is one
of the great landmarks of practical criticism in English.

Dryden had been preceded as a verse satirist in Restoration England by a writer of a very different kind, in spite of certain similarities
of cast of mind. This was Samuel Butler (1612–80), whose *Hudibras*
is perhaps the first great poetic satire in English. This burlesque
romance, of which the first part appeared in 1663, the second in
1664, and the third in 1678, was delightedly acclaimed at the Court
of Charles II as a brilliant attack on the Puritans, but in fact it was
something more complex and more interesting than that. Butler
had lived through a period of violent social, religious, and political
conflict, and had noted how different sects each proclaimed with
passion and conviction its own doctrine as the only true one; he saw
that ignorance or philosophical incapacity did not restrain men
from propounding their opinions with violence and intolerance; he
noted how easily catchwords, slogans, citation of texts, and every
kind of irrational manipulation of language replaced rational discourse, and came to the conclusion that the ultimate mysteries of
life were permanently concealed from men, for whom the only
useful intellectual activity was observation of the natural world
with a view to discerning its order and pattern. His view was thus
in some degree the same as Francis Bacon's, but he had little
sympathy with those followers of Bacon at the Royal Society who
were, in Butler's view, wasting their time with fantastic and unprofitable experiments. His main attack was directed against passion and
prejudice in religious argument; the attack was delivered from the
standpoint of a mild rationalism with many skeptical overtones. But
although passion and prejudice in religious argument, as exhibited
in the controversies of the Puritan sects, were Butler's principal
target, he also hit out against every kind of extravagance and folly

in contemporary thought and society; in the debates between Hudibras and his squire Ralph he mocks the scholastic and rhetorical
studies that still prevailed at Cambridge in his university days and
at the same time castigates theological pedantry, Presbyterian ri-
gidity, and the pretensions of mystical and hermetic thinkers. Few
of the religious sects of the seventeenth century escape his barbs.
Further, in its mock-heroic form (which derives both from *Don
Quixote* and perhaps also from Scarron's deliberate mockery of the
Aeneid the *Virgile travesti*) *Hudibras* is also a literary satire on
the pretentiousness of epic and romance and on all the extravagances
of passion and diction with which poets have been wont to treat
human situations. The poem, on its positive side, is an implicit plea
for common sense, reason, and the recognition of human limitations.

We do not, however, read *Hudibras* for its positive moral; we read
it, as it was read in its own day, for its brilliant satirical portraits and
for the wit and humor of its mock-heroic action. This preposterous
Puritan knight and his equally preposterous squire (each represents
a different kind of religious sectarianism and intellectual folly) are
involved in a series of ludicrous adventures which, by inflation to
epic proportions, are made to pour a continuous stream of witty
ridicule on all those pretensions and fatuities which Butler most
disliked. The set character sketches, too (as might be expected from
a writer who also worked in the seventeenth-century character-
writing tradition and produced some of the best examples of this
kind of writing, with a fine satiric twist), are expertly done. But perhaps the most important single element in Butler's satiric technique
was his use of the octosyllabic couplet, with its deliberate mixture of
pedantic and colloquial speech, the outrageous rhymes, the steady
trot of cumulative ridicule:

> Beside he was a shrewd Philosopher,
> And had read every text and gloss ever:
> Whate'er the crabbed'st Author hath
> He understood b' implicit Faith,
> What ever Sceptick could inquere for;
> For every *why* he had a *wherefore*; . . .
> He knew the seat of Paradise,
> Could tell in what degree it lies,
> And, as he was dispos'd, could prove it
> Below the Moon, or else above it.
> What Adam dreamt of when his Bride
> Came from her Closet in his side;
> Whether the Devil tempted her
> By a high Dutch interpreter;
> If either of them had a Navel;

Who first made Musick malleable;
Whether the Serpent at the Fall
Had cloven feet, or none at all. . . .
    For his Religion it was fit
To match his Leaning and his Wit:
'Twas Presbyterian true blew,
For he was of that stubborn Crew
Of Errant Saints, whom all men grant
To be the true Church Militant;
Such as do build their Faith upon
The holy text of Pike and Gun,
Decide all Controversies by
Infallible Artillery,
And prove their Doctrine Orthodox
By Apostolick Blows and Knocks,
Call Fire and Sword and Desolation
A *godly-thorough-Reformation,*
Which always must be carry'd on,
And still be doing, never done:
As if Religion were intended
For nothing else but to be mended. . . .

There is not a point here which does not glance at some seventeenth-century doctrine, controversy, or event, but, though a historical gloss greatly illuminates the passage, its more general satiric effect is recognizable without it.

If the Cavalier tradition was revived in England at the Restoration, and if in their different ways the Court Wits, the dramatists, John Dryden, and Samuel Butler represented various kinds of anti-Puritan feeling, this does not mean that the Puritan tradition in England was dead or even that it was seriously weakened. The Indian summer of the Cavaliers did not last long, and even while it did last the deeply entrenched Puritan *ethos* was flourishing below the polite surface. Concern with personal salvation, interest in the psychological processes involved in conversion, in the pattern of the true spiritual life and the stages through which the believer went in proving to himself and others that he really was a member of God's elect, and in techniques of preaching and persuasion—these continue to be reflected in Puritan literature from Arthur Dent's *Plain Man's Path-way to Heaven,* first published in 1601 and running into numerous editions throughout the seventeenth century, and Richard Bernard's prose allegory about sin, *The Isle of Man,* published in 1626 (it reached its twelfth edition in 1648), to the culmination of this kind of literature in the work of Bunyan. John Bunyan (1628–88) shows how generations of Puritan preaching could help to develop a prose style which owed something to the English Bible and perhaps more to the vigorous and homely vocabulary of popular exhortation. There had been a simple and popular strain in English preaching from the earliest times, and though more ornamental traditions had developed, this simple strain had never died out and was much cultivated by the Puritans. So while a conscious reformation of English prose was being undertaken by members of the Royal Society in the interests of scientific clarity and the psychology of John Locke was encouraging "clear and distinct ideas" expressed in a clear and distinct vocabulary, Puritan literature was moving in a similar direction for quite different reasons. The cogency and flexibility of Dryden's prose style and the colorful simplicity of Bunyan's represent two contemporary kinds of "plain" prose—sufficiently different from each other, but in the long run flowing together to provide a prose that would make the English novel possible.

If in some ways Bunyan's best work represents a culmination of certain kinds of seventeenth-century Puritan writing, in others it looks forward to the development of the English novel. His interest in spiritual autobiography and cautionary allegory stems from a long Puritan tradition which in turn had roots in medieval religious thought and expression; his method of translating his theological ideas into vivid, realistic, contemporary terms, reflecting with extraordinary immediacy the daily life and conversation of the ordinary people of England, shows the technique of the embryo novelist. Bunyan's own spiritual life followed a classic pattern of worldliness followed by conviction of sin (as a result of a preacher's effective work on him) and vocation or calling, followed in turn by various torturing doubts of his election that led him more than once to the brink of despair and at last through many turns and twists to settled conviction of his salvation, a firm saving faith, and steady progress in sanctification or holiness of life. He refused to conform to the various acts passed in the early and middle 1660's directed against the dissenters and particularly against the holding of preachings and religious meetings by unauthorized nonconformist preachers, and as a result spent some twelve and a half years of his life in jail, where he wrote some of his best work. Of humble origin, Bunyan had little theological or other learning besides an intimate knowledge of the Bible and of seventeenth-century Puritan devotional literature (including Dent's *Plain Man's Path-way to Heaven*). In the course of his career as a Baptist preacher he acquired much experience in the art of pressing home religious truths with concrete and vivid illustrations. Bunyan's spiritual autobiography, *Grace Abounding to the Chief of Sinners* (1666), was in a traditional Puritan mode which flourished especially between 1640 and 1660, but it is superior to its predecessors in its artful selection of concrete detail to illustrate states of mind. His Calvinist theology and his own psychological experiences in adjusting himself to the demands and implications of that theology are never discussed abstractly but through physical and sensual images that succeed in a remarkable degree in thrusting his own emotional states into the consciousness of the reader. Bunyan's genius lay in his ability to render spiritual experience in concrete and homely terms, to use his knowledge of ordinary daily life in making vivid his presentation of theological problems of salvation and damnation. It is true that, in Tillyard's words, "Bunyan was deficient in the middle ground between the spiritual and the quotidian"; there is a lack of intellectual and emotional complexity in all his writing, so that, while he can render with appealing force certain responses toward a dogmatic religious creed—and not only simple positive responses but all kinds of hesitations, obsessions, and self-tortures—he cannot provide a narrative texture rich enough to satisfy the reader who does not accept Bunyan's creed or the total validity of its psychological exploration of human dilemmas and states. But if there is this limiting naïveté in his work, there is the compensating virtue of colloquial liveliness and the brilliant handling of the concrete image.

The Pilgrim's Progress (1678) takes the archetypal theme of man's life as a journey and treats of Christian's journey from the City of Destruction to salvation and Heaven with raciness and color; and though there are moments when Bunyan strays out of familiar landscapes and personalities to indulge in too abstract or unrealized descriptions, for the most part he draws on the life and the people he knows and the narrative has concreteness of detail and even, on occasions, humor. The Holy War (1682) takes the other great archetypal allegory—that of man's life as a war between good and evil—and endeavors to handle the whole of divine and human history, the story both of the world in general and of the individual soul in its fight to attain salvation; and though again there are inevitable naïvetés and inconsistencies, the realism and humor with which the everyday world is brought in to illustrate spiritual and theological situations and problems constitute the greatest appeal of the work. We feel here as in The Pilgrim's Progress that while Bunyan used his own experience of life brilliantly, the limitations of his experience and of his imagination fail to provide "the middle ground between personal religious experience and the homely things he could see around him." But Tillyard, who makes this criticism, also asserts that *The Holy War* has a better claim than any other work to be called England's Puritan epic.

The second part of *The Pilgrim's Progress* (1684) deals with the pilgrimage of Christian's wife Christiana and her children from the City of Destruction to salvation. It has less power than the first part; Christiana's experiences are much less demanding; she has a companion, Mercy, and, after a while, a guide and protector, Great-heart. Much of her pilgrimage seems almost like a tourist's visit to the places where Christian underwent his ordeals: Bunyan seems concerned here more with community religious life, the less arduous position of the ordinary believer and church-goer, than with the spiritual struggles and temptations of the individual Christian soul. This must reflect in part the easier circumstances of dissenters in the 1680's, partly perhaps a relaxation of tension in the older, assured Bunyan, satisfied author of a religious best seller, partly the fact that Bunyan was writing now of the position of women in the religious community. The note of struggle, or *ascesis,* almost disappears; but the use of homely and vivid situations from the life he knew can still be found, giving that special Bunyanesque life to the work.

The diaries of John Evelyn (1620–1706) and Samuel Pepys (1633–1703) show kinds of autobiographical writing very different from the species of spiritual autobiography represented by Bunyan's *Grace Abounding.* Evelyn was a cultivated gentleman of wide curiosity who, as a young man, traveled in France and Italy as well as in England, and later held a variety of public positions. Travel, architecture, the arts of life, and inventions that might make life easier or more interesting, remained Evelyn's chief interests, and his diary records with continuous interestedness his experiences and observations. His self-possession, urbanity, quiet loyalty, and self-discipline remind us that the Restoration gallants shown in the comedy of the time do not altogether represent the Restoration gentleman: midway between the extremes of Court wit and Puritan soul-searcher stood the humane and eager mind of John Evelyn; his diary is in no sense a private confession but a confident, almost at times too consciously articulated, account of what he did, thought, and saw. Pepys' diary is more revealing, for it was written only for his private satisfaction, in shorthand which was not deciphered until the nineteenth century. Pepys too had a fund of intellectual curiosity, but as he reveals himself in his diary there is much more of ordinary human frailty—vanity, lust, ambition—in his make-up than Evelyn's more self-conscious recording reveals. He was, in habits and tastes, a little nearer the stereotype of Restoration gallant than Evelyn was; yet, in spite of aberrations, he had a deep love for his wife and reveals a humane intelligence as well as a strict practical efficiency in the management of both private and public affairs. His administrative duties as Secretary of the Navy Board were carried out with outstanding success, and a distinguished English historian has called him "perhaps the greatest administrator in the history of the British Navy." His career as a civil servant emerges from his diary in the midst of the vanities, trivialities, gossip, and domestic problems which he presents with engaging frankness. Pepys' diary is not literature, but it reveals a man and his age with fascinating particularity.

The essays and miscellaneous writings of Sir William Temple (1628–99) and of George Savile, first Marquis of Halifax (1633–95), reveal other aspects of the gentlemanly character of the period. Both writers helped to develop the quietly urbane prose that Addison later was to make the model of English prose style for generations; their work is part of that history of the simultaneous simplifying and polishing of English prose which has already been noted in the discussion of Dryden's critical essays. Temple was praised by Dr. Johnson as "the first writer who gave cadence to English prose," which, while not true, is nevertheless significant of Temple's influence on later writers. He took the side of the Ancients in the great debate between the Ancients and the Moderns, but he was no great scholar or critic and his most memorable writings are his graceful and charming essays in which his own tastes and personality are revealed in a quietly controlled prose. Temple, like Cowley (whose essay "Of Myself," published posthumously with his other essays in 1668, is one of the first truly confessional short pieces of prose in English), was a pioneer in the personal essay, which was not to become dominant in England until the early nineteenth century. Halifax, a somewhat more worldly character than Temple, is best known for his *Character of a Trimmer,* in which he expatiates on what later came to be regarded as the traditional English political virtues of compromise, moderation, and "trimming" between extremes, but a more intimate side of his character is revealed in his charming and affectionate letter to his daughter, *The Lady's New-Year's-Gift; or, Advice to a Daughter.* Halifax and more particularly Temple reveal yet another side of English thought and sensibility in the late seventeenth century. The conclusion of Temple's essay on poetry (1690) shows a world of thought and feeling very far from that which was at the same time being bodied forth by his contemporary William Congreve:

When all is done, human life is, at the greatest and the best, but like a froward child, that must be played with and humoured a little to keep it quiet till it falls asleep, and then the care is over.

CHAPTER SIXTEEN

The Augustan Age: Defoe, Swift, Pope

As the conflicts and enthusiasms of the mid-seventeenth century receded into the past and English society and culture settled down into a period of relative stability until political revolution in France and industrial revolution at home helped to produce another era of more rapid change and more violent conflict of ideas, it becomes possible to distinguish that view of life and letters which those who held it liked to consider "Augustan." We have seen how, in the latter part of the century, London became more and more the center of the literary and intellectual life of the country and writers came to look upon "polite" London society as their chief, if not their sole, audience. Aristocracy in the old sense has been transmuted into gentility, and wealth becomes (though rarely obviously and directly) the main motivating power in society. The old idealisms, by which men had lived and over which they had fought and died, appear to be gone forever; men—at least those men who write—are more civilized, more calculating perhaps, more complacent, more rational, more respectable. Those who have not the minimum of income to allow them to mingle in urban society remain out of sight and out of mind so far as the majority of writers and thinkers are concerned. Economics and ethics are finally separated. The new economists—their field is "political arithmetic"—prove to their own satisfaction that the individual desire to make money can produce in the long run nothing but good, and poverty can only be the result of idleness. Society refuses to take responsibility for those of its members who fall by the wayside. In London, the coffeehouse replaces the Court as the meeting place of men of culture. The journalist makes his appearance. Gossip and tittle-tattle make their way into print. Poetry becomes social and familiar. It must be remembered that there was a correlation between social class and education, between elegance and learning, that has not always existed in subsequent periods, and if poets were to use a fairly standardized body of references to the Latin and Greek classics as well as to events in the contemporary world of learning, they had to consider themselves addressing a very limited audience. Men were very much aware at this time of what man had made of himself by submitting his raw impulses to conventions and polishing his speech in accordance with the demands of those conventions. It was that sort of thing that made life livable, and that made personal and social relationships contribute to the agreeableness of existence. Civilization was very precious; it was the product of the refinement of primitive impulses by a series of conventions which were transmitted and improved upon by education. "We are refined," wrote Lord Chesterfield to his son, "and plain manners, plain dress, and plain diction, would as little do in life, as acorns, herbage, and the water of the neighbouring well, would do at table."

Poetry in such a period worked within relatively narrow limits. It was a civilized activity, and civilization demanded a certain kind of perspective in looking at things, a certain polish and elegance and consciousness of good society, wit, restraint, good taste, and the subordination of personal idiosyncrasy to a social norm. The heroic couplet becomes the standard—at times there seems to be a feeling that it is virtually the only—verse technique, partly because it is the best form for conveying that combination of elegance and wit, of ease and polish, which the age demanded, but also because it lent itself to the utterance of "what oft was thought but ne'er so well expressed" and encouraged a nice balance between individual insight and the rhetoric of social belief.

The atmosphere of the reign of Queen Anne (1702–14) was congenial to the genius of such a poet as Pope; it encouraged poets to write for a civilized urban group whose education they could take for granted, whose attitudes they understood, and whose standards of wit and elegance coincided with their own. The limitation of audience and of subject matter, and the careful assignment of the proper kind of diction to each kind of poetry, did not necessarily mean that a body of poetry inferior to that of the previous century would be produced. Limitations and conventions of this kind are a challenge to art, and art thrives on such challenges. The delicate satire and oblique wisdom developed by Pope in "The Rape of the Lock" show what perfect poetic achievements were possible in—were in fact encouraged by—a social atmosphere of this kind. Such an atmosphere also produced the kind of *vers de société* so happily exemplified in the poems of Matthew Prior, whose playful elegance (as well as graceful vulgarity) must be distinguished from Pope's more formal performances. Another aspect of early eighteenth-century civilization is caught perfectly by John Pomfret's poem, "The Choice" (1700), an immensely popular verse essay describing the gentleman's ideal way of life, a leisured, civilized "golden mean." We are reminded, as so often in this period, of the mood and tone of many of the poems of the Roman poet Horace, who was one of the favorite poets of the age; though it is true that there are aspects of Horace of which the early eighteenth-century writers showed themselves quite unaware. Closely related to admiration of the Horatian golden mean is the insistence that poetry should concern itself with *general* human nature, that it should take as the norm the highest common factor of civilized man. Such a view had its effect on tone and diction as well as on choice of subject matter and underlying philosophy.

If we say that gentility was replacing aristocracy as an ideal of the governing classes in early eighteenth-century England we must be clear about what was actually involved, because it affects the whole texture of the culture of the age. Throughout the century the merchants and tradesmen of the towns came to play a more and more important part in the life of the country—indeed, the steady rise in influence and numbers of the urban middle classes had been a feature of English history since the fifteenth century. But the middle classes were not yet the real rulers of the country. The political rulers were the landed aristocracy, the country gentlemen and big estate owners, though they ruled only with the permission of and in alliance with the commercial interests. When the alliance was broken not long afterward, it was broken only in a formal political sense, for by this time the landed aristocracy had become so absorbed in the upper strata of the middle classes that their interests had become identified. The long period of Robert Walpole's political rule (1721–42) lulled the squirearchy to sleep, and when they awoke they found themselves indistinguishable from upper-middle-class gentlemen. The fusion of interests was complete. Wealthy merchants bought their way into Parliament and purchased the estates of bankrupt landowners, and aristocracy developed into plutocracy. This process continued throughout the century, and we can see it taking place in the pages of Defoe's *Tour Through the Whole Island of Great Britain* (1724–27).

The "Glorious Revolution" of 1688, when James II was replaced by William of Orange and his wife Mary in a movement largely engineered by the middle-class, Protestant heart of England, represented a victory of the town over the Court. But if the town had defeated the Court and had rejected the Court's standards in manners and morals, it had now to find its own standards, to root itself in a social and ethical code. It needed educating in the trivialities of life, which hitherto had been the property of the Court. The new society had its philosophers and theologians, but as yet it had neither monitor nor dancing master. And it needed both—they were a rather bewildered company, these prosperous citizens with their wives and daughters. They had kept aloof from the courtly life of the Restoration, with its license and debauchery, and now that that had gone and correct conduct in a metropolitan society was coming to be a concern of their own they felt awkward and ignorant, and wanted advice. The town had defeated the Court, and now the town had to be educated up to its new position. The education and the entertainment (where possible, both together) of the middle classes now became a legitimate objective of literature. The differences between the courtesy books of the Renaissance and the essays of Addison and Steele in the early eighteenth century illustrate with quite startling clarity the differences between the old aristocratic education and the new genteel variety.

Although from the time of the Restoration London had been more and more the center of English cultural life, England was still essentially an agricultural country, and while the peasantry played little part in the literary life of the time, the squirearchy was continuously present in the imagination of those who wrote and thought about England. When Addison, in the first issue of *The Spectator* on March 1, 1711, had his Spectator introduce himself ("Thus I live in the world, rather as a spectator of mankind, than as one of the species"), he gave him a squirearchical background: "I was born to a small hereditary estate, which according to the tradition of the village, where it lies, was bounded by the same hedges and ditches in William the Conqueror's time that it is at present, and has been delivered down from father to son whole and entire, without the loss or acquisition of a single field or meadow, during the space of six hundred years." Addison and Steele, the great educators of the English middle class at the beginning of the eighteenth century, were at the same time concerned to bridge the gap between town and country, represented at the Restoration by the courtly fashion of sneering at the uncouthness and simplicities of visiting squires, and also to unite past and present, to re-establish the continuity of English history. Sir Roger de Coverley, first introduced by Steele in the second issue of *The Spectator,* was an old-fashioned country gentleman ("His grandfather was inventor of that famous country-dance which is called after him") who had in his youth "often supped with my Lord Rochester and Sir George Etherege, fought a duel upon his first coming to town, and kicked Bully Daw-son in a public coffee-house for calling him youngster"; but as his character was developed by Addison in subsequent numbers, he becomes an eccentric and lovable Tory squire whose foibles are held up for the sympathetic amusement of a Whig audience. He eventually becomes a symbol of an ideal feudal paternalism in his relation with his servants and tenants: "I am the more at ease in Sir Roger's family, because it consists of sober and staid persons; for as the knight is the best master in the world, he seldom changes his servants; and as he is beloved by all about him: by this means his domestics are all in years, and grown old with their master. You would take his *valet-de-chambre* for his brother, his butler is grey-headed, his groom is one of the gravest men that I have ever seen, and his coachman has the looks of a privy-counsellor. You see the goodness of the master even in the old house-dog, and in a gray pad that is kept in the stable with great care and tenderness out of regard to his past services, though he has been useless for several years." This is a significant change from the man who once supped with my Lord Rochester; the softening and even sentimentalizing of the character of this old Tory squire represents an attempt to heal the breach between two traditions in English history that had long been at war and is another facet of the interpenetration of squirearchy and middle classes which is represented on the more purely physical level by wealthy merchants buying estates in the country and becoming themselves members of the landed gentry. Addison and Steele introduced into their *Spectator* essays other characters representing different social classes; there is, for example, Sir Andrew Freeport, "a merchant of great eminence in the city of London," whose "notions of trade are noble and generous"; and this too is part of their attempt to educate and unite English society. But the development of Sir Roger is the clearest example of the change that had taken place—or rather, that Addison and Steele wished would take place and helped to effect—from the days when the country squire was mercilessly ridiculed on the stage and despised both by the city merchant and the Court wit.

Joseph Addison (1672–1719) and Richard Steele (1672–1729) effectively pooled their talents to achieve extraordinary success in their endeavor "to enliven morality with wit, and to temper wit with morality." Their aim was frankly educational. Addison writes of his readers in the tenth *Spectator*: ". . . And to the end that their virtue and discretion may not be short, transient, intermittent starts of thought, I have resolved to refresh their memories from day to day, till I have recovered them out of that desperate state of vice and folly into which the age is fallen." He added: "I shall be ambitious to have it said of me, that I have brought philosophy out of closets and libraries, schools and colleges, to dwell in clubs and assemblies, at tea-tables and coffee-houses." This was a moral and educational program for post-Restoration English society, particularly for the *nouveaux riches* and the rising middle classes in general. Steele was the pioneer. More warmhearted, more sentimental, more sympathetic with bourgeois morality and at the same time more erratic and impulsive than Addison, he started his essay periodical *The Tatler* in 1709. There had been earlier periodical sheets giving news, social gossip, and general discussion of the affairs of the town; this kind of journalism had developed in the last decade of the seventeenth century; but Steele's was to be different. "Though the other papers which are published for the use of the good people of England have certainly very wholesome effects, and are laudable in their particular kinds, they do not seem to come up to the main design of such narrations, which, I humbly presume, should be principally intended for the use of politic persons, who are so public spirited as to neglect their own affairs to look into transactions of State. Now these gentlemen, for the most part, being men of strong zeal and weak intellects, it is both a charitable and necessary work to offer something, whereby such worthy and well-affected members of the commonwealth may be instructed, after their reading, *what to think;* which shall be the end and purpose of this my paper: . . . I have also resolved to have something which may be of entertainment to the fair sex, in honour of whom I have taken the title of this paper." The irony here is good-natured and does not conceal an underlying moral seriousness. Steele tended to jolly his readers along in a way that Addison, with his cooler and at times almost condescending style, never quite achieved or wanted to achieve. Gradually the amount of news in *The Tatler* diminished, and more and more it came to be a periodical essay devoted to comment on manners, morals, and literature. Addison read the early *Tatlers* in Ireland, where he was for a short time secretary to the Lord Lieutenant, recognized Steele's hand, and offered contributions which were happily accepted. It was largely under Addison's influence that the gossip was reduced and the essays turned more and more to the direct discussion of men and books. Steele, however, was the more cunning journalist, and it was he who originated most of the bright ideas and thought of new ways of insinuating moral or other teaching under the guise of entertainment. It was he who invented the club of eccentrics in the *Tatler's* Trumpet Club. But it was Addison who developed many of these devices to their ultimate perfection, just as he developed the character of Sir Roger de Coverley from Steele's first sketch. In *The Tatler* Addison had been Steele's assistant and contributed 42 of the total of 271 papers which were put out between April, 1709, and January, 1711, when the periodical ceased publication. In *The Spectator*, which ran to 555 numbers between March, 1711, and December, 1714, Addison was the senior partner and produced 274 papers to Steele's 240.

The Spectator covered everything necessary to a proper social education, from what kind of hats ladies should wear to how to appreciate Milton. In the fifth *Spectator* Addison laughed at the extravagances and absurdities of Italian opera, then so fashionable in London. In numbers 58 to 62 he developed John Locke's distinction between wit and judgment into a discussion of wit and its various forms that is of the first importance in understanding the approach to poetry of the majority of thoughtful readers of the period. The first kind of false wit is the arranging of poems in the shapes of physical objects; the second involves doing tricks with letters; the third is illustrated by anagrams and acrostics and *bouts rimés* (writing verses to set rhymes) as well as the kind of double rhymes used by Samuel Butler in *Hudibras* for comic and satiric effect. A whole essay is reserved for an attack on punning, "a conceit arising from the use of two words that agree in the sound, but differ in the sense." This is "false wit" to anyone who has John Locke's approach to language, and the fact that the pun disappeared from serious poetry at the beginning of the eighteenth century not to return until the second decade of the twentieth is significant of the change in the attitude to language that developed with the "Age of Reason." For Shakespeare, and for all the great sixteenth- and seventeenth-century poets before Dryden, the pun was a serious literary device which could be used to illustrate the complexity of experience, the simultaneous coexistence of different levels of thinking and feeling, and the tentative and exploratory nature of language itself. But once wit and judgment have been sharply separated, and once all knowledge and understanding is based on Locke's "clear and distinct ideas" and words are taken to have a one-for-one correspondence with the things or ideas they refer to, the pun becomes regarded as mere verbal exhibitionism, and so Addison, Dr. Johnson, and most other critics regarded it for two hundred years.

True wit, for Addison, consisted in the "resemblance and congruity of ideas," while false wit drew on accidental, physical resemblance and congruity between letters, words, and the shapes of sentences. A third kind, "mixed wit," is illustrated by one of Cowley's more metaphysical treatments of simile; a partial resemblance between two things is treated as a total resemblance and all kinds of ingenious developments of the analogy are thus made possible. What Addison condemns is precisely what most modern critics admire; it is what John Crowe Ransom calls, in admiration, "miraculism," which "arises when the poet discovers by analogy an identity between objects which is partial, though it should be considerable, and proceeds to an identification which is complete." Addison was teaching his readers to dislike the seventeenth-century metaphysical style; his attitude was part effect and part cause (but more effect than cause) of the revolution in poetic taste that T. S. Eliot has linked with the "dissociation of sensibility," the inability to experience thought as an emotion, and vice versa, which manifested itself in English poetry toward the end of the seventeenth century and remained more or less until the twentieth.

In the 70th *Spectator* Addison taught his readers that the old ballads were not to be despised. Though they do not obey the rules of the literary critics, the rules themselves are based on "nature" (i.e., on human nature and the permanent qualities of men and things) and so even a rude poet who follows nature will find himself doing, in however humble a way, what the great classical poets did. So the old ballad of "Chevy Chase" really obeys the neoclassic rules for heroic poetry. In the 81st issue, he laughs at the female habit of wearing patches on the face. In the 249th he discusses laughter, and remarks: "If the talent of ridicule were employed to laugh men out of vice and folly, it might be of some use to the world; but instead of this, we find that it is generally made use of to laugh men out of virtue and good sense, by attacking every thing that is solemn and serious, decent and praiseworthy in human life." In paper 267 and on the next eleven Saturdays, Addison discusses *Paradise Lost,* laying down the proper requirements of an epic poem and proceeding to show by concrete illustrations how Milton's epic fulfills them. This is the most solid criticism in *The Spectator,* and shows a clear neoclassic mind at work demonstrating how *Paradise Lost* meets Aristotle's specifications for an epic (with some minor exceptions) and why therefore it is proper to admire Milton. Neither the method nor the points made were original with Addison; but only Addison could have treated such a subject with acceptance for such a wide audience. In numbers 411 to 421, treating of the "pleasures of the imagination," Addison again applied the ideas of Locke in an ambitious attempt to develop a theory of beauty in both art and nature. Here once more if he was not a pioneer, the scale and manner of his treatment was original.

These examples will give some idea of the range of the *Spectator* essays. It is difficult to determine the precise degree to which Addison and Steele succeeded in their attempt to educate their age, but there can be no doubt of the influence and popularity of *The Spectator*. The essays were collected in eight volumes in 1712–15, twice in seven volumes in 1714, and once again in the same year in eight volumes, and the collection continued to be reprinted steadily—there were well over fifty editions before 1800. Generations of readers were subjected to *The Spectator's* views of manners, morals, and literature. Generations, too, read Addison's poised and lucid prose, which had a permanent influence for good on English prose style. Throughout the eighteenth century it was admired and imitated, and Jane Austen's cool and balanced prose owes much to it. Johnson summed up the achievement of *The Tatler* and *The Spectator* when he remarked that they "adjusted . . . the unsettled practice of daily intercourse by propriety and politeness" and the treatment of a variety of topics was "happily varied with elegant fictions and refined allegories, and illuminated with different changes of style and felicities of invention." As for Addison's prose, Johnson considered it "the model of the middle style," and concluded that "whoever wishes to attain an English style, familiar but not coarse, and elegant but not ostentatious, must give his days and nights to the volumes of Addison."

Addison mediated between town and country, between landed gentry and prosperous citizen, even—to use the terminology of an older generation—between Cavalier and Puritan. Daniel Defoe (1660–1731) is the representative of only one side of this equation, the middle-class dissenting Englishman (by "dissenting" is meant membership of a nonconformist Protestant sect, characteristic of large numbers of the English trading class). Defoe's remarkably varied career included several trade and business projects, which somehow always seemed to end in financial disaster or at least difficulty, a number of journalistic enterprises, and secret service work for the Government. In 1697 he published his *Essay on Projects,* in which he put forward an impressive number of practical proposals which included the establishment of a society "to encourage polite learning, to polish and refine the English tongue, and advance the so much neglected faculty of correct language, and to purge it from all the irregular additions that ignorance and affectation have introduced"; an academy for women, for "I have often thought of it as one of the most barbarous customs in the world . . . that we deny the advantages of learning to women"; and proposals for the more adequate care of mental defectives, the management of insurance, the reform of the banking system and of the bankruptcy laws, and

the building of roads. The book was clearly the work of a shrewd and
humane mind. In 1701, Defoe produced a verse satire, *The True-
Born Englishman*, in which he answered those who objected to the
occupation of the English throne by the Dutch King William by
ironically describing the mixed stock from which the English people
derived—"a race uncertain and uneven, /Derived from all the nations under heaven." The poem, which was crude enough so far as
the technique of versification went, had an immense success and
brought Defoe the friendship of the King, who, however, died
shortly afterward, so that Defoe could not profit from the royal
patronage. His next work was a pamphlet entitled *The Shortest Way
with the Dissenters* (1702) in which he satirized the Anglican Tory
attitude to the nonconformists by ironically suggesting extreme
measures of persecution to be taken against them (a technique which
was to give the hint to Swift in his much more brilliant *Modest Proposal*). Irony, as Defoe discovered to his cost, is a dangerous weapon;
both Tories and Dissenters took Defoe literally, so that he was attacked by both sides and had to serve a short jail sentence and stand
in the pillory for sedition. Enterprising and inventive as ever, he
emerged from jail to begin a new career in journalism and secret government work: his periodical *The Review*, which ran from 1704–13,
was conducted in the interests of Robert Harley, Earl of Oxford, a
moderate Tory who, during the reign of Queen Anne, induced his
party to pass the Act of Settlement which fixed the succession to the
throne on the House of Hanover in the event of Anne's death without
children. Defoe published pamphlets in favor of the Hanoverian succession, to which as a dissenting Protestant and a bourgeois he was
committed (high Anglicans, Roman Catholics, and certain of the
landed gentry, cast a lingering look back to the exiled Stuart line).
In 1706 he published a minutely realistic account of a supernatural
occurrence, *A True Relation of the Apparition of One Mrs. Veal*,
which showed his journalist's eye for detail and his mastery of the
art of realistic reporting.

The Hanoverian succession was assured by George I's ascent to
the throne in 1714, and Defoe then worked in oblique ways for a
variety of Whig ministers. The difficulties involved in these activities
eventually proved too much for him, and he turned his talents to the
writing of fiction, producing his first novel, *Robinson Crusoe*, in 1719,
when he was almost sixty years old. Defoe had already demonstrated
his talents as a reporter and observer in a great variety of writings,
but *Robinson Crusoe*, written almost with nonchalance as a means
of making money, revealed something more—the ability to organize
and present detail in order to implement a view of the relation be-

tween man and nature that sprang from the depths of the English
middle-class view of life. The novel, narrated in the first person as
though it were an actual autobiographical account, shows the ship-
wrecked trader on his desert island endeavoring to remold in his distant isolation the whole pattern of the material and moral civilization
he had left behind him, and in doing so adding a new kind of romantic interest to the common necessities of life. The middle-class de-
cencies of living are here wrested from nature, and in the process acquire new meaning and dignity. It is significant that Crusoe did not
take advantage of the loneliness that was thrust upon him to indulge
in introspection or to think out afresh man's relation to the universe:
he had gone on his journey as a trader, in order to make money and
increase his material comforts, and when he found himself on a
desert island his only thought was to recreate as best he could something at least of the material civilization he had left behind him. The
pieties of middle-class life also found their way onto the island—a
sober, businesslike religion, due gratitude to God for His mercies
together with a belief that God helps those who help themselves.
Crusoe is not an adventurer who goes to sea in search of excitement,
but a sober and prudent merchant engaged in a business enterprise.
Prudence rather than heroism is the key to his actions; he is, in fact,
the first significant example in English literature of the prudential
hero. His common sense and prudence are not set against romantic
extravagance (as that of Sancho Panza is set against the behavior of
Don Quixote) and so never appear mean-spirited or comic. Crusoe
has his author's respect and admiration throughout.

The success of *Robinson Crusoe* led Defoe to write many other
works of fiction, again presented as true accounts of what happened
to real people rather than frankly as fiction. These include *Captain
Singleton* (1720), *Moll Flanders* and *Colonel Jack* (1722), *Roxana*
(1724), and *Captain George Carlton* (1728). In 1722 he published
also his *Journal of the Plague Year,* a minutely realistic account of
the Great Plague of 1665 supposed to be a diary kept by a London
saddler but in fact a working of a variety of sources into an original
narrative so vividly circumstantial that the reader feels convinced
that the author must be describing what he had himself lived
through. The most interesting of his novels after *Robinson Crusoe* is
Moll Flanders, the autobiography of a prostitute, done with the most
lively realistic detail, in the handling of which Defoe showed his
knowledge of English social and economic life. Moll uses her beauty
to try and achieve financial security; her sex is a commodity which
she is continually trying to sell in the highest market. Though she is
penitent at the end, and is thus allowed to find happiness and peace

after her multifarious adventures, she has no moral sense at all, only a deep and constant sense of the value of money. Everything is reduced sooner or later to its monetary value, and the financial accounts and calculations with which the novel teems not only give an air of actual reporting to the story (as though this were a transcript of evidence given before a bankruptcy court), but also exposes with cheerful ruthlessness the economic basis of so much human activity —and so much social evaluation.

Defoe is a novelist almost in spite of himself. His intention was to reduce all literature to journalism, to tell invented things as though he were a reporter writing an account for the press. His eye for detail, his fascination with material things and with the surface of human behavior, and his deep roots in the English middle class, combined to make his best fiction both historically important and intrinsically interesting. But he had no imaginative understanding of the real springs of human behavior. Moll Flanders talks with authentic liveliness and tells her story with a matter-of-fact precision that compels assent; but she lives only as a figure in a social scene, not as a fully-developed, doing-and-suffering human being. And even *Robinson Crusoe* does not really absorb his frightening experiences: his long years of living alone produce no moral or psychological change. He is merely a vehicle for the persuasive recording of an attempt to impose on the alien world of nature the familiar world of English middle-class civilization, and though we respond with excitement to such a vivid scene as Crusoe's first discovery of the naked human footprint on the supposedly uninhabited island, it is the nature of the situation not its meaning in terms of the action as a whole that interests us. Defoe was deficient both in creative imagination and in a sense of structure. Yet he had his own kind of imagination, the ability to lie like the truth. His fiction shows with convincing clarity the way in which the developing English novel was linked with the habits of mind and literary needs of the rising middle classes. Defoe is not called "the father of the English novel" for nothing. The greatness of *Robinson Crusoe* is perhaps accidental, but the novel is not only the first full-length piece of prose fiction written in the plain style of early eighteenth-century expository prose with continuous colloquial overtones; it is also the first English popular novel (as distinct from romance, legend, *fabliau*, allegory, and other varieties of narrative) and the first to have as hero a man who seeks comfort and safety rather than honor or an object made valuable by some idea attached to it rather than its intrinsic material value. Stories before had often been based on the quest, whether it was the quest for the Holy Grail or the quest for something undefined by the seeker or the quest for riches or reputation or happiness or redemption. Crusoe does not search for far-off things, he improves what is there. And Moll Flanders, with her shrewd awareness of the relation between cash and reputation, points forward to Becky Sharp and those characters in Victorian fiction whose behavior and fortunes show the gap between gentility and morality. She even suggests her chronologically nearer neighbor, Richardson's Pamela, who also knows the financial equivalent of moral virtues and in the end makes a much shrewder bargain than Defoe's heroine.

An age which saw man as a rational creature achieving civilization by the calm exercise of common sense laid itself open rather obviously to disillusion. The political passions and intrigues of the early eighteenth century were not marked by sweet reasonableness, nor was the struggle for positions of power or profit in Church and State characterized in this period by any less unscrupulousness, selfishness, and hypocrisy than such struggles generally show. A keen look at *homo sapiens* in the Augustan Age, especially when the look was directed by a disappointed or frustrated man, was not likely to yield a vision of disinterested rationality producing an ideal civilization. And if the man who looked was also a master of irony, a political pamphleteer of genius, a wounded moralist who never forgave the world for not being what its optimistic philosophers said it was, possessor of an imagination both brilliant and bitter and of a narrative and expository style characterized by clarity, cogency, and an eloquent plainness, then something new and terrible in the way of satire could be expected. Jonathan Swift (1667–1745) was such a man, and he shows the other side of Augustan complacency with at times a masochistic energy. Born in Dublin of English parents, Swift as a young man came to work in the household of Sir William Temple as secretary and poor relation. Temple was a Whig and a supporter of the Ancients in the Ancients versus Moderns controversy, and it was in support of Temple that Swift wrote his *Battle of the Books,* a lively squib written in 1696–98 and published together with *A Tale of a Tub* (written about the same time) in 1704. In the "Apology" which he prefixed to the latter book in the fifth edition of 1710, Swift explained his purpose:

The author was then young, his invention at the height, and his reading fresh in his head. By the assistance of some thinking, and much conversation, he had endeavoured to strip himself of as many real prejudices as he could; I say real ones, because, under the notice of prejudices, he knew to what dangerous heights some men have proceeded. Thus prepared, he thought the numerous and gross corruptions in religion and learning might furnish matter for a satire, that would be useful and diverting. He resolved to proceed in a manner that should be altogether new, the world having been already too long nauseated with endless repetitions upon every subject. The abuses in religion, he proposed to set forth in the Allegory of the Coats and the three Brothers, which was to make up the body of the discourse. Those in learning he chose to introduce by way of digressions . . .

The tale is of three sons, Peter, Martin, and Jack, representing respectively the Roman Catholic Church, the Church of England, and the Protestant dissenters, who have each been left by their father the legacy of a coat with specific instructions as to how to wear and look after it. He then proceeds to give an ironic history of the development of Christianity by means of accounts of the various ways in which each brother behaves with respect to his coat and also in other matters. The device of translating developments in theology and in ritual into a parody of the purely physical accompaniments of such things struck deeper than Swift intended, for once religion is discussed in such ludicrous terms it is impossible to restrict the destructive satire to the abuses of what Swift considered popish superstition on the one hand and dissenting fanaticism on the other: religion itself becomes ludicrous, and equated with its most external and trivial trimmings. So long as Swift keeps to obvious abuses, such as the deliberate addition by the brothers of ornaments expressly forbidden in their father's will, the satire is specific and limited:

A while after there came up all in fashion a pretty sort of flame-coloured satin for linings; and the mercer brought a pattern of it immediately to our three gentlemen. . . . Upon this, they fell again to rummage the will, because the present case also required a positive precept, the lining being held by orthodox writers to be of the essence of the coat. After long search, they could fix upon nothing to the matter in hand, except a short advice of their father's in the will, to take care of fire, and put out their candles before they went to sleep. [Swift explained: "That is, to take care of hell; and, in order to do that, to subdue and extinguish their lusts."] This, though a good deal for the purpose, and helping very far towards self-conviction, yet not seeming wholly of force to establish a command; and being resolved to avoid further scruple, as well as future occasion for scandal, says he that was the scholar, "I remember to have read in wills of a codicil annexed, which is indeed a part of the will, and what it contains hath equal authority with the rest. Now, I have been considering of this same will here before us, and I cannot reckon it to be complete for want of such a codicil: I will therefore fasten one in its proper place very dexterously: I have had it by me some time; it was written by a dog-keeper of my grandfather's [this refers to the Apocrypha, which includes the story of Tobit and his dog], and talks a great deal (as good luck would have it) of this very flame-coloured satin.

The "flame-coloured satin" in this passage refers to the doctrine of Purgatory.

Even in making these quite specific references to doctrines with which he disagreed, however, Swift, by his tone, is reducing all religious belief to something arbitrary and trivial. It was all very well for him to protest in his "Apology": "Why should any clergyman of our church be angry to see the follies of fanaticism and superstition exposed, though in the most ridiculous manner; since that is perhaps the most probable way to cure them, or at least to hinder them from farther spreading?" If differences in the interpretation of Christianity are reduced to this level, then Christianity itself is reduced. The satire in *A Tale of a Tub* is often ingenious and brilliant, but only an agnostic could fully relish all of it. One of Swift's favorite satiric devices is to insist that there is no difference between the sign or symbol of a thing and the thing itself. " 'Tis true, indeed, that these animals, which are vulgarly called suits of clothes, or dresses, do, according to certain compositions, receive different appellations. If one of them be trimmed up with a gold chain, and a red gown, and a white rod, and a great horse, it is called a Lord-Mayor: if certain ermines and furs be placed in a certain position, we style them a Judge; and so an apt conjunction of lawn and black satin we entitle a Bishop." This is an effective way of puncturing human pride (and human pride was always one of Swift's main targets); but if one insists that there is no reality at all behind any of the symbols and rituals with which man surrounds his beliefs, practices, and institutions, the implication cannot be confined to satire of bad beliefs or practices or defective institutions or of anything less than the total nature of man. Swift spoke in the name of reason against pride and fanaticism; at the same time he was a stout supporter of the Church of England and opposed too tolerant treatment of dissenters. But exactly the same tools with which he destroyed the position of those with whom he disagreed could have been, and indeed were (though he did not fully realize it), used by him against his own. Pure unalloyed reason could not have justified the Anglican position as the only tenable Christian position for an Englishman. It is Peter and Jack who are attacked in *A Tale of a Tub;* but Martin is really equally vulnerable.

Some of the most brilliant parts of *A Tale of a Tub* are the digressions, in which Swift carried on his war against the pride and emptiness of modern scholars and the wicked folly of "religious enthusiasm" (a word defined by Dr. Johnson in his dictionary as "a vain confidence of divine favour or communication" and used to denote especially any conviction of personal inspiration which would lead a man away from the decent worship of the Anglican Church to the individual extravagancies of dissenting sects). The "Digression concerning the Original, the Use, and Improvement of Madness in a Commonwealth" is particularly revealing. Madness is humorously attributed to the rising of certain vapors from lower parts of the body into the brain. It is this kind of madness which has been responsible for "the greatest actions that have been performed in the world, under the influence of single men, which are, the establishment of new empires by conquest, the advance and progress of new schemes in philosophy, and the contriving, as well as the propagating, of new religions." (But Swift stops short of applying this theory to the origin of Christianity: it applies only to modern innovations.) The collection of vapors in the brain disturbs human reason, and then fancy takes control and common sense is turned out:

... if the moderns mean by madness, only a disturbance or transposition of the brain, by force of certain vapours issuing up from the lower faculties, then has this madness been the parent of all those mighty revolutions that have happened in empire, in philosophy, and in religion. For the brain, in its natural position and state of serenity, disposeth its owner to pass his life in the common forms, without any thought of subduing multitudes to his own power, his reasons, or his visions; and the more he shapes his understanding by the pattern of human learning, the less he is inclined to form parties after his particular notions, because that instructs him in his private infirmities, as well as in the stubborn ignorance of the people. But when a man's fancy gets astride of his reason, when imagination is at cuffs with the senses, and common understanding, as well as common sense, is kicked out of doors; the first proselyte he makes is himself; and when that is once compassed, the difficulty is not so great in bringing over others; a strong delusion always operating from without as vigorously as from within. . . .

"Cant and vision," Swift goes on to say, "are to the ear and eye the same that tickling is to the touch." It is a significant collocation. The entertainments and pleasures that men value most in life "are such as dupe and play the wag with the senses." Proof of this is found in the fact that "happiness . . . is a perpetual possession of being well deceived." Delusion is stronger than things as they appear "in the glass of nature." Credulity is better than curiosity, and superficial acceptance of the surface of things better than "that pretended philosophy, which enters into the depth of things, and then comes gravely back with information and discoveries, that in the inside they are good for nothing." We should, Swift ironically informs us, be content with what we can know by sight and touch only, and ignore reason which comes "officiously with tools for cutting, and opening, and mangling, and piercing, offering to demonstrate, that they are not of the same consistence quite through." Let us therefore be content with the outside. "Last week I saw a woman flayed, and you will hardly believe how much it altered her person for the worse." Swift is here attacking the human propensity to be taken in by the surface of things, by mere clothes and decorations; his method is to suggest that this is wholly desirable, for the use of reason to go below the surface may reveal unpleasant things. "Yesterday I ordered the carcass of a beau to be stripped in my presence, when we were all amazed to find so many unsuspected faults under one suit of clothes. Then I laid open his brain, his heart, and his spleen; but I plainly perceived at every operation, that the farther we proceeded, we found the defects increase upon us in number and bulk; from all which, I justly formed this conclusion to myself; that whatever philosopher or projector can find out an art to sodder and patch up the flaws and imperfections of nature, will deserve much better of mankind, and teach us a more useful science, than that so much in present esteem, of widening and exposing them. . . ." The man who is content to enjoy the surface of things "creams off nature, leaving the sour and the dregs for philosophy and reason to lap up. This is the sublime and refined point of felicity, called the possession of being well deceived; the serene peaceful state, of being a fool among knaves."

This is brilliantly savage stuff; but Swift's contrast between the happily deluded fool who is content to know the surface of things and the rational man who uses his reason to inquire into what lies below the surface has already been weakened by his earlier contrast between reason on the one hand and imagination, vision, enthusiasm, fancy (all these terms are used at one point or another in the argument) on the other. The reason that is perpetually suspicious of imagination is surely precluded from going very far below the superficial surface of things. Swift was exacerbated with his fellow men because he believed in reason; he believed that man was, if not a rational creature in all his doings, at least *rationis capax*, capable of reason, and it was therefore all the more tragic that he should allow his fancy to get astride of his reason. This of course is to accept the separation of fancy and judgment made by Hobbes and Locke—perhaps an illogical position in one who so fiercely attacked the moderns in philosophy. Ultimately it reduces the province of reason to something so narrow that it is incapable of really achieving anything. The exaltation of reason easily turns into anti-intellectualism, which finds its fullest expression in *Gulliver's Travels* where the Brobdingnagians are obliquely praised for knowing only morality, history, poetry, and mathematics and being incapable of apprehending the least notion of "ideas, entities, abstractions and transcendentals," while the noble Houyhnhnms cannot believe that a member of their species can take any pleasure in Gulliver's company, though it is an empirical fact that one of them does, because "such a practice was not agreeable to reason or nature, or a thing ever heard of before among them." Indeed, there is an inescapable dilemma in the thought of Swift and of his age. If belief in reason and nature means a belief in the common sense of mankind, then what the common sense of mankind believes is reasonable and natural and true. Anything new must be wrong. "It is impossible for us," wrote Addison in *The Spectator*, "who live in the latter ages of the world, to make observations in criticism, morality, or in any art of science, which have not been touched upon by others. We have little else left us, but to represent the common sense of mankind in more strong, more beautiful, or more uncommon lights." But most men are fools and knaves, according to Swift, and so the common sense of mankind, which he also believed in as an ultimate criterion, in fact leads to folly and knavery. Again, reason teaches us to be suspicious of imagination, of vision, of enthusiasm; we must stick to those simple rational truths that the calm application of common sense discovers. At the same time we must go below the surface and not be taken in by the mere appearances of things. Sometimes reason seems to lead to a simple empiricism: we must allow no knowledge that we cannot immediately test by our own experience. At other times a simple empiricism leads to delusion, for things are not as they seem and we must probe deeper to get at reality. We must beware of all abstractions, generalizations, transcendental ideas; yet this advice is given in the name of "reason and nature," themselves abstract general ideas—not to mention Swift's position as a devout member of the Church of England, whose theology certainly could not deny the transcendental. Brilliant in its play of irony as *A Tale of a Tub* is, it demonstrates some of the intellectual and moral dilemmas of the Age of Reason more clearly than anything else of its time.

On Sir William Temple's death in 1699 Swift went into public life, and hoped for some substantial position in the Church, whose prerogatives he strongly defended against both dissenters and deists. He obtained minor preferments in Ireland, but made frequent visits to London where he made friends with the important Whig writers (notably Addison) of the time. His ecclesiastical pamphleteering, however, brought him no reward, and, annoyed with the Whigs both for their neglect of him and for their benevolence toward dissenters, he joined the Tories in 1710 and wrote for them some of his most successful political pamphlets, including *The Conduct of the Allies* (1711), which prepared the public for the peace which concluded the War of the Spanish Succession. He was now intimate with most of the "Queen Anne wits," including Pope, Gay, Prior, Thomas Parnell, and Dr. Arbuthnot, and estranged from his former Whig friends. But Queen Anne herself was suspicious of the author of *A Tale of a*

Tub, and in spite of Swift's prominent position as the leading Tory pamphleteer and intimate of the Tory political leaders (who were solidly in power during the last years of Queen Anne's reign) he was never able to secure a more important position in the Church than the Deanery of St. Patrick's Cathedral, Dublin. The death of Queen Anne in 1714 meant the eclipse of the Tories and the triumph of the Whigs with the accession of George I; and this was the end of Swift's chances of an important ecclesiastical position. He retired to Ireland, his natural misanthropy increased by deep personal frustration.

Swift's misanthropy was of a peculiar kind. "I have ever hated all nations, professions, and communities," he wrote in a letter to Pope, "and all my love is towards individuals: for instance, I hate the tribe of lawyers, but I love Counsellor Such-a-one, and Judge Such-a-one: so with physicians . . . soldiers, English, Scotch, French, and the rest. But principally I hate and detest that animal called man, although I heartily love John, Peter, Thomas, and so forth; . . ." His hatred of that animal called man and his contempt for the Irish did not prevent him from being moved by the economic plight of the Irish people and producing in his *Drapier's Letters* (1724) a hard-hitting attack on the government's proposal for a new Irish coinage, which led to his becoming immensely popular among the Irish. Among his other pamphlets written on behalf of the Irish is his *Short View of the Present State of Ireland* (1727) and *A Modest Proposal for Preventing the Children of Poor People from being a Burthen to their Parents or Country* (1729). In the former he temporarily abandoned his favorite ironic method, because his heart was "too heavy to continue this irony longer." But the latter is the most brilliant use in English of the ironic device that Defoe had used in *Shortest Way with the Dissenters*. His proposal is simply that both parents and children would suffer infinitely less than they do at present if young children were fattened and sold for food. The opening is direct and somber:

> It is a melancholy object to those who walk through this great town or travel in the country, when they see the streets, the roads and cabin-doors crowded with beggars of the female sex, followed by three, four, or six children, all in rags, and importuning every passenger for an alms. These mothers instead of being able to work for their honest livelihood, are forced to employ all their time in strolling to beg sustenance for their helpless infants, who, as they grow up, either turn thieves for want of work, or leave their dear native country, to fight for the Pretender in Spain, or sell themselves to the Barbadoes.

But the note soon changes:

> As to my own part, having turned my thoughts, for many years, upon this important subject [the kind of provision that should be made for the children

of pauper parents], and maturely weighed the several schemes of other projectors, I have always found them grossly mistaken in their computation. It is true, a child just dropped from its dam may be supported by her milk for a solar year with little other nourishment, at most not above the value of two shillings, which the mother may certainly get, or the value in scraps, by her lawful occupation of begging; and it is exactly at one year old that I propose to provide for them in such a manner, as, instead of being a charge upon their parents, or the parish, or wanting food and raiment for the rest of their lives, they shall, on the contrary, contribute to the feeding and partly to the clothing of many thousands.

The phrase "dropped from its dam," language usually used only in discussing animals, prepares us for the proposal which follows. This proposal is couched in terms of quietly realistic humanitarianism, and the details are expounded with all the calm reasonableness of a merchant persuading his customers of the superior quality of a particular kind of article or a political economist advocating an economic nostrum:

I am assured by our merchants, that a boy or a girl before twelve years old is no saleable commodity, and even when they come to this age, they will not yield above three pounds, or three pounds and half a crown at most, on the exchange; which cannot turn to account either to the parents or kingdom, the charge of nutriment and rags having been at least four times that value.

I shall now therefore humbly propose my own thoughts, which I hope will not be liable to the least objection.

I have been assured by a very knowing American of my acquaintance in London, that a young healthy child well nursed is at a year old a most delicious nourishing and wholesome food, whether stewed, roasted, baked, or boiled; and I make no doubt that it will equally serve in a fricassie or a ragout.

I do therefore humbly offer it to public consideration, that of the hundred and twenty thousand children, already computed, twenty thousand may be reserved for breed, whereof only one fourth part to be males; which is more than we allow to sheep, black cattle, or swine, and my reason is, that these children are seldom the fruits of marriage, a circumstance not much regarded by our savages; therefore, one male will be sufficient to serve four females. That the remaining hundred thousand may at a year old be offered in sale to the persons of quality and fortune, through the kingdom, always advising the mother to let them suck plentifully in the last month, so as to render them plump, and fat for a good table. A child will make two dishes at an entertainment for friends, and when the family dines alone, the fore or hind quarter will make a reasonable dish, and seasoned with a little pepper or salt will be very good boiled on the fourth day, especially in winter.

The mask of complete indifference to the distinction between animals and children conceals, of course, a savage indignation at the conditions under which these children have to live. The quiet and matter-of-fact tone of Swift's proposals reveals much more effectively than any rhetoric the appalling fact that these children would really be better off if treated like cattle than under their present conditions. The calm is really a white heat. The whole devastating pamphlet is a brilliant example of one of Swift's favorite ironic devices—that of role-taking, pretending to be someone very different from the person he really is and speaking earnestly in that person's voice. The tone continues to the deadpan conclusion:

> I profess in the sincerity of my heart that I have not the least personal interest in endeavouring to promote this necessary work, having no other motive than the public good of my country, by advancing our trade, providing for infants, relieving the poor, and giving some pleasure to the rich. I have no children, by which I can propose to get a single penny; the youngest being nine years old, and my wife past child-bearing.

This disclaimer of any personal advantage is a ferocious parody of the hypocrisy of politicians in making similar statements; the ferocity is not however in the language, which in itself is quiet and factual, but in the whole implicit set of comparisons and contrasts which the discussion has set going. Swift had used this kind of irony before, notably on his *Argument Against Abolishing Christianity*, but irony in ecclesiastical discussion, as Defoe also found out, is dangerous: the gap between what is said and what is implied is not always discernible. The arguments against abolishing Christianity which Swift advocated on the assumption that their very absurdity would disqualify them and render ridiculous the kind of thinking of which this was a parody or a *reductio ad absurdum* have not always been found absurd. But in *A Modest Proposal* the appalling nature of the suggestions put forward in such a perfect imitation of the accents of the politicians and "projectors" of the time bring the disturbing analogies at once to the forefront of the reader's mind. The reader is forced to draw conclusions which are never once directly suggested by the writer.

A *Modest Proposal* shows Swift's curious combination of bitterness and compassion, as though his misanthropy were based on frustrated love. Frustrated ambition also plays its part, for Swift sought a position of power and influence which he never attained and which, after 1714, there was no likelihood of his attaining. Between 1710 and 1714, when he was a power in Tory politics and intimate with the most influential politicians and writers of the day, he indulged in a kind of literary high spirits that he was not to show again. He was the leading spirit in the founding of the Scriblerus Club, whose members included Pope, Arbuthnot, Gay, and Harley, a development of the earlier Tory Club in which he had also been active —"We take in none but men of wit and interest," Swift had written to Stella of the former in 1711. The objective of the Scriblerus Club was to satirize abuses in learning in the person of an absurd pedant,

Martin Scriblerus. It was a joint enterprise, and *The Memoirs of Martinus Scriblerus,* first published in the second volume of Pope's *Prose Works* (1741), was a cooperative production which contained germs of several ideas later developed by individual members.

A quite different side of Swift is revealed in his *Journal to Stella,* letters written daily between September, 1710, and June, 1713, to Esther Johnson, illegitimate daughter of Sir William Temple. Swift's precise relations with Stella are still argued about by his biographers; they may have been secretly married; but there is no doubt of their mutual love and of the fact that Stella's death in 1728 left Swift a broken man. The journal covers the period of Swift's change from the Whigs to the Tories and his rise to a position of influence among the Tory government leaders. The letters give the most intimate details of political discussions and intrigues of the period; they are sometimes frank and gossipy, sometimes tender and whimsical, sometimes welling up into an embarrassingly sentimental intimacy which on occasions expresses itself in a species of baby talk. Sometimes one feels that Swift had an impossibly idealistic view of the world and when he found that his own experience of men did not bear this out he reversed his original view with savage masochism. Sometimes he appears to be the frustrated sentimentalist. Stella had earlier gone to Ireland to be near Swift (but with a female companion, for respectability's sake), and the *Journal* was posted fortnightly to her from London. She was not the only girl to follow Swift to Ireland; Hester Vanhomrigh, whom Swift called Vanessa, fell in love with him and pursued him to Dublin—an embarrassing situation which Swift tried to deal with sometimes by jocularity, sometimes by anger. He was never cruel, except to mankind in general.

Swift's long exile in Ireland did not improve either his health or his character, and in his last years "sunk by public as well as personal vexation" as he once put it in a letter to Pope, he was ruined in mind as well as in body; in Johnson's grim phrase, "Swift expires a driveller and a show." Yet his Irish years produced his masterpiece, *Gulliver's Travels* (published anonymously in 1726, after a visit to England) and, in the early 1730's, a group of remarkable poems. The paradox of Swift's most comprehensive and brilliantly worked out satire of man and his civilization having become a children's classic has often been remarked on; but it is not hard to understand why the first two books of *Gulliver's Travels,* which show the hero's adventures first among tiny little people and then among enormous giants, with the most meticulous attention to scale in each case, should attract children, for whom dolls and small-scale models of things always have a special fascination. Among the Lilliputians Gulliver is among dolls, and among the Brobdingnagians he is a doll himself, and these facts are in themselves superficially intriguing. Though Swift himself had a childlike fascination with shifts in scale, that is not, of course, the main interest of even the first two books of *Gulliver*. Swift's object in Book I is to deflate human pride by showing all the pomp and circumstance of human pretension, all the stylization of cruelty, the vanities, rituals, political catchwords, meaningless controversies, that characterize man in society, existing in a community of minute creatures and so appearing as wholly contemptible. Conversely, when Swift places his hero among giants and makes him, now himself a tiny creature, boast about the way his civilization works to contemptuously amused grown-ups, they can only react to his absurd boastings with the crushing comment that Gulliver's people must be "the most pernicious race of little odious vermin that Nature ever suffered to crawl upon the surface of the earth." But Swift's attack is not simply on men in general, nor does he make his points only by reducing the scale of the world we know and so making man as we know him ridiculously petty. The enormous size of the Brobdingnagians, who are observed with minute closeness by Gulliver as he is handled by them, enables Swift to vent his disgust with the flesh, with man as a physical animal who sweats and excretes—a disgust which grew on Swift until it became thoroughly obsessive. The Brobdingnagians are sometimes shown as living in a state of simple virtue in sharp contrast to the corruptions of European civilization, at other times their grossness simply emphasizes the horribleness of the human animal. Again, Swift is as much concerned to expose particular abuses of his own time as to attack mankind, and though most of the detailed political satire is lost on the ordinary reader today, there is, especially in Book I, a complex political allegory at work, based on Swift's own experience of politics in Queen Anne's reign. But even without knowledge of these references the full power of the work can be realized.

The form of *Gulliver's Travels* was suggested to Swift by the great popularity of books of voyages and travel. He took Lemuel Gulliver, "first a surgeon and then a captain of several ships" and had him give his account of "travels into several remote nations of the world" in a plain and factual manner, introduced by his cousin and editor, who, in a note to the reader, explains: "The author of these travels, Mr. Lemuel Gulliver, is my ancient and intimate friend; there is likewise some relation between us by the mother's side. . . ." And so he testifies to his veracity. The quiet factualness of the narrative is reminiscent in some respects of Defoe, but Gulliver is a very different kind of person from Robinson Crusoe and his succession of experiences, unlike those of Crusoe, gradually change him until in the end he is totally disgusted with his own kind and full of admiration for the rational virtues of the noble Houyhnhnms. The whole process of Gulliver's education by his experiences is central to the book. At the beginning he has all the presuppositions and prejudices of someone brought up as he has been, son of a small landowner, educated at Cambridge, apprenticed to a surgeon in London, then student of navigation before marrying a respectable girl and settling down. He went to sea as ship's surgeon when his "business began to fail," and continued his education by reading the best authors, ancient and modern, in his hours of leisure. Swift is careful not to make the voyage to Lilliput the first of Gulliver's voyages; earlier voyages are briefly referred to, as having been more or less uneventful. Then, with the same quiet precision, the voyage begins which is to end in Lilliput: ". . . I accepted an advantageous offer from Captain William Prichard, master of the *Antelope*, who was making a voyage to the South Seas. We set sail from Bristol, May 4, 1699, . . ." The account of his shipwreck and swimming ashore on the coast of Lilliput is told in the same style. The sheer fascination of the detail carries the reader on with the account of the tiny people of Lilliput and how Gulliver gets on with them. Before we realize that any satire is intended we have been brought right into the story and escape is impossible. Swift handles every practical difficulty, from explaining how Gulliver learned the language to the most detailed accounts of the various ways in which he adjusted his vast bulk to the tiny scale of the country in which he found himself. As Swift proceeds with his account of the Lilliputians the satire begins to develop. There is a deliberate inconsistency in the way in which the satire operates. Sometimes the Lilliputian ways are described in such a way as to make the reader realize how stupid and vicious the European ways are. "The nurseries for males of noble or eminent birth, are provided with grave and learned professors, and their several deputies. The clothes and food of the children are plain and simple. They are bred up in the principles of honour, justice, courage, modesty, clemency, religion and love of their country; they are always employed in some business, except in the times of eating and sleeping, which are very short, and two hours for diversions, consisting of bodily exercises. They are dressed by men till four years of age, and then are obliged to dress themselves, although their quality be ever so great; . . ." Lilliput is sometimes Utopia and sometimes eighteenth-century England made utterly contemptible by the small size of the people who exhibit the same vices and follies as the English. The account of Lilliputian politics, with the quarrel between

the High-Heels and the Low-Heels and between the Big-Enders and
the Little-Enders, is clearly a parody of English politics. On the
other hand, the chapter on Lilliputian laws and education is almost
wholly Utopian. "In choosing persons for all employments, they have
more regard to good morals than to great abilities; . . . they thought
the want of moral virtues was so far from being supplied by superior
endowments of the mind, that employments could never be put into
such dangerous hands as those of persons so qualified; . . ." The
irony lies not so much in that here is a Utopian system which shows
up our own; but rather that here, put into actual practice, is what
we all profess to believe in but nobody would ever dream of acting on.

The voyage to Brobdingnag begins in the same circumstantial way
as the earlier voyage, but we move more immediately into the satire.
Deserted by the rest of the crew of the longboat on a foreign shore,
Gulliver finds himself in a country where everything is of enormous
size; the first man he sees "appeared as tall as an ordinary spire
steeple, and took about ten yards at every stride." He realizes that
he appears as ridiculous to these people as the Lilliputians had
seemed to him. He is discovered by a farmer, who "considered a
while with the caution of one who endeavours to lay hold on a
small dangerous animal in such a manner that it shall not be able
either to scratch or bite him, as I myself have sometimes done with
a weasel in England. . . . I apprehended every moment that he
would dash me against the ground, as we usually do any little hateful
animal which we have a mind to destroy." In a few words man as
Swift knew him is rendered animal, contemptible, and cruel.

Gulliver becomes the domestic pet of the farmer's nine-year-old
daughter, and how he fares in these circumstances is detailed in the
same circumstantial way as the Lilliputian adventures, with careful
account of the scale of everything and the means devised to enable
Gulliver to manage in this enormous world. Gulliver is part pet,
part freak of nature to be exhibited for profit, part baby, and part
doll, and in each of these aspects his experiences enable Swift to
indulge in satirical exposure of human pride and pretension. Gulliver
is then summoned to court, where the Queen buys him. He pleads his
cause before her (having learned the language from the farmer's
daughter) and she is "surprised at so much wit and good sense in so
diminutive an animal." The King at first conceives him to be a clock-
work toy, but on hearing him speak concedes that he is a rational
creature—an ironic conclusion in the light of the remainder of the
book. Gulliver becomes a pet of the royal family, and has his own
miniature furniture and utensils in a portable wooden box that serves
as a bedchamber. He tells the King about English civilization. "But,

I confess, that after I had been a little too copious in talking of my own beloved country, of our trade, and wars by sea and land, of our schisms in religion, and parties in the state; the prejudices of his education prevailed so far, that he could not forbear taking me up in his right hand, and stroking me gently with the other, after an hearty fit of laughing, asked me, whether I were a Whig or a Tory." The attack on human pride is relentless: ". . . he observed how contemptible a thing was human grandeur, which could be mimicked by such diminutive insects as I. 'And yet,' said he, 'I dare engage, these creatures have their titles and distinctions of honour, they contrive little nests and burrows, that they call houses and cities; they make a figure in dress and equipage; they love, they fight, they dispute, they cheat, they betray.' And thus he continued on, while my colour came and went several times, with indignation to hear our noble country, the mistress of arts and arms, the scourge of France, the arbitress of Europe, the seat of virtue, piety, honour, and truth, the pride and envy of the world, so contemptuously treated." Gulliver's education has barely begun. It proceeds apace in Chapter 7, where he boasts of his country and its customs only to arouse in the King extreme contempt. "Nothing but an extreme love of truth," this chapter begins, "could have hindered me from concealing this part of my story." It tells of the ultimate humiliation not only of himself but of the civilization he represented. Here is corrupt man facing humane reasonableness. ". . . I remember very well, in a discourse one day with the King, when I happened to say there were several thousand books among us written upon the art of government, it gave him (directly contrary to my intention) a very mean opinion of our understandings. He professed both to abominate and despise all *mystery, refinement,* and *intrigue* either in a prince or a minister. He could not tell what I meant by *secrets of state,* where an enemy or some rival nation were not in the case. He confined the knowledge of governing within very *narrow bounds;* to common sense and reason, to justice and lenity, to the speedy determination of civil and criminal causes; with some other obvious topics, which are not worth considering. And he gave it for his opinion, that whoever could make two ears of corn or two blades of grass to grow upon a spot of ground where only one grew before, would deserve better of mankind, and do more essential service to his country, than the whole race of politicians put together." The ideal nature of the Brobdingnagians becomes ever clearer in this section. Even their prose style "is clear, masculine, and smooth, but not florid." Gulliver discovers a book treating "of the weakness of human kind," which was "in little esteem, except among the women and the vulgar." And reading here further matter to diminish human pride he is led for the first time to "believe, upon a strict inquiry, those quarrels might be shown as ill grounded among us, as they are among that people."

When Gulliver's box is carried off by an eagle and dropped into the sea, whence he is rescued by an English ship, the Brobdingnagian adventure ends; but it has left more permanent marks on Gulliver than the Lilliputian. The kindness of the ship's captain to Gulliver passes without comment, although it seems to contradict the indictment against humankind which runs through the book (the same can be said to the even greater kindness of the captain of the Portuguese ship that rescues him in Book IV). It takes Gulliver a long time to get used to the littleness of "the houses, the trees, the cattle, and the people" once he is back in England. That as far as the people are concerned it is a moral littleness, he is not fully aware until after his last voyage. And yet there are the two ships' captains, models of kindness and sympathy: it is almost as though Swift were illustrating his remark to Pope that he hated man but loved individuals.

Book III of *Gulliver's Travels*, the Voyage to Laputa, is less interesting both because of its lack of unity and because the objects of Swift's satire are here more particular to his age. He is attacking every kind of impractical scholarship and vain philosophy and the absurd and pretentious schemes of economists and "promoters." It is here that we see most clearly how Swift's exaltation of reason leads to anti-intellectualism. Speculative thought is ridiculous. "With these bladders they now and then flapped the mouths and ears of those who stood near them, of which practice I could not then conceive the meaning; it seems the minds of these people are so taken up with intense speculations, that they neither can speak, nor attend to the discourses of others, without being roused by some external taction upon the organs of speech and hearing; . . ." The Laputans neglect practical matters to indulge in theory. "Their houses are very ill built, the walls bevil, without one right angle in any apartment, and this defect ariseth from the contempt they bear to practical geometry, which they despise as vulgar and mechanic, those instructions they give being too refined for the intellectuals of their workmen, which occasions perpetual mistakes. And although they are dexterous enough upon a piece of paper in the management of the rule, the pencil, and the divider, yet in the common actions and behaviour of life, I have not seen a more clumsy, awkward, and unhandy people, nor so slow and perplexed in their conceptions upon all other subjects, except those of mathematics and music." Yet "imagination, fancy, and invention, they are wholly strangers to, nor have any words in their language by which those ideas can be expressed." Their intellectual interests are confined to mathematics and music.

From Laputa Gulliver goes to Balnibarbi and its capital Lagado, and in the description of the Academy of Projectors in Lagado, Swift satirizes inventors and promoters of schemes for improving everything. "In these colleges the professors contrive new rules and methods of agriculture and building, and new instruments and tools for all trades and manufactures, whereby, as they undertake, one man shall do the work of ten; a palace may be built in a week, of materials so durable as to last for ever without repairing." Swift has a great deal of fun with his description of the professors of the Academy and their pursuits. "A new method of teaching was for a proposition and demonstration to be fairly written on a thin wafer, with ink composed of a cephalic tincture. This the student was to swallow upon a fasting stomach, and for three days eat nothing but bread and water. As the water digested, the tincture mounted to his brain, bearing the proposition along with it." The satire here is more comic than bitter, except in the passage explaining their method of proving the guilt of persons suspected of plotting against the state. The anagrammatic method of exposing a plot is illustrated thus: "So for example if I should say in a letter to a friend, *Our brother Tom has just got the piles*, a skilful decipherer would discover that the same letters which compose that sentence may be analysed into the following words: *Resist, a plot is brought home; The tour* [tower]. And this is the anagrammatic method." The matter-of-fact final sentence is what rams home the preposterousness of the whole thing.

Nevertheless, the satire in the third book is for the most part either confused or ephemeral or relatively trivial. It is with Book IV, "A Voyage to the Country of the Houyhnhnms" that Swift's satire rises to its most shattering, though at the same time it tends to destroy itself. The Houyhnhnms are a race of noble horses who live according to the laws of "reason and nature." Serving them and despised by them are the beastly Yahoos, a degenerate species of man. Gulliver himself recognizes how detestable the Yahoos are before he realizes, to his "horror and astonishment," that those "abominable animals" had perfect human figures. Gulliver this time makes no attempt to assert the superiority or even the decency of the human race, being content to try to persuade the Houyhnhnms of the relationship between human beings and horses in his own country. In giving an account of the state of England Gulliver speaks directly with Swift's own voice: "Now your Honour is to know, that these judges are per-

sons appointed to decide all controversies of property, as well as for
the trial of criminals, and picked out from the most dexterous lawyers, who are grown old or lazy, and having been biased all their
lives against truth and equity, lie under such a fatal necessity of
favouring fraud, perjury, and oppression, that I have known several
of them to have refused a large bribe from the side where justice lay,
rather than injure the faculty, by doing anything unbecoming their
nature or their office." As Gulliver proceeds with his account of England, he speaks more and more from the point of view of the Houyhnhnms who regarded British institutions as the plain results of "our
gross defects in reason, and by consequence, in virtue." He apolo-
gizes to the reader for "giving so free a representation of my own
species," but explains that "the many virtues of those excellent quad-
rupeds placed in opposite view to human corruptions, had so far
opened my eyes and enlarged my understanding, that I began to
view the actions and passions of men in a very different light, and to
think the honour of my own kind not worth managing; . . ." Disgust
for the human species increases steadily as the narrative proceeds,
and Gulliver learns to live as a humble admirer and servant of the
Houyhnhnms.

The life of reason as led by the Houyhnhnms is curiously dead.
George Orwell has argued that the "reason" which governs them is
really a desire for death. "They are exempt," says Orwell, "from love,
friendship, curiosity, fear, sorrow, and—except in their feeling towards the Yahoos, who occupy rather the same place in their community as the Jews in Nazi Germany—anger and hatred." They show
no fondness for their colts or foals; reason ousts any demonstration of
love except an abstract and universal benevolence. They take no
pleasure in sex, producing two children out of rational duty and
thereafter abstaining. Their poetry is wholly didactic, usually containing "some exalted notions of friendship and benevolence, or the
praises of those who were victors in races, and other bodily exercises." Orwell comments: "The Houyhnhnms, creatures without a
history, continue for generation after generation to live prudently,
maintaining their population at exactly the same level, avoiding all
passion, suffering from no diseases, meeting death indifferently,
training up their young in the same principles—and all for what? In
order that the same process may continue indefinitely." It is indeed
a "dreary Utopia," and one cannot help feeling that the motive behind its creation is more contempt for the Yahoos than love of the
Houyhnhnms. There are contradictions, too. Gulliver is appalled by
the bestiality of the Yahoos, recoiling from them as creatures for
whom he has a natural antipathy. Yet it is demonstrated that the

Yahoos are men, although completely degenerate men. If Swift is trying to tell us that men as we know them are really more like Yahoos than we realize, whence comes Gulliver's instinctive horror of them? Gulliver's revulsion is the measure of the Yahoos' difference from himself, but Swift wants to make it also the measure of the degeneracy to which man who does not use his capacity to lead the life of reason will inevitably sink. It is difficult for him to have it both ways. Again, though the obvious difference between men and Yahoos is what makes the thought of their ultimate or potential similarity so shocking (and is where the force of the satire resides), by the end of the book Swift is cheerfully calling the English Yahoos and leaving it at that. Gulliver concludes the book by describing his difficulty in reconciling himself to life among Yahoos in England after his experience with the noble Houyhnhnm race, and he ends with a final broadside against human pride:

My reconcilement to the Yahoo-kind in general might not be so difficult, if they would be content with those vices and follies only which Nature hath entitled them to. I am not in the least provoked at the sight of a lawyer, a pickpocket, a colonel, a fool, a lord, a gamester, a politician, a whoremaster, a physician, an evidence, a suborner, an attorney, a traitor, or the like; this is all according to the due course of things: but when I behold a lump of deformity, and diseases both in body and mind, smitten with *pride*, it immediately breaks all the measures of my patience; neither shall I be ever able to comprehend how such an animal and such a vice could tally together.

The collocation of pickpockets, fools, lords, politicians, etc., is a savage repudiation of all human institutions; the very length of the list and the extremes it contains indicates the violence with which Swift rejects all human attempts to make distinctions between kinds of behavior and of function. All are subsumed in a single absurd and contemptible image—the Yahoo actually being proud of his Yahooness. One cannot argue Swift out of this nihilistic position by contending that after all men are *not* Yahoos or by emphasizing the kindness of the Portuguese captain. Nor can one say that Swift withdraws himself from the obsessed Gulliver (whose education in morality and reason has ended by making him unfit for human company) and is now being ironical at Gulliver's expense. This is clearly Swift's voice speaking, powerful and compelling and sounding with genius, but at the same time distorted and terrifying.

Swift's poetry has a dry ironic force of its own, a quality more admired today than it was in earlier periods. "A Description of the Morning" and "A Description of a City Shower" achieve poetic force by calm precision of the detail—an etching rather than a painting—

The turnkey now his flock returning sees,
Duly let out a-nights to steal for fees:
The watchful bailiffs take their silent stands,
And schoolboys lag with satchels in their hands.

Or this:

Sweeping from butchers' stalls, dung, guts, and blood,
Drowned puppies, stinking sprats, all drenched in mud,
Dead cats and turnip-tops come tumbling down the flood.

He can be humorous and intimate, as in his poems on Stella's birthday. But he is most impressive in his strong, ironic octosyllabic couplets, notably in "The Beasts' Confession" and "Verses on the Death of Dr. Swift," both dating from the early 1730's. The former concludes:

Our author's meaning, I presume is,
A creature *bipes et implumis*
Wherein the moralist designed
A compliment on humankind:
For here he owns that now and then
Beasts may *degenerate* into men.

The "Verses on the Death of Dr. Swift" present an ironic self-portrait which is at the same time a criticism of society, done with a restrained satirical touch quite unlike the savagery of the last part of *Gulliver,* and at the same time quite without self-pity:

. . . Behold the fatal day arrive!
"How is the Dean?"—"He's just alive."
Now the departing prayer is read.
"He hardly breathes"—"The Dean is dead."
   Before the passing-bell begun
The news through half the town has run.
"Oh! may we all for death prepare!
What has he left? and who's his heir?"
"I know no more than what the news is;
'Tis all bequeathed to public uses."
"To public use! a perfect whim!
What had the public done for him?
Mere envy, avarice, and pride:
He gave it all—but first he died.
And had the Dean in all the nation
No worthy friend, no poor relation?
So ready to do strangers good,
Forgetting his own flesh and blood?" . . .
   My female friends, whose tender hearts

Have better learned to act their parts,
Receive the news in doleful dumps:
"The Dean is dead (and what is trumps?) . . .
　"Perhaps I may allow the Dean
Had too much satire in his vein;
And seemed determined not to starve it,
Because no age could more deserve it.
Yet malice never was his aim;
He lashed the vice, but spared the name;
No individual could resent,
Where thousands equally were meant;
His satire points at no defect,
But what all mortals may correct; . . .
　If vice can ever be abashed,
It must be ridiculed or lashed.
If you resent it, who's to blame?
He neither knew you nor your name.
Should vice expect to 'scape rebuke,
Because its owner is a duke?
　"He knew an hundred pleasant stories,
With all the turns of Whigs and Tories:
Was cheerful till his dying day;
And friends would let him have his way.
　"He gave the little wealth he had
To build a house for fools and mad;
And showed by one satiric touch,
No nation wanted it so much.
That kingdom he hath left his debtor,
I wish it soon may have a better."

These are Swift's last words on himself, and they may stand.

The career and writings of Swift reveal some of the contradictions of the Augustan Age; Alexander Pope (1688–1744), the dominant poetic figure among the Augustans, reflects, in his view of his art and in his practice of it, the social tone of the urban literary world of his day, and at the same time reveals a personality as sharply idiosyncratic as Swift's, though very different. Thus, the optimistic deism of the *Essay on Man*, the stylized elegance of the *Pastorals*, the deliberate conventionality of *Windsor Forest*, the chiseled formulations of the *Essay on Criticism*, all suggest the urbane self-confidence of an age pleased with its own civilization, drawing confidently on classical precedent with a happy sophistication and the assurance that comes from writing for a relatively small audience of similar education. On the other hand, the delicate sadness underlying *The Rape of the Lock*, the savagely pessimistic tone of some of the satires and epistles, the disgusted vituperation of the *Dunciad*, reveal an atti-

tude far removed from the optimistic self-congratulation on having
reached a pinnacle of civilization which is often regarded as a mark
of the Augustan writer. Pope can write in the *Essay on Man:*

> All Nature is but Art, unknown to thee;
> All Chance, Direction, which thou canst not see;
> All Discord, Harmony not understood;
> All partial Evil, universal Good:
> And, spite of Pride, in erring Reason's spite,
> One truth is clear, WHATEVER IS, IS RIGHT.

He can also write, in the *Epilogue to the Satires:*

> Lo! at the wheels of her triumphal car,
> Old England's Genius, rough with many a scar,
> Dragged in the dust! his arms hang idly round,
> His flag inverted trails along the ground!
> Our youth, all liveried o'er with foreign gold,
> Before her dance: behind her, crawl the old!
> See thronging millions to the pagod run,
> And offer country, parent, wife, or son!
> Hear her black trumpet thro' the land proclaim,
> That NOT TO BE CORRUPTED IS THE SHAME. . . .
> See, all our nobles begging to be slaves!
> See, all our fools aspiring to be knaves!
> The wit of cheats, the courage of a whore,
> Are what ten thousand envy and adore:
> All, all look up, with reverential awe,
> At crimes that 'scape, or triumph o'er the law:
> While truth, worth, wisdom, daily they decry—
> "Nothing is sacred now but villainy."

And again:

> Here, last of Britons! let your names be read;
> Are none, none living? let me praise the dead,
> And for that cause which made your fathers shine,
> Fall by the votes of their degen'rate line.

Pope was a Roman Catholic at a time when Roman Catholics in
England still suffered civil disabilities; he was also sickly and mal-
formed. These two facts may go a little way toward explaining the
individual qualities of Pope's work as opposed to what one might call
the social and Augustan qualities. One can also note a chronological
shift, the earlier poems showing more urbanity and optimism, the
later (with a notable exception in the *Essay on Man*) displaying an
almost Swiftian contempt for his fellows. Yet—while it is salutary to
remember that the age of Pope was also on the one hand the age of

Addison and on the other the age of Swift—Pope is never truly Swift-ian; his campaign against dullness, folly, and venality was waged against persons who represented those qualities, not against man-kind, and he rarely suggested that human society was inherently cor-rupt. He became disgusted with men, not with Man; with Swift it was the other way round—"I hate and detest that animal called man, although I love John, Peter, Thomas and so forth." In the earlier part of his career, Pope was a member of an intimate circle of writers (in-cluding Swift, Arbuthnot, Gay, and Bolingbroke). With the fall of the Tories on the death of Queen Anne in 1714, Swift retired to Dublin, and though he paid a long visit to Pope in 1726, his absence made a difference. Further, during the premiership of Sir Robert Walpole (1721–42), a man with no use for writers save as hacks to produce party political propaganda, Pope and his friends inevitably became more and more antigovernment; the promise of Augustan civilization held out in the last four years of Queen Anne's reign seemed utterly frustrated; and Pope became even more proud, sensitive, and quar-relsome. Gay died in 1732; Arbuthnot, the Scottish physician, Pope's closest friend, died in 1735; and in 1745 Swift died after some years of progressive mental and physical degeneration. It is not difficult to see why Pope felt lonely and embittered in the last years of his life. But such biographical explanations remain unsatisfactory. The fact that Pope was both spokesman for the Augustan Age and its chief scourge must also be related to some inner contradictions in the civili-zation of the age itself. Another aspect of those contradictions can be seen in the poetry of Matthew Prior, where the line between as-sured urbanity and condescending vulgarity is often uncertain, and in Gay's *Beggar's Opera*, where a society made up of nasty swagger and sordid self-interest is presented as an ironic commentary on the political life of the time, by a poet who could write simple-minded verse fables and elegant songs about Daphnis and Chloe or Damon and Cupid and who expected a government sinecure in recognition of his poetic talents.

Pope was first encouraged in his poetic ambitions by a group of older writers—including Walsh, Wycherley, and Congreve—who sur-vived from the age of Dryden and who helped to formulate Pope's early critical notions in terms of the hopes of that age. "About fif-teen," Pope told Joseph Spence, "I got acquainted with Mr. Walsh. He used to encourage me much, and used to tell me, that there was one way left of excelling: for though we had several great poets, we never had any one great poet that was correct; and he desired me to make that my study and aim." The rhetorical facility of much of Dry-den's work produced its own kind of masculine eloquence; but its repetitive cadences, indiscriminate use of the alexandrine, and concentration on the total effect of a verse paragraph rather than on the polish, balance, and variety of the individual couplet, left much for Pope to do in "correcting" English versification:

> Ev'n copious Dryden wanted, or forgot,
> The last and greatest Art, the Art to blot.

Walsh's advice suited Pope's genius; he had a subtle ear for variety within unity, as well as the kind of wit which sought and achieved most effective expression in those verbal devices which, by varying delicately the balance or progression of the thought to which the verse had been leading, at the same time demonstrated technical virtuosity and created new overtones of meaning. For the most part, Pope stuck to the heroic couplet, and his verse is monotonous only in the sense that he does not commonly seek other measures. In his use of the heroic couplet his achievement was to subtilize that verse form and substitute for the superficial smoothness of Waller or the rhetorical *élan* of Dryden something approaching metaphysical wit.

The poems which aroused the interest of Walsh and others in the young Pope were pastorals, written, Pope later claimed, at the age of eighteen. These were printed in 1709 by the publisher Tonson in one of his *Miscellanies*. Pope wrote a prefatory "Discourse on Pastoral Poetry" in which he declared that "simplicity, brevity and delicacy" were the proper qualities of a pastoral poem, and added: "If we would copy Nature, it may be useful to take this Idea along with us, that Pastoral is an image of what they call the golden age. So that we are not to describe our shepherds as shepherds at this day really are, but as they may be conceived then to have been; . . ." The four pastoral dialogues—one for each season, beginning with Spring—which Pope gives us are derivative and artificial enough, but the versification is remarkably assured, if wholly lacking in the subtlety of the later Pope. The stately stylization is sufficiently indicated by the passage from "Summer" which has been kept alive by Handel's matching music:

> Where'er you walk, cool gales shall fan the glade;
> Trees, where you sit, shall crowd into a shade;
> Where'er you tread, the blushing flowers shall rise,
> And all things flourish where you turn your eyes.

Messiah: A Sacred Eclogue, which appeared in the *Spectator* on May 14, 1712, is an attempt to combine Virgil's Fourth Eclogue with the messianic parts of Isaiah in couplet verse of high formal gravity.

Comparison with the effective simplicity of the biblical original is inevitable, and such a rhetorical exercise as

> Hark! a glad voice the lonely desert cheers;
> Prepare the way! a God, a God appears:
> A God, a God! the vocal hills reply,
> The rocks proclaim th' approaching Deity

seems obviously inflated when compared to the third verse of the fortieth chapter of Isaiah: "A voice crieth in the wilderness: Prepare a way for the Lord, make straight in the desert a highway for our God." Nor can Pope's

> And boys in flowery bands the tiger lead

stand beside the biblical: "and a little child shall lead them." The neoclassic theory of "kinds" and insistence on decorum demanded that verse on a high religious theme should be deliberately stately in diction and movement. The same theory demanded that satirical verse should be vigorously colloquial in tone, as Pope's always was. The theory is sensible enough, and generally works in Pope's application of it. The messianic theme, however, with its biblical background, posed special problems, which Pope at this stage of his career was hardly equipped to tackle.

More interesting is *Windsor Forest*, published in 1713 and apparently written at two separate periods, the first part in 1704 and the second in 1713. This kind of descriptive and reflective poetry—what Dr. Johnson called "local poetry"—goes back to Denham's "Cooper's Hill" and Waller's briefer poem "On St. James's Park." One described the scene, and reflected on its geography and history. Pope's poem has little unity; it is a collection of scenes and apostrophes; but some of the descriptive passages have a fine heraldic gloss which marks the high point of this kind of art. The shot pheasant is a heraldic bird:

> Ah! what avails his glossy, varying dyes,
> His purple crest, and scarlet-circled eyes,
> The vivid green his shining plumes unfold,
> His painted wings, and breast that flames with gold.

The fish, too, have a similar formal beauty:

> Our plenteous streams a various race supply,
> The bright-eyed perch with fins of Tyrian dye,
> The silver eel, in shining volumes rolled,
> The yellow carp, in scales bedropped with gold,
> Swift trouts, diversified with crimson stains,
> And pikes, the tyrants of the watery plains.

The formality of diction càn add grace and charm to an account of a rural scene, in spite of—or because of—the artificiality:

> Nor yet, when moist Arcturus clouds the sky,
> The woods and fields their pleasing toils deny.
> To plains with well-breathed beagles we repair,
> And trace the mazes of the circling hare; . . .
> With slaught'ring guns th' unwearied fowler roves
> When frosts have whitened all the naked groves;
> When doves in flocks the leafless trees o'ershade,
> And lonely woodcocks haunt the watery glade.
> He lifts the tube, and levels with his eye;
> Straight a short thunder breaks the frozen sky:
> Oft, as the mounting larks their notes prepare,
> The clam'rous lapwings feel the leaden death:
> Oft, as the mounting larks their notes prepare,
> They fall, and leave their little lives in air.

The "Ode on St. Cecilia's Day" (published in 1713 and said by Pope, possibly wrongly, to have been written in 1708) is an exercise in the irregular ode in the manner of Dryden's odes; the rapid shifts in mood and tone, variation in line lengths, and general striving after emotional effect results in a curious piece of verse posturing, very untypical of its author. Two other early poems written in stanza form are the "Ode on Solitude," a deftly turned Horatian imitation, and "The Dying Christian to his Soul" a three-stanza adaptation and amplification of the Emperor Hadrian's address to his soul, *"Animula, vagula, blandula."* The "Ode on Solitude" has a quiet grace in the modulation of the lines:

> Happy the man whose wish and care
> A few paternal acres bound,
> Content to breathe his native air,
> In his own ground. . . .

The *Essay on Criticism,* published in 1711, is Pope's first full-dress work. It is essentially a turning into polished epigrammatic couplets of the main critical ideas of the time. Part I announces the place of Taste, the relation between Art and Nature, the meaning and function of the Rules, and the importance of the Ancients. True taste is as rare in a critic as a true genius in a poet,

> Yet if we look more closely, we shall find
> Most have the seeds of judgment in their mind:
> Nature affords at least a glimm'ring light;
> The lines, tho' touch'd but faintly, are drawn right.

"Nature" here means something like "common sense," though its meaning throughout the poem is often more comprehensive than this, indicating both the whole state of things as they are and the ideal which serves as a model for imitation in both life and art, and it can also mean simply the normal. So when Pope goes on to say

> First follow Nature, and your judgment frame
> By her just standard, which is still the same,

he is referring to an ideal implicit in the way the world goes on. Nature is

> At once the source, and end, and test of Art.

The rules discovered by the ancient critics (chiefly Aristotle) simply reveal to us the true pattern and universality of Nature:

> Those Rules of old discovered, not devis'd,
> Are Nature still, but Nature methodiz'd;
> Nature, like liberty, is but restrain'd
> By the same laws which first herself ordain'd.

To obey the rules, to copy Homer or Virgil, and to follow Nature amount to the same thing; for the rules methodize Nature, and Homer and Virgil show how Nature can best be followed:

> Learn hence for ancient rules a just esteem;
> To copy Nature is to copy them.

There are, however, graces beyond the reach of art which only the "great wit" can achieve:

> Great wits sometimes may gloriously offend,
> And rise to faults true Critics dare not mend.

Pope then goes on in Part II to show

> the Causes which conspire to blind
> Man's erring judgment, and misguide the mind.

Pride, imperfect learning ("A little learning is a dangerous thing . . ."), judging by the parts instead of looking at the whole, wrong emphasis of one kind or another, excessive enthusiasm or excessive censoriousness, and different kinds of prejudice, are the culprits, and each is illustrated with an adroit reference or explained by a witty description. Critics, he concludes, should cultivate good nature together with good sense, and realize that the chief object of censure is obscenity, while dullness and obscenity together are unpardonable

(Charles II's reign is used as an illustration here). Part III gives positive rules for good critical behavior, somewhat abstractly, in spite of the illustrations; truth and candor, diffidence, good breeding, civility, and sincerity are all necessary. The case of Appius, who "reddens at each word you speak" (Pope was attacking John Dennis) is cited as an awful warning, giving us the first of those brief satiric character sketches that Pope was later to develop so characteristically. Finally, Pope presents a thumbnail history of criticism, from Aristotle, "the mighty Stagirite," to William Walsh, and the poem ends with a eulogy of his recently dead friend:

> Such late was Walsh—the Muse's judge and friend,
> Who justly knew to blame or to commend;
> To failings mild, but zealous for desert;
> The clearest head, and the sincerest heart. . . .
> Careless of censure, nor too fond of fame;
> Still pleas'd to praise, yet not afraid to blame,
> Averse alike to flatter, or offend;
> Not free from faults, nor yet too vain to mend.

The *Essay on Criticism* is not a serious contribution to critical theory, nor was it meant to be. It is the stringing together, in the most apt and pointed verse expression of which Pope was capable, of a number of commonly held ideas, with certain personal digressions.

The Rape of the Lock, published in 1712 and revised in 1714, is the masterpiece of Pope's earlier life and perhaps of his whole career. This mock-heroic poem on Lord Petre's cutting off a lock from Miss Arabella Fermor's hair, written to laugh the two families out of the quarrel that resulted, brought out in Pope a combination of qualities that he never again displayed together. Delicate imagination, subtly ironic wit, mock-heroic extravagance, the most perfect control over cunningly manipulated verse—these qualities go together with an almost tenderly affectionate humor, a criticism of female (and male) vanity at once indulgent and penetrating, and the faintest breath of underlying melancholy at the inevitable disparity between human professions and the realities of social life. A true relish of the epic devices in this "heroic-comical poem" is perhaps lost to a generation which has not been brought up with that sense of literary decorum that demands an appropriate diction and tone for every sort of poetry and every degree of formality. To make a trivial drawing-room episode into an epic theme and to treat the social customs of the Age of Queen Anne with an assumed epic seriousness, was to set going certain tensions and ironies which the early eighteenth century was especially fitted to appreciate. A looser, more individualistic, romantic theory and practice of poetry would have made this kind of poetic jest impossible. But *The Rape of the Lock* is more than a jest; it is, in Arnold's phrase, a criticism of life, "under the conditions fixed by the laws of poetic truth and poetic beauty."

The mock-epic tradition is an old one, going back to the pseudo-Homeric *Batrachomyomachia* ("Battle of the Frogs and Mice") and, nearer to Pope's time, to Alessandro Tassoni's *Rape of the Bucket* (*La Secchia Rapita*), Vida's *Game of Chess*, and Boileau's *Lutrin*. Pope took what he needed from the suggestions of earlier writers (e.g., the game of ombre from Vida's chess) but his use of the epic tradition as he knew it in Homer, Virgil, and Milton, varying in kind from direct parody to indirect suggestion, is essentially his own. More important, the *tone* of the poem is wholly original, the blend of burlesque, wit, humor, irony, and morality being a distillation we find nowhere else in English poetry. Something of the nature of the irony can be seen in the opening statement of the theme:

> Say what strange motive, Goddess! could compel
> A well-bred Lord t' assault a gentle Belle?

—where the obvious irony of the epic appeal to the goddess in the manner of Homer is crossed by the subtler irony of expressing surprise that a lord should assault a belle. Further, he specifies a well-bred lord and a gentle belle—thus suggesting that not all lords were well-bred nor all belles gentle. Or consider the first few lines of the opening of the story proper:

> Sol thro' white curtains shot a tim'rous ray,
> And oped those eyes that must eclipse the day:
> Now lap-dogs give themselves the rousing shake,
> And sleepless lovers, just at twelve, awake:
> Thrice rung the bell, the slipper knock'd the ground,
> And the press'd watch return'd a silver sound.

The mock formality of the first of these lines gives way to the delicacy of the last. "Those eyes" in the second line are the eyes of Belinda, the heroine, and the high compliment involved in saying that they must "eclipse the day" partakes only faintly of the irony of the mock-heroic: there is an element of real admiration here. The obvious irony of the lap-dogs and the sleepless lovers is rendered less obvious by the artful poise of the verse in which it is expressed, while the quiet, steady run of the last line (referring to Belinda's pressing her repeater watch to hear it sound the hour) provides the calmly confident social tone. Yet it is that social tone which the poem as a whole criticizes—criticizes without blaming, almost, for Pope is not condemning any specific society, but being gently ironical about the social surface of life in general. The description of Belinda's dressing table—

> Here files of pins extend their shining rows,
> Puffs, Powders, Patches, Bibles, Billet-doux—

is humorously indulgent, but at the same time the confusions between real and pretended interests are not only Belinda's. Similarly, the equal weighting of moral disaster and minor social accident which the fashions and conventions of any society are bound to produce in some degree is artfully ticked off in the well-known lines:

> Whether the nymph shall break Diana's law,
> Or some frail china jar receive a flaw;
> Or stain her honour or her new brocade;
> Forget her pray'rs, or miss a masquerade;
> Or lose her heart, or necklace, at a ball;   [Shock: the
> Or whether Heav'n has doom'd that Shock must fall.   lap-dog]

The epic machinery ("The Machinery, Madam," wrote Pope in his dedication of the poem to Arabella Fermor, the original of Belinda, "is a term invented by the Critics to signify that part which the Deities, Angels, or Daemons are made to act in a Poem") was introduced in the revised edition of 1714, and though it seemed risky to interfere with such a delicately wrought work, the presence of the Sylphs gave Pope the opportunity to introduce, with the lightest of touches, further elements of half-ironic, half-serious moral overtones which add to the total pattern of meaning of the poem. The epigrams which are woven into the texture of the poem are not isolated exercises of wit, but part of this total pattern: "And wretches hang that jurymen may dine" is a comment on the relation between the real and the professed which is one of the strands woven right through. The deliberate juxtaposition of Bibles and billet-doux is matched again and again by similar lines referring to different areas of social life—e.g.

> Here Britain's statesmen oft the fall foredoom
> Of foreign Tyrants and of Nymphs at home;
> Here thou, great Anna! whom three realms obey,
> Dost sometimes counsel take—and sometimes Tea.

(The rhyming of "foredoom" with "home" and of "obey" with "tea" was not false in the pronunciation of Pope's day.)

The brilliance of the description of the game of ombre (where an actual card game, in specific detail, is described in terms drawn from epic conflict yet which specify every movement in the game with complete accuracy) has often been noted, but the skill involved here is not only the counterpointing of the contemporary social and the traditionally heroic; there are also moral overtones reflecting back on the principal characters. Perhaps the greatest skill of all is that displayed in using mock-heroic diction to provide an atmosphere both ritualistic and cheerfully social in describing the activities of high society—as, for example, in the celebrated description of the serving of coffee:

> For lo! the board with cups and spoons is crown'd,
> The berries crackle, and the mill turns round;
> On shining Altars of Japan they raise
> The silver lamp; the fiery spirits blaze:
> From silver spouts the grateful liquors glide,
> While China's earth receives the smoking tide:
> At once they gratify their scent and taste,
> And frequent cups prolong the rich repast.

The epic climax of the poem, when the peer cuts off the lock in spite of the vain interposition of a guardian Sylph, is both mock-heroic and somehow suggestive of genuine sadness:

> The Peer now spreads the glitt'ring Forfex wide,
> T' inclose the Lock; now joins it, to divide.
> Ev'n then, before the fatal engine clos'd,
> A wretched Sylph too fondly interpos'd;
> Fate urg'd the shears, and cut the Sylph in twain,
> (But airy substance soon unites again)
> The meeting points the sacred hair dissever
> From the fair head, for ever, and for ever.

The remainder of the poem is full of variety and of evidence of Pope's special kind of mock-heroic skill, from the brilliant description of the Cave of Spleen to the final translation of the lock into the skies. Clarissa's speech, which Pope added in 1717 to emphasize the moral (or so he alleged), adds just that touch of gravity needed to bring out the moral echoes throughout the poem as a whole. One expects them to be too heavy for the poem, but, surprisingly, they are not. The lines

> Oh! if to dance all night, and dress all day,
> Charm'd the small-pox, or chas'd old-age away . . .

bring into the open, briefly and not too sententiously, a theme implicit in the whole poem—the vanity of social life. But though vain and even in some respects ridiculous, social life has its charm and its graces; and Belinda, though subject to the vanities characteristic of all belles, is truly beautiful. Vanity, and the decorated surface of social life, are a necessary part of *la condition humaine,* and the poem manages to combine irony, sadness, acceptance, and affection.

In 1717 Pope published a collected volume of his poems, thus marking the end of what might be considered his early period. This volume included the "Elegy to the Memory of an Unfortunate Lady" and "Eloisa to Abelard," two poems which reveal him choosing themes and poetic attitudes not usual with him. The "Elegy" is a somewhat melodramatic poem in which the poet addresses and meditates over the ghost of an unfortunate lady of great spirit, beauty, and noble blood who, after an unhappy love affair and cruel treatment by her family (especially a wicked uncle), killed herself abroad. The situation appears to have been largely imaginary, and the inspiration rhetorical rather than personal. There are some fine rhetorical couplets in the poem, though some of them verge on the ludicrous in their extravagance, and the subdued conclusion, in which the poet speaks of himself in a quieter elegiac cadence—

> Poets themselves must fall, like those they sung,
> Deaf the prais'd ear, and mute the tuneful tongue.
> Ev'n he, whose soul now melts in mournful lays,
> Shall shortly want the gen'rous tear he pays. . . .

modulates the poem to an effective close. "Eloisa to Abelard," modeled on the Heroic Epistles of Ovid, derives its situation from an English translation of the Latin letters of Heloise and Abelard which had appeared in 1713; but the handling of the material, the controlled passion of the tone, the masterly ordering of detail, are of course Pope's own. There is no suggestion of melodrama here, and the slow march of the couplets builds up cumulatively an impressive picture of a psychological state. The fluctuations of mood, which contribute so happily to the total effect, are conveyed as much by subtle variations within the line as by the content. Here again the poet becomes quietly personal at the end, turning the poem at last into an oblique declaration of love, probably to Lady Mary Wortley Montagu:

> And sure, if fate some future bard shall join
> In sad similitude of griefs to mine,
> Condemn'd whole years in absence to deplore,
> And image charms he must behold no more;
> Such if there be, who loves so long, so well;
> Let him our sad, our tender story tell;
> The well-sung woes will sooth my pensive ghost;
> He best can paint 'em who shall feel 'em most.

Pope's translation of Homer's *Iliad* appeared in six volumes between 1715 and 1720. In spite of the fact that this ambitious undertaking involved Pope in bitter quarrels with Addison's "Little Senate" at Button's coffeehouse, arising out of a complex mixture of personal, literary, and political factors, the success of the translation was immediate, enabling Pope to buy his house and garden at Twickenham in 1718 and live there in financial independence for the rest of his life. Pope was no great Greek scholar (as his enemies kept reminding him), and his *Iliad* is not, and was not intended to be, an accurate rendering, but rather a poetic paraphrase in a highly theatrical poetic idiom of which Pope was complete master. "It's a very pretty poem, but you mustn't call it Homer," the great classical scholar Richard Bentley is said to have remarked to Pope, and this is in its way true, and in its way irrelevant. For Pope the language of a true heroic poem must be elevated and never mean, and the elevated heroic style which he developed for his Homer owes something to a tradition of poetic diction that goes back to Sylvester's Du Bartas and George Sandys' translation of Ovid as well as to Milton. But to be elevated is not to be stilted: Pope admired Homer's "spirit and fire" and he contrived his own kind of spirit and fire in his translation. The poetic craftsmanship which subsumed all the immense variety of Homer—the epic vigor, the combination of brooding on fate and meticulously realistic rendering of details of human activities, the nobility and the whole unsentimental acceptance of men as they are —into a single style in which all the original earthiness has been translated into a spirited refinement, represents a remarkable achievement. Homer's fly becomes Pope's "vengeful hornet," because "our present idea of the fly is indeed very low." Simple naming of animals, parts of the body, ordinary behavior, are heightened and generalized in Pope's cunning couplets; but they do not lose vitality in the process; they gain a new kind of vigor. Here, for example is a literal translation of a passage from Book IX, with Pope's rendering of it:

Then the swift-footed Achilles answered him: "Zeus-born Ajax, son of Telamon, all that you say is very much my own opinion, but my heart swells with anger when I think of those things, how Atreides heaped insult on me among the Argives, as though I were a foreigner with no rights. But now go and deliver my message; for I will not think of bloodshed and war again until noble Hector, son of the wise Priam, comes to the huts and ships of the Myrmidons, slaying Argives on his way, and sets the fleet on fire. I think, though, that, furious for battle though he may be, Hector will be held."

> "Oh soul of battles, and thy people's guide!"
> To Ajax thus the first of Greeks replied:
> "Well hast thou spoke; but at the tyrant's name
> My rage rekindles and my soul's on flame;
> 'Tis just resentment, and becomes the brave;
> Disgraced, dishonoured, like the vilest slave!

Return then, heroes! and our answer bear,
The glorious combat is no more my care;
Not till amidst yon sinking navy slain,
The blood of Greeks shall dye the sable main;
Not till the flames, by Hector's fury thrown,
Consume your vessels, and approach my own;
Just there, the impetuous homicide shall stand,
There cease his battle, and there feel our hand."

Pope's version has tremendous rhetorical *élan,* and a high accent of its own; but the accent is very far from Homer's.

The heroic style which Pope worked out for the *Iliad* (and in fact originally tried out in some specimen renderings from the *Odyssey*) served him equally well in his rendering of the *Odyssey* (in five volumes, 1725–26), for which, however, his hired assistants Elijah Fenton and William Broome did a great deal of the versifying. The fact that it was possible to delegate much of the work to assistants indicates that Pope's heroic style lent itself to mechanical application; it was indeed an imitable style, and though Fenton and Broome never reached the high points to which the master often attained, they did well enough to demonstrate what might be called the tricks of the trade.

The rest of Pope's work, which includes much of his most characteristic as well as his most distinguished writing, is mostly moral and satirical, especially the latter. The *Essay on Man,* in four "Epistles" addressed to Henry St. John, Viscount Bolingbroke, appeared in 1733 and 1734. This brilliant verse essay, which moves with speed and wit and is couched (unlike his Homer) in a diction which combines formality of expression with overtones of easy colloquial discourse, is not, of course, valuable for its original philosophy. Vindication of the state of things by pointing to man's position in the "vast chain of being"; the duty of self-knowledge rather than of vain speculations; the interpenetration of vice and virtue to produce an automatic system of checks and balances; the relation between the individual and society; the necessity of virtue for true happiness; and above all the insistence that all apparent evil or injustice is part of the inevitable and necessary ultimate order of things—these are commonplaces of eighteenth-century thought. In handling them, Pope is neither original nor consistent; the arguments adduced in the different epistles are neither welded into a unity nor individually explored to any depth. The justification of "whatever is" by what has been called the principle of plenitude, which maintains that God required the utmost range and diversity of created things and thus created everything, however unnecessary or harmful it might seem to man, in its proper place, does not necessarily imply a facile optimism; man is in an intermediate place in the great chain and cannot see the total pattern, which had not been created for man's happiness but to achieve maximum plenitude with order. Yet Pope also sees an automatic control system ordering things for the best among individual human passions; the control, however, only alleviates man's lot, it does not guarantee virtue or happiness. There is little point in inquiring closely into the philosophical notions of the *Essay on Man,* or of examining Pope's debt to Bolingbroke, Shaftesbury, and other thinkers. The literary value of the *Essay* lies in the splendid and witty ease with which the couplets speed along, sparkling with epigrams and with an intellectual brilliance that arises not from profundity but from sheer liveliness of mind linked with a balanced liveliness of verbal expression.

The *Essay on Man* was part of a larger and vaguer project which was never fully defined or developed but which produced also four other verse essays, the "Moral Essays, in four epistles to several persons." The first of these is on "the knowledge and characters of men," the second on the characters of women, and the third and fourth on the use of riches. The tone of these is satirical rather than didactic, and as the satiric passion rises the colloquial speed of the verse increases and the wit becomes more devilishly brilliant. In the first essay he has not quite got up speed, though the characteristic note of these essays is already sounded:

> See the same man, in vigour, in the gout;
> Alone, in company; in place, or out;
> Early at Business, and at Hazard late;
> Mad at a Fox-chase, wise at a Debate;
> Drunk at a Borough, civil at a Ball;
> Friendly at Hackney, faithless at Whitehall.

This is very knowing verse, ironic comment on man as a social animal by one who knows contemporary high society through and through. The pose in all these essays is that of the man who sees through all human actions. The second of them ("To a Lady"—i.e., Martha Blount) is a devastating attack on the female character that opens with the lines

> Nothing so true as what you once let fall,
> "Most women have no characters at all"

and turns round in the end to pay a brilliant compliment to the sex:

> And yet, believe me, good as well as ill,
> Woman's at best a Contradiction still.
> Heav'n, when it strives to polish all it can
> Its last best work, but forms a softer Man;
> Picks from each sex, to make the Fav'rite blest,
> Your love of Pleasure, our desire of Rest:
> Blends, in exception to all general rules,
> Your Taste of Follies, with our Scorn of Fools:
> Reserve with Frankness, Art with Truth allied,
> Courage with Softness, Modesty with Pride;
> Fixed Principles, with Fancy ever new;
> Shakes all together and produces—You.

> Be this a Woman's Fame: with this unblest,
> Toasts live a scorn, and Queens may die a jest.
> This Phoebus promised (I forget the year)
> When those blue eyes first opened on the sphere;
> Ascendant Phoebus watched that hour with care,
> Averted half your Parents' simple Prayer;
> And gave you Beauty, but denied the Pelf
> That buys your sex a Tyrant o'er itself.
> The gen'rous God, who Wit and Gold refines,
> And ripens Spirits as he ripens Mines,
> Kept Dross for Duchesses, the world shall know it,
> To you gave Sense, Good-humour, and a Poet.

To turn a general satire into an individual compliment in this way shows a high art. And the language of this extract ought to be studied by those who believe that the eighteenth-century poets always used an artificial poetic diction.

The two moral essays on the use of riches are mostly concerned with the misuse of riches, illustrated with some sparkling ironical character sketches of both types and individuals. The portraits of Sir Balaam in Epistle III and of Timon in Epistle IV are (unlike the idealized portrait of the Man of Ross in Epistle III) among Pope's best productions of this kind. Epistle IV ends on a more positive note, with a fine Horatian description of the proper use of riches. A fifth verse epistle, "To Mr. Addison, occasioned by his Dialogues on Medals," was written much earlier than the others with which, together with the Epistles to Oxford and to Arbuthnot, it was later included. The others were composed (in the opposite order to that in which they were later arranged) in the early 1730's, while the *Epistle to Addison*, originally written in 1715, is a wholly independent poem, remarking in relatively uninspired verse on the ravages of time and the usefulness of medals in preserving the forms and names of "Gods, Emp'rors, Heroes, Sages, Beauties." It ends with a compliment to Addison which is in sharp contrast to the brilliantly satirical portrait of him as Atticus in the *Epistle to Dr. Arbuthnot*.

The *Epistle to Dr. Arbuthnot* (which Pope later regarded as the prologue to his satires) was mostly written at speed in 1734, though some passages, notably the portrait of Atticus, had been written earlier. This is Pope's formal *apologia* as a satirist. He presents himself as a man of peace goaded into satire by the intolerable behavior of fools and knaves. This picture is not altogether false; Pope was indeed much attacked from the time that the first volume of his *Iliad* appeared in 1715, and kept quiet for a long time. Nevertheless his pose as the contented, peace-loving poet besieged on all sides by flatterers, poetasters wanting his approval or his assistance, dramatists urging him to write prologues for their plays, writers of all kinds asking for introductions to publishers or to noble patrons, is deliberately heightened in its presentation of the author as above the literary battle of his day and only drawn in by force. From the very opening line, the tone of contempt toward the mob of ordinary writers is maintained:

> Shut, shut the door, good John! fatigued, I said,
> Tie up the knocker, say I'm sick, I'm dead.
> The Dog-star rages! nay 'tis past a doubt,
> All Bedlam, or Parnassus, is let out:
> Fire in each eye, and papers in each hand,
> They rave, recite, and madden round the land. . . .
>   Is there a Parson, much bemused in beer,
> A maudlin Poetess, a rhyming Peer,
> A Clerk, foredoomed his father's soul to cross,
> Who pens a Stanza, when he should *engross?*
> Is there, who, locked from ink and paper, scrawls,
> With desp'rate charcoal round his darkened walls?
> All fly to Twit-nam, and in humble strain
> Apply to me, to keep them mad or vain.

The intimate air he adopts in addressing his close friend Arbuthnot preserves a colloquial strain throughout the poem, which moves with great speed and variety. The justification of his writing—

> Why did I write? what sin to me unknown
> Dipt me in ink, my parents', or my own?

which goes on to tell how Walsh, Congreve, and others encouraged him as a youngster, is done with a simple dignity, but is itself the pro-

logue to a fiercer turn of the satire. The set piece on Atticus is too
well known to require quotation; it is a masterly satirical portrait,
recognizably Addison, true enough to sting without the obvious exaggeration which enables the victim to laugh it off. The memorable
lines

> Damn with faint praise, assent with civil leer,
> And without sneering teach the rest to sneer;

refer to Addison's unwillingness or inability to restrain his "little Senate" from attacking Pope. The conclusion of this perfectly manipulated poem, in which the heroic couplet is used with a flexibility and
a playful yet deadly wit to a degree not easily found in Pope's earlier
work, is a moving benediction on his friend, who was to die less than
two months after the Epistle to him was published.

Horace was for the early eighteenth century, as for Ben Jonson, the
type of the civilized poet, and most poets of the time tried in some
degree to affect a Horatian air. Much of Pope's satirical verse apart
from the *Dunciad* was described as imitations of Horace; they were
imitations in the eighteenth-century sense of adaptations of Horace's
satires to contemporary English conditions. Pope's genius was never
more happily employed: the discursiveness of the form, the combination of moral principle and personal chat, the challenge to wit and
ingenuity in finding the proper English equivalents for Horace's
Roman references, the opportunities for personal attacks and personal compliments, all helped to stimulate him to produce that relaxed yet fast-moving verse in which his mastery of the couplet was
so well demonstrated. He "imitated" six of Horace's satires and
epistles, and these, together with his "versification" (i.e., turning into
verse of his own style) of two of Donne's satires, and two Dialogues
originally entitled *One Thousand Seven Hundred and Thirty-eight*
and later called simply *Epilogue to the Satires*, stand with his *Moral
Essays* and the *Epistle to Dr. Arbuthnot* to constitute the main body
of his shorter satirical poems. *The First Epistle of the Second Book
of Horace: to Augustus* is perhaps the most consistently sparkling of
Pope's Horatian imitations, though the skill with which he manipulates references to contemporary persons and events can only be appreciated by a reader who has some familiarity with the history of
the period. The poem contains some interesting sidelights on Pope's
view of English literary history, worked in neatly enough in a discussion of the relation between the past and present of England; but
the poem reaches its true summit when the satire of George II (who
is the modern Augustus—the ancient-modern relationship is deftly

manipulated throughout the poem) is presented, at the end, in tones of apparent panegyric:

> Oh! could I mount on the Mæonian wing,
> Your arms, your actions, your repose to sing!
> What seas you traversed, and what fields you fought!
> Your country's peace, how oft, how dearly bought!
> How bar'brous rage subsided at your word,
> And nations wondered while they dropped the sword!
> How, when you nodded, o'er the land and deep,
> Peace stole her wing, and wrapped the world in sleep
> Till earth's extremes your mediation own,
> And Asia's tyrants tremble at your throne—
> But verse, alas! your Majesty disdains;
> And I'm not us'd to panegyric strains:
> The zeal of fools offends at any time,
> But most of all, the zeal of fools in rhyme.
> Besides, a fate attends on all I write,
> That when I aim at praise, they say I bite,
> A vile encomium doubly ridicules:
> There's nothing blackens like the ink of fools.
> If true, a woeful likeness; and if lies,
> "Praise undeserv'd is scandal in disguise":
> Well may he blush, who gives it or receives;
> And when I flatter, let my dirty leaves
> (Like journals, odes, and such forgotten things
> As Eusden, Philips, Settle, writ of Kings)
> Clothe spice, line trunks, or flutt'ring in a row,
> Befringe the rails of Bedlam and Soho.

Even without knowing who Eusden, Philips, and Settle were (that they were in Pope's view bad poets is clear from the text), or realizing that Bedlam and Soho were districts where dealers in old books gathered, we can savor the wicked wit of this passage. The placing of "repose" in the second line and of "bought" in the fourth are highly effective, if relatively obvious, satiric devices. The shift in tone with "But verse, alas! your Majesty disdains" introduces a subtler satiric variation, and the deliberate bathos of the conclusion adds its final comment. The Epilogue to the Satires, especially the second Dialogue, gives us Pope's most fully worked up picture of the injured poet who subsumes private revenge in zeal for the public welfare and becomes a spokesman for virtue, wherever it is found, against vice and folly wherever practiced. "When truth or virtue an affront endures, /Th' affront is mine, my friend, and should be yours" sounds somewhat priggish, perhaps; but there is nothing priggish about

Pope's beautifully modulated claim to have earned the fear of those who lack even the fear of God:

> Yes, I am proud; I must be proud to see
> Men not afraid of God, afraid of me:
> Safe from the bar, the pulpit, and the throne,
> Yet touched and shamed by ridicule alone. . . .

Pope's most sustained satirical work is *The Dunciad*, a mock-heroic poem whose history is both complex and (in spite of the efforts of generations of scholars) somewhat obscure. Designed originally as a contribution to the war against dullness and pedantry carried on by the members of the Scriblerus Club, it went through various stages of development during each of which Pope indulged in so many mystifications that a complete account of what went on can only be conjectural. It was at first intended to conclude a volume of *Miscellanies* by Swift and Pope in 1728, but it soon outgrew these limits and was omitted from the volume, Pope substituting a prose satire, *Peri Bathous: or, the Art of Sinking in Poetry*, in which he attacked bad poets and literary enemies. The first edition of *The Dunciad* appeared anonymously in 1728; a new edition, with a burlesque "critical apparatus" which enabled Pope to take many more digs at his enemies while at the same time attacking pedantry and parodying learned editions, came out the following year; and a major revision was prepared for the collected edition of Pope's works prepared by his friend William Warburton: this version of the poem, which appeared in 1743, is the form in which it has ever since been read. Book IV of the finally revised version first appeared separately in 1742 as *The New Dunciad*. These changes, revisions, and expansions resulted from the way in which Pope's quarrels with the "dunces" developed. As first published, *The Dunciad* had as its hero Lewis Theobald, who had incurred Pope's enmity by publishing, in 1726, a sharp attack on Pope's edition of Shakespeare, entitled *Shakespeare Restored, or a Specimen of the many Errors as well committed as unamended by Mr. Pope in his late edition of this Poet*. Pope's edition, published in 1725, was an "improving" edition, tidying up and amending the text according to his own literary lights and showing no awareness of the principles of textual and bibliographical scholarship. Theobald had a much better understanding of editorial principles as they are now understood, and much of his criticism of Pope as editor was perfectly sound. But Pope took it as symptomatic of the worst kind of antiquarian and verbal pedantry, a major form of "dullness" as he and his friends understood the term. "Dunces" to Pope were either pedants or fools, or both, and by his performance Theobald qualified in Pope's view for the part of hero in a poem dedicated to the mock-heroic celebration of such persons. Pedantry, like bad poetry, was associated with dullness and boredom, and the soporific effect of the work of the duncs is an important theme in *The Dunciad*. In his major revision of the poem, carried out in 1742–43, Pope substituted Colley Cibber for Theobald as hero. Pope had had a long quarrel with Cibber, and Warburton, who was editing Pope's collected works, had been a friend of Theobald's; there were also other reasons for the substitution, but any account of the personalities and the quarrels involved belongs to a specialized monograph.

The Dunciad has no fully developed mock-heroic action such as we find in *The Rape of the Lock;* it is a collection of episodes each one of which is a self-contained unit and deals, often brilliantly, both with literary dullness and pedantry in general and with specific writers guilty of these vices. Book I is the only book in which the hero is the principal figure. The goddess Dullness contemplates her realm of confusion and bad poetry on the day of the Lord Mayor's Show, and thinks of the long succession of bad poets to the City of London, of whom the latest, Elkanah Settle, had died in 1724. She decides on Bays (Cibber) as the obvious successor to the throne of Dullness, and we are presented with a picture of him:

> Swearing and supperless the Hero sate,
> Blasphemed his gods, the dice, and damned his fate;
> Then gnawed his pen, then dashed it on the ground,
> Sinking from thought to thought, a vast profound!
> Plunged for his sense, but found no bottom there;
> Yet wrote and floundered on in mere despair.
> Round him much embryo, much abortion lay,
> Much future ode, and abdicated play;
> Nonsense precipitate, like running lead,
> That slipped thro' cracks and zig-zags of the head; . . .
> Next o'er his books his eyes began to roll,
> In pleasing memory of all he stole,
> How here he sipped, how there he plundered snug,
> And sucked all o'er, like an industrious bug. . . .

Unpopular and despairing, Cibber decides to sacrifice his unsuccessful plays to the goddess, but as he sets fire to the pile of books she quenches the flames with a volume of Ambrose Philips and then crowns him King of the Dunces. The verse in which all this is described is packed with allusions to places and persons, many of which are solemnly explained, generally with an oblique irony, in the footnotes. Yet, as so often in Pope, sheer brilliance of technique makes the main points clear even to the reader who is ignorant of the precise meaning of the allusions, and the different kinds of contempt, mockery, laughter, and castigation are communicated by the manipulation of the language and the movement of the lines.

Book II describes the public games and sports instituted by the goddess to celebrate Cibber's coronation. The mock-heroic element is at its strongest here, from the opening parody of Milton—

> High on a gorgeous seat, that far out-shone
> Henley's gilt tub, or Flecknoe's Irish throne,

to the account, deliberately filthy with cloacal images, of the race between the booksellers Lintot and Curl. The objects of attack here are numerous, and all are employed in an atmosphere of mud and filth in what is perhaps the most brilliantly nasty verse in the language. Conventional poetic epithets are put into contexts which force the reader into an awareness of unpleasant literal meanings, and the more one knows of the history of poetic diction in the seventeenth and eighteenth centuries the more kinds of irony one sees in Pope's handling of language. From one point of view Book II of *The Dunciad* represents the apotheosis of schoolboy humor, with its concentration on sewage and excrement; but there is a delicacy of technique in the midst of the coarseness of imagery and a constant play of wit that both startles and amuses. The book ends with a contest in reading from dull books until all the contestants fall asleep.

Book III describes Cibber's vision of the past, present, and future triumphs of Dullness, which gives Pope the opportunity to vent his anger against a great many people and institutions he dislikes. Book IV is the most expansive of all, describing (in the words of Pope's "argument" prefixed to it) "the Goddess coming in her majesty to destroy Order and Science, and to substitute the Kingdom of the Dull upon earth." The imagery here is somewhat more abstract and the attack on movements and tendencies, on evils and abuses, more than on individuals. The poem concludes with a picture of the triumph of Dullness and the resulting disintegration of civilization:

> She comes! she comes! the sable throne behold
> Of Night primaeval and of Chaos old!
> Before her, Fancy's gilded clouds decay,
> And all its varying rainbows die away.
> Wit shoots in vain its momentary fires,
> The meteor drops, and in a flash expires.
> As one by one, at dread Medea's strain,
> The sick'ning stars fade off th' ethereal plain;
> As Argus' eyes by Hermes' wand opprest,
> Closed one by one to everlasting rest;

Thus at her felt approach, and secret might,
Art after Art goes out, and all is Night.
She skulking Truth to her old cavern fled,
Mountains of casuistry heaped o'er her head!
Philosophy, that leaned on Heaven before,
Shrinks to her second cause, and is no more.
Physic of Metaphysic begs defence,
And Metaphysic calls for aid on Sense.
See Mystery to Mathematics fly!
In vain! they gaze, turn giddy, rave, and die.
Religion blushing veils her sacred fires,
And unawares Morality expires.
Nor public flame, nor private, dares to shine;
Nor human spark is left, nor glimpse divine!
Lo! thy dread empire, Chaos! is restored;
Light dies before thy uncreating word;
Thy hand, great Anarch! lets the curtain fall,
And universal Darkness buries all.

This ending goes beyond satire to achieve a tragic sense of doom, as though Pope had, in the end, genuinely given up hope for civilization—a strange climax for the author of the *Essay on Man* and poet of the optimistic Age of Reason. But Pope, like Swift, was deeply involved in the contradictions of the Augustan Age. There is, however, nowhere in Pope anything like the savage masochism of the last book of *Gulliver's Travels*. In spite of the real gloom of the ending, *The Dunciad* as a whole reveals a satiric poet enjoying to the full the exercise of his art; it is a high-spirited work, and it is the high spirits that allow us to accept the personalities and the malice which might otherwise have spoiled it. Pope's failure to distinguish between enemies of Pope and enemies of poetry, his calm assumption that his cause and the cause of literature and of civilization were one and the same, may show a certain lack of humility, but it is this which gives scope and depth to his satire and makes it still interesting and impressive. *The Dunciad* may have been in its day primarily a blow by Pope against his enemies; but it survives as a blow for civilization— the most artful and cunning use of the mock-heroic idiom in defense of culture that English literature has produced. The art and the cunning remain almost miraculous, and even those who dislike a defense of culture undertaken by means of an attack on its enemies (or of individuals forced by the poet into the role of its enemies) can relish the poem's remarkable virtuosity.

The tone of the age of Queen Anne was rendered less brilliantly and comprehensively by Matthew Prior (1664–1721), but even Prior's poems reveal some of the age's complexities and contradictions. He combined elegance and vulgarity in a rather striking manner, using, in his poems of compliment and love, both Anacreontic properties (Venus and her doves, Cupid and her arrows, myrtle, laurel bays, etc.) and contemporary colloquialisms. He writes poems to Cloe, Phyllis, Celia, and Leonora, but in spite of the classical apparatus the tone is generally familiar:

> As Cloe came into the room t'other day,
> I peevish began: where so long could you stay?
> In your life-time you never regarded your hour;
> You promised at two; and (pray look, child) 'tis four. . . .

He can use this rocking anapaestic rhythm to strengthen the colloquial element:

> Dear Cloe, how blubbered is that pretty face;
>   Thy cheek all on fire, and thy hair all uncurl'd;
> Pr'ythee quit this caprice; and (as old Falstaff says)
>   Let us e'en talk a little like folks of this world. . . .
>
> Then finish, dear Cloe, this pastoral war;
>   And let us, like Horace and Lydia, agree:
> For thou art a girl as much brighter than her,
>   As he was a poet sublimer than me.

He also tells stories based on late classical mythology in archly familiar verse and produces stilted pastoral dialogues between Damon and Alexis. He can write

> Tell, dear Alexis, tell thy Damon why
> Dost thou in mournful shades obscurely lie?

And he can also write:

> In sullen humour one day Jove
> Sent Hermes down to Ida's grove,
> Commanding Cupid to deliver
> His store of darts, his total quiver;
> That Hermes should the weapons break
> Or throw 'em into Lethe's lake.
>   Hermes, you know, must do his errand:
> He found his man, produced his warrant;
> Cupid, your darts—this very hour—
> There's no contending against power.
>   How sullen Jupiter, just now,
> I think I said; and you'll allow
> That Cupid was as bad as he:
> Hear but the youngster's repartee. . . .

He can be prurient and suggestive with stories comparing his mistress to Venus and detailed accounts of Cupid's tricks. He can also be racy in the ballad style. The opening of "Down Hall" shows his breezy use of classical reference in a contemporary English context:

> I sing not old Jason, who travelled through Greece,
> To kiss the fair maids and possess the rich fleece;
> Nor sing I Æneas, who, led by his mother,
> Got rid of one wife and went far for another.
>   Derry down, down, hey derry down.
>
> Nor him who through Asia and Europe did roam,
> Ulysses by name, who ne'er cried to go home,
> But rather desir'd to see cities and men,
> Than return to his farms and converse with old Pen.
>
> Hang Homer and Virgil! Their meaning to seek
> A man must have poked in the Latin and Greek;
> Those who love their own tongue, we have reason to hope,
> Have read them translated by Dryden and Pope.
>
> But I sing exploits that have lately been done
> By two British heroes, called Matthew and John; . . .

Anacreon and the English street ballad, songs of Cavalier courtliness and leering suggestiveness, polish and vulgarity—Prior's poems are in some ways a strange mixture. He was fond of the octosyllabic couplet and used it frequently, both in descriptive and in narrative verse. "An Epitaph" shows him forgetting the classics to deal with a purely English theme with considerable charm:

> Interred beneath this marble stone,
> Lie sauntering Jack and idle Joan. . . .

It concludes:

> Nor good, nor bad, nor fools, nor wise;
> They would not learn, nor could advise:
> Without love, hatred, joy, or fear,
> They led—a kind of—as it were:
> Nor wished, nor cared, nor laughed, nor cried;
> And so they lived; and so they died.

He can also be pensive in a subdued elegiac way, as in his lines "Written in the Beginning of Mezeray's History of France." And he can be solemn and pretentious as in a number of odes on serious themes and in blank verse translations of two hymns of Callimachus. He wrote a long didactic poem, *Solomon, or the Vanity of the World* (1718) in decasyllabic couplets which has been properly neglected and a more interesting long poem, *Alma, or the Progress of the Mind* (1718) in which he employs octosyllabic couplets to develop somewhat playfully his ideas about human nature.

It is as a writer of short "occasional" pieces that Prior is at his best, though one longer piece, "Jinny the Just," in thirty-five stanzas of three anapaestic rhyming lines each, is one of his most attractive: it is a lively and sympathetic picture of the life and character of an ordinary English countrywoman. Man of the world and diplomat, he was at home in the European society of his time. His charming little poem, "The Secretary," written when he was secretary to the English Ambassador at the Hague, gives an attractive picture of himself

> In a little Dutch chaise on a Saturday night,
> On my left hand my Horace, a nymph on my right: . . .

which sums up much of his character. He was employed first by the Whigs and later by the Tories, and on the fall of the Tories in 1714 he joined the company of those other Queen Anne wits for whom the new Whig government meant the end of all political hopes.

Where Prior manages to balance elegance and familiarity, as he does in his best poems, he speaks for his age in a rather special way, for that balance represented exactly what the Augustan writers sought. To be both polite and easy was their ideal. Their theories of decorum led them to prescribe different kinds of poetic diction for different kinds of themes and occasions, and this explains why Augustan diction is most interesting and subtle when the theme and occasion is complex (as where the intention is mock-heroic), and also why so many of these poets are at their weakest when they are being simply solemn and must therefore use a diction that is *merely* elevated. It would be unfair to remember Prior by his unsuccessful solemnities, but it is interesting to see what he made of the simple biblical eloquence of the thirteenth chapter of I Corinthians, "Though I speak with the tongues of men and of angels, and have not charity . . ." Here is the beginning of Prior's verse paraphrase:

> Did sweeter sounds adorn my flowing tongue,
> Than ever man pronounced, or angel sung;
> Had I all knowledge, human and divine,
> That thought can reach, or science can define;
> And had I power to give that knowledge birth,
> In all the speeches of the babbling earth; . . .
> Yet gracious charity, indulgent guest,
> Were not thy power exerted in my breast,
> Those speeches would send up unheeded prayer;

That scorn of life would be but wild despair;
A tymbal's sound were better than my voice,
My faith were form, my eloquence were noise.

The vocabulary here is not in fact very elaborate; it is the use of periphrasis that strikes the modern ear so unhappily. Pope could use a special kind of periphrasis in his *Homer* to give a special kind of energy, but used as Prior here uses it periphrasis is mere poeticizing, mere decorative drawing out of a set theme, a kind of literary exercise more appreciated then than it has been since. Prior was a better poet when he had his eye, not on eternal truths, but on his friends. And that says something about his age as well as about his temperament.

John Gay (1685–1732), friend of Pope and Swift, was a writer of altogether milder powers whose greatest success was in some degree a happy accident. His earliest work shows him somewhat timidly employing one of the standard Augustan styles on simple subjects. His *Rural Sports* (1713), dedicated to Pope, has a certain stylized charm in its pastoral imagery reminiscent of Pope's *Pastorals;* this is conventional stuff, but nevertheless it bears the marks of Gay's own personality:

Or when the ploughman leaves the task of day,
And trudging homeward whistles on the way;
When the big uddered cows with patience stand,
Waiting the strokings of the damsel's hand;
No warbling cheers the woods; the feathered choir
To court kind slumbers to their sprays retire;
When no rude gale disturbs the sleeping trees,
Nor aspen leaves confess the gentlest breeze; . . .
Here pensive I behold the fading light,
And o'er the distant billow lose my sight.

This is a half-humorous use of poetic diction; "feathered choir" and "rude gale" are standard Augustan periphrases for "birds" and "wind" respectively, but here they are used less to give dignity and generality to the subject than to give a touch of almost whimsical beauty. In his description of fishing, Gay talks, as other poets of his time did, of "the finny brood," but in describing the catching of fish in this quietly elevated diction he achieves a note which is both quizzical and serene:

Far up the stream the twisted hair he throws
Which down the murm'ring current gently flows;
When if or chance or hunger's powerful sway
Directs the roving trout this fatal way,

> He greedily sucks in the twining bait,
> And tugs and nibbles the fallacious meat: . . .

> Those baits will best reward the fisher's pains,
> Whose polish'd tails a shining yellow stains:
> Cleanse them from filth, to give a tempting gloss,
> Cherish the sullied reptile race with moss;
> Amid the verdant bed they twine, they toil,
> And from their bodies wipe their native soil.

Or in the description of hunting:

> Nor less the spaniel, skilful to betray,
> Rewards the fowler with the feathered prey,
> Soon as the lab'ring horse with swelling veins,
> Hath safely housed the farmer's doubtful gains,
> To sweet repast th' unwary partridge flies,
> With joy amid the scattered harvest lies;
> Wand'ring in plenty, danger he forgets,
> Nor dreads the slavery of entangling nets.
> The subtle dog scours with sagacious nose
> Along the field, and snuffs each breeze that blows,
> Against the wind he takes his prudent way,
> While the strong gale directs him to the prey;
> Now the warm scent assures the covey near,
> He treads with caution, and he points with fear; . . .

This suggests what Gay's *Shepherd's Week* confirms, that all Augustan poetry tends toward the mock-heroic. The most successful eighteenth-century adaptations of Milton's elevated and generalizing language (and much eighteenth-century poetic diction comes ultimately from Milton) are in most un-Miltonic contexts, where there is some degree of humor or mockery. The *Shepherd's Week* (1714) was intended as mock-pastorals, mocking the rural simplicities of Ambrose Philips (1674–1749), whose Pastorals seemed to Pope and others ridiculously insipid. But, though Gay proclaims his humorous intention by the names he gives his characters (Bumkinet, Bouzybee, Blouzelind, Lobbin Clout, Cloddipole, etc.), the poems turn out to be something more than (or at least different from) the burlesques they set out to be: the description of country custom is persuasive, lively and sometimes moving in its own right. The diction, which is sometimes colloquial and sometimes quaintly elevated, succeeds in conveying an affectionate interest in the subject. Augustan doctrines of decorum and of general nature forbade poets to consider the realistic description of humble life as a proper subject for poetry. Pope more than once mocked the idea of such descriptions, and in an essay on Philips' *Pastorals* in *The Guardian* he introduced a verse dialogue between two rustics, Cicely and Roger, in a broad Somerset dialogue (remarking with mock praise that "it may be observed, as a further beauty of this pastoral, the words *Nymph, Dryad, Fawn, Cupid,* or *Satyr,* are not once mentioned through the whole") in order to demonstrate the utter absurdity of trying to make poetry out of real contemporary rustic behavior. Pope was speaking for his age and for the whole neoclassic tradition when he wrote in his "Discourse on Pastoral Poetry" a passage we have already quoted: "If we would copy Nature, it may be useful to take this Idea along with us, that Pastoral is an image of what they call the golden age. So that we are not to describe our shepherds as shepherds at this day really are, but as they may be conceived then to have been; when the best of men followed the employment." So Gay, both in his *Rural Sports* and in his *Shepherd's Week,* could only describe country people as they really are in the form of burlesque; but the burlesque is often only a matter of diction, and sometimes not even of that.

Gay's *Trivia, or the Art of Walking the Streets of London* (1716), which clearly owes something to Swift's "Description of a City Shower" and other pieces, again has a mock-heroic element: it is a lively, realistic description of life on the London streets:

> For ease and for dispatch, the morning's best;
> No tides of passengers the streets molest.
> You'll see a draggled damsel here and there,
> From Billingsgate her fishy traffic bear; . . .

"Fishy traffic" for "fish" represents an Augustan device to give elevation to a common subject; but as used here it has a suggestion of burlesque and also serves to particularize an activity. *Trivia* is interspersed with stories of the classical gods and goddesses, again to indicate the mock-heroic element; but the most appealing parts of the poem (which is quite long, and is divided into three books) are the straightforward descriptions of London sights, sounds, and smells.

Gay's *Fables,* told in brisk octosyllabic couplets, reflect a fairly simple-minded moralism and show a mild technical competence but nothing more. His miscellaneous songs and ballads are much more interesting; although some ("Damon and Cupid," "Daphnis and Chloe") are the usual Augustan kind of artificial classicizing love song; others ("Sweet William's Farewell to Black-eyed Susan," "Newgate's Garland," "Molly Mog") get their form and tempo from the popular street tradition, and go rollicking along:

> The school-boys delight in a play-day;
> The school-master's joy is to flog;
> Fop is the delight of a lady,
> But mine is in sweet Molly Mog.

But his great triumph was (and is) *The Beggar's Opera* (1728), deriving from a suggestion from Swift for a "Newgate pastoral." Here, in an opera about a highwayman and his mistresses, Gay presented a picture of the world of politics and high society: the immoralities and treacheries of highwaymen, crooks, and trollops were no different from those of their so-called betters—the difference was only one of social class. Macheath the highwayman was Sir Robert Walpole, the head of the government (who boasted that "every man has his price," and was generally proved right), and there were all sorts of political and social parallels between Gay's plot and the life of his time. Yet on the surface this is a gay, swaggering, wholly amoral work, where the author with merry cynicism twists the plot to a happy ending to prevent the work from turning into a tragedy. A beggar who comes on the stage toward the end remarks: "Through the whole piece you may observe such a similitude of manners in high and low life, that it is difficult to determine whether (in the fashionable vices) the fine gentlemen imitate the gentlemen of the road, or the gentlemen of the road the fine gentlemen.—Had the play remained, as I at first intended, it would have carried a most excellent moral. 'Twould have shown that the lower sort of people have their vices in a degree as well as the rich: and that they are punished for them." Gay filled his opera with bright lyrics set to popular airs (thus also striking a blow at the fashionable Italian opera), and his dialogue and situations gave a brilliantly vivid picture of the London underworld. The town was delighted, and Gay made a fortune. The sequel, *Polly*, was equally popular, but only in published form, as the Lord Chamberlain forbade its presentation because it reflected on the Court. Neither of these works is subtle or profound in its satire; Gay remained a simple-minded moralist. But perhaps only a simple-minded moralist could have achieved so many kinds of parallel between the underworld and high society in a work of such attractive exuberance. Critics have found all sorts of symbolic implications in Macheath's name and character and in the action of *The Beggar's Opera* as a whole; but Swift's phrase "Newgate pastoral" indicates the opera's real nature. The deliberate violation of decorum by taking low scoundrels as heroes and heroines was a criticism both of literature and of society. The Augustan Age, which formulated so clearly its notions of propriety in both life and letters, was always seeking for ways of getting by its rules without actually breaking them. The neoclassic theory of kinds postulated the heroic as the highest form of poetry and implied certain views about the appropriate diction for heroic poetry as for other kinds; but the age was really more interested in poetry that was both intimate and satirical —the very reverse of heroic. Like Pope, only very much in his own smaller way, Gay found that he could only be himself by playing different neoclassic "kinds" against each other.

CHAPTER SEVENTEEN

Poetry from Thomson to Crabbe

THOUGH THE AUGUSTAN poets believed that the proper study of mankind was man, they were far from indifferent to the beauties of Nature, and throughout the eighteenth century is found a strain of descriptive and meditative poetry in which natural description prompts moral reflections on the human situation. The pioneer here was James Thomson (1700–48), whose four long poems on the seasons—*Winter* (1726), *Summer* (1727), *Spring* (1728), and *Autumn*, which appeared in 1730 in the collected volume—employ a quasi-Miltonic blank verse in describing the countryside at different times of the year and interlarding his descriptions with meditations on man. In his Preface to *Winter* Thomson expressed a view of his subject which was to become increasingly popular:

> I know of no subject more elevating, more amusing, more ready to awake the poetical enthusiasm, the philosophical reflection, and the moral sentiment, than the works of Nature. Where can we meet with such variety, such beauty, such magnificence? All that enlarges and transports the soul? What more inspiring than a calm, wide survey of them? In every dress Nature is greatly charming—whether she puts on the crimson robes of the morning, the strong effulgence of noon, the sober suit of the evening, or the deep sables of blackness and tempest! How gay looks the spring! how glorious the summer! how pleasing the autumn! and how venerable the winter!—But there is no thinking of these things without breaking out into poetry; which is, by the bye, a plain and undeniable argument of their superior excellence.
>
> For this reason the best, both ancient and modern, poets have been passionately fond of retirement and solitude. The wild romantic country was their delight. And they seem never to have been more happy than when, lost in unfrequented fields, far from the little busy world, they were at leisure to meditate, and sing the works of Nature.

Thomson was born in the Scottish Border country and came to seek literary fortune in London after studying at Edinburgh University; it may be that the country environment in which he grew up permanently affected his imagination. But he is emphatically an

English rather than a Scottish poet; if he brought to Augustan poetry something if not altogether new yet somewhat different from what was most in favor with the literary men of the time, he absorbed from the climate of early eighteenth-century English opinion the view of an ordered universe directed by universal laws framed by the original designer, God, and discovered by Newton, and the phenomena of Nature which he describes are seen as parts of this ordered system. His "Poem Sacred to the Memory of Sir Isaac Newton" expresses this view clearly:

> O unprofuse magnificence divine!
> O wisdom truly perfect! thus to call
> From a few causes such a scheme of things,
> Effects so various, beautiful, and great,
> A universe complete! And O beloved
> Of Heaven! whose well purged penetrative eye
> The mystic veil transpiercing, inly scanned
> The rising, moving, wide-established frame.

And the Hymn with which he concluded *The Seasons* sees the phenomena of Nature as the result of the benevolent contrivance of God:

> These, as they change, Almighty Father, these
> Are but the varied God! The rolling year
> Is full of Thee. Forth in the pleasing Spring
> Thy beauty walks, Thy tenderness and love.
> Wide flush the fields; the softening air is balm;
> Echo the mountains round; the forest smiles;
> And every sense, and every heart, is joy.
> Then comes Thy glory in the Summer months,
> With light and heat refulgent. . . .
> Thy bounty shines in Autumn unconfined,
> And spreads a common feast for all that lives.
> In Winter awful Thou! with clouds and storms
> Around Thee thrown, tempest o'er tempest rolled,
> Majestic darkness! . . .
> Mysterious round! what skill, what force divine,
> Deep felt in these appear! a simple train,
> Yet so delightful mixed, with such kind art,
> Such beauty and beneficence combined,
> Shade, unperceived, so softening into shade,
> And all so forming an harmonious whole
> That, as they still succeed, they ravish still.

The ideas expressed in *The Seasons* were not new, but the sensibility reflected in the poem was, at least in some degree. The age admired the kind of "local poetry" represented by Denham's "Cooper's Hill," but Denham and his imitators were content to embellish description—in Dr. Johnson's phrase—"by historical retrospection, or incidental meditation." Thomson's meditations went deeper, and the deliberate cultivation of pensiveness in the contemplation of Nature showed a quite different kind of sensibility:

> Thus solitary, and in pensive guise,
> Oft let me wander o'er the russet mead,
> And through the saddened grove, where scarce is heard
> One dying strain, to cheer the woodman's toil. . . .
> He comes! he comes! in every breeze the Power
> Of Philosophic Melancholy comes!
> His near approach the sudden-starting tear,
> The glowing cheek, the mild dejected air,
> The softened feature, and the beating heart,
> Pierced deep with many a virtuous pang, declare.
> O'er all the soul his sacred influence breathes;
> Inflames imagination, through the breast
> Infuses every tenderness, and far
> Beyond dim earth exalts the swelling thought. . . .
> As fast the correspondent passions rise,
> As varied, and as high: Devotion, raised
> To rapture and divine astonishment;
> The love of Nature unconfined, and, chief,
> Of human race; the large ambitious wish
> To make them blest; the sigh for suffering worth
> Lost in obscurity; the noble scorn
> Of tyrant-pride; the fearless great resolve; . . .
> The sympathies of love and friendship dear,
> With all the social offspring of the heart.
>   Oh, bear me then to vast embowering shades,
> To twilight groves, and visionary vales,
> To weeping grottoes and prophetic glooms,
> Where angel-forms athwart the solemn dusk
> Tremendous sweep, or seem to sweep, along;
> And voices more than human, through the void
> Deep-sounding, seize th' enthusiastic ear!

(Autumn)

The use of "enthusiastic" here, without any of the reservations or suspicions with which Shaftesbury or Pope or Johnson would have used the term is significant. Yet Thomson's optimistic Deism derives in large measure from Shaftesbury, who had also hailed Nature in rapturous terms, as one of the speakers in his dialogue entitled *The Moralists: A Rhapsody* (1709) illustrates: "Ye fields and woods, my refuge from the toilsome world of business, receive me in your quiet sanctuaries and favour my retreat and thoughtful solitude. Ye verdant plains, how gladly I salute ye. . . . O glorious Nature! supremely fair and sovereignly good! All-loving and all-lovely, all-divine! . . . To thee this solitude, this place, these rural meditations are sacred; whilst thus inspired with harmony of thought, though unconfined by words, and in loose numbers I sing of Nature's order in created beings, and celebrate the beauties which resolve in thee, the source and principle of all beauty and perfection." And Dr. Johnson was to pay tribute to Thomson's ability to reveal things which, once revealed, were seen to be of universal application: "The reader of the *Seasons* wonders that he never saw before what Thomson shows him, and that he never yet has felt what Thomson impresses." And Pope and his circle admired and encouraged Thomson. We must not therefore see Thomson as representing a pre-Romantic enthusiasm in his treatment of Nature which was opposed to the more sophisticated polite poetry of an age. Though in his feeling for the sights and sounds of the countryside and the affectionate detail with which he could describe them he displays a sensibility rather different from that which we readily associate with the spirit of the age, in his moralizing, his using natural description as a jumping-off place for generalizations about man, and his deistic view of order, he spoke with the voice of his age and pleased his contemporaries. Only Swift objected to the want of action in the poems: "I am not over fond of them, because they are all descriptions, and nothing is doing," he wrote to a friend in 1732; and Dr. Johnson, in his "Life of Thomson," was to combine admiration with the remark that "the great defect of the *Seasons* is want of method."

It is interesting that in Johnson's account of *The Seasons* he is so taken up with the attraction of Thomson's descriptions that he uses Thomson's word "enthusiasm" in Thomson's sense, not in the pejorative sense which he gives it in his own dictionary:

His descriptions of extended scenes and general effects bring before us the whole magnificence of Nature, whether pleasing or dreadful. The gaiety of *Spring*, the splendour of *Summer*, the tranquillity of *Autumn*, and the horror of *Winter*, take in their turns possession of the mind. The poet leads us through the appearances of things as they are successively varied by the vicissitudes of the year, and imparts to us so much of his own enthusiasm, that our thoughts expand with his imagery, and kindle with his sentiments. Nor is the naturalist without his part in the entertainment; for he is assisted to recollect and to combine, to arrange his discoveries, and to amplify the sphere of his contemplation.

This is interesting evidence of the way in which *The Seasons* struck the eighteenth-century reader. Johnson seems to be expressing with his usual cogency the common opinion of Thomson in his own time.

Thomson's diction is deliberately elevated, to give dignity to his descriptions. Johnson called it "florid and luxuriant" in the highest degree. Sometimes the pseudo-Miltonic Latinizations have an almost comic effect.

> At last
> The clouds consign their Treasures to the fields,
> And, softly shaking on the dimpled pool
> Prelusive drops, let all their moisture flow,
> In large effusion, o'er the freshened world.
> The stealing shower is scarce to patter heard,
> By such as wander through the forest walks,
> Beneath the umbrageous multitude of leaves.

His description of fishing in *Spring* has something of the half-burlesque quality of Gay's similar description in *Rural Sports,* though it is not intended:

> Now when the first foul torrent of the brooks,
> Swelled with the vernal rains, is ebbed away,
> And, whitening, down their mossy tinctured stream
> Descends the billowy foam; now is the time,
> While yet the dark-brown water aids the guile,
> To tempt the trout. The well-dissembled fly,
> The rod fine-tapering with elastic spring,
> Snatch'd from the hoary steed the floating line,
> And all thy slender watery stores, prepare.
> But let not on thy hook the tortured worm,
> Convulsive, twist in agonising folds; . . .
> When with his lively ray the potent sun
> Has pierced the streams and roused the finny race,
> Then, issuing cheerful, to thy sport repair; . . .

The tricks of diction and phrasing which Thomson got from Milton derive from the most superficial aspects of Milton's style: as Dr. Johnson put it, "His blank verse is no more the blank verse of Milton, or of any other poet, than the rhymes of Prior are the rhymes of Cowley." The use of dignified periphrasis in the description of homely or rustic things has, as we have seen, its burlesque element, and to tell the rural fisherman to "throw, nice-judging, the delusive fly" sounds somewhat absurd; but Thomson can use this diction to give real weight and feeling to his verse:

> With broadened nostrils to the sky upturned,
> The conscious heifer snuffs the stormy gale.
> Even as the matron, at her nightly task,
> With pensive labour draws the flaxen thread,

> The wasted taper and the crackling flame
> Foretell the blast. But chief the plumy race,
> The tenants of the sky, its changes speak.
> Retiring from the downs, where all day long
> They picked their scanty fare, a blackening train
> Of clamorous rooks thick-urge their weary flight,
> And seek the closing shelter of the grove.
> Assiduous in his bower, the wailing owl
> Plies his sad song.
>
> (Winter)

In his choice of descriptive detail to suggest a mood and in building up the mass of his verse to carry the weight of the mood, Thomson is at his best. In his frequent apostrophes, reflections, moralizings, invocations, and rhetorical questions his verse is at its most turgid and tedious.

Thomson's other important poem is *The Castle of Indolence* (1748), a descriptive-narrative poem in two cantos written in Spenserian stanzas and with an intermittent and half-hearted attempt at a Spenserian vocabulary. Thomson did however succeed in capturing something of Spenser's mood and movement:

> A pleasing land of drowsy-head it was
> Of dreams that wave before the half-shut eye;
> And of gay castles in the clouds that pass,
> For ever flushing round a summer sky.
> There eke the soft delights, that witchingly
> Instil a wanton sweetness through the breast,
> And the calm pleasures, always hovered nigh;
> But whate'er smackt of noyance or unrest
> Was far, far off expelled from this delicious nest.

Thomson was aware of the half-humorous effect of using Spenser's language (or traces of it) in the eighteenth century. In the "Advertisement" prefixed to the poem he wrote: "This poem being writ in the manner of Spenser, the obsolete words, and a simplicity of diction in some of the lines which borders on the ludicrous, were necessary to make the imitation more perfect." Nevertheless, in spite of some deliberately humorous flickers in the handling of language and in portraits of his friends, the sleepy movement of the first canto of the poem—reminding us at times of Tennyson's "The Lotos-Eaters"— is intended as a serious poetic effect, and it is so. The second canto, where the knight Sir Industry overthrows the Castle of Indolence, shows Thomson turning to a favorite theme, the progress of the arts and industry in Britain (treated in his dull blank-verse poem, *Liberty*); it is less successful than the first, lacking its music and sleepy

movement and concentrating on an allegorical action of little subtlety and on Sir Industry's exhortation to the inhabitants of the castle
to rouse themselves and *do* something. That Thomson should choose
the Spenserian stanza and the form of the allegorical romance, however uncertainly serious his mood, is interesting testimony to the
search for new models and wider poetic horizons that was going in
in the very heart of the Augustan Age.

Poets of this period seem to have been fascinated by the half-
burlesque, half-serious effects produced by applying elevated periphrastic poetic language to rustic or familiar things. John Dyer
(1699–1757) produced in *The Fleece* a poem in four books describing the care and shearing of sheep, the winding of wool, weaving
past and present, the cloth industry and the various countries to
which British woollen manufactures were exported. Though Dyer's
tone is wholly serious throughout, he can hardly have been unaware
of the near-comic effects he sometimes achieved:

> The ingenious artist, learned in drugs, bestows
> The last improvement; for the unlaboured fleece
> Rare is permitted to imbibe the dye.
> In penetrating waves of boiling vats
> The snowy web is steeped, with grain of weld,
> Fustic, or logwood, mixed, or cochineal,
> Or the dark purple pulp of Pictish woad,
> Of stain tenacious, deep as summer skies,
> Like those that canopy the bowers of Stow
> After soft rains, when birds their notes attune,
> Ere the melodious nightingale begins. . . .
>   That stain alone is good, which bears unchanged
> Dissolving water's, and calcining sun's,
> And thieving air's attacks. . . .

Or this:

> See that thy scrip have store of healing tar,
> And marking pitch and raddle; nor forget
> The sheers true-pointed, nor the officious dog,
> Faithful to teach the stragglers to return: . . .

Sometimes the Miltonisms (or pseudo-Miltonisms) of the eighteenth century were frankly burlesque, as in *The Splendid Shilling* by
John Philips (1676–1709):

> Happy the man who void of cares and strife
> In silken or in leathern purse retains
> A splendid shilling: he nor hears with pain
> New oysters cried, nor sighs for cheerful ale,

> But with his friends, when nightly mists arise,
> To Juniper's, Magpie, or Town-Hall repairs,
> Where, mindful of the nymph whose wanton eye
> Transfixed his soul and kindled amorous flames,
> Chloe or Phyllis, he each circling glass
> Wisheth her health and joy and equal love. . . .

Philips' *Cyder* (1708), a long poem on the growing of apples and the making of cider, uses the same kind of language, but rather more seriously; as with Dyer's *Fleece*, the burlesque is sometimes unconscious and never continuous. He is obviously being deliberately humorous when, describing rustic merrymaking, he writes:

> Meanwhile, blind British bards with volant touch
> Traverse loquacious strings, . . .

but this is not the consistent tone of the poem. Later imitators of the style of Thomson's *Seasons* developed the solemn periphrasis to ludicrous proportions with no apparent comic intention at all. John Armstrong's *Art of Preserving Health* (1744) provides an extreme example of stylized periphrasis giving a false dignity to a didactic and expository poem: when a versifying doctor writes a long poem on hygiene in which cheese is described as "tenacious paste of solid milk" something rather odd has happened to the poetic tradition. Samuel Garth, an earlier versifying doctor, produced in his *Dispensary* (1699) a mock-heroic account of a quarrel among the College of Physicians in couplets which owed much to Dryden's satires; but the deliberate mock-heroic must be distinguished from the half-burlesque note of Dyer and Philips as well as from the quite unconscious burlesque achieved by later perpetuators of a stereotyped periphrastic poetic diction. It was these last who led more than Wordsworth to believe that it was time for a change.

Dyer's best known and best liked work was "Grongar Hill" (1726), a poem in octosyllabic couplets describing a landscape in his native Carmarthenshire. The whole touch is lighter than Thomson's, but, like Thomson, Dyer combines description and reflection, if more superficially:

> And see the rivers, how they run
> Through woods and meads, in shade and sun;
> Sometimes swift, sometimes slow,
> Wave succeeding wave, they go
> A various journey to the deep
> Like human life to endless sleep!
> Thus is Nature's vesture wrought,

> To instruct our wandering thought;
> Thus she dresses green and gay,
> To disperse our cares away.

The language here is less elevated than Thomson's, or than Dyer's elsewhere: it is more the language of late seventeenth-century verse, based on the conversation of gentlemen.

Octosyllables remained a popular verse form throughout this period. Matthew Green (1696–1737) produced in *The Spleen* (1737) a witty poem on melancholy and its cure written in octosyllables with colloquial liveliness:

> Hunting I reckon very good
> To brace the nerves and stir the blood,
> But after no field honours itch,
> Achieved by leaping hedge and ditch. . . .

Yet even in this poem there are occasional burlesque Latinisms of diction or mock-heroic personifications.

Thomson's hailing of philosophic melancholy was symptomatic of a developing strain of meditative poetry. This fashion grew rapidly in the middle of the century. Edward Young (1683–1765), impelled by private grief, produced in his *The Complaint; or Night Thoughts on Life, Death, and Immortality* (1742–46) an account of his broodings over his sorrow, his thoughts on mortality and immortality, in a carefully wrought gloomy context of night:

> Night, sable goddess! from her ebon throne,
> In rayless majesty now stretches forth
> Her leaden sceptre o'er a slumbering world.
> Silence, how dead! and darkness, how profound!
> Nor eye nor listening ear an object finds;
> Creation sleeps.

And having set the scene he proceeds with his meditations:

> How poor, how rich, how abject, how august,
> How complicate, how wonderful is man!

Young's vocabulary, while consistently dignified, is not Miltonic or pseudo-Miltonic. Though a rhetorical note often emerges in the midst of his meditations there is never any suggestion of possible burlesque. Young follows specific traditions of Christian meditation and his vocabulary aims at intensity rather than polite periphrasis:

> Yet why complain? or why complain for one?
> Hangs out the sun his lustre but for me,
> The single man? Are angels all beside?
> I mourn for millions: 'tis the common lot;

> In this shape or in that has fate entailed
> The mother's throes on all of woman born,
> Not more the children, than sure heirs, of pain.

The personal note is stronger than in Thomson's *Seasons:* the meditations spring directly out of personal sorrow and the tone of the poem is largely that of self-communing.

The fashion for gloomy meditation in verse spread apace. Robert Blair (1699–1746), a Scot who remained in Scotland, drew on his reading of English poets and dramatists to produce in *The Grave* a meditation on death written in a blank verse quite un-Miltonic and suggesting rather the verse of Jacobean drama and sometimes of Restoration tragedy:

> Tell us, ye dead! will none of you, in pity
> To those you left behind, disclose the secret?
> Oh! that some courteous ghost would blab it out
> What 'tis you are, and we must shortly be.
> I've heard that souls departed have sometimes
> Forewarned men of their death. 'Twas kindly done
> To knock and give the alarum. But what means
> This stinted charity? 'Tis but lame kindness
> That does its work by halves. Why might you not
> Tell us what 'tis to die? Do the strict laws
> Of your society forbid your speaking
> Upon a point so nice? I'll ask no more.

Blair shows a positive relish in contemplating the horrors of dissolution, but it is all in the interests of piety. Piety even more pronounced dominates the prose *Meditations among the Tombs* (1745–47) of James Hervey, whose high-pitched sentiment and florid style appealed to numerous readers.

Thus the Age of Reason modulated gradually into the Age of Sensibility, with no contradiction discernible to contemporaries. In Thomson sensibility is related to admiration of Nature's order, rationally explained by Newton, so that reason and sensibility are dependent on each other. But dissatisfaction both with the coolly rational religion of the deists and with the mechanical rituals of the Church of England (which in the eighteenth century was more a social than a religious institution, and looked suspiciously on any exhibition of deep religious feeling) produced a more deliberate cultivation of the emotions. The brothers John and Charles Wesley brought a new emotional power into religion and the Methodist Movement which they founded (first within the Church of England and then, as a result of the Church's hostility, as an independent sect) was in many respects a reaction against the ideals of moderation and good sense which had prevailed in the Augustan Age. John Wesley (1703–91) recorded his experiences and activities in his *Journal* which makes abundantly clear how far he had gone from the Augustan suspicion of "enthusiasm." The Bishop of Exeter who died in 1762 is praised in his epitaph on the wall of the Choir of Exeter Cathedral as "a successful exposer of pretence and enthusiasm," and indeed he wrote a book called *The Enthusiasm of Methodists and Papists Compared.* But Methodism appealed to large numbers of people whose emotions had been starved by orthodox religion, and the popularity of the Evangelical movement in the latter part of the eighteenth century suggests a break-out after long repression.

Notions of the picturesque in both painting and gardening also developed rapidly throughout the century so as to increase emphasis on individual sensibility. Pope, in a letter to a friend in 1712, remarked: "Mr. Philips has two lines, which seem to me what the French call very Picturesque:

> All hid in snow, in bright confusion lie,
> And with one dazzling waste fatigue the eye."

By the middle of the century the term "picturesque" was associated with the wild, the romantic, the "Gothic." Addison in *The Spectator* tried to laugh his readers out of belief in witches. John Wesley observed in 1768 that "the giving up of witchcraft is in effect the giving up the Bible." And yet these changes were not so violent as the quotations might suggest. Admiration for Gothic ruins could well up in the breast of a contemporary of Pope, and Dr. Johnson, while he had no use for religious enthusiasm, wrote prayers for his own use that were deeply personal and deeply devout. The shifts that developed as the century progressed were shifts of emphasis. Earlier, the Gothic was admired as wild and irregular, something appropriate to a dark and barbarous age—rather in the way that Shakespeare was admired. "I will conclude by saying of Shakespeare, that with all his faults, and with all the irregularity of his drama, one may look upon his works, in comparison of those that are more finished and regular, as upon an ancient majestic piece of Gothic architecture, compared with a neat modern building. The latter is more elegant and glaring, but the former is more strong and more solemn." So wrote Pope in his "Preface to Shakespeare," balancing majesty against elegance in a way characteristic of him and of his age. But the balance, like so much in Augustan thought, was a precarious one, and could not long be maintained. Reason discovering objects on which the sensibility might operate; rational benevolence encouraging sentimentality; arguments for the existence of God the great designer supporting belief in revealed Christianity; belief in progress and in the superiority of the present age nourished by veneration of the Latin and Greek classics—all this represented an unstable equilibrium. The stability which English thought and society regained at the end of the seventeenth century could not in the nature of things be long maintained: contradictions and complexities soon revealed themselves. Melancholy, interest in the uncivilized and the odd, a sense of change and of the impossibility of keeping civilization static—some or all of these attitudes are seen quite early in the century; and by the time we get to Gray and Goldsmith and Cowper some of them are almost standard. The enclosing of village ground in the interest of big landowners and relatively large-scale farmers produced change and unrest in the countryside (as Goldsmith's "Deserted Village" records), and the beginnings of the Industrial Revolution in the latter part of the century produced a very different view of the value of life in urban society from that reflected in, say, Pope's *Rape of the Lock.*

That exaltation of the imagination and cultivation of philosophical and meditative verse did not necessarily go with an interest in the picturesque or the Gothic is shown by Mark Akenside (1721-70) whose *Pleasures of the Imagination* (1744) discusses the sublime and the beautiful in Thomsonian blank verse and at the same time turns sternly away from Gothic barbarism to the "Genius of ancient Greece," to whom at the end of Book I he expresses his determination to "tune to Attic themes the British lyre." Akenside's verse is more consistently expository and less descriptive than Thomson's, and the poem is in large measure versified philosophy drawing on ideas that were popular in the age: it is an excellent poem for study by the student of eighteenth-century thought. His "Hymn to Science" (1739) shows his enthusiasm for the world of knowledge that had been opened up by Newton and Locke:

> Science! thou fair effusive ray
> From the great source of mental Day,
>   Free, generous, and refined!
> Descend with all thy treasures fraught,
> Illumine each bewilder'd thought,
>   And bless my lab'ring mind. . . .
>
> Give me to learn each secret cause;
> Let number's, figure's, motions's laws
>   Revealed before me stand;
> These to great Nature's scenes apply,
> And round the globe, and through the sky,
>   Disclose her working hand.

> Next, to thy nobler search resigned,
> The busy, restless, human mind
>   Through ev'ry maze pursue;
> Detect Perception where it lies,
> Catch the ideas as they rise,
>   And all their changes view.

Akenside's *Odes on Several Subjects* (1745) show his classical interests as well as his patriotism; they exhibit a certain metrical fluency. Occasionally in his shorter poems Akenside strikes a quietly personal note that is faintly Wordsworthian, as in the conclusion to his "Ode to the Evening Star":

> O sacred bird, let me at eve,
>   Thus wandering all alone,
> Thy tender counsel oft receive,
> Bear witness to thy pensive airs,
> And pity nature's common cares
>   Till I forget my own.

William Shenstone (1714–63) exhibits more obvious signs of changing tastes and attitudes. The Horatian pose of the cultivated gentleman in his quiet country retreat (as in Pomfret's "Choice") has become somewhat Gothicized:

> Bear me, ye winds, indulgent to my pains
> Near some sad ruin's ghastly shade to dwell!
> There let me fondly eye the rude remains
> And from the mouldering refuse build my cell!

This is from his poem "To the Winds," while in "To a Friend" he wrote

> O loved Simplicity! be thine the prize!
> Assiduous Art correct her page in vain!

He has many poems of rural content which differ from earlier poems of the kind by being less pastoral in the literary sense and in emphasizing the pleasures of Nature unrefined by Art:

> Hark, how the wood-lark's tuneful throat
>   Can every studied grace excel;
> Let art constrain the rambling note,
>   And will she, Laura, please so well?

Though the emphasis is on simplicity, the lady still has a literary name; similarly, the song "The Landskip" refers to Daphne, though the stanza form is simple and the scene English:

> How sweetly smiled the hill, the vale,
> And all the landskip round!
> The river gliding down the dale!
> The hill with beeches crowned.

This is far removed in tone and in style from Pope's "Ode on Solitude." His lyrics however often have a lapidary quality that is the result of considerable artfulness, for all his depreciation of art as opposed to Nature. Some of his most attractive verses are "inscriptions," written for a particular object or place. Sometimes, as in "Written at an Inn at Henley," he sounds the Horatian note with graver overtones:

> Whoe'er has travelled life's dull round,
> Where'er his stages may have been,
> May sigh to think he still has found
> The warmest welcome at an inn.

Shenstone's most engaging poem is *The Schoolmistress* (1737), a descriptive poem "in imitation of Spenser" in which he followed Thomson's example in using the Spenserian stanza and some deliberately "quaint" Spenserian words to achieve a half-humorous effect. He said himself of the poem that it was intended to be "somewhat more grave than Pope's Alley ["The Alley," a burlesque piece of Spenserian imitation] and a good deal less than Mr. Thomson's *Castle of Indolence*." The tone is one of affectionate amusement, and the Spenserian archaisms are meant simply to raise a smile:

> Lo now with state she utters the command!
> Eftsoons the urchins to their tasks repair;
> Their books of stature small they take in hand
> Which with pellucid horn secured are,
> To save from finger wet the letters fair;
> The work so gay, that on their back is seen,
> St. George's high achievements does declare;
> On which thilk wight that has y-gazing been
> Kens the forthcoming rod, unpleasing sight, I ween!

This is fundamentally quite un-Spenserian, more so than the first canto of *The Castle of Indolence:* nothing could be further removed from the tone and intention of *The Faerie Queene*.

Shenstone was a gentleman of taste whose way of thinking, of feeling, and of living illustrates the development of taste in the mid-eighteenth century. His country estate of Leasowes was famous for its landscape gardening—and the development of landscape gardening is an important clue to the history of taste. Joseph Heely, in his

Letters on the Beauties of Hagley, Envil and the Leasowes (1777), gives an account of Shenstone's former estate which is very much in the spirit of the time: "The moment I entered this quiet and sequestered valley, the superlative genius of Shenstone stood confessed on every object, and struck me with silent admiration. I turned to a bench under the wall, and sat so absorbed with the charms of a cascade, so powerfully conducted in the very image of nature herself, plunging down a bed of shelving rock and huge, massy stones, that for a long while my attention was lost to everything else." Shenstone's own *Unconnected Thoughts on Gardening* (1764) presents his view of natural beauty and the picturesque. "Ruinated structures appear to derive their power of pleasing from the irregularity of surface which is variety, and the latitude they afford to the imagination to conceive an enlargement of their dimensions or to recollect any events or circumstances appertaining to their pristine grandeur, so as far as concerns grandeur and solemnity." The numerous books on gardening which appeared throughout the century (they include Horace Walpole's important *Essay on Gardening*, 1771) show the picturesque and the romantic which are reflected in the literature of the time.

With Joseph Warton (1722–1800) and Thomas Warton, Jr. (1728–90), sensibility and the love of older literature leads to a conscious break with the ideals of Pope. Joseph Warton's *Essay on the Genius and Writings of Pope* (Vol. I, 1756, Vol. II, 1782) first formulated a view of poetry that became the dominant one for over 150 years. "We do not, it should seem, sufficiently attend to the difference there is betwixt a *man of wit*, a *man of sense*, and a *true poet*. Donne and Swift were undoubtedly men of wit and men of sense: but what traces have they left of *pure poetry?* . . . The sublime and the pathetic are the two chief nerves of all genuine poesy. What is there transcendently sublime or pathetic in Pope? . . . Our English poets may, I think, be disposed in four different classes and degrees. In the first class I would place our only three sublime and pathetic poets: Spenser, Shakespeare, Milton. In the second class should be ranked such as possessed the true poetical genius in a more moderate degree, but who had noble talents for moral, ethical, and panegyrical poetry. At the head of these are Dryden, Prior, Addison, Cowley, Waller, Garth, . . . In the third class may be placed men of wit, of elegant taste, and lively fancy in describing familiar life, though not the higher scenes of poetry. Here may be numbered Butler, Swift, Rochester, Donne. . . . In the fourth class the mere versifiers . . . should be disposed." The function of the *Essay* is to determine to which class Pope belongs. He is no Spenser or Milton. "He who

would think *The Faerie Queen, Palamon and Arcite, The Tempest,*
or *Comus* childish and romantic might relish Pope. Surely, it is no
narrow and niggardly encomium, to say he is the great Poet of Reason, the first of ethical authors in verse." He concludes that Pope,
"considering the correctness, elegance, and utility of his works, the
weight of sentiment, and the knowledge of man they contain,"
should be assigned "a place next to Milton, and just above Dryden."
Pope is top of the second class.

Joseph Warton's own verse shows him endeavoring to use his recipe for sublime and pathetic poetry. "The Enthusiast, or the Lover of
Nature" proclaims its intentions clearly enough in its title. It is not
Nature to advantage dressed that Warton admires, but Nature un-
improved by man:

> Can Kent [a landscape gardener] design like Nature? Mark
>   where Thames'
> Plenty and pleasure pours through Lincoln's meads;
> Can the great artist, though with taste supreme
> Endued, one beauty to this Eden add?
> Though he, by rules unfettered, boldly scorns
> Formality and method, round and square
> Disdaining, plans irregularly great.

Put this beside Pope's advice on planning a garden in Epistle IV of
his *Moral Essays* and we see how the term "Nature" has shifted its
meaning:

> To build, to plant, whatever you intend,
> To rear the column or the arch to bend,
> To swell the terrace, or to sink the grot;
> In all, let Nature never be forgot.
> But treat the goddess like a modest fair,
> Nor over-dress, nor leave her wholly bare;
> Let not each beauty everywhere be spied,
> Where half the skill is decently to hide.
> He gains all points who pleasingly confounds,
> Surprises, varies, and conceals the bounds.

Warton, too, appeals to Nature, but in very different terms:

> Oh taste corrupt! that luxury and pomp,
> In specious names of polished manners veiled,
> Should proudly banish Nature's simple charms.
> All beauteous Nature! by thy boundless charms
> Oppressed, O where shall I begin thy praise,
> Where turn th' ecstatic eye, . . .

As the Enthusiast or Lover of Nature continues his meditations and apostrophes, it becomes clear that Pope's great ideal of correctness has been abandoned in favor of spontaneity and grandeur:

> What are the lays of artful Addison,
> Coldly correct, to Shakespeare's warblings wild?

In the same poem there is a picture of the poet as contemplative lover of the night that derives (as much of this kind of verse in the mid-eighteenth century derives) from Milton's "Il Penseroso":

> But let me never fail in cloudless nights,
> When silent Cynthia in her silver car
> Through the blue concave slides, when shine the hills,
> Twinkle the streams, and woods look tipt with gold,
> To seek some level mead, and there invoke
> Old Midnight's sister, Contemplation sage
> (Queen of the rugged brow, and stern-fixt eye)
> To lift my soul above this little earth,
> This folly-fettered world: to purge my ears,
> That I may hear the rolling planets' song,
> And tuneful turning spheres: . . .

The mood was infectious. His brother Thomas, in his poem on "The Pleasures of Melancholy" similarly echoes "Il Penseroso":

> Nor let me fail to cultivate my mind
> With the soft thrillings of the tragic Muse,
> Divine Melpomene, sweet Pity's nurse,
> Queen of the stately step, and flowing pall. . . .

Thomas Warton's poem is in the tradition of melancholy brooding among ruins that has already been noticed:

> Beneath yon ruined abbey's moss-grown piles
> Oft let me sit, at twilight hour of eve,
> Where through some western window the pale moon
> Pours her long-levelled rule of streaming light; . . .
> I choose the pale December's foggy glooms.
> Then, when the sullen shades of ev'ning close,
> Where through the room a blindly-glimm'ring gleam
> The dying embers scatter, . . .

There are not here the religious overtones of Young or the intensive pieties of Blair; the ruins may be ecclesiastical but they are chosen not for their religious associations but for their picturesqueness. Sensibility is here indulged in for its own sake. And its indulgence is associated with disparagement of Pope and praise of Spenser, Shakespeare, and Milton:

Through Pope's soft song though all the Graces breathe
And happiest art adorn his Attic page;
Yet does my mind with sweeter transport glow,
As at the root of mossy trunk reclined,
In magic Spenser's wildly warbled song
I see deserted Una wander wide
Through wasteful solitudes, and lurid heaths,
Weary, forlorn; . . .

The Wartons are not distinguished poets, but they are of the first importance in the history of taste. Thomas Warton was also a scholar whose work on earlier English poetry was to have the most important consequences for the future of poetry and of criticism in England. He published in 1754 his *Observations on the Faerie Queene of Spenser,* seeing in Spenser imagination at work unfettered by judgment and concluding that "if the critic is not satisfied, yet the reader is transported." He pleaded that critics of older literature should read the books "which were in repute about the time in which each author wrote, and which it is most likely he had read" and urged that Spenser, who, like Ariosto, "did not live in an age of planning, should not be judged by the laws of composition developed by the moderns." This is really a plea for critical relativism, and it was supported by Bishop Hurd's *Letters on Chivalry and Romance* (1762) which pleaded that *The Faerie Queene,* as a Gothic poem, should be judged by the rules appropriate to Gothic art. Hurd went further, and suggested that there might be something intrinsically more poetical in the Gothic manner. "Or may there not be something in the Gothic Romance peculiarly suited to the views of a genius, and to the ends of poetry?" He concluded: "What we have gotten by this revolution . . . is a great deal of good sense. What we have lost, is a world of fine fabling." This was very much Thomas Warton's conclusion too, and neither critic was quite happy about this opposition between good poetry and good sense. Warton went on from antiquarian and critical studies of earlier poetry to produce his vast and sprawling *History of English Poetry from the Twelfth to the Close of the Sixteenth Century* (Vol. I, 1774; Vol. II, 1778; Vol. III, 1781), a pioneer work made possible by the development of scholarship, editing, and the cataloguing of libraries throughout the century. It remained unfinished, and Warton was never quite able to manipulate his imagination–judgment antithesis so as to provide a proper dialectic for a literary history: he comes nearest to it when he suggests that the glories of Elizabethan literature were made possible because the age was close enough to the Gothic superstition to enjoy its poetic advantages and close enough on the other side to the refinement and order of the modern world to enable its writers to give form to their imaginings—a very unstable equilibrium indeed. Behind Warton's antiquarian and scholarly interests, and behind his love of earlier poetry, lay a development in literary taste that had the most far-reaching consequences. He himself kept wavering between love of Gothic wildness and appreciation of the beauty and order of the neo-classic world; and it is significant that after years of absorbing himself in older literature in order to write his history he finally recanted. His "Verses on Sir Joshua Reynolds's Painted Window at New College, Oxford," show him coming down in the end on the side of order and elegance:

> For long, enamoured of a barbarous age,
> A faithless truant to the classic page;
> Long have I loved to catch the simple chime
> Of minstrel-harps, and spell the fabling rhyme;
> To view the festive rites, the knightly play,
> That decked heroic Albion's elder day;
> To mark the mouldering halls of barons bold,
> And the rough castle, cast in giant mould;
> With Gothic manners Gothic arts explore,
> And muse on the magnificence of yore.
>
> But chief, enraptured have I loved to roam,
> A lingering votary, the vaulted dome,
> Where the tall shafts, that mount in massy pride,
> Their mingling branches shoot from side to side; . . .
> Where Superstition with capricious hand
> In many a maze the wreathed window planned,
> With hues romantic tinged the gorgeous pane,
> To fill with holy light the wondrous fane; . . .
> Ah, spare the weakness of a lover's heart!
> Chase not the phantoms of my fairy dream,
> Phantoms that shrink at Reason's painful gleam!
> That softer touch, insidious artist, stay,
> Nor to new joys my struggling breast betray!
>
> Such was a pensive bard's mistaken strain.—
> But oh, of ravished pleasures why complain?
>
> No more the matchless skill I call unkind,
> That strives to disenchant my cheated mind.
> For when again I view thy chaste design,
> The just proportion, and the genuine line;
> Those native portraitures of Attic art,
> That from the lucid surface seem to start;
> Those tints, that steal no glories from the day,
> Nor ask the sun to lend his streaming ray:
> The doubtful radiance of contending dyes,

> That faintly mingle, yet distinctly rise; . . .
> Sudden, the sombrous imagery is fled,
> Which late my visionary rapture fed:
> Thy powerful hand has broke the Gothic chain,
> And brought my bosom back to Truth again; . . .

This conclusion, like Hurd's, makes it clear that the change in taste that was proceeding during the middle of the century had no strong or clear critical principles behind it. Indeed, there was an air of dilettantism about all this idolizing of older poets, even though a good deal of respectable scholarship went on. The position of Warton and his friends was neither genuinely relativistic nor genuinely for the free play of the uncontrolled imagination, nor really anything else. They made some attempt to balance the extremes of imagination and reason, but the opposition was a simple-minded one and reflected unresolved problems of sensibility rather than the foundation of a new position with respect to life and letters.

A more interesting imagination, and a more poetic use of materials drawn from older literature, is found in the poetry of William Collins (1721–59), who shared the Wartons' love of Spenser, Shakespeare, and Milton and was also devoted to the Greek tragic dramatists. His earliest published work, the *Persian Eclogues* (1742), are somewhat frigid exercises in a conventional mode given a superficial novelty by the Persian names and setting: the effect can be almost ridiculous:

> Thus sung the swain, and eastern legends say,
> The maids of Bagdat verified the lay: . . .

His *Odes on Several Descriptive and Allegorical Subjects* (1746) were originally planned to appear in a joint volume with odes by Joseph Warton, but the scheme fell through; they appeared alone and had no contemporary success. Collins' odes often show a contrived extravagance of utterance that seems to represent an attempt to be vatic in some grand old way; yet he can also be restrained and delicate. Sometimes the tone is calm while the language is wild:

> Come, Pity, come, by Fancy's aid,
> Ev'n now my thoughts, relenting maid,
>   Thy temple's pride design:
> Its southern site, its truth complete
> Shall raise a wild enthusiast heat,
>   In all who view the shrine.

(Ode to Pity)

In his "Ode to Fear" Collins tries hard to raise a "wild enthusiast heat." As the "Ode to Pity" celebrates Euripides, the "Ode to Fear" pays tribute to the effects achieved by Aeschylus and Sophocles in a language that strangely combines stylized eighteenth-century poetic diction and a more melodramatic and personal utterance:

> Wrapt in thy cloudy veil th' incestuous queen
> Sighed the sad call her son and husband heard,
> When once alone it broke the silent scene,
> And he the wretch of Thebes no more appeared. . . .

> Thou who such weary lengths hast past,
> Where wilt thou rest, mad nymph, at last?
> Say, wilt thou shroud in haunted cell,
> Where gloomy Rape and Murder dwell?

His "Ode on the Poetical Character" is the most complex of his odes in imagery and thought, but, as so often in Collins, the passionate note sounds forced. Collins was very fond of the device of personification, which he sometimes used in an exclamatory and rhapsodic fashion ("Ah Fear! Ah frantic Fear! /I see, I see thee near") but occasionally with quiet dignity and control, as in the perfectly wrought "Ode" written in the beginning of 1746:

> How sleep the brave, who sink to rest,
> By all their country's wishes blest!
> When Spring, with dewy fingers cold,
> Returns to deck their hallowed mould,
> She there shall dress a sweeter sod,
> Than Fancy's feet have ever trod.

> By fairy hands, their knell is rung,
> By forms unseen their dirge is sung;
> There Honour comes, a pilgrim grey,
> To bless the turf that wraps their clay,
> And Freedom shall a while repair,
> To dwell a weeping hermit there!

The perfection of this finely carved piece makes one wonder whether the kind of thing Collins did in such a poem as "The Passions: an Ode for Music" was not the result of applying in a doctrinaire fashion theories of poetry that were not really congenial to his own creative genius. There is, it is true, a certain power, but there is also a melodramatic extravagance, in such lines as:

> With eyes upraised, as one inspired,
> Pale Melancholy sat retired,
> And from her wild sequestered seat
> In notes by distance made more sweet,

> Poured through the mellow horn her pensive soul
>   And dashing soft from rocks around,
>   Bubbling runnels joined the sound; . . .

The "Ode on the Popular Superstitions of the Highlands of Scotland," incomplete and posthumously published, is one of the first attempts in English literature to exploit the romantic aspects of Scottish scenery and legend; yet the diction is that of conventional elevated eighteenth-century poetic speech:

> What though far off, from some dark dell espied
>   His glimm'ring mazes cheer th' excursive sight,
> Yet turn, ye wand'rers, turn your steps aside,
>   Nor trust the guidance of that faithless light;
> For watchful, lurking 'mid th' unrustling reed,
>   At those mirk hours the wily monster lies, . . .

The movement, however, is far from that of the Popeian couplet and almost as far from that of Thomson's blank verse; it has a slow, somber quality, which Collins manages better in this poem than in most of his others. Sometimes Collins' interest in older poets could yield a new simplicity of verse-form and in some degree of diction, as in his "Song from Shakespeare's Cymbeline," and sometimes he can use the poetic diction of his age in such a way as to achieve a tone of simple elegy, as in his "Ode on the Death of Mr. Thomson":

> In yonder grave a Druid lies
>   Where slowly winds the stealing wave!
> The year's best sweets shall duteous rise
>   To deck its Poet's sylvan grave!

(The poem would probably read better if one omitted Collins' exclamation marks, but they are worth leaving in as indicative of his exclamatory and emotional approach.)

Perhaps the most technically successful of all Collins' poems (after "How sleep the brave") is his "Ode to Evening," one of the few successful examples in English of the unrhymed lyric, where the skillful handling of vowel sounds and rhythmic effects compensates for the lack of rhyme:

> If aught of oaten stop or pastoral song
> May hope, chaste Eve, to soothe thy modest ear,
>   Like thy own solemn springs,
>   Thy springs, and dying gales,
> O nymph reserved, while now the bright-haired sun
> Sits in yon western tent, . . .

Collins' career petered out in depression and madness, a fate all too common among eighteenth-century writers (Swift, Cowper, Christopher Smart). He never quite came to terms with his genius nor did he fully assimilate the different elements of scholarship and imagination that he brought to his poetry. He could combine an extreme artificiality of diction with a content asserting the enthusiastic and spontaneous nature of his utterance; we feel sometimes that he was between two worlds, and sometimes that he worked too hard at being a poet.

Thomas Gray (1716–71) is another poet whose scholarship and breadth of literary and intellectual interests helped to fashion his poetic ideals and practice. A retiring scholar in temperament and habit of life, Gray experimented with a number of different kinds of poetry based on or illustrative of various older kinds. His Pindaric odes followed the construction of Pindar in their tripartite pattern of strophe, antistrophe, and epode. His poems on Celtic and Norse subjects were intended as illustrations of older modes for an unwritten history of English poetry. Like Collins, he tried to combine a highly stylized diction with a note of intense passion, and while he sometimes succeeded rather better than Collins did, he frequently risks falling into bombast. Gray's contemporaries found his odes obscure, and in an "advertisement" prefixed to the edition of 1768 Gray somewhat testily remarked that he had been recommended to subjoin some explanatory notes but he "had too much respect for the understanding of his readers to take that liberty." Some of the odes combine generalized description, meditation, and moralizing in a way calculated to please contemporary taste, the "Ode on the Spring," for example:

> Still is the toiling hand of care:
> The panting herds repose:
> Yet hark, how through the peopled air
> The busy murmur glows!
> The insect youth are on the wing,
> Eager to taste the honied spring,
> And float amid the liquid noon:
> Some lightly o'er the current skim,
> Some show their gaily-gilded trim,
> Quick-glancing to the sun.

The meditation and moralizing play a more prominent part in the well-known lines from the "Ode on a Distant Prospect of Eton College":

> Alas, regardless of their doom
> The little victims play!
> No sense have they of ills to come,
> Nor care beyond to-day:
> Yet see how all around them wait
> The ministers of human fate,
> And black misfortune's baleful train!
> Ah, show them where in ambush stand
> To seize their prey the murderous band!
> Ah, tell them they are men!

The use of apostrophe was very much in the rhetorical mode of the time—mid-eighteenth-century verse is a forest of exclamation marks. Gray also uses personification much as Collins does:

> These shall the fury Passions tear,
> The vultures of the mind,
> Disdainful Anger, pallid Fear,
> And Shame that skulks behind;
> Or pining Love shall waste their youth,
> Or Jealousy with rankling tooth, . . .

The Eton College ode manages these devices well. Essentially a contemplative poem, it starts off as an address to the College and moves through a recollection of the poet's own youth there, through thoughts on what is in store for youth in general, to come to rest on what is really a note of self-pity; but the deliberately elevated style depersonalizes or at least generalizes the emotion. The personifications, the invocations, the apostrophes, the elevation of language in such a phrase as "To chase the rolling circle's speed /Or urge the flying ball" help to provide the proper esthetic distance. It is worth noting that this kind of stylization was as far from the Pope tradition as it was from the Wordsworthian; Johnson was speaking for the former when he complained of the poet's apostrophe to Father Thames to tell him who were now disporting themselves on his banks: "His supplication to father Thames, to tell him who drives the hoop or tosses the ball, is useless and puerile. Father Thames has no better means of knowing than himself." This is unfair—Gray is quite explicit on the reasons why he expects Father Thames to know—and is based on a misunderstanding of the kind and degree of conventionality employed by the poem.

Gray's poem "On the Death of a Favourite Cat" is a deliberate application of highly formal diction to commonplace incident, in the tradition of mock-heroic and burlesque use of formal styles in the eighteenth century. The "Hymn to Adversity" aims at an Aeschylean grandeur, but is really in the tradition of moralizing apostrophe to be found in Thomson, Young, and others, although the movement of the verse is quite different from that of Thomson's or Young's blank verse:

> Daughter of Jove, relentless Power,
> Thou tamer of the human breast,
> Whose iron scourge and torturing hour
> The bad affright, afflict the best! . . .

Gray uses a variety of stanza forms in his poetry, and avoids both the heroic couplet and blank verse, thus helping to restore stanzaic variety to English poetry.

"The Progress of Poesy" is one of Gray's most ambitious Pindaric odes, highly wrought, deliberately "grand," and with a sustained rhetorical excitement. The ideas in it were already commonplaces, but the attempt at grandeur was Gray's own:

> Awake, Aeolian lyre, awake,
> And give to rapture all thy trembling strings,
> From Helicon's harmonious springs
> A thousand rills their mazy progress take:
> The laughing flowers, that round them blow,
> Drink life and fragrance as they flow.
> Now the rich stream of music winds along
> Deep, majestic, smooth, and strong,
> Through verdant vales, and Ceres' golden reign:
> Now rolling down the steep amain,
> Headlong, impetuous, see it pour:
> The rocks and nodding groves rebellow to the roar.

The mood and tone varies with each stanza; there is deliberate rising and falling; the language sometimes mounts to ecstatic heights that tremble on the verge of the ludicrous (but never quite fall over) and is sometimes content with rather pedestrian periphrasis. It is perhaps rather a remarkable poetic exercise than a great poem.

"The Bard" (meant as an example of the style of old Celtic poetry) and "The Fatal Sisters" (illustrating the heroic Norse style), ironically called by Dr. Johnson "the Wonderful Wonder of Wonders," are more difficult to come to terms with. "The Bard" is even more highly rhetorical in style than "The Progress of Poesy." Most of the poem represents the bitter prophecy addressed by a Welsh bard to Edward I when his conquering army entered Wales, and Gray attempts to sustain the high note of heroic denunciation. The poem certainly has rhetorical splendor, but Gray has not been able to avoid a suggestion of strained histrionics. "The Fatal Sisters," adapted from a

Latin version of a Norse poem, is not a Pindaric, but written in simple four-line stanzas with alternating rhyme and trochaic beat (seven syllables to a line): it has a melodramatic air in spite of (or perhaps because of) its ballad suggestions. "These odes," remarked Johnson of these two poems, "are marked by glittering accumulations of ungraceful ornaments; they strike, rather than please; the images are magnified by affection; the language is laboured into harshness. The mind of the writer seems to work with unnatural violence. *Double, double, toil and trouble.* He has a kind of strutting dignity, and is tall by walking on tiptoe." One can understand exactly why Johnson says this without altogether agreeing with him. We are rather too conscious of Gray's straining after effect ("his art and his struggle are too visible," said Johnson) and the high rhetorical notes sometimes wobble. It is significant that both Johnson and Wordsworth castigated Gray for the artificiality of his diction.

The poem of Gray's that Wordsworth objected to was his sonnet on the death of Mr. Richard West; but in fact the artificiality of diction to which Wordsworth took exception is part of the carefully wrought texture of a happily stylized poem. The sonnet was not a form used in any degree by neoclassic poets, and in employing it Gray was again helping to restore to English poetry one of its lost resources. But the conventions on which the poem is built are wholly neoclassic.

> In vain to me the smiling mornings shine,
> And redd'ning Phoebus lifts his golden fire;
> The birds in vain their amorous descant join,
> Or cheerful fields resume their green attire.
> These ears, alas! for other notes repine,
> A different object do these eyes require:
> My lonely anguish melts no heart but mine,
> And in my breast the imperfect joys expire.
> Yet morning smiles the busy race to cheer,
> And new-born pleasure brings to happier men;
> The fields to all their wonted tribute bear;
> To warm their little loves the birds complain:
> I fruitless mourn to him that cannot hear,
> And weep the more, because I weep in vain.

The treatment of grief is highly conventional (nature is beautiful, but it is no longer beautiful to me) and the Latinized diction adds a further note of stylization. Yet it is the conventionality and the stylization that make the poem.

Gray's most popular poem, and for long the most popular poem in the English language, is his "Elegy Written in a Country Church-yard," which Dr. Johnson rejoiced to concur with the common reader in praising. The simple and slow-moving stanza form is here handled with great skill. The poem opens effectively by gradually emptying the landscape of both sights and sounds as dusk descends, and the elegiac, meditative tone is sustained throughout a variety of turns in the thought. It is in the tradition of graveyard contemplation which has already been discussed, but here the handling of the setting and of the development of the meditation is done with high art. The poem moves with ease from a contemplation of the landscape to a consideration of "the short and simple annals of the poor" to suggest moral ideas which arise from this consideration. The alternation between generalized abstractions and individual examples is adroitly done, and the whole poem gives a sense of personal emotion universalized by form. There was in fact a deeply personal feeling behind it, and it was not all written at one time, which accounts for the somewhat unexpected turn the poem takes as it moves to its conclusion. The poet turns to address himself in the twenty-fourth stanza and to move the poem round until it reveals his own epitaph, and this involves a certain break in the continuity which is never wholly justified by developments in the tone or the structure.

Gray was as interested as Thomas Warton in the history of English poetry, though he never carried out his plan to write one. He was aware of the Celtic and the Norse traditions and had read widely in the literary and historical scholarship of his time. He is an interesting example of the way in which scholarship and poetic imagination reinforce each other, and also shows how the continued investigation of poets who lived before "the reform of our numbers" helped to shift poetic taste and widen literary horizons and break down some of the Augustan assurance. He is, however, less a transitional figure between the Augustans and the Romantics than a highly idiosyncratic poet who responded to the intellectual and esthetic currents of his time in his own way.

The Wartons, Gray, and Collins show an interest in older English literature that is symptomatic not only of a restlessness about Augustan taste but also of a curiosity about primitive poetry in general. "Primitive poetry" to many critics of the middle and late eighteenth century was a vague term; it included biblical poetry—discussed by Bishop Lowth in his influential Oxford lectures, *De Sacra Poesi Hebraeorum*, published in 1753—as well as Celtic and Norse poetry, ballads, and other folk literature, and the real or supposed literature of Laplanders, Indians, and Peruvians. It was thought to be highly metaphorical and to reflect certain kinds of enthusiasm and sensibility which disappeared with the development of a more polished civilization. Interest in primitive poetry often went together with an interest in the origins of poetry, concerning which there was much speculation, theorizing, and dogmatizing. When therefore James Macpherson (1736–96) brought out his flamboyant prose poems as translations of ancient Gaelic epic poetry there was tremendous excitement, for this seemed to prove that a great primitive epic had existed and that it revealed primitive man graced with all the sensibility with which the theorists had endowed him. The very possibility of a primitive epic of any real literary merit and interest was of course inconceivable to the neoclassic mind; literature to the Augustans was the product of civilization and art; and Dr. Johnson, who spoke for civilization on this issue, roundly condemned Macpherson's productions as rank forgeries. But others not only believed in their authenticity but hailed them as in any case great poetry. Macpherson was urged on by the Scottish writers Hugh Blair, the Edinburgh critic and professor, and John Home, the dramatist to whom Collins had dedicated his "Ode on the Popular Superstitions of the Scottish Highlands." He published his *Fragments of Ancient Poetry Collected in the Highlands of Scotland and Translated from the Gaelic or Erse Language* in 1760 and then, anxious to confirm his friends' views that these fragments indicated the existence of a great primitive Gaelic epic, obligingly produced the epic, *Fingal, An Ancient Epic* (1761). This was followed by *Temora, An Epic Poem* (1763) and the collected edition, entitled *The Poems of Ossian*, appeared in 1765.

It is now known that though Macpherson did draw on fragments of genuine Gaelic ballad poetry his work was substantially a fabrication and its whole tone and treatment far removed from anything found in older Gaelic literature. It was precisely this tone and treatment which enchanted so many contemporary readers and made "Macpherson's Ossian" such a popular and influential work on the Continent. Against a landscape based vaguely on that of the Scottish Highlands but more misty and "sublime," Macpherson set heroic actions reflecting current ideas about the nobility of natural man. The characters, in the elevated rhetoric of their speech and the tragic nobility of their behavior, in their sensitivity to nature and their apostrophes to the sun, the moon, and the winds, vindicated the theories of the primitivists and flattered the national pride of those Scots who had based their claims to possess a national literature on the existence of a great Gaelic epic. It is an odd reflection on the whole literary situation in Scotland that while the Ossian controversy raged, the revival of Gaelic poetry by a handful of contemporary Gaelic poets (for the Gaelic language still flourished in the Highlands) passed unnoticed, and while the literary world became excited over Macpherson's doctored and synthetic epics, the first genuine translation of a Gaelic ballad, by Jerome Stone, which appeared in the *Scots Magazine* in 1755, appears to have aroused no interest at all (though it may have helped to set Macpherson on to his own task).

The rhythms of Macpherson's rhetorical prose-poetry were derived partly from the Bible, with some overtones from Miltonic blank verse and partly, it would seem, from the cadences of Highland preaching. The brooding melancholy and prevailing sentimentality of the work represents Macpherson's concession to the graveyard tradition and to current notions of the sublime as well as of the primitive. How far removed the tone and imagery of *The Poems of Ossian* is from genuine epic poetry of the heroic age can be seen from a single extract:

It is night; I am alone, forlorn on the hill of storms. The wind is heard in the mountain. The torrent pours down the rock. No hut receives me from the rain; forlorn on the hill of winds!

Rise, moon! from behind thy clouds. Stars of the night arise! Lead me, some light, to the place, where my love rests from the chase alone! his bow near him, unstrung: his dogs panting around him. But here I must sit alone, by the rock of the mossy stream. The stream and the wind roar aloud. I hear not the voice of my love! Why delays my Salgar, why the chief of the hill, his promise? Here is the rock, and here the tree! here is the roaring stream! Thou didst promise with night to be here. Ah! whither is my Salgar gone? With thee I would fly, from my father; with thee, from my brother of pride. Our race have long been foes; we are not foes, O Salgar!

Cease a little while, O wind! stream, be thou silent awhile! let my voice be heard around. Let my wanderer hear me! Salgar! it is Colma who calls. Here is the tree, and the rock. Salgar, my love! I am here. Why delayest thou thy coming? Lo! the calm moon comes forth. The flood is bright in the vale. The rocks are gray on the steep. I see him not on the brow. His dogs come not before him, with tidings of his near approach. Here I must sit alone!

A less practically successful but a more genuinely poetic forger of an antique style was Thomas Chatterton (1752–70), the unfortunate youth who committed suicide when his false claim to have discovered genuinely medieval poems was refuted. Chatterton is yet another symptom of the increasing interest in older poetic styles. But whereas earlier eighteenth-century poets had been content to burlesque or imitate older styles, he tried to write poetry that he could pass off as genuinely fifteenth-century. He had pored over documents in the muniment room of the church of St. Mary Redcliffe in Bristol, and this gave him ideas and inspiration, but, though his head was stuffed with medieval romance and medieval imaginings, he never quite caught the real tone, and no instructed reader could mistake his preposterous spelling and strangely histrionic melancholy for the genuine medieval lyrics and ballads composed, as he claimed, by one Thomas Rowley. But Chatterton's Rowley poems have an interest and a merit of their own. There is a real lyric gift at work, and though the feeling is sometimes mawkish, the images exaggerated, and the medieval properties too blatant, some of them show at least a promise of a poetic style that might have developed into something original in its own romantic way:

> O! synge untoe mie roundelaie,
> O! droppe the brynie teare wythe mee,
> Daunce ne moe atte hallie daie,
> Lyke a reynynge ryver bee;
>> Mie love ys dedde,
>> Gon to hys death-bedde,
>> Al under the wyllowe tree.

Crude enough, perhaps; but as the work of an impoverished youngster fifteen or sixteen years old far from despicable, and indicative of a rising strain in English sensibility which was to have interesting results in the nineteenth century.

The poetry of Oliver Goldsmith (1730–74) is more centrally in the tradition of mid-eighteenth-century verse, moralizing and descriptive and often sententious; but Goldsmith preferred the heroic couplet in his serious verse and looked askance at the extension of verse forms that was taking place. In his dedicatory letter to *The Traveller* (1764) he broke out: "What criticisms have we not heard of late in favour of blank verse, and Pindaric odes, choruses, anapaests and iambics, alliterative care and happy negligence! Every absurdity has now a champion to defend it, . . ." *The Traveller* surveys the different European countries in heroic couplets that are metrically competent but have none of Pope's plasticity and sparkle. The tone is both meditative and rhetorical:

> When thus creation's charms around combine,
> Amidst the store, should thankless pride repine?
> Say, should the philosophic mind disdain
> That good which makes each humbler bosom vain?

He finds the advantages and disadvantages, the virtues and vices, of different countries canceling each other out, and at the end, turning to Britain, attacks the vice of luxury, a favorite theme of his:

> Have we not seen, round Britain's peopled shore,
> Her useful sons exchanged for useless ore?
> Seen all her triumphs but destruction haste,
> Like flaring tapers brightening as they waste?

> Seen opulence, her grandeur to maintain,
> Lead stern depopulation in her train, . . .

Goldsmith's poetic language is highly abstract even when he is dealing with particular scenes and situations:

> And over fields where scattered hamlets rose
> In barren solitary pomp repose . . .
>
> With food as well the peasant is supplied
> On Idra's cliffs as Arno's shelvy side; . . .
>
> The shuddering tenant of the frigid zone . . .

When we find a couplet that rings with the force of a proverb, we
learn that it was inserted by Dr. Johnson:

> How small, of all that human hearts endure,
> That part which laws or kings can cause or cure!

Goldsmith lacks wit, and his use of abstractions and generalizations
often seems to be the result of no compelling poetic need but to be
merely a mechanically skillful use of convention. This is clearly seen
in his most popular poem, ₁ ₁e *Deserted Village*, where there are not
only enormously generalized descriptions—

> Where smiling spring its earliest visit paid,
> And parting summer's lingering blooms delayed,

but also a mingling of abstract and concrete terms in the same phrase
which reveal a superficial handling of poetic diction:

> For talking age and whispering lovers made
>
> A bloated mass of rank, unwieldy woe.

"Age" becomes too abstract when set beside the concrete "lovers,"
though both are highly general terms; and the abstract "woe" becomes the emptier, not the richer, term when preceded by strong
physical terms like "bloated mass" and "rank." He sometimes succeeds with the proverbial or epigrammatic touch:

> Ill fares the land, to hastening ills a prey,
> Where wealth accumulates and men decay.

But even here the repetition of "ill" and "ills" is not happy; it is
neither a balance, a contrast, nor an effectively cumulative progression. Goldsmith falls back, too, on words of minimal meaning
and maximum conventionality all too often—such a word as "train,"
for example:

> But times are altered; trade's unfeeling train
> Usurp the land, and dispossess the swain; . . .

> She only left of all the harmless train,
> The sad historian of the pensive plain.

> His house was known to all the vagrant train;
> He chid their wanderings, but relieved their pain; . . .

> Yes! let the rich deride, the proud disdain
> These simple blessings of the lowly train; . . .

> The dome where Pleasure holds her midnight reign,
> Here, richly decked, admits the gorgeous train; . . .

> Do thine, sweet Auburn, thine, the loveliest train—
> Do thy fair tribes participate her pain?

This argues a general sloppiness in the handling of language. Yet the poem has a kind of charm. Some of the inset pictures of village characters are done with affectionate humor—the account of the village schoolmaster, for example:

> . . . While words of learned length and thundering sound
> Amazed the gazing rustics ranged around;
> And still they gazed, and still the wonder grew
> That one small head could carry all he knew.

But in his more serious portraits, such as his account of the dispossessed and emigrant poor, his melodramatic generalities are tedious. Every unfortunate old peasant is a "good old sire," his daughter must be "lovely," the daughter's husband "fond," and so on, while the account of the "poor houseless shivering female" betrayed by a proud rich man is sentimental melodrama at its grossest:

> Her modest looks the cottage might adorn,
> Sweet as the primrose peeps beneath the thorn;
> Now lost to all—her friends, her virtue fled—
> Near her betrayer's door she lays her head
> And, pinched with cold, and shrinking from the shower,
> With heavy heart deplores that luckless hour,
> When idly first, ambitious of the town,
> She left her wheel and robes of country brown.

The imaginary geography of the distant regions to which the wretched country folk are forced to emigrate is quite absurd, and the concluding attack on luxury lacks force because of the strained melodramatic context out of which it emerges. This is Augustan verse weakened by sententious rhetoric.

Goldsmith's lighter pieces are appealing in a somewhat superficial way, the swinging anapaestic "Retaliation," where with genial satire he replies to mock epitaphs perpetrated on him by his friends, the lively and colloquial "Haunch of Venison," the mock-ballad "Elegy on the Death of a Mad Dog" (much more successful than the serious ballad, "The Hermit," with its false elegance of tone), and the handful of colloquial pieces in octosyllabic couplets. On the whole it can be said that Goldsmith as a poet is more interesting as a symptom than as a wholly successful practitioner.

If sententious rhetoric weakens Goldsmith's verse, it strengthens Dr. Johnson's. Johnson (1709–84) developed a technique in the handling of the heroic couplet for purposes of moralizing description that brought a new strength and balance to this verse form. His early satirical poem "London" (1739), "a poem in imitation of the third satire of Juvenal," shows it less fully developed than "The Vanity of Human Wishes" (1749; suggested by Juvenal's tenth satire), yet even "London" shows a power and a control in the couplet that had not been seen since Pope, though the verse is essentially different from Pope's:

> For arts like these preferred, admired, caressed,
> They first invade your table, then your breast;
> Explore your secrets with insidious art,
> Watch the weak hour, and ransack all the heart; . . .

Here the balancing of the literal "table" by the metaphorical "breast" is not the result of a weak conventionality; it is a satiric device and operates as such, as does the balancing of "watch . . . hour" and "ransack . . . heart" in the last line of the quotation. The rhetorical question is employed with grim effectiveness, not as a mere empty flourish:

> Has heaven reserved, in pity to the poor,
> No pathless waste, or undiscovered shore?
> No secret island in the boundless main?
> No peaceful desert yet unclaimed by Spain?
> Quick let us rise, the happy seats explore,
> And bear oppression's insolence no more.
> This mournful truth is everywhere confessed:
> SLOW RISES WORTH BY POVERTY DEPRESSED:
> But here more slow, where all are slaves to gold,
> Where looks are merchandise, and smiles are sold;
> Where won by bribes, by flatteries implored,
> The groom retails the favours of the lord.

This gives a new dimension to the moralizing verse of the mid-eighteenth century. The ironic side glance at Spain in the fourth line, the movement to get up and hasten to the Utopia he pretends has been suggested to him, to be checked on the realization of "this mournful truth" which rings out like a proverb, the rhymes themselves strengthening the feeling and punctuating the thought, as well as such devices as the qualification of a general truth by remarking that it is even more true here ("Slow rises worth . . . but here more slow"), all denote a new kind of mastery of the heroic couplet.

This mastery is seen perfectly wielded in "The Vanity of Human Wishes." Here the rhymes chime out at the end of each pair of lines to give emphasis and moral weight to the verse; balance and antithesis are used to force the reader into attention by exploring all sides of the situation and showing how everything contributes to the same dark pattern; while, at the end of a sequence of carefully balanced lines, a single line, marching forward without a pause to its ringing conclusion, sums up or brings to an effective climax a whole series of points.

The opening couplet—

> Let Observation, with extensive view,
> Survey mankind from China to Peru,

is deliberately grandiloquent and general, with the poet's eye sweeping across the whole world: this is to be a poem about man as a whole, not about any particular phase of civilization. And having established the geographical inclusiveness of the scene, Johnson goes on to establish its historical inclusiveness by taking examples of the vanity of human wishes from different periods in history. The reader is caught relentlessly, one might almost say, in the atmosphere which the poem sets up. Whether we consider man's hopes or his fears, his adventurousness or his vacillation, his reason or his obstinacy, his natural gifts or his artificial graces, the result is the same:

> Remark each anxious toil, each eager strife,
> And watch the busy scenes of crowded life;
> Then say how hope and fear, desire and hate,
> O'erspread with snares the crowded maze of fate,
> Where wavering man, betrayed by venturous pride
> To tread the dreary paths without a guide,
> As treacherous phantoms in the mist delude,
> Shuns fancied ills, or chases airy good.
> How rarely reason guides the stubborn choice,
> Rules the bold hand, or prompts the suppliant voice;
> How nations sink, by darling schemes oppressed,
> When vengeance listens to the fool's request.

> Fate wings with every wish the afflictive dart,
> Each gift of nature, and each grace of art;
> With fatal heat impetuous courage glows,
> With fatal sweetness elocution flows;
> Impeachment stops the speaker's powerful breath,
> And restless fire precipitates on death.

There is a remarkable use of antithesis in such lines as

> Where wavering man, betrayed by venturous pride

and

> Shuns fancied ills, or chases airy good.

(Here "shuns" contrasts with "chases" and "ills" with "good," while "fancied" and "airy" correspond to one another: ills and good are both largely illusory, and whether we shun the former or chase the latter, the result is equally vain.) In such a couplet as

> Where wavering man, betrayed by venturous pride
> To tread the dreary paths without a guide

the second line lacks the balanced pauses of the first, but runs on to establish the inclusive pattern—*which ever* side you take, whether you concentrate on the wavering or the venturous, the end is the same. The end of each verse paragraph uses this kind of climactic line, without the pause, even more strongly, and sometimes the whole couplet is treated in this way, as at the end of the first verse paragraph:

> Impeachment stops the speaker's powerful breath,
> And restless fire precipitates on death.

The end of the verse paragraph is not always marked by a rising line without a pause, however; sometimes a balanced line can be used as a climax just as effective, e.g.,

> The dangers gather as the treasures rise

or

> One shows the plunder, and one hides the thief.

In the latter of these lines the antithesis between "shows" and "hides" is part of the trap set by the complete couplet: light and darkness are equally fatal to the rich traveler; either way he is in for trouble:

> Nor light nor darkness brings his pain relief,
> One shows the plunder, and one hides the thief.

The poem moves in a series of verse paragraphs each of which plays its part in the cumulative building up of the total picture. The handling of the transitions is skillful—"But scarce observed, . . ." "Let history tell, . . ." "Yet still one general cry . . ." "Such was the scorn . . ." Sometimes the choice of noun or verb can provide an implicit metaphor, as in

> Delusive fortune hears the incessant call,
> They mount, they shine, evaporate, and fall,

where the image suggested by the succession of verbs is that of exploding fireworks and also that of the water of a fountain. And what ironic force Johnson can get by concentrating everything on a single line (not balanced this time), as in

> And ask no questions but the price of votes.

Personification is used with skill and tact, never overdone, just enough to suggest a vivid image, to conjure up in the reader's mind a concrete example. When Johnson writes

> Unnumbered suppliants crowd Preferment's gate

he is not so much personifying Preferment as suggesting a picture of seekers after office crowding round the doors of some influential person—a common enough scene in Johnson's day. And when he writes

> Hate dogs their flight, and insult mocks their end

he is not using the device of personification in a strict and formal way ("insult" is not capitalized), but conjuring up a picture of an eighteenth-century crowd mocking at a disgraced politician or a condemned criminal (the two are implicitly associated). In his account of the disgraced politician's picture being removed from the wall—

> The form distorted justifies the fall
> And detestation rids the indignant wall,

we find a remarkably powerful use of the abstract noun and the device of the "pathetic fallacy." "The form distorted" is the kind of compressed statement we often find in Latin, with the perfect participle passive, and "the indignant wall," by attributing human feelings to an inanimate object, helps to give the passage its fierce compactness.

The inset stories of great heroes who came to sad ends are done with a similar compactness, and they are cunningly placed so as both to vary and to illustrate the generalizations about human life which abound in the poem. No two of these stories are constructed in exactly the same way; the variations between the general and the particular statements are subtly maneuvered. One might compare a climax such as

> Wreaths which at last the dear-bought right convey
> To rust on medals, or on stones decay

with the conclusion of the story of "Swedish Charles":

> His fall was destined to a barren strand,
> A petty fortress, and a dubious hand;
> He left a name at which the world grew pale,
> To point a moral or adorn a tale.

And these in turn might be compared with the quite different sort of effect achieved by the last line of the account of the miser:

> Unlocks his gold, and counts it till he dies.

Different again is the savagely particular illustration of generalizations concerning "life's last scene";

> In life's last scene what prodigies surprise;
> Fears of the brave, and follies of the wise!
> From Marlb'rough's eyes the streams of dotage flow,
> And Swift expires a driv'ler and a show.

Another kind of effect is the combination of mournfulness and fierce contempt in

> Now Beauty falls betrayed, despised, distressed,
> And hissing infamy proclaims the rest.

There is a pause before the concluding twenty-six lines of the poem, which form a "coda" in a somewhat different key: still somber, but gentler in tone now and slower and quieter in movement, the lines round out the poem with a subdued profession of faith in the ability of the individual to come to terms with the world by cultivating the proper frame of mind. In the end it is the proper frame of mind alone that matters:

> With these celestial Wisdom calms the mind,
> And makes the happiness she does not find.

There is an antithesis in this final line of the poem between "makes" and "find," but it is not as violently expressed as some of the earlier statements in this form, nor does it divide the line into two. It is a gentle stress in "find"—all the gentler because the last word chimes with the preceding line's "calms the mind"—on which the poem comes to an end. Indeed, the final gentle stress is on the whole phrase—

> and *makes* the happiness she *does not find*.

This provides just the right note of mingled confidence and pessimism for the conclusion of a poem of this kind.

None of Johnson's other poems are as carefully wrought as "The Vanity of Human Wishes"; many of them are mere exercises, and some are burlesques. The most successful of his shorter lyrics is his poem "On the Death of Dr. Robert Levet," where he uses a simple four-line stanza with weight and dignity:

> Condemned to Hope's delusive mine,
> As on we toil from day to day,
> By sudden blasts, or slow decline,
> Our social comforts drop away.

This has the simple gravity of a hymn.

Johnson's two great satires, "London" and the "Vanity," are not typical of the satirical poetry of the period. Johnson's are moral satires on human delusions and frailties; true to his critical principles, he was not numbering the streaks of the tulip but enunciating general truths in a particular way. But for the most part mid-eighteenth-century satirical verse was petty and political. There was a great deal of it, much of it appearing in short-lived periodicals in the interests of one party or faction or another. It was a way of making a living, and though Johnson despised it there were many who embraced it. Perhaps the most able of these minor verse satirists was Charles Churchill (1731–64), who at different times attacked the Scots (as a result of the unpopularity of the government headed by Lord Bute, a Scotsman), in *The Prophecy of Famine, a Scots Pastoral* (1763), satirized the London theater and London actors in *The Rosciad* (1761), laughed at the fuss about the story of the Cock-Lane Ghost, which Dr. Johnson took a hand in investigating, in *The Ghost* (1762–63) (which contains an attack on Johnson), and took part in various political controversies in *The Duellist* (1764), *Gotham* (1764), and *The Candidate* (1764). Churchill's couplets have both wit and strength, though his wit is not as complex as Pope's nor his strength as impressive as Johnson's. Much of his verse was concerned with topicalities, and his poetic vigor, though considerable, was never really great enough to give larger scope and interest to his themes.

An isolated and in many ways quite remarkable poetic figure of the middle of the eighteenth century was Christopher Smart, whose poems were long considered the fascinating but wholly disordered products of a crazed imagination. But, though Smart did suffer from a religious mania which was taken to imply mental disorder, his poetic imagination was far from being hopelessly confused. The long, rhapsodic "Song to David" has its own principle of order and the poem moves in clearly conceived progression in spite of the abandoned effect of its profuse imagery. The eloquence and abandon of the verse is like nothing else in the eighteenth century:

> He sung of God—the mighty source
> Of all things—the stupendous force
>   On which all strength depends;
> From whose right arm, beneath whose eyes,
> All period, power, and enterprise
>   Commences, reigns, and ends.
>
> Angels—their ministry and meed,
> Which to and fro with blessings speed,
>   Or with their citterns wait;
> Where Michael with his millions bows,
> Where dwells the seraph and his spouse,
>   The cherub and her mate.
>
> Of man—the semblance and effect
> Of God and love—the saint elect
>   For infinite applause—
> To rule the land, and briny broad,
> To be laborious in his laud,
>   And heroes in his cause.
>
> The world—the clustering spheres he made,
> The glorious light, the soothing shade,
>   Dale, champaign, grove, and hill;
> The multitudinous abyss,
> Where secrecy remains in bliss,
>   And wisdom hides her skill. . . .

The range of Smart's imagery and its allusiveness are extraordinary; he uses archetypal images drawn from the recondite as well as obvious sources in an almost Blakeian way. His most extraordinary production is his *Jubilate Agno* ("Rejoice in the Lamb") in which, with amazing particularity, he calls on all creation to join in the worship of God: the passage about his cat Jeoffry—far too long to quote in its entirety—is remarkable in its exuberant detail:

For I will consider my cat Jeoffry.

For he is the servant of the Living God, duly and daily
serving him.

For at the first glance of the glory of God in the East he
worships in his way.

For is this done by wreathing his body seven times round
with elegant quickness.

For then he leaps up to catch the musk, which is the
blessing of God upon his prayer.

For he rolls upon prank to work it in.

For having done duty and receiving blessing he begins to
consider himself.

For this he performs in ten degrees.

For first he looks upon his fore-paws to see if they are
clean.

For secondly he kicks up behind to clear away there.

For thirdly he works it upon stretch with the forepaws
extended.

For fourthly he sharpens his paws by wood.

For fifthly he washes himself.

For sixthly he rolls upon wash.

For seventhly he fleas himself, that he may not be
interrupted upon the beat.

For eighthly he rubs himself against a post.

For ninthly he looks up for his instructions.

For tenthly he goes in quest of food.

For having considered God and himself he will consider his
neighbour.

For if he meets another cat he will kiss her in kindness.

For when he takes his prey he plays with it to give it a
chance.

For one mouse in seven escapes by his dallying.

For when his day's work is done his business more properly
begins.

For he keeps the Lord's watch in the night against the
adversary.

For he counteracts the powers of darkness by his electrical
skin and glaring eyes.

For he counteracts the Devil, who is death, by brisking
about the life.

For in his morning orisons he loves the sun and the sun
loves him.

For he is of the tribe of Tiger. . . .

His contemporaries locked Christopher Smart up as mad and regarded his writings as the ravings of a lunatic. To later generations
he appears to have possessed an astonishingly brilliant and original

poetic gift. But it was not the kind of poetic gift that the critical theory of the time was prepared to come to terms with.

Religious sensibility operated in a very different way on the poetic mind of William Cowper (1731–1800). A melancholy and devout man, he early retired from the world to a life of rustic seclusion, where he engaged in gardening, reading, writing, and religious exercises. His tendency to religious melancholia developed at times into insanity, but at other periods his native piety, controlled by the new Methodist religious movement, of which he was the first English poet to be spokesman, led him to exploit a vein of descriptive and reflective verse which, at its best, has a gentle charm far removed from the more formal meditations of most other eighteenth-century poets. His *Table Talk* (1782) consists of somewhat dull pietistic chat in couplets, and the contemporary reviewer who complained that Cowper was here "travelling on a plain, flat road with great composure, almost through the whole long and tedious volume" was not wide of the mark, though there are occasional flashes of livelier verse, notable among which is his reference to Pope:

> Then Pope, as harmony itself exact,
> In verse well disciplined, complete, compact,
> Gave Virtue and Morality a grace,
> That, quite eclipsing Pleasure's painted face,
> Levied a tax of wonder and applause,
> E'en on the fools that trampled on their laws.
> But he (his musical finesse was such.
> So nice his ear, so delicate his touch)
> Made poetry a mere mechanic art;
> And every warbler has his tune by heart.

This is paralleled by a remark in one of Cowper's letters to his publisher: "A critic of the present day serves a poem as a cook serves a dead turkey, when she fastens the legs of it to a post and draws out all the sinews. For this we may thank Pope; but unless we could imitate him in the closeness and compactness of his expression, as well as in the smoothness of his numbers, we had better drop the imitation, which serves no other purpose than to emasculate and weaken all we write. Give me a manly rough line, with a deal of meaning in it, rather than a whole poem full of musical periods, that have nothing but their oily smoothness to recommend them."

The "manly rough line" for which Cowper pleaded is seen less in his rhymed couplets than in the blank verse of *The Task* (1785), a long poem in four books in which he ranges over a variety of subjects but which is notable chiefly for its intimate and precisely etched

pictures of country scenes and domestic interiors. At the opening of
Book I ("The Sofa") he adopts the mock-heroic style of so many of
the eighteenth-century imitators of Milton:

> I sing the SOFA. I, who lately sang
> Truth, Hope, and Charity, and touch'd with awe
> The solemn chords . . .
>   Time was, when clothing sumptuous or for use,
> Save their own painted skins, our sires had none.
> As yet black breeches were not; satin smooth,
> Or velvet soft, or plush with shaggy pile:
> The hardy chief upon the rugged rock
> Washed by the sea, or on the grav'ly bank
> Thrown up by wintry torrents roaring loud,
> Fearless of wrong, reposed his weary strength.
> Those barb'rous ages past, succeeded next
> The birth-day of invention; weak at first,
> Dull in design, and clumsy to perform.
> Joint-stools were then created; on three legs
> Upborn they stood . . .
>   At length a generation more refined
> Improved the simple plan; made three legs four,
> Gave them a twisted form vermicular,
> And o'er the seat, with plenteous wadding stuffed,
> Induced a splendid cover, green and blue,
> Yellow and red, of tap'stry richly wrought,
> And woven close, or needle-work sublime.

This is mildly humorous, and is meant to be; but the style soon
changes when Cowper, by an easy transition, leaves the sofa to turn to
a description of the countryside by the river Ouse. As long as he is
discussing the sofa, the tone is mock-heroic and the style mock-
Miltonic. The run of the verse, as well as the tone, changes when he
moves from the sofa to the countryside:

> Here Ouse, slow winding through a level plain
> Of spacious meads with cattle sprinkled o'er,
> Conducts the eye along its sinuous course
> Delighted. There, fast rooted in their bank,
> Stand, never overlook'd, our fav'rite elms,
> That screen the herdsman's solitary hut; . . .

Cowper had a landscape painter's eye for scenery and a remarkable sense of perspective. He always balances his foreground with
a background filled in on a diminishing scale. The passage just
quoted continues:

> While far beyond, and overthwart the stream
> That, as with molten glass, inlays the vale,
> The sloping land recedes into the clouds;
> Displaying on its varied side the grace
> Of hedge-row beauties numberless, square tow'r,
> Tall spire, from which the sound of cheerful bells
> Just undulates upon the list'ning ear,
> Groves, heaths, and smoking villages, remote.

His eye for natural scenery was precise and affectionate; he described with loving detail the configuration of the landscape and related the picture to a moral sense of rustic peace. Sometimes he intersperses his rural descriptions with inset pictures of characters, occasionally, as with the picture of crazy Kate, in a manner reminiscent of Crabbe—a man of a very different kind of sensibility yet some aspects of whose work Cowper in some degree foreshadows.

The moralizing is frequent, yet agreeably subdued to the descriptive pattern, so that we feel none of the impatience that afflicts most readers of *Table Talk*. The meticulous picture of his garden in Book III ("The Garden") with his careful account of pruning and framing and looking after the greenhouse is set against a background of gentle piety and, sometimes, of mildly melancholy autobiography, as in the famous "stricken deer" passage:

> I was a stricken deer, that left the herd
> Long since; with many an arrow deep infixt,
> My panting side was charged, when I withdrew
> To seek a tranquil death in distant shades. . . .

It is in Book III, too, that we find the most eloquent expression of that religious humanitarianism which Methodism nourished:

> . . . I was born of woman, and drew milk,
> As sweet as charity, from human breasts.
> I think, articulate, I laugh and weep,
> And exercise all functions of a man.
> How then should I and any man that lives
> Be strangers to each other? Pierce my vein,
> Take of the crimson stream meand'ring there,
> And catechise it well; apply thy glass,
> Search it, and prove now if it be not blood
> Congenial with thine own: and, if it be,
> What edge of subtlety canst thou suppose
> Keen enough, wise and skilful as thou art,
> To cut the link of brotherhood, by which
> One common Maker bound me to the kind?

The tone here is very different from that of Pope's *Essay on Man*. There is a new vein of humanitarianism here, reflected also in Cowper's affection for animals and his protest against hunting them for sport. And his sense of rustic content is equally different from the consciously Horatian mood of earlier extollers of the happy mean, such as John Promfret in his "The Choice." Cowper's is a grateful awareness of a precarious peace won by a disciplined content in the shadow of the Fall. Even the deep satisfaction he felt in rural labor—in both performing it and watching it—is sudued to a sense of Adam's doom softened into a blessing—

> 'Tis the primal curse
> But soften'd into mercy; made the pledge
> Of cheerful days, and nights without a groan.

His descriptions of rustic content are punctuated by attacks on urban luxury which were common enough at this time, but in Cowper they ring with a sincerity not often found among eighteenth-century handlers of this theme. And how utterly different from the rhetorical tradition of abuse so effectively drawn on by Dr. Johnson in his "London" is Cowper's

> God made the country, and man made the town.
> What wonder then that health and virtue, gifts
> That can alone make sweet the bitter draught
> That life holds out to all, should most abound
> And least be threaten'd in the fields and groves?

If this strain is far removed from the Horatian urbanity of Pomfret and the literary pastoralism of many seventeenth- and eighteenth-century poets, it is equally far from any pre-Romantic primitivism or glorification of the noble savage or the uncorrupted peasant. There is a quietly humorous realism in Cowper which saves him from any such extravagance. His attitude to Nature is, of course, quite un-Wordsworthian: Nature is not an educational force in itself, but at best a congenial setting for attractive human behavior. Further, Cowper, for all his dislike of cities, never adopted the fashion of idealizing solitude. Book IV of *The Task* ("The Winter Evening") is in large part devoted to the pleasures of the proper kind of society. "Fireside enjoyments, home-born happiness, /And all the comforts that the lowly roof /Of undisturbed retirement and the hours /Of long uninterrupted evening know" are as much the joys of rustic life as outdoor activities, and the retirement is not a lonely one. Indeed, some of Cowper's most effective verse is in his description of warm domestic interiors, full of the proper kind of social cheerfulness, that he sets against the picture of the wintery weather outside. His art here is reminiscent of the Flemish genre painters.

Cowper's humor, mild at best, is found intermittently in his letters (which have a great deal of quiet charm) and at its most sustained in "The Diverting History of John Gilpin," which also shows the influence on him of the simple ballad measure. His hymns (*Olney Hymns*, 1779) show an ability to adapt a personal religious sensibility (often on the verge of profound melancholia) to communal purposes. As hymns should, they have a simple, ballad-like meter and rhyme scheme and resolve the personal emotion into resounding general truths:

> God moves in a mysterious way,
>   His wonders to perform;
> He plants his footsteps in the sea,
>   And rides upon the storm.

Cowper's most remarkable lyrical poem, however, is not to be found among his hymns, but is a more personal utterance in which he expressed that desolating sense of loneliness and loss that always lay beneath the surface of his religious conviction. "The Castaway" (written in 1799 and first published posthumously in 1803), with its relentlessly marching rhythms and its powerfully detailed description of a sailor washed overboard and left alone in the midst of the ocean to swim vainly for an hour before drowning, is a strangely compelling work: its last lines are continually quoted by Mr. Ramsay in Virginia Woolf's *To the Lighthouse*, a novel much concerned with human loneliness. The turn from the sailor to the poet himself is done with a somber eloquence wholly different from the conversational informality of the best parts of *The Task:*

> I therefore purpose not, or dream,
>   Descanting on his fate,
> To give the melancholy theme
>   A more enduring date:
> But misery still delights to trace
> Its semblance in another's case.
>
> No voice divine the storm allayed,
>   No light propitious shone;
> When, snatched from all effectual aid,
>   We perished, each alone:
> But I beneath a rougher sea,
> And whelmed in deeper gulphs than he.

Something of the same sense of personal desolation, though subdued to a more quietly elegiac mood, is found in the slow-moving couplets of his "On the Receipt of My Mother's Picture out of Norfolk" (written in 1790 and published in 1798).

Cowper must remain one of the minor English poets, but he is a remarkable and a versatile one. In his use of simple ballad measures, in flexible descriptive and meditative verse, in his attitude toward nature and his humanitarianism, in the lyrical expression of a somber and haunted imagination, in his ability to write a swinging, singable hymn—in all these diverse achievements he was in his way notable. And if the psychological critic can see in him an illuminating example of a certain kind of religious sensibility reacting to various stimuli, undergoing various modifications, and expressing itself in various ways, the literary historian can note in his work some important developments and changes in the view of the proper subject matter for poetry, the attitude of the poet to his subject and to his public, and the relation of the poet's private to his public personality. If it is a simplification to call Cowper a pre-Romantic, we can at least call him with confidence an innovator and concede that his kind of poetic sensibility was, for all its points of contact with the spirit of the age, a highly original one.

Unmoved by any of the newer modes of sensibility, George Crabbe (1754–1832) is often considered a belated Augustan surviving into the Romantic world; his early work was praised by Burke and Dr. Johnson, and he lived to be praised by Byron as "Nature's sternest painter, yet the best." In his handling of the heroic couplet he did indeed owe a great deal both to Pope and to Johnson, and this verse form remained his favorite throughout his career. His characteristic genius as the narrator of verse tales with a quietly disillusioned clarity of observation cannot however usefully be discussed in terms of any Classic-Romantic antithesis. His interest in his characters can be compared neither to Wordsworth's interest in the leech-gatherer and the idiot boy nor to the sentimental portrayal of misfortune by such a writer as Henry Mackenzie. He was a moralist and psychologist who believed that stories illustrative of the various ways in which human character manifested itself in behavior would arouse the sympathetic curiosity of the reader, who would gain from them both new understanding and the pleasure of recognizing fellow human beings in action. His first important poem, *The Village* (1783), concentrating as it did on the poverty and bleakness of life in the Suffolk coastal region where he grew up, and deliberately setting the harsh truth about village life against such sentimental versions as Goldsmith's *Deserted Village* ("By such examples taught, I paint the Cot /As Truth will paint it, and as Bards will not"), has earned for him the reputation of the poet of poverty and misery. In fact, however, much of his best work deals, not with the poor and wretched, but with what he himself called the "middling classes," in whom, he believed, "more originality, more variety of fortune, will be met with; because, on the one hand, they do not live in the eye of the world, and, therefore, are not kept in awe by the dread of observation and indecorum; neither, on the other, are they debarred by their want of means from the cultivation of mind and the pursuits of wealth and ambition, which are necessary to the development of character displayed in the variety of situations to which this class is liable." This is, of course, far from the classical or the neoclassical view of what constitutes suitable subjects for serious literature; we see here the acceptance of the "middling classes" as the most interesting for the writer which is so markedly reflected in the rise of the novel.

Crabbe, however, was no novelist (he destroyed the few prose novels he attempted). His descriptions of town and village life and his stories illustrating the ironies of character and fate (always related in Crabbe) deliberately eschew the discursiveness of prose presentation for the sharper yet more neutral-toned accents of couplet verse. *The Parish Register* (1807), which he described as "an endeavour once more to describe village manners, not by adopting the notion of pastoral simplicity, or assuming ideas of rustic barbarity, but by more natural views of the peasantry, considered as a mixed body of persons," is simply a series of sketches of general conditions in the village, of the types of people who lived there, and of individual characters and incidents, with no more coherent form than that (to use Crabbe's own analogy) of a picture gallery. Similarly, *The Borough* (1810), which takes the form of a series of letters to a friend in the country describing the writer's town and its inhabitants, is a fairly miscellaneous collection of anecdotes, character sketches, and stories. *Tales in Verse* (1812) makes no attempt to provide links between the different verse stories, but *Tales of the Hall* (1819) introduces the scheme of two half-brothers meeting after a long separation and telling each other stories of what they have experienced and encountered. This last device is unexpectedly successful; the relation between the brothers, which shifts as the tales are told, gives an extra dimension to the work as a whole and the scheme enables Crabbe to change interestingly and effectively the reader's distance from what is being presented.

Crabbe's couplets are not as pointed as Pope's or as weighty as Johnson's. He interprets his material less by witty observation or moral generalizations than by the careful way he alternates description and action, letting each comment on the other so that a cumulative moral pattern is built up. He tries to keep the tone of his narrative calm and neutral; his indignation or his blame is expressed by a sly juxtaposition or the introduction of a quiet phrase which indicates, say, some disparity between a character's pretensions and the truth about his moral nature. His natural descriptions—and his accounts of the Suffolk coast are justly famous—are not set pieces to be detached from the stories in which they occur; they take their coloring from the moral and psychological tone of the character to whom the particular description is related, as in the well-known tale of *Peter Grimes* (in *The Borough*). Some of his most skillful work is in *Tales of the Hall*, where the unobtrusive alternation of description and action sometimes succeeds in building up a much richer and more subtle moral pattern than a rapid reading of the tale might reveal. In Crabbe's poetry we see some of the forces that went to the development of the English novel, but both his vision and his handling of language differed significantly from the novelist's. He was a poet in his own dry and cunning way, using a development of an eighteenth-century verse technique for wholly original purposes.

CHAPTER EIGHTEEN

The Novel from Richardson
to Jane Austen

THE ENGLISH NOVEL, destined to become the most popular and prolific of all English literary forms, first fully emerged in the eighteenth century. It was in large measure the product of the middle class, appealing to middle-class ideals and sensibilities, a patterning of imagined events set against a clearly realized social background and taking its view of what was significant in human behavior from agreed public attitudes. From Richardson until the early twentieth century the plot patterns of English fiction were based on the view (shared by reader and writer) that what was significant was what altered a social relationship—love followed by marriage, quarreling and reconciliation, gain or loss of money or of social status. The class consciousness shown by the novel from the beginning, the importance of social and financial status and the use of the rise or fall from one class to another as reflecting critical developments in character and fortune, indicate the middle-class origin of this literary form. Like the medieval *fabliau*, also a product of the urban imagination, the novel tended to realism and contemporaneity in the sense that it dealt with people living in the social world known to the writer.

Many currents came together to produce the English novel. Elizabethan prose tales, picaresque stories, and accounts of the urban underworld represented one; the character-writers of the seventeenth century developed a technique of psychological portraiture which was available to Addison and Steele in their creation of Sir Roger de Coverley, Sir Andrew Freeport, Will Honeycomb, and the rest of the portrait gallery in *The Spectator* and which inevitably led to the anecdote illustrative of character; the straightforward narrative style used by Bunyan in *The Pilgrim's Progress* and the somewhat similar factual style of Defoe's journalistic and pseudo-autobiographical writings also helped to make the fully realized novel possible. The tradition of heroic romance represented by Sidney's *Arcadia* and its imitators and the debased tradition of French heroic romance which produced in late seventeenth-century England long and infinitely tedious narratives about characters with classical names suffering a bewildering variety of adventures in remote lands (the French practitioners of this kind of fiction were notably the Sieur de Gomberville, La Calprenède, and Mademoiselle de Scudéry, and the English imitations included Roger Boyle's *Parthenissa*, Sir George Mackenzie's *Aretina*, and John Crowne's *Pandion and Amphigenia*)—these have often figured in accounts of the genealogy of the English novel, but they really represent a different line. William Congreve's *Incognita* (1692) is a drama in the form of a prose tale which combines romantic action with occasional ironic (or mock-heroic) comment, a symptom rather than a cause of the growing interest in prose fiction, while Mrs. Aphra Behn's two prose romances *Oroonoko* and *The Fair Jilt* (both published in 1698) place romantic action in contemporary society; the former, with its idealization of the noble savage, is more important as a document in the history of sensibility than as a contribution toward the English novel. Certain *Spectator* papers, the writings of Defoe, and Swift's *Gulliver's Travels* provide the more immediate and obvious background for the emergence of the English novel, and the story of the novel in the modern sense of the term properly begins here.

Whether Defoe was "properly" a novelist is a matter of definition of terms, but however we define our terms we must concede that there is an important difference between Defoe's journalistic deadpan and the bold attempt to create a group of people faced with complex psychological problems. Defoe's interest in character was minimal, and the novel only grew up when it learned to combine Defoe's sense of social and material reality with some awareness of the complexities of human personality and of the tensions between private moral and public social forces, between morality and gentility. With the novels of Samuel Richardson (1689–1761) we first find this combination.

Richardson was a prosperous London printer, who discovered his talent as a novelist at the age of fifty-one when he was in the process of compiling a volume of letters designed to serve as models for humble people not sufficiently educated to be able to write easily and confidently on those occasions when letters might be called for.

He was working on this collection in 1739—probably writing letter number 138, entitled "A Father to a Daughter in Service, on hearing of her Master's attempting her Virtue"—when it occurred to him that he might work up a complete novel out of a series of letters written by a virtuous servant girl to her parents in the intervals of dodging her master's attempt at rape. He remembered a true story of a virtuous servant girl who eventually married her master after successfully repulsing his more irregular approaches, and this exemplary combination of prudence and virtue appealed to him. He temporarily dropped his collection of letters and in two months produced *Pamela* (1740). The theme of the novel is basically a folk theme, but the treatment is very different from anything to be found in folk literature. The class background is far from being the simple one of low-born maiden and high-born lord. Richardson's class was committed to the view that worth depended on individual effort rather than on status, yet they were fascinated by status and could not help admiring and envying it. This gives an ironic ambivalence to the whole moral pattern of the novel (which is presented in the form of letters from Pamela to her parents). Squire B., whose mother had employed Pamela as her maid, is bent first on seduction and then on rape; he is dishonest, malevolent, cruel, and persecuting. He does everything he can to get Pamela into his physical power, and at one stage is on the point of committing rape when Pamela providentially falls into fits and scares him off. Yet, after Mr. B. has relented and sent Pamela home, she returns voluntarily when he sends for her, loving and admiring him all the time, though disapproving of his attempts to dishonor her. Whenever he relaxes his attempts for a moment, she is all respect and admiration for him; and when he finally convinces her that her continued successful resistance has led him to offer marriage, she is all humble love and passionate gratitude. Successful resistance turns lust to love; once Squire B. has got over his weakness for seduction and rape he is seen by Richardson as a wholly admirable person, not only worthy of the love of a virtuous girl like Pamela but deserving of her humblest obedience and veneration. If a man is a wealthy landowner, and handsome and graceful in manner to boot, he must be considered wholly good so long as he is not being actively bad. Printers do not become angels by merely ceasing to threaten girls with sexual violence, but evidently squires do. Richardson, of course, would have been horrified by such a comment. He claimed that he was showing a genuine reformation of character, wrought by Pamela's virtue in a young man who had the advantage of an excellent moral grounding in childhood. But the reader knows better.

This counter pattern which crosses the moral pattern which Richardson consciously planned for the work does not, of course, spoil the novel; on the contrary, it makes it richer and truer. Human nature is like that; motivation is complex, and the relation between our moral professions and the full psychological explanation of our actions is far from simple. Sometimes it almost seems that Richardson knew this and was deliberately writing a sly, ironic novel. After Mr. B.'s first attempts on her, before she has been deceitfully carried off to the country house where Mrs. Jewkes presides, Pamela very properly decides to go to her parents and leave the scene of temptation; but she finds excuse after excuse for not going, and postpones her departure until Mr. B. has managed to mature his plan for tricking her into going instead to the house he has waiting for her. And though she professes to prefer honest poverty to vicious luxury, she makes it quite clear in her letters home that she has grown used to a much better way of life than her parents can afford in their humble cottage. She notes all the fine clothes given her by her late mistress and her master, and, having completed an inventory of what she has, noting what she can in conscience retain, makes such remarks as "First, here is a calico night-gown, that I used to wear o' mornings. 'Twill be rather too good for me when I get home; but I must have something. . . . And here are four other shifts, one the fellow to that I have on; another pretty good one, and the other two old fine ones, that will serve me to turn and wind with at home, for they are not worth leaving behind me; and here are my two pairs of shoes; I have taken the lace off, which I will burn, and maybe will fetch me some little matter at a pinch, with an old silver buckle or two." Most suggestive of all, she gives up the fine clothes her lady had given her, determined not to sail under false colors, and provides herself with a new, simpler outfit.

And so when I had dined, upstairs I went, and locked myself in my little room. There I dressed myself in my new garb, and put on my round-eared ordinary cap, but with a green knot, my home-spun gown and petticoat, and plain leather shoes, but yet they are what they call Spanish leather; and my ordinary hose, ordinary I mean to what I have been lately used to, though I should think good yarn may do very well for every day, when I come home. A plain muslin tucker I put on, and my black silk necklace, instead of the French necklace my lady gave me; and put the earrings out of my ears. When I was quite equipped, I took my straw hat in my hand, with its two blue strings, and looked in the glass, as proud as any thing. To say truth, I never liked myself so well in my life.

O the pleasure of descending with ease, innocence, and resignation!—Indeed, there is nothing like it! An humble mind, I plainly see, cannot meet with any very shocking disappointment, let Fortune's wheel turn round as it will.

And down she trips, looking, as she very well knows, more ravishing than ever, and runs straight into her master, who pretends not to recognize the "pretty neat damsel."

He came up to me, and took me by the hand, and said, "Whose pretty maiden are you? I dare say you are Pamela's sister, you are so like her. So neat, so clean, so pretty! Why, child, you far surpass your sister Pamela."

I was all confusion, and would have spoken, but he took me about the neck: "Why," said he, "you are very pretty, child: I would not be so free with your *sister*, you may believe; but I must kiss *you*."—"O Sir," said I, "I am Pamela, indeed I am: indeed I am Pamela, *her own-self!*"

This, and scenes like this, are admirably done, whatever Richardson thought he was really doing. It is as though Richardson knows Pamela so well that he has simply to let himself *be* Pamela in order to write the letters. He does not have to understand her or to analyze her motives, any more than she understands and analyzes herself. She sets herself out to attract her master from the beginning, though she herself does not realize it and perhaps her creator does not; but prudence as well as morality demand that she keep herself unravished while keeping his interest in her at fever pitch. She thinks she is trying to escape his clutches, but allows herself to be deflected from her attempts at escape by the slightest obstacles (even to the point of supposing an inoffensive cow to be a fierce bull), and when he finally lets her go she flies back to him at his summons.

When he releases her, she leaves with a reluctance that surprises herself. "I think I was loth to leave the house. Can you believe it?— What could be the matter with me, I wonder. I felt something so strange at my heart! I wonder what ailed me." She writes home in this troubled state of mind from a village where the coach has paused. "Here I am, at a little poor village, almost such a one as yours!" The smallness and poverty of the village (and by implication of her parents' home) are mentioned more than once. And when Mr. B.'s letter arrives, asking her to return (though only in the most oblique way promising marriage) she writes in her journal, "O my exulting heart!" She knows now what she has wanted all along.

Part II of *Pamela*, added in 1742 to replace and discredit continuations (both serious and satirical) by other hands, is a dull marriage manual showing the ideal couple in action, with a mild and temporary break in perfect felicity when Squire B. becames involved with a widowed countess at a masked ball. Pamela becomes the oracle, dispensing wisdom in her letters on everything from the state of the drama to Locke's view on education. The most interesting part of *Pamela* is over by the time her marriage is accomplished.

Clarissa appeared in eight volumes in 1748. It is a subtler and profounder work than *Pamela*, and by general agreement Richardson's masterpiece. The deployment of the plot is a remarkable achievement. Clarissa, the virtuous, beautiful, talented younger daughter of the wealthy Harlowes, with a fortune of her own left her by her grandfather (but which she has filially surrendered to her father), is manipulated from a position which combines the height of virtue with the height of material good fortune to one in which she is despised and rejected, becoming an almost Christlike figure of the Suffering Servant. This is achieved by no sudden and dramatic reversal of fortune, but by a brilliantly deployed series of little incidents which combine to deny Clarissa the fruits of prudence without actually making her an imprudent character and eventually close in on her to prevent any return to the world of material happiness. Clarissa is maneuvered into sainthood by a cunningly woven mesh of circumstance which seems always until almost the very end to allow the possibility of escape back into the world of lost prosperity. She is given the appearance of guilt without real guilt; she is made to appear to fall without having really fallen; almost everybody comes at one time or another to doubt the purity of her motives or the perfection of her character. Then, in the end, when public opinion seems to have disposed of her for ever, she rises in death from her degradation to shine on high in glorious resurrection.

The first major phase of the action concerns the Harlowe family's sustained attempt to force Clarissa to marry the stupid, ugly, and mean-spirited Mr. Solmes. The leading spirit here is her contemptible brother, who sees financial advantage to himself in the match, while her jealous sister Arabella, suspicious that Clarissa is in love with Lovelace (whom Arabella loves but pretends to hate), is equally determined to have her married off to Solmes. Her father, a gouty autocrat, finds his authority and what he calls his honor involved, and insists on the match. Her mother, weakly giving in to pressure from the rest of the family, adds her persuasions. Meanwhile, Clarissa's brother has insulted Lovelace, who has overcome and wounded him in a duel, while Clarissa reluctantly consents to a clandestine correspondence with Lovelace in order to prevent him from taking a bloody revenge on the Harlowe family. Clarissa is in continuous correspondence with her friend Anna Howe, to whom she recounts each day's events.

The situation here developed enables Richardson to unfold a much richer moral pattern than anything to be found in *Pamela*. Clarissa, the perfection of whose character is made clear from the beginning, finds herself obliged to disobey her parents and at the same time involved in a clandestine correspondence with a rake. Richardson is here exploring, as fully as he can, the borderland of his moral universe. Children must obey their parents; but on the other hand parents must never force a child into marriage against the child's inclinations. These principles Richardson had already made clear elsewhere, but they are clear enough in the story. Clarissa offers to give up all thoughts of marriage and to live single either on the estate her grandfather had left her or anywhere else acceptable to her parents. She is suspected of being really in love with Lovelace, but she protests that she will have nothing more to do with him or any other man if she is allowed to remain free of Solmes. But her brother has organized the family to press for her marriage with Solmes, and she is confined to her room and subjected to every kind of pressure in the hope that she will consent to the marriage, in connection with which the most elaborate and (to the Harlowe family) favorable settlements have been drawn up. The picture of family pressure operating on Clarissa is drawn with magnificent vividness. The spiteful brother and sister, the tender but insistent mother, the hectoring uncles, and in the background the father egotistically insistent on his parental rights—all this comes through with vividness and immediacy from Clarissa's letters to Anna Howe. At the same time Anna herself is revealed in her replies as a sprightly and witty girl whose chief pleasure in life (to Clarissa's distress) is teasing the worthy gentleman whom her mother wants her to marry and whom, it is clear, she will eventually marry.

We also get occasional glimpses of Lovelace, who is revealed as the master mind behind the preposterous behavior of the Harlowe family. By bribing servants to report his intention of performing various rash acts in pursuit of his vengeance against the Harlowes and his love for Clarissa, he whips the family into a fury of determination that Clarissa shall marry the odious Mr. Solmes at the earliest possible moment. Pressure on Clarissa grows stronger and stronger; Lovelace presents himself continually as a source of refuge, offering to provide unconditional sanctuary for the persecuted girl among the ladies of his family (who, of course, all adore her, though by reputation only). Finally, when it looks as though Clarissa is to be forced by physical compulsion into marriage with Solmes, she momentarily yields to Lovelace's suggestion of rescue, only to revoke her acceptance of his offer shortly afterward. But Lovelace refuses to take cognizance of her letter of revocation and awaits her at the garden gate with all necessary equipment for her escape. On her going out to inform him that she cannot take advantage of his offer, he contrives a scene which enables him to whisk her off, and henceforth she is in Lovelace's power.

The second movement of the novel deals with the struggle between Clarissa and Lovelace. He is a rake, and therefore is reluctant to marry, though he adores Clarissa. He contrives matters so that she is made more and more dependent on him, and eventually brings her to London, to an apparently respectable lodging house which is in fact a brothel run by an old friend of his and staffed by girls whom he has ruined. After much coming and going, and a complex series of movements in Clarissa's heart toward and away from Lovelace—the documentation of this shows us Richardson at the height of his powers—he attempts her virtue by arranging a mock fire and bringing her out of her room in her nightdress to escape the supposed conflagration. She sees his purpose, discovers his trick, and successfully repulses him, shaken to the core by his villainy. He is repentant, and offers immediate marriage, which she proudly rejects. She despises him now, and will not marry a man whom she despises. He plays a variety of tricks in order to try to regain favor in her eyes and succeeds to the point of maneuvering her back to the house of ill-fame, and there, with the cooperation of the inmates, he first drugs and then violates her. Now that he has won his bet with himself, as it were, and scored up another triumph for rakery, he is prepared to concede Clarissa's true virtue and to marry her. (He had pretended to be dying to marry her all the time, but had adroitly phrased his offers so as to compel her refusal on each occasion.) After illness and hysteria she escapes from him, and ignores his frenzied appeals for forgiveness and immediate marriage. Meanwhile her friends and relations consider her a ruined woman who has wilfully contributed to her own dishonor. Her family regard her as a wicked runaway who deliberately chose ruin at the hands of a rake.

The third and final movement of the book deals with Clarissa's vindication and sanctification. By means of letters appropriately copied and circulated, the truth begins to emerge. But her family are prevented from knowing the truth until after her death, while her dear friend Anna Howe is kept from her by a number of contrived circumstances, and even her sympathetic cousin Morden, who finally arrives home from Italy, is not allowed to come to see her until her death is inevitable. All this time the unfortunate Lovelace is frantically pleading for forgiveness and marriage, backed by his powerful family. But Clarissa remains alone, in lodgings, befriended by strangers, cut off from friends and relations. And there, having made all suitable preparations, she dies, before an audience of new-found admirers. Her death is a studied presentation of *ars moriendi,* a high example of the art of dying like a Christian. Her family, on finally learning the whole truth about her conduct, are consumed by remorse, and her funeral is the occasion of its exhibition. Every single wicked character in the book then meets with an appropriate sticky end.

Before her violation Clarissa had been prepared to consider marriage to the fascinating Lovelace for the purpose of reforming him, and Lovelace himself cunningly played on his need for reformation by such means. But that temptation is over once the rape has taken place; marriage is henceforth unthinkable to Clarissa (but not to her friends), whose thoughts are more and more centered on the next world. Attempted violation is one thing; successful violation is another. Richardson is not as clear as he might be on the relation between guilt and misfortune. Sometimes he suggests that Clarissa (though through no fault of her own) is "ruined," made permanently unfit for matrimony by having been forcibly rendered a fallen woman. Like so many of his generation and later, Richardson had a purely technical view of chastity. Clarissa, though a saint, had lost her chastity, so she must give up hope of accommodation with this world. She could not, of course, consider marriage with her violator (Richardson is a cut above many nineteenth-century moralists in this), but neither could she respect any other man willing to marry a woman who had lost her "honor," however innocently.

It would be naïve to argue that Clarissa, if she had really wanted to, could have escaped from the house in which Lovelace had her confined. By the time the need for escape is apparent, that house has become a microcosm of the world, and Clarissa's confinement in it is a symbol of her confinement in this wicked mundane sphere; the only escape now can be into the next world. After her violation, *all* men are vile: nothing in the novel is more psychologically convincing than Clarissa's horror of anything in trousers after her experience at Lovelace's hands. This world, in whose social duties man may, with luck, imitate heavenly felicity and anticipate his ultimate reward, has become for Clarissa a den of iniquity. Her family, obedience to whom is a condition of earthly prosperity, have made her obedience impossible. She cannot go back to them. She is going home to her father, as she tells Lovelace in a deliberately ambiguous note, but it is her Heavenly Father; her family relationship is subsumed in the higher relationship to God, the Father of all.

Lovelace is a more interesting character than Squire B., though no more convincing. He is a mild and timid man's picture of the ideal rake, of Satan as gentleman, witty, boisterous, adventurous, courageous, ruthless. His letters to his friend Belford are preposterous enough, showing him as they do congratulating himself on being a rake and introspecting on his rakishness with incredible self-consciousness. To the modern reader he is less a fascinating villain than a cad and a fool, who does not even know how to handle his women. But he serves his purpose, which is little more than that of catalyst.

Richardson's final novel was *Sir Charles Grandison*, published in seven volumes in 1754. The relative lack of moral conflict in this work makes it less interesting than the other two. Further, Richardson is here concerned with high life, which was unfamiliar to him, and the result is a stiffness that compares most unfavorably with Pamela's vulgar self-revelations. Who can be convinced by a hero who has absolutely everything life has to offer—fortune, supreme good looks, perfect virtue, and perfect prudence? He goes through life settling other people's affairs with calm assurance, making friends of enemies, arranging marriages, making up quarrels, mingling seemly mirth with graceful reproof. Nowhere else in Richardson is the public nature of the emotional life made so apparent. Everyone reveals his (or, more often, her) inmost emotions to everyone else. Letters are shown, copied, exchanged. Sir Charles, who first meets the beautiful and virtuous Harriet Byron through rescuing her from being carried off by the villainous Sir Hargrave Pollexfen, soon reveals to her the complicated story of his emotional entanglements in Italy, and she is referred to letters in the hands of Sir Charles' chaplain for further details. The Italian subplot is melodramatic and artificial, and the lovely Clementina, who would have married Sir Charles (indeed, all the ladies are in love with him) but for a difference in religion, is an odd creature to find in Richardson's pages. But in high life anything can happen, and Sir Charles speaks Italian perfectly. The book is not, however, as dull as this description might lead one to suppose. Lady G.'s accounts of her tiffs with her husband are often lively and amusing, and there are other "humours" in the book to relieve the complacent virtue of the hero.

The ideals that Richardson employs and manipulates in his novels are: prudence and virtue, gentility and morality, reputation and character. The relation between them is often complex. Gentility is sometimes opposed to morality, sometimes a sign of morality. Reputation is generally the reward of good character but not always a guarantee of it. Prudence and virtue often go together, but sometimes (as in the latter part of *Clarissa*) lead in opposite directions.

Richardson is very much aware of the social context, even obsessed with it. Rank mattered to him; the difference between classes was something he could never forget, and his moral patterns are built up against a background of social relationships which provide the most real and ineluctable facts about human life. For Richardson, all the tests of life are public, carried out in full view of society. Eden for him is no garden but an estate, and Adam is a landlord with tenants, Eve a lady with social duties and dangers, and the serpent a neighboring squire who violates the rules of the game by combining the genuine attractiveness of rank with an immoral character. There is no private wrestling with one's soul or with the Devil here; Richardson's moral dramas are acted out on a public stage, and any moments of private anguish are promptly communicated by the sufferer to a friend in a letter. The epistolary technique is no incidental device: it is bound up with the social context of Richardson's moral patterns. And if there is no purely private anguish, there is similarly no purely private victory. Virtue must be recognized to be real, and Clarissa's death is made into a moral victory and indeed a beatification in virtue of the universal recognition of her saintliness which it produces. Richardson was the first important English writer to deal with basic moral problems in a detailed social context.

This, then, is what is meant by the claim that Richardson's novels enshrine an eighteenth-century bourgeois morality. Virtue is consistently related to prudence on the one hand and to reputation on the other, and the arena of moral struggle is the stratified society of contemporary England. Further, in the eyes of Richardson and his fellows the aristocracy is still a class to be envied and aspired to. Pamela, the serving maid, has her virtue rewarded by marrying into the squirearchy; Clarissa's upper-middle-class family want to consolidate their position as property owners and achieve a title, and Clarissa's pursuer, the aristocratic Lovelace, has never any doubt that marriage to him is a desirable thing for her. Prosperous tradesmen and master craftsmen may have believed that their class was the sole repository of true virtue and respectability in the nation, but the aristocracy was still admired and looked up to as the class which the successful bourgeois hoped ultimately to enter. The implications of this double view of the aristocracy—as representing both rakishness and the heights of that worldly felicity which was the proper reward of a life of combined prudence and virtue—can be seen again and again in the working out of Richardson's plots.

Richardson's volume of model letters—*Letters Written to and for particular friends, . . . Directing . . . the Requisite Style and Forms To be Observed in writing Familiar Letters . . .* (1741)—

reveals, or at least suggests, the moral world in which his novels are set. It is a world in which *relationships* are of the first importance: the relation between master and servant, between parents and children, between debtor and creditor, between suitor and sought—these and other relationships condition what is proper in human behavior, and they are all, in some sense, symbolic of the relationship between man and God. They reveal a nexus of rights and duties, the rights being parental and proprietary, the duties being filial and, in a sense, feudal. Interspersed with the letters revealing, and indeed commanding, these rights and duties, are calls to repentance and amendment addressed to those who have gone astray. The rewards for duty well done are clearly defined; they are both earthly and heavenly. Family and social relationships in this world being a microcosm of the larger relationship between man and God, there is an obvious analogy between prosperity in this world (the result of the proper management of human relationships) and eternal felicity in the next. The analogy between the two worlds is, throughout Richardson's work, complex but consistent. One moves into the next world only if the present world fails one. Pamela was able to combine prudence with virtue and, literally, make the best of both worlds. The title of the novel is *Pamela: or, Virtue Rewarded.* Clarissa, cheated out of prudence, fails to secure earthly prosperity but is instead rewarded in Heaven. Prudence guarantees earthly happiness, while virtue guarantees heavenly happiness, and the truly fortunate are those to whom circumstances allow both. Respectability is the outward and visible sign of prudence, and often, but not always, of true virtue. (Clarissa loses her external respectability while fully preserving her true virtue.) Similarly, gentility is the social behavior and the conventions within which virtue is likely to flourish but does not necessarily flourish. *Clarissa* shows that otherworldliness is not a virtue until this world has failed one. Good management, economy, methodical disposition of one's time, prudence and efficiency in managing property and business, are important qualities in all Richardson's heroes and heroines; Clarissa has them all at first, and, though Lovelace cheats her into the imprudent act of going off with him, she retains them to the end, changing only the objects to which she applies them: she gets ready for death with exemplary efficiency, even ordering and paying for her coffin in advance. If, like Pamela, one can combine prudence, virtue, and beauty, one is truly secure in both worlds. If, like Clarissa, one has virtue and beauty but is cheated by the Devil out of the exercise of prudence on one critical occasion, one can compensate by raising virtue to the level of saintliness and, confident of the next world, cheerfully repudiate this one. Pamela is held up for our imitation (though Richardson makes it very clear that only a most exceptionally gifted servant girl can hope to marry her master), Clarissa for our adoration. The latter is the true saint's life.

Richardson's epistolary method was not only a natural one for him, and an inevitable one in view of the road by which he approached the novel; it was also the appropriate one for a novelist concerned with the moment-to-moment recording of the fluctuations of emotion in the midst of moral struggle. It serves a similar purpose to that of the soliloquy in drama and the so-called stream of consciousness technique in modern fiction. We are brought immediately and directly into the consciousness of the character. It is, of course, a convention, in itself no better and no worse than other conventions in fiction. There is no point in speculating on how the characters found time or mental composure to write the innumerable letters that make up the novels. That Lovelace, rake and daredevil and man of action, should write long letters to his friend giving the most intimate details of his plots against Clarissa and reporting progress at every stage, is of course improbable, but this kind of improbability does not touch the level of probability at which the novel moves. Pamela's and Clarissa's letters take the reader into the heart of the developing situation and enable him to follow with extraordinary immediacy the psychological implications of the working out of the moral pattern.

One great difference there is between the epistolary technique and the stream of consciousness method: the latter emphasizes the privateness, the uniqueness, of individual experience, and is therefore appropriate for novels in which the essential loneliness of the individual is stressed and the impossibility of adequate communication between individuals is a major problem. The great theme of the eighteenth- and often of the nineteenth-century novelist is the relation between gentility and virtue; that of the modern novelist is the relationship between loneliness and love. The former theme requires a more public kind of elaboration than is appropriate for the latter, and letters are a most effective way of publicizing private experience. Publicity is important for Richardson; virtue must be publicly known and admired. Clarissa's death scene is most carefully staged; it is a device for demonstrating saintliness in action. For the saint to arrange such a demonstration implies a certain degree of self-approval, but that was no problem for Richardson, for whom self-approval must always coexist with virtue, even with modesty. Clarissa is humble, yet she is full of conscious superiority, which she expresses quite unaffectedly, and the same can be said of Sir Charles Grandison. The moral life is a public life; it is an *exemplum*, something to be seen, approved, and imitated or at least admired. Martyrdom would be useless if no one knew of it, and the exemplary life could not be exemplary if no one observed it. Clarissa represents the former, Pamela the latter.

Popular as *Pamela* was, there were not lacking contemporary readers who showed uneasiness at the moral implications of the heroine's preserving her chastity until she could exchange it for a marriage that would raise her to financial and social heights and of Squire B.'s easy transition from a villainous rake to a desirable husband. Henry Fielding (1707–54), who came to the novel after a career as a writer of comedies, burlesques, and satirical plays, a journalist, and a barrister (he became a Justice of the Peace for Middlesex and helped to initiate important social and legal reforms), voiced this uneasiness in his *Joseph Andrews* (1742), "written in imitation of the manner of Cervantes, author of *Don Quixote*." Ostensibly this novel is a parody of *Pamela*. Its hero is supposed to be a brother of Pamela, a servant in the household of Lady Booby, whom Fielding makes an aunt of Richardson's Squire B. Chaste, handsome, gifted with all graces and all virtues, Joseph in his behavior and fortunes allows his creator to laugh at Richardson's moral world through the adventures and misadventures he encounters. But the element of parody in the novel soon disappears. Fielding, too, was writing a moral novel, and it soon becomes evident that he is developing and illustrating a moral code of his own, not as fundamentally different from Richardson's as he thought but different enough, and revealing another aspect of the moral sensibility of the age. Joseph's virtue is attempted by his widowed mistress, Lady Booby, and when he repulses her she dismisses him from her service. To treat male chastity with the seriousness with which Richardson treated female chastity is to treat it comically, but the very fact that such treatment inevitably turns out to be comic is a comment on the moral confusions implied in Richardson's position. A reformed rake makes the best husband, but a girl who has once lost her virtue, even in the most minimal technical sense, is undone forever. The origins of this view go behind eighteenth-century attitudes and conventions to a view of marriage and of the relation between the sexes that goes far back in Western European history and has persisted into the present century. Fielding's main purpose is not, however, to criticize this view, but to develop his own view on the difference between real and supposed virtue, between true goodness and public esteem. For Richardson, virtue and reputation went together, except for unhappy accidents; for Fielding, they rarely go together, for virtue is a matter of innate disposition and intention—the good heart—rather than of public demonstration, and the signs of morality which are publicly approved bear little relation, or are even related in inverse proportion, to real goodness.

Fielding explains his general purpose in the preface to *Joseph Andrews:*

. . . The Ridiculous only . . . falls within my province in the present work. . . . The only source of the true Ridiculous (as it appears to me) is affectation. But though it arises from one spring only, when we consider the infinite streams into which this one branches, we shall presently cease to admire at the copious field it affords to an observer. Now, affectation proceeds from one of these two causes, vanity or hypocrisy: for as vanity puts us on affecting false characters, in order to purchase applause, so hypocrisy sets us on an endeavour to avoid censure, by concealing our vices under an appearance of their opposite virtues. . . .

From the discovery of this affectation arises the Ridiculous, which always strikes the reader with surprise and pleasure; and that in a higher and stronger degree when the affectation arises from hypocrisy, than when from vanity; for to discover any one to be the exact reverse of what he affects, is more surprising and consequently more ridiculous, than to find him a little deficient in the quality he desires the reputation of. . . .

Now, from affectation only, the misfortunes and calamities of life, or the imperfections of nature, may become the objects of ridicule. Surely he hath a very ill-framed mind who can look on ugliness, infirmity, or poverty, as ridiculous in themselves: nor do I believe any man living, who meets a dirty fellow riding through the streets in a cart, is struck with an idea of the Ridiculous from it; but if he should see the same figure descend from his coach and six, or bolt from his chair with his hat under his arm, he would then begin to laugh, and with justice. . . . Much less are natural imperfections the object of derision; but when ugliness aims at the applause of beauty, or lameness endeavours to display agility, it is then that these unfortunate circumstances, which at first moved our compassion, tend only to raise our mirth.

The exposure of affectation, as when lustful women pretend to be chaste or selfish and greedy landlords pretend to be charitable or worldly and self-seeking clergymen claim to be thinking only of the Christian virtues and to be motivated only by spiritual ideals, is indeed a source of the comic in Fielding. But it is not the only or the most important source. Hypocrisy is an old established butt of satirists, and if Fielding had done nothing more than write satirical novels concerned with exposing the difference between what his characters really were and what they pretended to be, his works would have been neither original nor especially interesting. But he had learned something from Swift about the use of the mock-heroic in exposing the differences between what men are and what they think they are or claim to be, and something from Cervantes in exploring the relation between the privately good and the publicly ridiculous, with the result that in *Joseph Andrews* he produced a novel in which the dangers of convention and the ambiguities of innocence are explored for the first time in English fiction. Richardson, it is true, had shown an awareness of the gap between what Pamela was really doing and what she thought she was doing; in her letters there is clear evidence of self-deception; but Richardson is content merely to indicate his awareness of this and to pursue it no further. It neither invalidates Pamela's claims to supreme virtue nor allows any play of the comic spirit. But for Fielding these ambiguities and contradictions are the essence of the novel and the true stuff of comedy.

Fielding also draws on the picaresque tradition to set his characters on the road and by involving them in a great variety of adventures by the roadside, at inns, and in various places through which they pass, gives a sense of the color and variety of English life (whereas Richardson's novels are much more concentrated on the emotions and sensibilities of the individual and on the behavior of one small group of people). By contriving it so that Joseph Andrews, his sweetheart the beautiful and innocent servant girl Fanny, and the quixotic Parson Adams are all on the road together, he involves different kinds of innocence in the snares of the world and makes moral capital —as well as high comedy—out of the result. In some respects Parson Adams has a greater claim to be considered the hero of the novel than Joseph himself: the original title is *The History of the Adventures of Joseph Andrews and of his friend Mr. Abraham Adams*. Adams represents what Fielding had learned from Cervantes, but whereas Cervantes' hero mistook the real world because he lived in a world of the imagination created by his reading of old romances, Parson Adams mistakes the real world because he lives in the world of Christian values which everybody else professes to live in but which in fact everybody else ignores. Innocence of the world, and simple-minded astonishment and horror whenever he discovers how people in the real world actually behave, are bound up with Parson Adams' goodness. Goodness, innocence, and ignorance of the world go together. "I prefer a private school [to a public school], where boys may be kept in innocence and ignorance," Adams declares in a conversation with Joseph. The notion that innocence and ignorance go together has had an interesting history in Western thought (it was challenged, among others, by Milton, who maintained that after the Fall man could only know good by evil and that "a fugitive and cloistered virtue" was not true virtue) and is seen at its most extreme as applied to women in so many Victorian novels in which women who know even the most elementary "facts of life" are therefore inevitably bad, and the innocent and virtuous are also wholly ignorant.

But the Victorians restricted this equation of innocence and ignorance to genteel women and to matters of sex. In Fielding, there is
no ignorance of sex on anybody's part, and knowledge of the "facts
of life" is taken for granted in Fanny as it is in Richardson's Pamela:
how could women resist the ravisher if they did not know what the
ravisher planned? Pamela guards her premarital chastity like a hawk,
but she is not a prude; she knows exactly what Squire B. is after and
has no hesitation in talking about it. Fielding's Fanny, though wholly
virtuous and innocent, is well aware of the excitement her physical
proximity produces in Joseph (and in herself). Innocence for Fielding
meant ignorance of the disparity between what men profess and
what they are; it meant believing literally in Christian charity.
Adams is described as being "as entirely ignorant of the ways of this
world as any infant just entered into it could possibly be. As he never
had any intention to deceive, so he never suspected such a design in
others. He was generous, friendly, and brave, to an excess; but simplicity was his characteristic." He did not believe that malice and
envy existed in mankind. His lack of knowledge of the world kept
him in perpetual poverty, and no experience (and he has many in the
novel) could root out his native innocence and credulity.

We can see here a revolt against the idealization of sophistication
found, for example, in Lord Chesterfield's letters to his son. Not that
Chesterfield was a wicked man, but he believed, as so many of his
generation did, that the rituals and conventions of civilization were
what made life tolerable, and that it was only by strictly observing
the social code of the day that men were able to demonstrate their
distinguishing qualities as men rather than animals. The revolt
against this is of course bound up with ideas about the noble savage
and the natural man that had been developing since the seventeenth
century and which by the middle of the eighteenth century were
having a steadily increasing influence on literature. If one meaning
of sentimentality is belief in untutored innocence as opposed to
worldly wisdom, then Fielding was infinitely more sentimental than
Richardson. Yet the doctrine of the "moral sense" was an Augustan
one and was held by some of the most eminent eighteenth-century
philosophers. Fielding is not, however, merely illustrating in characters like Parson Adams (and Squire Allworthy in *Tom Jones*) the
operation of the moral sense; he is asserting that true goodness is
ignorant and gullible. Even when he proceeds in *Tom Jones* to illustrate in the character of the hero the view that the good heart is all,
that sins of the flesh are venial compared with hardness of the spirit—
selfishness, cruelty, lack of compassion—he makes this hero also in
some degree gullible, and it is his gullibility and even more that of

Squire Allworthy that really starts the action and helps to keep it moving. (Yet Allworthy is maliciously deceived, and it is his excessive confidence in his own knowledge of men, rather than simple naïveté, that helps him to be deceived.)

Fielding's moral code is thus no profounder than Richardson's, though most later readers have found it the more attractive. But *Joseph Andrews* is a comic novel and it is for the comic potentialities of his moral code that it is interesting. This code enables him to present Adams as both silly and admirable, comically ludicrous and almost saintly. Even his faults—his simple-minded vanity, his proneness to give advice about the duty of resigning oneself to the will of Providence when he himself responds with violent emotion to any personal sorrow or joy—are treated affectionately and do not detract from his essential goodness. Yet Fielding does not spare him the most ludicrous situations; we see him, his cassock in tatters, his wig stuck on upside down, with somebody accidentally upsetting a chamber pot over his head—one of innumerable characteristic moments—and he seems to be a character in pure farce. Similarly, the mock-heroic descriptions of fights and quarrels seem at first merely to render everything ludicrous. This does not happen, however; the moral pattern is not destroyed, and while we think Joseph a goose and Adams a "sucker," the glory of their innocence shines through. Fielding makes it quite clear that *he* (and his readers) know the world, even if Adams does not. He does not identify himself altogether with any of his good characters. The mock-heroic has among its several functions that of separating the author from his characters.

A novel that sets out as parody and soon develops into a comic moral novel in its own right is bound to suffer from some lack of unity of tone; but in fact *Joseph Andrews* suffers less than might have been expected. The parody of *Pamela* is subsumed into the larger purpose without any real gap. And when, in the latter part of the book, Fielding introduces Pamela and Squire B. (now Squire Booby) and gives them a significant part in the action, the laugh at Richardson, though it is real, is less important than the developing texture of the plot, both richly comic and seriously moral. Some of the most direct of the thrusts in the book are in minor characters and incidents: Joseph, stripped naked by robbers and left in a ditch as dead, is passed by respectable people afraid of being involved or simply too mean to help; nobody will even supply him with a coat; "and it is more than probable poor Joseph, who obstinately adhered to his modest resolution [not to enter a coach naked] must have perished, unless a postilion (a lad who hath since been transported for robbing a henroost) had voluntarily stripped off a great-coat, his only garment, at the same time swearing a great oath (for which he was rebuked by the passengers) 'that he would rather ride in his shirt all his life, than suffer a fellow-creature to lie in so miserable a condition.' "

The life and color of the novel, the vivid pictures of characters and accounts of scenes on the road, the sense of the English countryside, help to give it freshness and vitality. Though the characters are all types rather than fully realized individuals, they are vividly colored types. "I declare here once for all," Fielding confides to his readers in the novel, "I describe not men, but manners; not an individual, but a species. Perhaps it will be answered, Are not the characters then taken from life? To which I answer in the affirmative; . . ." There are inset stories in which characters tell their life histories and enable Fielding to point his moral in a new way. The long autobiography of Mr. Wilson, for example, ending in an account of his quiet country life (a subdued and more Christian version of Pomfret's "Choice") and including an account of the economic struggles of the professional writer in the 1730's and early 1740's, has both moral, sociological, and dramatic interest. It is also full of stock sentimental situations (the ruined girl, the descent and recovery of the wastrel, a careful patterning of cruelties and benevolences) that were to recur again and again in eighteenth-century literature. The glimpses of social and economic life are often most illuminating. The whole position of "Grub Street" with its hack writers working for booksellers, is clarified in Wilson's story, as is also the decline of literary patronage soon to be so signally symbolized by Johnson's letter to Lord Chesterfield. "Many a morning," Mr. Wilson tells his hearers in tones that remind us of Johnson's letter, "have I waited hours in the cold parlours of men of quality; where, after seeing the lowest rascals in lace and embroidery, the pimps and buffoons in fashion, admitted, I have been sometimes told, on sending in my name, that my lord could not possibly see me this morning: . . ." This is part of Fielding's attack on the lack of charity among great persons, but it is also a record of an important part of the social history of the age. For Fielding, the writing of social history was necessary if he was to produce his kind of moral social comedy; it is never introduced simply for its own sake; yet it is there, and gives an extra dimension to his work.

In *Tom Jones* (1749) Fielding developed the comic epic on a more impressive scale and found the proper kind of expansive form for his characteristic genius. Like *Joseph Andrews,* it is a novel both comic and moral. Fielding set forth his moral aim quite explicitly in his dedicatory preface to Lord Lyttleton:

. . . I hope my reader will be convinced, at his very entrance on this work, that he will find in the whole course of it nothing prejudicial to the cause of religion and virtue, nothing inconsistent with the strictest rules of decency, nor which can offend even the chastest eye in the perusal. On the contrary, I declare, that to recommend goodness and innocence hath been my sincere endeavour in this history. . . .

Besides displaying that beauty of virtue which may attract the admiration of mankind, I have attempted to engage a stronger motive to human action in her favour, by convincing men that their true interest directs them to a pursuit of her. For this purpose I have shown that no acquisitions of guilt can compensate the loss of that solid inward comfort of mind, which is the sure companion of innocence and virtue; nor can in the least balance the evil of that horror and anxiety which, in their room, guilt introduces into our bosoms. And again, that as these acquisitions are in themselves generally worthless, so are the means to attain them not only base and infamous, but at best incertain, and always full of danger. Lastly, I have endeavoured strongly to inculcate that virtue and innocence can scarce ever be injured but by indiscretion; and that it is this alone which often betrays them into the snares that deceit and villainy spread for them. . . .

For these purposes I have employed all the wit and humour of which I am master in the following history; wherein I have endeavoured to laugh mankind out of their favourite follies and vices. . . .

Fielding's insistence that nothing in Tom Jones "can offend even the chastest eye on perusal" sprang in part from his awareness that the kind of morality he was preaching—goodness of heart rather than technical virtue, with sins of the flesh regarded much more lightly than sins against generosity of feeling—might be superficially shocking to at least some of his readers: he was protesting that despite what might appear to be evidence to the contrary, his book was both chaste and moral. The hero was no Joseph Andrews; Tom Jones is a lusty, passionate, highly sexed young man, as well as impulsively generous and easily moved by others' sufferings. "He was besides active, genteel, gay, and good-humoured, and had a flow of animal spirits which enlivened every conversation where he was present." In tracing the fortunes of this kind of hero Fielding could come more satisfactorily to terms with the moral complexities of the world as it is than he could with the simple-minded virtue of Joseph Andrews and Parson Adams, whose behavior required the embarrassing equation of innocence, ignorance, and goodness on the one hand and experience, knowledge, and evil on the other.

Tom Jones is a comic epic in prose, with mock-heroic invocations and descriptions scattered throughout the narrative. But the comic and "mock" element serves an important artistic purpose. It is not simply a joke at the expense of neoclassic categories. It enables Fielding to make certain points about society, to deflate certain kinds of pretentiousness, to communicate his relish of the color and variety

of human life simultaneously with his ironic perception of the underlying identity of high-class duelling or battling and low-class brawling and of other parallels between the "high" and the "low" which
the high would never admit and the low never surmise. More than
this, it enables him to bring his hero into a series of situations where
his imprudence and lack of discretion give power to his enemies and
seem to be about to destroy him, without causing the reader serious
anxiety, for the gay mock-heroics of the omniscient narrator reas-
sures the reader from the outset that Tom will come through. Not
that the reader follows Tom's varying fortunes without suspense as
time and time again his recklessness or indiscretion seems to be on
the point of leading him to destruction; but it is a comic suspense if
one may use the term, a suspense seasoned with comic awareness of
the absurdities and fatuities of life and a genial sympathy with Tom's
ways of getting himself into trouble.

The full title of the book is *The History of Tom Jones, a Foundling,* and the choice of a common English name together with the description of the hero as "a foundling" indicate with belligerent clarity
that Fielding is not going to follow the normal procedure of epic histories but will deal with English society as it is. Of course, the story
of a foundling who turns out to be of noble blood after all is an
archetypal folk theme, and Fielding's use of it here illustrates how
what Northrop Frye calls the "low mimetic mode" of fiction can move
back to myth through irony. The plot is constructed with the greatest
ingenuity. From one point of view, it is built round the question of
the identity of Tom, who is found as a new-born infant in the bed of
the benevolent Squire Allworthy and brought up by that good man
until the evil machinations of the Squire's nephew, Blifil, who also
lives with Allworthy and has been brought up by him, result in Tom's
being banished in disgrace for crimes he did not commit but which
his imprudence and his passionate nature make it easy for the malevolent Blifil to fasten on him. The central third of the book follows
Tom's adventures on the road, and the final third is set in London,
whither all the major characters are brought to achieve the denouement. It turns out in the end that Tom is really a half brother of
Blifil, though illegitimate, and in the light of this knowledge the
reader is able to look back and see clues to Tom's real identity artfully planted throughout the book. But the real interest of the reader
is not sustained by the desire to discover Tom's real identity, a question kept in the background throughout most of the novel. What
keeps the plot going is Tom's continuous betrayal by his indiscretions
(which include various casual sexual experiences) into the hands
either of his enemies or of fortune. Each time the consequences of

his imprudence or folly (it is never worse than folly) seem to be leading to disaster, until in the end he is in prison about to be accused
of murder and apparently hopelessly at the mercy of Blifil's evil
schemes; but the consequences are never as bad or as permanent as
they seem always about to be, and in the end Tom wins through to
reconciliation with Allworthy (who turns out to be his uncle), to fortune, and to the hand of the beautiful and virtuous Sophia.

The plot thus summarized seems neither original nor interesting,
but in fact it is much more complex and ingenious than any such
summary can indicate, and it is related to character and to the moral
pattern of the novel in a highly original manner. Allworthy is the
Good Squire, a type rather than an individual, but not a mere type of
innocence or benevolence. If he is imposed upon, it is less out of
complete ignorance of the world (such as Parson Adams showed)
than because of his *hamartia*, his overconfidence in his own knowledge of men. It is his errors of judgment rather than mere naïveté
that help to precipitate Tom's unjust expulsion. Yet he is shown as a
completely good man. Fielding indeed seems to have involved himself in certain contradictions in trying to maintain both Allworthy's
perfect innocence and his knowledge of the world. He is gullible, if
not to the same extent as Adams. Yet there are moments when Fielding tries to persuade the reader that Allworthy knows very well the
moral weaknesses of the people who surround him. The two tutors
whom he hired for Tom and Blifil, Thwackum and Square, are caricatures of two kinds of contemporary thinker.

Square held human nature to be the perfection of all virtue, and that vice was a
deviation from our nature, in the same manner as deformity of body is.
Thwackum, on the contrary, maintained that the human mind, since the Fall,
was nothing but a sink of iniquity, till purified and redeemed by grace. In one
point only they agreed, which was, in all their discourses on morality never to
mention the word goodness. The favourite phrase of the former was the natural
beauty of virtue; that of the latter was the divine power of grace.

But Fielding is not content to satirize these opposing views in the
persons of those who hold them; he makes both Square and
Thwackum also unscrupulous careerists interested primarily in ad-
vancing their own material interests and capable of twisting their
creeds to support any course of action that will yield them material
gain. When Tom is caught poaching on a neighbor's game preserve
he refuses to betray Black George, the gamekeeper who initiated and
shared the enterprise. Thwackum wants Tom thrashed for this (all
Thwackum's meditations "were full of birch") and argues with Allworthy against "wicked lenity." Allworthy, recognizing the gener-

osity of Tom's motive, though he considered it misguided, forbids Thwackum to birch Tom, and Thwackum obeys with the greatest reluctance. Now it is made quite clear in this scene that Allworthy sees through both Thwackum and Square; yet if he does so and refuses to dismiss them he is partly responsible for Tom's sufferings at the hands of these gentlemen. (Blifil never suffers at their hands; he knows how to flatter and play the hypocrite, so as to let each think that Blifil is his devoted disciple.) So, a few pages further on, Fielding has to tell the reader that Allworthy does *not* see through the tutors. In discussing his relation to Thwackum he tells us that at first Thwackum "was extremely agreeable to Allworthy," but

upon longer acquaintance and more intimate conversation, this worthy man saw infirmities in the tutor which he could have wished him to have been without; though as those seemed greatly overbalanced by his good qualities, they did not incline Mr. Allworthy to part with him: nor would they indeed have justified such a proceeding; for the reader is greatly mistaken, if he conceives that Thwackum appeared to Mr. Allworthy in the same light as he doth to him in this history.

Fielding adds: "Of readers who from such conceits as these, condemn the wisdom or penetration of Mr. Allworthy, I shall not scruple to say, that they make a very bad and ungrateful use of that knowledge which we have communicated to them."

We can see here that Fielding is trying to modify his earlier position with regard to the relation between innocence and ignorance. Allworthy is gullible, but only because he does not know things which he could not be expected to know and which the reader only knows because the author, in his omniscience, has revealed them to him. Allworthy is deliberately deceived and misled by Blifil and others, and it is only partly his innocence and virtue that allow him to be so deceived. Fielding tells us again in his account of the conversation between Allworthy and his irascible, bibulous, extrovert fox-hunting neighbor, Squire Western, concerning Sophia Western's love for Tom and her father's insistence that Sophia should marry Blifil, that Allworthy "perfectly well knew mankind." How then was he so long deceived in Blifil, whose general nastiness was visible immediately to even such a sheltered innocent as Sophia? It is perhaps a kind of vanity which plays into Blifil's hands and enables him, by acting out in the most superficial manner the character of a respectful and virtuous nephew, to fool his uncle. Yet when at the end of the book the full extent of Blifil's villainy is revealed, Allworthy is shocked but not incredulous; he is of course disappointed in Blifil but not disillusioned in mankind; and his response to his new knowledge is immediate and tough.

The benevolence and generosity of Allworthy, the Good Squire, is contrasted with the impetuous selfishness of Squire Western, whose character represents a rollicking caricature of a type of English country gentleman—interested only in his bottle and his hounds—who has had a long life in English literature, and justifiably so, for he was based on long-continued fact. Squire Western is not a villain; he is a comic character, whose violent moods, Somerset dialect, mock-epic quarrels with his sister, and selfish love of his daughter are treated with tremendous comic gusto. Yet, when Tom is disinherited and exiled and Western, who has hitherto liked Tom, turns against him and seeks Blifil as his son-in-law, this comic squire's persecution of his daughter (who loves the rejected Tom and detests Blifil) leads to Sophia's running away with her maid in order to seek refuge with a cousin in London. The scenes where the Squire alternately pleads with and abuses his daughter are full of violence; but it is a comic violence, and there is no suggestion that Sophia is really treated cruelly, even though she is locked up in her room. Indeed, the sinister arguments of Squire Western's sister are more difficult to take than Western's blustering. Sophia is persecuted, yet we cannot take her persecutors seriously as villains: neither Western nor his sister ever step out of their comic roles. Though the reader is full of indignation at Sophia's treatment, as he is to an even greater extent at Tom's, that indignation is never great enough to make him see even Blifil as a serious villain. Blifil, as R. S. Crane has pointed out, is no Iago; his villainy is a kind of nasty cleverness which is bound to overreach itself sooner or later. And Western's treatment of Sophia is itself so much a comic caricature of the behavior of that kind of father under that sort of circumstance that, without losing our feeling for Sophia, we relish the comedy in the very scenes where she is being abused. Fielding uses exaggeration and caricature as devices for allowing us to enjoy the comedy without losing our concern and sympathy for the hero and heroine.

Once Fielding has got both his hero and his heroine on the road (where their paths cross but they never meet) he can indulge in the picaresque aspect of his novel and give us, on a larger scale than that of *Joseph Andrews,* the diversity and color and vitality of the English scene. With Tom separated both from his beloved Sophia and from Squire Allworthy, whom he still loves, he becomes a soldier of fortune and his adventures acquire a new kind of interest. Yet we never lose sight of the main threads of the plot, and throughout Tom's wanderings with his companion Partridge, characters (Partridge himself is one of them) from his past weave in and out and the materials not only for the final solution of the problem of Tom's real identity but also (what the reader at this stage is far more interested in) for the rehabilitation of his character, his reconciliation with Allworthy, the exposure of Blifil, and Tom's marriage with Sophia, are gradually assembled. The final third of the book, with Tom and Sophia both in London, shows Tom on the one hand exhibiting his real character (whose main characteristic was generosity) to a sufficient number of people in order to build up a convincing collection of witnesses to his virtue when the testing times comes, and on the other hand provoking fortune by his imprudence to lead him to further miseries. But in the end the building up of character witnesses and the provocations of fortune come together to achieve the denouement. When Allworthy and Blifil come to London after Western has found his daughter there, the threads begin to converge and at the lowest moment of Tom's fortunes we can already begin to see the pattern of his release and triumph. The various bits of the truth are brought together by the fortunate—and carefully manipulated—conjunction of the relevant characters, and so the novel moves to its close.

Fielding occasionally betrays a certain amount of timidity in exercising his satirical comic powers. He finds it necessary to explain that in his portraits of Thwackum and Square "it is not religion or virtue, but the want of them, which is here exposed. Had not Thwackum too much neglected virtue, and Square, religion, in the composition of their several systems, and had not both utterly discarded all natural goodness of heart, they had never been represented as the objects of derision in this history." He is afraid lest an audience which acclaimed Richardson's *Pamela* might not realize that he, Fielding, was equally on the side of religion and morality. His main attack, as always, was on hypocrisy and on that cold-blooded self-interest that acts out virtue on the public stage but is privately selfish and cruel. And attacks on hypocrisy can always be misconstrued by the superficial reader as attacks on the virtues which the hypocrite is counterfeiting. "A treacherous friend," Fielding informs the reader in one of the many personal essays on life, literature, and morality which he intersperses throughout the book (often in mock-heroic style, but sometimes wholly seriously),

is the most dangerous enemy; and I will say boldly, that both religion and virtue have received more real discredit from hypocrites than the wittiest profligates or infidels could ever cast upon them: nay, further, as these two, in their purity, are rightly called the bands of civil society, and are indeed the greatest of blessings, so when poisoned and corrupted with fraud, pretence, and affectation, they have become the worst of civil curses, and have enabled men to perpetrate the most cruel mischiefs to their own species.

In his hatred of cruelty and hypocrisy and his love of frankness and generosity even when accompanied by weakness of the flesh, Fielding is consciously rebelling against the tendency to equate morality with sexual control which had long been a feature of Puritan and middle-class thought and was long to continue to be so, and he is rebelling, too, against the equation of virtue and outward respectability. But even he never considers having a single standard in sexual behavior for both men and women: though the various women in *Tom Jones* who are guilty of unchaste behavior are generally treated with compassion and understanding (but not if they are guilty also of hypocrisy) it would be unthinkable for Fielding to have as his heroine a girl who was not perfectly chaste and modest. Sentimentalizing over fallen women had already become a fashion, and the "good" prostitute, more sinned against than sinning, has a long history in eighteenth- and nineteenth-century fiction; but it is one thing to be compassionate and understanding about female lapses from chastity and another to make a girl guilty of such a lapse into a genuine heroine. Defoe's Moll Flanders is a low-life character whose adventures are a matter of sociological interest, but Moll is a heroine neither in the sense that Pamela or Sophia is nor in the sense that Hardy's Tess was to be.

Whether the mock-heroic elements in *Tom Jones,* and other features which Fielding took over from the traditions of narrative available to him (such as the long inset story of the Man of the Hill) and which the modern reader may find otiose or irritating, represent the most adequate devices for the presentation of a novel both comic and moral of the kind Fielding was endeavoring to write is perhaps debatable. So is the effectiveness of the numerous personal digressions, many written in a tone of high-spirited burlesque. But Fielding was working with the traditions and devices he found in the literary past he knew or was able to invent by modifications and permutations of such traditions and devices. The resultant comic epic in prose may not have helped in developing new forms for the English novel; in some respects the form of *Tom Jones* was naïve and anachronistic, and has neither the psychological brilliance of *Clarissa* nor the moral subtlety we might expect from one who objected to Richardson's morality. There are moments in the novel when the moral intention interferes with the psychological one—as when Tom is made a good classical scholar, able to expound Latin poetry to the ex-schoolteacher Partridge (though he is not the brilliant classicist which Parson Adams, with similar doubtful appropriateness, is made out to be) because the use of the classics in this way represents a "good" use of education: the high-spirited open-air boy that Tom is represented as being would not have lapped up his Latin like that. All Fielding's heroes are in danger of becoming prigs, at least on occasion. But that is a danger that the English novel found difficulty in avoiding right through the nineteenth century. And in spite of whatever may be urged against it, *Tom Jones* remains a remarkable achievement; its vitality, scope, brilliance of plotting, and handling of the comic element so as to keep the reader's suspense from falling into genuine anxiety and at the same time to enrich the moral pattern, show art of a high kind.

Fielding had already tried his hand at a novel in which his moral feeling would be conveyed by a purer brand of irony than the plot and method of *Tom Jones* made desirable or possible. This was his *History of the Life of the late Mr. Jonathan Wild the Great* (1743) in which the life of a notorious highwayman is told as from the point of view of one who agreed with the ideals implicit in a life of unscrupulous egotism, with any temptation to deviate into the weakness of kindness or disinterestedness treated as the conventional moralist treats temptations to evil. The standards of the world, the standards not openly professed but actually followed by those "who have lived long in cities, courts, gaols, or such places," are here accepted as real standards; goodness and unselfishness are presented as weak and contemptible, and the artistry with which cunning villainy can operate at the expense of the weak or unfortunate in order to achieve material prosperity is described as though it were genuinely heroic. Fielding was doing here something similar to what Gay did in *The Beggar's Opera,* showing how the life of the criminal and the behavior of those who occupied high places in politics and society were really the same, except that the latter were hypocrites and professed to believe in ideals which they did not follow. But he was doing something more: he was trying to shock his readers into an awareness of the cruelty of the world and the vulnerable position in it of the generous and kindhearted. The result is a *tour de force* rather than a classic of irony. The limitations imposed by the method constrict the scope of the novel, though it does show Fielding's characteristic vitality and humor, the latter sometimes of a grim quality not elsewhere found in his work.

Fielding's last novel, *Amelia* (1751), is altogether different in tone from any of his previous fiction. Pathos replaces humor, moral gravity rather than comic violence or irony sets the mood. The heroine, a latter-day Patient Griselda, is drawn with a tenderness and a personal sympathy quite new in Fielding. The patient sufferings of the virtuous wife are treated against a background of quietly and precisely drawn middle-class life, and in the course of the action

Fielding draws attention to a variety of social abuses. There is no breath of epic here; the emphasis is domestic, and all the moral feeling is lavished on the good and gentle heroine, whose character and behavior shine in a naughty world to justify and redeem human nature. Amelia's husband, Mr. Booth, is neither hero nor villain, but an erring man of the sort who, as has been said, "exist to be forgiven." *Amelia* for all its charm suffers from its lack of vitality and may reflect its author's declining health, which led him to take a voyage to Portugal, where he died. His *Journal of a Voyage to Lisbon*, published posthumously in 1755, is an appealing account of this last journey.

Fielding's younger contemporary Tobias Smollett (1721–71) was content to work in the picaresque tradition—he translated Le Sage's *Gil Blas*—and to take a hero through a series of violent, brawling adventures on land and sea in the course of which he could render with vigorous realism aspects of the social life of his time. A Scot who came to London to seek his literary fortune in London after studying surgery in Glasgow, Smollett never got over his disappointment at the failure of his first tragedy, which he attributed, as he attributed everything that went wrong, to the malice and jealousy of individuals. He quarrelled with almost everybody, and vented his anger and his spleen in his writings. Unable to take London by storm, he served as surgeon's mate on one of the ships of the Cartagena expedition of 1741—a mismanaged and unsuccessful naval episode in the maritime war with Spain that accompanied war against France in the War of the Austrian Succession—and acquired experience there of the horror and brutality of life aboard an eighteenth-century man-of-war that he was able to put to good purpose in fiction. *Roderick Random*, his first novel, appeared in 1748. Here Smollett followed the outlines of his own life, but crammed the story with innumerable invented incidents and episodes, many of them violent and cruel. His hero is a young Scot who, after the disappearance and supposed death of his father who had married without *his* father's consent, is left unprovided for and goes to London to embark on a series of adventures which includes an astonishing variety of mishaps in London, being press-ganged aboard a man-of-war before achieving the position of surgeon's assistant there, and a wealth of violent, tender, colorful, grim, or sordid experiences by land and sea in different parts of the world; eventually he discovers his father in Paraguay, marries his beloved Narcissa, and returns to Scotland to recover his paternal estate and live happily ever after. The plot is episodic, and the incidents follow one another with breathless haste. Though Smollett displays a comic relish of the coarseness of daily life (he shares

Fielding's fondness for emptying chamber pots over people), he lacks altogether Fielding's pervasive humanity and his joyful gusto. His pictures of the brutalities of life in London and at sea are, it is true, prompted by moral indignation, but there is a masochistic note in this catalogue of beatings, diseases, betrayals, and hoaxes. And the art is a surface one; there is no subtlety or complexity either of moral and psychological patterning or of structure.

Smollett acknowledges his debt to *Gil Blas* in his preface to *Roderick Random* and then goes on to explain his purpose:

> I have attempted to represent modest merit struggling with every difficulty to which a friendless orphan is exposed from his own want of experience, as well as from the selfishness, envy, malice, and base indifference of mankind. To secure a favourable prepossession, I have allowed him the advantages of birth and education, which, in the series of his misfortunes, will, I hope, engage the ingenuous more warmly in his behalf; and, though I foresee that some people will be offended at the mean scenes in which he is involved, I persuade myself the judicious will not only perceive the necessity of describing those situations to which he must of course be confined, in his low estate, but also find entertainment in viewing those parts of life, where the humours and passions are undisguised by affectation, ceremony, or education, and the whimsical peculiarities of disposition appear as Nature has implanted them.

Smollett's preface to his third novel, *Ferdinand, Count Fathom* (1753) gives a more explicit statement of his view of the novel:

> A novel is a large, diffused picture, comprehending the characters of life, disposed in different groups, and exhibited in various attitudes, for the purposes of an uniform plan, and general occurrence, to which every individual figure is subservient. But this plan cannot be executed with propriety, probability, or success, without a principal personage to attract the attention, unite the incidents, unwind the clue of the labyrinth, and at last close the scene, by virtue of his own importance.

The labyrinth in Smollett is not however a genuine labyrinth, and the unwinding of the clue is nearly always a superficial matter stuck on at the end.

The Adventures of Peregrine Pickle (1751) is the longest and most rambling of Smollett's novels, told in the third person this time, and so losing some of the immediacy of *Roderick Random*. The speed and variety of the incidents, and the violence and coarseness of many of them, give the novel the characteristic Smollett color. The hero himself, a swashbuckling adventurer, is less sympathetic than Roderick, but Commodore Trunnion, a sympathetically drawn naval character (like the goodhearted Lieutenant Tom Bowling in

Roderick Random), has an important place in the history of the "old salt" as a humorous character type in English fiction. Bowling and Trunnion are almost Jonsonian "humours"—"The commodore and your worship," says a publican to Peregrine Pickle before Peregrine first meets the commodore, "will in a short time be hand and glove: he has a power of money, and spends it like a prince, that is, in his own way; for, to be sure, he is a little humoursome, as the saying is, and swears woundily, though I'll be sworn he means no more harm than a sucking babe." His conversation is mostly picturesque naval oaths: "Damn my heart and liver! 'tis a land lie, d'Ye see; and I will maintain it to be a lie, from the sprit-sail yard to the mizen-top-sail haulyards! Blood and thunder! . . . Damn my limbs! I have been a hard-working man, and served all offices on board, from cook's shifter to the command of a vessel. Here, you Tunley, there's the hand of a seaman, you dog." It is all very picturesque and vigorous, but the character behind this lively play of words is not fully developed.

The Adventures of Ferdinand, Count Fathom is the history of a scoundrel, something in the style of Fielding's *Jonathan Wild* and probably suggested by it (though Smollett abused and maligned Fielding viciously, and accused Fielding of stealing from him). The account of the adventures, devices, fortunes and misfortunes of villainy unrelieved by humor and done at times with a masochistic savagery has less interest today than any other of Smollett's novels. Smollett was determined to be "low," and in his opening chapter belligerently addressed his readers on the subject of lowness, pointing out that while they enjoy lowness in Ovid, Petronius, *Don Quixote, Gil Blas,* Swift, Pope, and Rabelais, yet if a modern writer ventures to be equally low they "will stop their noses, with all the signs of loathing and abhorrence, at a bare mention of the china chamber-pot." Those "who applaud Catullus, Juvenal, Persius, and Lucan, for their spirit in lashing the greatest names of antiquity" nevertheless "when a British satirist, of this generation, has courage enough to call in question the talents of a pseudo-patron in power, accuse him of insolence, rancour, and scurrility." Smollett s satire, both that introduced incidentally in his novels and that found in his many works of miscellaneous journalism, was violent, personal, and often outrageous; but he never understood why he was not hailed as a great satirist.

The major part of Smollett's literary life was taken up with journalistic enterprises of many kinds, from translating *Don Quixote* to editing the *Critical Review* and compiling a continuation of Hume's *History of England*. His interest in Cervantes led him to attempt an imitation: *The Adventures of Lancelot Greaves* (1761) brings a knight errant in armor to contemporary Britain; but Smollett was wholly incapable of the kind of irony we find in *Don Quixote*, and though there are some impressively realistic descriptive scenes the book fails to make proper literary capital out of its central situation.

Smollett's most popular and most attractive novel is his last, *Humphrey Clinker* (1771), written in relaxation in Italy, where he seemed to be recuperating from a variety of diseases and where he certainly was mellower in mood than during most of his life, before his sudden death in 1771. The form is still picaresque in that the principal characters are traveling through England and Scotland for most of the novel. But the principal figure, the outwardly crusty and misanthropic but really kindhearted and generous Matthew Bramble, is a middle-aged gentleman traveling for health and recreation with his selfish and vain spinster sister (on the lookout always for a husband), his nephew and niece, and his sister's maid. The novel is carried on by means of letters, and the characters are defined by their different reactions to the adventures they encounter during their travels. Into the mouth of Bramble (who is a Welshman), Smollett puts many of his own grumbling complaints about luxury, social pretension, lack of hygiene, and other matters. But though there are the usual coarse hoaxes and, especially in Bramble's letters, profusion of cloacal imagery, the tone is never bitter or malicious, as it often is in the earlier novels. Bramble emerges as a more and more attractive character, whose complaints are amusing—almost endearing—aspects of his character. When he complains about the noises, smells, infections, and social climbers of Bath, he is in amusing contrast to the raptures of his niece, who sees in the same scene only liveliness and gaiety. And the peevish selfishness of his sister cannot arouse in the reader any genuine moral indignation, because she is (in Bramble's words) such a "fantastical animal" that every scene in which she plays a part is turned into high comedy. This is indeed Smollett's only genuinely comic novel, yet it is comic in a special sense. The superficial plot—concerning the niece's love affair with a player who turns out in the end to be a gentleman in disguise and son of an old friend of Bramble's, and the picking up on the road of the impoverished and faithful stray, Humphrey Clinker, who turns out to be the illegitimate son of Bramble himself—is silly, sentimental, and extravagant, and the number of incidents of a similar kind which punctuate the action—long-lost sons suddenly returning to succor aged parents and similar recognitions and reconciliations—are equally absurd; but the real plot of the novel concerns the releasing in Bramble of his essential kindliness and charm as he moves north-

ward to the author's native Scotland. When Smollett gets his characters to his own native region, a note of pastoral peace emerges, and
from this point on a sense of men at work in their own communities,
carrying on fruitful and industrious lives in a smiling countryside,
pervades the novel. Smollett's Scottish patriotism led him to introduce into Bramble's letters from Scotland much information about
Scottish topography and economy in such a way as to produce an
eloquent defense of the country and the people against their detrac-
tors. But it is all part of the unfolding kindliness of Bramble's character. Stronger pleas for Scotland, her grievances against England,
statements of the wrongs she has suffered at the hands of England,
are put into the mouth of the eccentric Scottish lieutenant, Obadiah
Lismahago; such arguments may be shown as the products of a per-
verse desire to be paradoxical in opinion, yet (significantly), they
are unanswerable by Bramble, who has to confess himself impressed
by Lismahago's arguments. Various kinds of eccentric and "humorous" characters as well as a number of real historical persons appear
throughout the story. Part gallery of Jonsonian humors, part gazet-
teer, part sentimental romance, *Humphrey Clinker* is perhaps most
of all a novel of comic character and incident in which the characters
react to their environment and adventures, as well as to each other,
in such a way as to suggest both the varieties and contradictions of
human nature and the lines on which it may best achieve happiness.
The persons whose actions and experiences produce the story, form
a microcosm of human society, so that in the end the novel turns out
to be Smollett's recipe for man. The recipe is at bottom not unlike
Fielding's: the good heart is the most important thing. But it is not
everything: industry and good management are important too, and
Humphrey Clinker abounds in incidents and situations which show
how only the combination of goodness and prudence can produce a
satisfactory life.

Fielding's notion of the comic epic in prose had infused new blood
into the picaresque tradition in England, but Smollett did not follow
Fielding in this and, except for his last novel, was content to follow
the traditional picaresque mode and bring his hero's adventures to
an end when he had carried through as many adventures as his own
experience and invention enabled him to produce. But for both
writers, as indeed for all writers of stories hitherto, the narrative line
was important and events ordered in chronological order provided
the external framework and the formal structure of the work.

Laurence Sterne (1713–68) was an altogether more original figure.
His *Life and Opinions of Tristram Shandy,* published in nine volumes
between 1759 and 1767, revealed a wholly new concept of form in

fiction as well as a kind of sentimental comedy equally removed from
Fielding's comic epic and the didactic humors of *Humphrey Clinker*.
Told in the first person by a narrator whose personality and train of
association determine the tone and organization of the narrative (and
who is not born until near the end of the third volume), *Tristram
Shandy* is on the surface a rambling and eccentric patchwork of
anecdotes, digressions, reflections, jests, parodies, and dialogues
centering on the character and opinions of the narrator's father,
Walter Shandy, and those of his brother, the narrator's Uncle Toby,
with other characters and caricatures introduced to provide humorous or sentimental incidents. The punctuation consists largely of
dashes, and the book is interlarded with asterisks, blanks, and a
variety of typographical and other eccentricities including pages that
are solid black, entirely blank, or marbled. The chapters vary in
length from several pages to a single short sentence. The author's
own views are conveyed partly in his own person and partly in the
person of Yorick, a sentimental and jesting person. There are passages of extreme sentimentality, in Sterne's own sense of that term:
for Sterne, to be sentimental was to be self-consciously responsive
to the slightest emotional stimulus, to relish every sensation and feeling. This self-conscious responsiveness was both comic and moral.
It made its possessor both sympathetic with the feelings of others
and so helped to make him charitable and affectionate, and at the
same time led to awareness of the ludicrous and promoted genial
laughter at the idiosyncrasies and private fantasies of individuals.
Sterne's treatment of idiosyncrasy is more than humorous in the
Jonsonian sense. He had learned from John Locke, his favorite
philosopher, that the consciousness of every individual is conditioned
by his private train of association; thus every man in a sense lives in
a world of his own, with his own "hobby horse" (as Sterne called a
private obsession) in the light of which he interprets (or misinterprets) the actions and conversations which other people's hobby
horses have led them to engage in. Every man is the prisoner of his
private inner world, which in turn is the product of his own "association of ideas which have no connection in nature." It is only by a
conscious exertion of fellow-feeling that one man can make contact
with another. Walter Shandy's main obsession (he has several) is his
theory of names, and Uncle Toby's is the theory and practice of
fortification and siege warfare; when Walter harangues Toby about
his pet theory Toby misinterprets him and imagines he is talking
about the theory of fortification, and in the same way Walter misunderstands Toby. Only the rush of affection can bridge the gulf that
lies between individual consciousnesses. One might almost say that

for Sterne one must be sentimental to escape from the prison of the private self.

The superficial evidence of chaos in the style and organization of *Tristram Shandy* is wholly misleading. Sterne knew what he was doing in his multiple digressions and inset anecdotes and tales. He deliberately eschews chronological order, partly because he knows that the past exists in present consciousness and colors and conditions it (we *are* our memories) and partly because he realizes that time as marked off by experiencing man is not the same as time as ticked off by the clock—a short clock-time can seem, and *be,* much longer in experience than a much longer clock-time. He has the chronology of his story firmly fixed in his mind; he is writing long after the events he is presenting took place, when some of the main characters are dead, so that he can occasionally leap forward to the present and see his story as history and at times stay with the moment whose events he is describing. A firm skeleton of dates lies underneath the author's jumping about in time. Uncle Toby's death is described in volume six, but he is alive at the end of volume nine, as is Yorick, who has the last word in the novel, yet who at several earlier points in the book is looked back on as long dead. The author's whimsical, sentimental personality—at once moralist and clown, alternately tender and prurient—controls the whole story, and the digressions not only determine the comic and moral scope of the novel but also, because they are promised, produced, looked back on, in different parts of the book, help to keep the tone personal and even intimate. The suggestiveness, the appeals to the reader (often done very slyly, assuming that the reader is a woman at some moments and at others addressing him as a man), the asterisks and blanks for the reader to interpret and fill up as he wishes, also help to implicate the reader in the novel. The reader is made a conspirator with the writer in producing the work.

The society in provincial England created by Sterne in *Tristram Shandy* consists largely of the inhabitants of Shandy Hall and certain neighbors; it is, however, sufficiently lively, varied, and representative to stand as a microcosm of human society as a whole. Sterne vents some private dislikes and prejudices throughout the novel, notably in the ludicrous character of Dr. Slop, the man-midwife, but there is nothing of Smollett's violent malice in these attacks. Everything is subdued to the comic–sentimental–moral picture of individuals in their oddities, obsessions, and fundamental loneliness teasing, misunderstanding, ignoring, amusing, or loving each other. There is also throughout the book a pervasive sense of human inadequacy. Walter Shandy begets the hero with a certain amount of difficulty:

he is already a middle-aged man who is worried by thoughts of impotence. His plans for his child (based on his own obsessive theories about names, about the importance of long noses, and other eccentric ideas) go ludicrously astray. He is never understood .and rarely understands any one else. His wife goes quietly about her business without ever responding to his frequent pedantic arguments, for she never knows what he is talking about. Yorick, the jesting sentimentalist, is misunderstood and ill used. Only Uncle Toby and his man Trim, simpletons both, enjoy (for the most part) living in their private world; their gentle emotional natures cannot understand evil and deceit, and they alone in the book never realize that they are prisoners of their private consciousnesses.

Tristram Shandy is packed with humorous pedantry and mock-pedantry. Nothing more readily illustrates the idiosyncrasies of the human mind than the obsessive love of scholars for their own theories. Walter Shandy is himself an eccentric pedant, and in his conversation Sterne can both parody the solemn disputations of scholars and create his favorite kind of comic moral dilemma. Sterne learned from Rabelais, Cervantes, Burton's *Anatomy of Melancholy*, Swift, and numerous obscure minor works of learning he found in the extraordinary library of his friend John Hall-Stevenson, and he puts his remarkable fragments of erudition together with all sorts of extravagant, fantastic, and sometimes simply nonsensical elements to achieve a chorus of parodied pedantry which sometimes swells out into a full-scale mock-treatise and at other times recedes to a muttering reference or two. Throughout the book he treats sex as both ridiculous and a little sad. He has been often attacked for his prurience and for his mingling of sentimental idealism with low sexual innuendo. But the combination belongs to the essence of his art and his attitude. Man is absurd, and nothing about him is more absurd than his sexual behavior. The novel opens with Mrs. Shandy inquiring of her husband, at the very moment when Tristram is about to be procreated, whether he had remembered to wind the clock. Mr. Shandy had been accustomed to wind the clock the first Sunday night of the month "and being somewhere between fifty and sixty years of age, at the time I have been speaking of,—he had likewise gradually brought some other little family concernments to the same period, in order, as he would often say to my uncle Toby, to get them all out of the way at one time, and be no more plagued and pestered with them the rest of the month." The two activities are thus associated in Mrs. Shandy's mind, even though as it happened this particular occasion, her husband having been away from home, was during the second week of the month. But the association had been set up, hence the question asked at such an unseasonable moment. Now this serves to make sex ludicrous, but not at all (as with Swift) disgusting. Dirty jokes are thus jokes at the expense of human absurdity. They are never obscene in the proper sense of the term, nor are they cruel. They are part of the comic sadness of the human situation.

The sentimentality sometimes rises to heights which offend the modern reader: anecdotes and inset stories of people of the most tender sensibilities weeping in each others' arms are not as popular now as they once were. But this element in *Tristram Shandy* (generally associated with Uncle Toby and Trim) is bound up both with its comic and its moral elements. Uncle Toby gently releasing a fly out of the window because he does not want to hurt the creature illustrates the comic simplicity of his character and at the same time presents the moral that kindness both to his fellow men and to other creatures is man's only way of escaping from the prison of self to become a member of God's creation. That Uncle Toby is a retired soldier who spends all his time building models of fortifications and conducting mock sieges makes his tenderheartedness comic in a special way: Uncle Toby would never have thought of applying his pacific principles to a consideration of war, because war as a theoretical art was his private obsession. The paradox helps to illustrate the nature of all human obsession; but it does not make Uncle Toby a hypocrite: his eloquent speech in defense of the military profession is wholly sincere—it omits, however, most of the really relevant considerations.

"Writing, when properly managed (as you may be sure I think mine is), is but a different name for conversation." This is one of many remarks which Sterne makes to the reader about his method of writing in the course of the novel. The tone of informal conversation or anecdote is sustained throughout the book. The author's personality pervades all, and the multifarious elements which make up this fantastic novel combine into a unity as a result. Sterne thus contrived to create a quite new kind of novelistic form, and gave the novel a kind of freedom it had never previously enjoyed and which novelists were not to take advantage of again until the twentieth century. He is in many ways—in his attitude to time, to the individual consciousness, his use of shifts in perspective—the most modern of eighteenth-century novelists. But the lesson he learned from Locke about human loneliness and the relativity of time was not what other men of his century learned from that philosopher. For other eighteenth- and nineteenth-century novelists, reality remained public and socially recognizable. It was left for twentieth-century novelists, learning from their own philosophers and psychologists lessons similar to that which Sterne had learned from Locke, to develop the novel further along the lines that Sterne had indicated.

In *A Sentimental Journey through France and Italy* (1768) Sterne tried to placate those who complained of his mixing bawdiness with moral feeling in *Tristram Shandy*. Here he is essentially the man of feeling, writing a quite new kind of travel book in which he describes not famous buildings and picturesque scenes but intimate glimpses in the character and emotions of people he happens to meet. It has none of the exuberance, variety, and trickery of *Tristram Shandy*, being both much shorter and in the same key throughout. The humor is still here, but it is mixed more gently with the sentimentality, and even when the author is thrown into comic predicaments with relation to a young lady (as in the concluding scene, when he has to share the one available bedroom in an inn with a Piedmontese lady and finds himself in the end accidentally holding hands with the lady's *fille de chambre*), the sigh of feeling is always heard. The famous account of the poor man lamenting his dead ass is a studied exhibition of the kind of feeling for which the book implicitly pleads and which its whole tenor illustrates. Yet the narrative moves with speed and is full of surprises. The style, proliferating with dashes, is essentially that of *Tristram Shandy*, and the pauses, turns, interruptions, and sudden developments in the action, while not as elaborate or extravagant as in the earlier novel, still maintain continuous interest and help to establish that intimate relationship between writer and reader that was so important to Sterne. The exhibitionist exploitation of the author's own generosity and charity is more in evidence in *A Sentimental Journey* than in *Tristram Shandy*, for now he is determined to vindicate his character. Yet there is humorous self-deprecation as well, which counterbalances the exhibitionism.

"Feeling" in *A Sentimental Journey* means something more than the expression of one's own emotions and sensibilities. It is essentially *Einfühlung*, the ability to feel oneself into someone else's situation and to be moved by the emotions of others—indeed, sometimes to feel others' emotions more strongly than they do themselves. It is morally good because it is bound up with generosity and Christian charity. Smollett, in his *Travels Through France and Italy* (1766), had vividly expressed his own feelings, but they were feelings of exacerbation and anger, altogether different from Sterne's state of mind. Sterne refers to Smollett's travel book in his own:

The learned Smelfungus travelled from Boulogne to Paris—from Paris to Rome—and so on—but he set out with the spleen and jaundice, and every object he passed by was discoloured or distorted—He wrote an account of them, but 'twas nothing but the account of his miserable feelings. . . .

I popp'd upon Smelfungus again at Turin, in his return, and a sad tale of sorrowful adventures he had to tell, . . .—he had been flea'd alive, and be-devilled, and used worse than St. Bartholomew, at every stage he had come at—

—I'll tell it, cried Smelfungus, to the world. You had better tell it, said I, to your physician.

Tristram Shandy was followed by many imitations, none of which showed anything like the genius of the original. There were at the same time other manifestations of the cult of feeling in fiction. Be-lief in a moral sense, professed by some of the most important eighteenth-century philosophers, is not far removed from the view that virtue is related to sensibility. Thus sentimentality—the deliber-ate cultivation of tender feelings and the venting of emotion on even the slightest object—had a certain philosophical foundation. Fielding's belief in the Good Heart and in generosity as the highest of the virtues is in a sense sentimental, or related to sentimentality; Parson Adams, Squire Allworthy, Uncle Toby, are all in their differ-ent ways sentimental characters. So is the hero of Oliver Goldsmith's *The Vicar of Wakefield* (1766), a deliberately simple-minded novel, done with quiet grace of style, about innocence and worldliness. Dr. Primrose, the vicar of Wakefield, a man who combines learning with innocence and whose greatest happiness is found by the domestic hearth with his wife and children, is led by the activities of the worldly and the vicious (as well as by a number of accidents) from one misfortune to another. His fortune is lost, his elder daughter is apparently seduced and "ruined" by the local squire, he is cheated, put upon, deceived in numerous ways until he finds himself in the county jail with his eldest daughter apparently dead and his eldest son a fellow prisoner accused of severely injuring a man in a duel. To all these misfortunes the worthy vicar responds (except for an oc-casional outbreak of cursing of the villains who are responsible, which he at once repents) with gentle resignation and the fortitude of "one whose chief stores of comfort are drawn from futurity." But by rapid and implausible contrivance the novel is huddled at last to a happy ending; the lost fortune is restored, the ruined daughter is found to be alive and really married to the squire after all (though the squire is still a villain, and Goldsmith shows no qualms about this kind of happy solution), the younger daughter marries a wealthy baronet, and the eldest son marries his moneyed first love after hav-ing lost her for the better part of the book. "I had nothing now on this side of the grave to wish for; all my cares were over, my pleasure was unspeakable." There is a folk element in this simple tale of extreme misfortune followed (as in the Book of Job) by rapid restitution. But in spite of the deliberate naïveties of the story, the moralizings, sentimentalities, and exhibitions of feeling, there is real art in the way the tale is told in the first person and in the slight but effective differentiations in character between the various members of the vicar's family. The mild worldliness of Mrs. Primrose and the elder daughter is drawn with some humor, and the vicar's differences of opinion with his wife over matters of dress and social ambition are gently comic. But it is all rather pallid, with none of the comic gusto of Fielding or the virtuosity of Sterne—nor the complex and dexterous ironies of Jane Austen. Mrs. Primrose is a far cry from Mrs. Bennet of *Pride and Prejudice*—Jane Austen had a much deeper insight into the nature and behavior of motherly worldliness on behalf of a daughter than Goldsmith ever had—but there is a very faint family resemblance.

The cult of feeling in England was immensely strengthened by the influence of Rousseau, whose novel *Julie, ou la nouvelle Héloïse* (1761) is a story of two young lovers who follow the promptings of the heart, love each other because of the response of her lively sensibility to his tenderness of feeling (and vice versa), and suffer because they are too tenderhearted. Sentiment rather than reason guides the hero and heroine, and if it brings about an unhappy ending—well, as Julie puts it, "C'est dans mon trop sensible coeur qu'est la source de tous les maux et de mon corps et de mon âme." *La nouvelle Héloïse* is the classic novel of sentimentalism of Europe, and the *Contes moraux* of Jean François Marmontel developed the tradition of the sentimental novel in France with stories of the redemptive effects of association with a man of feeling, of life in the country led according to "Nature," of innocence and simplicity, and such tales as that of a beautiful country maid with a noble and dignified old father wronged by a thoughtless gallant and at last restored to honor and happiness by the conversion, through the influence of innocence and natural nobility, of the villain. The most single-minded practitioner of the cult of feeling in Britain was the Scottish writer Henry Mackenzie (1745–1831), whose novel *The Man of Feeling* (1771) is the purest example of its kind. The hero, Harley, whose story is told in a series of scattered papers supposed to have been recovered by accident, is a professional man of feeling, tenderhearted, innocent, inclined to melancholy, and wholly gullible. His attempts to make his way in the world naturally fail, for success in the arts of self-advancement belongs only to the worldly and the hardhearted. In the course of his adventures he visits a madhouse and meets there a young lady whose wits have been turned by misfortune in love (Sterne had introduced such a lady, and an interest in madness is one of the marks of the sentimental novel), befriends an unfortunate prostitute and hears her unhappy story, meets and hears the affecting adventures of Old Edwards, who had offered himself to the press gang in place of his son and has just returned from India, falls in love with an heiress but is too timid to declare himself, and finally dies while still a young man, after telling a friend that "this world . . . was a scene in which I never much delighted. I was not formed for the bustle of the busy, nor the dissipation of the gay: . . . I leave it to enter on that state, which I have learned to believe, is replete with the genuine happiness attendant upon virtue." On his death-bed he declares his love for the heiress, who reciprocates. The narrator concludes: "I sometimes visit his grave; I sit in the hollow of the tree. It is worth a thousand homilies; every noble feeling rises within me! every beat of my heart awakens a virtue!—but it will make you hate the world—No: there is such an air of gentleness around, that I can hate nothing; but, as to the world —I pity the men of it." There is much of Sterne in this, as there is throughout the book, together with an occasional incident from Smollett and echoes of Rousseau and Marmontel. *The Man of Feeling* is written to a formula to appeal to a particular taste. It is in many ways an absurd novel; but it is important in the history of sentimentalism in English literature. Mackenzie's next novel, *The Man of the World* (1773), is similarly sentimental and moral and uses many of the stock properties of the sentimental tradition. His third and last, *Julia de Roubigné* (1777), is the most elaborately contrived, "memoirs of sentiment and suffering" in the form of an epistolary novel in which a virtuous girl, in love with a man of feeling, marries another for wholly virtuous reasons who murders her as a result of a series of misunderstandings before committing suicide. These novels were highly popular in their day, and had a host of imitators. Titles such as *The Tears of Sensibility, The Orphan Swains, The Benevolent Man, or the History of Mr. Belville, The Tender Father, Julia Benson, or The Sufferings of Innocence, Edwin and Julia, The Delicate Objection or Sentimental Scruple,* abound in the fiction lists of the 1770's.

This kind of novel is quite different from the sort of thing Dr. Johnson produced in *Rasselas* (1759), a didactic tale with a Middle Eastern setting in which the principal characters search for happiness, under the guidance of a sage, only to find in the end that "human life is everywhere a state, in which much is to be endured, and little to be enjoyed." Gravely probing the sources of human discontents and coming sometimes almost to the brink of despair, *Rasselas* is a philosophical fable about the conditions of human life and the proper activities of man told with a somber disillusionment which is never melodramatic and never sentimental; the tone is much more the realistic pessimism of *Ecclesiastes* than the sentimental moralizing of the novelists of the 1770's.

Growing interest in the "Gothic" and in the possibilities for emotional excitement provided by the ages of superstition and romance, which we have noted in the account of the poetry of this period, also affected the novel, though in a superficial way. The "Gothic novel" is the product of a dilettante interest in the potentialities of the Middle Ages for picturesque horror. Horace Walpole (1717–97) was an irrepressible dabbler in the medieval, as his fake Gothic house at Strawberry Hill testifies. His novel *The Castle of Otranto* (significantly subtitled, *a Gothic Story: translated by William Marshal, Gent., from the original Italian of Onuphrio Muralto, Canon of the Church of St. Nicholas at Otranto*), published in 1765, was a piece of nonsense which founded a new kind of fiction, the Gothic novel or novel of terror. It professed to be taken from a book printed in black letter in Naples in 1529 and referring to events of the twelfth or thirteenth century. In his preface to the second edition Walpole talked of his "attempt to blend the two kinds of Romance, the ancient and the modern. In the former, all was imagination and improbability: in the latter, nature is always intended to be, and sometimes has been, copied with success." But in fact the whole thing is pure, if ingenious, tushery, beginning with the enormous magic helmet, shaded with black feathers, which slays young Prince Conrad on his wedding day, introducing a little further on a portrait which steps out of its frame and descends to the floor "with a grave and melancholy air," and continuing in melodramatic starts to tell a story of a usurping tyrant, his dead son's fiancée (whom the tyrant wants to marry), with mysterious strangers, holy men, visiting knights, engaged in a general emotional turmoil, egged on at critical moments by various supernatural manifestations, until finally the usurping Prince of Otranto, having murdered his daughter in the belief that she was someone else, reveals his usurpation and retires to a monastery leaving his princedom to the newly revealed legitimate heir. There are moments in the story that are meant to be Shakespearean—the conversation of domestics, the confrontation of a Hamlet-like ghost—but, though Walpole professed to have followed "that great master of nature, Shakespeare," they are not Shakespearean at all.

The fact is that Horace Walpole's literary imagination was unable to come to terms with the medley of Gothic and other material he had assembled; but the assemblage of the material was important in the history of English literature, for it helped to found a tradition which was later to run in more fruitful channels—the medievalism of Keats' "Eve of St. Agnes," for example. In the early nineteenth century *The Castle of Otranto* was overvalued for a variety of reasons; Byron talked of it with the highest respect, and Scott spoke of "the applause due to chastity and precision of style, to a happy combination of supernatural agency with human interest, to a tone of feudal manners and language, sustained by characters strongly drawn and well discriminated"—which only shows how Walpole's fake medievalism had imposed on the later novelist and indeed helped to lead his imagination astray, for Scott's medieval novels are his least good and he is at his best in dealing with the recent past of his own country.

There were many imitations of *The Castle of Otranto*, many of them by women who combined Gothic sensationalism with the cult of feeling. Clara Reeve's *The Champion of Virtue, a Gothic Story* (1777; in the second edition the novel was entitled *The Old English Baron*), Charlotte Smith's *Emmeline, or the Orphan of the Castle* (1788), Sophia Lee's *The Recess* (1785) are some of the many novels which this fashion produced. William Beckford's fantastic oriental romance, *Vathek* (1786), originally written in French, is not really in the Gothic tradition, though it has points of resemblance with some Gothic novels. It is more exotic and more original. Its oriental setting enables Beckford to indulge an imagination sometimes fantastic, sometimes magnificent, sometimes humorous; he can raise exaggeration to the level of epic extravaganza. The oriental tale was common enough in the eighteenth century (even Johnson sets his *Rasselas* in Abyssinia), but only Beckford was able to use the remoteness of the setting as a justification for a new kind of probability in fiction: in *Vathek* he created and inhabited a world of ideal fantasy. The work had little real influence: it took a highly individual kind of imagination to use his materials as Beckford did.

The most successful practitioner of the Gothic novel was Mrs. Anne Radcliffe (1764–1823); her novels, while historically inaccurate and psychologically crude, have a certain verve in their employment of standard Gothic properties—secret passages, vaults, sliding panels, old moldering manuscripts unexpectedly discovered, all the tricks so happily laughed at by Jane Austen in *Northanger Abbey*. Her supernatural incidents are all explained away in the end as produced by natural causes, but not before she has extracted the maximum of suspense and excitement from them. Her characters are men—and women—of feeling, and her combination of generosity of feeling and romantic misanthropy in male characters represents an early manifestation of the Byronic hero. Her most popular novels were *The Mysteries of Udolpho* (1794), set in late sixteenth-century France and Italy but really acted out in a generalized distant time and place, and *The Italian* (1797), dealing with a diabolical monk at the time of the Inquisition.

Mrs. Radcliffe's caution in handling the supernatural is not followed by the writers who brought the Gothic novel or novel of terror to its highest pitch. These are Matthew Gregory Lewis (1775–1818), whose novel *The Monk* (1796) draws both on Radcliffian properties and on new romantic horror material from Germany and reaches extreme heights of sensationalist terror, and Charles Robert Maturin (1782–1824), whose *Melmoth the Wanderer* (1820) is the richest of all English terror novels in its combination of the usual Gothic apparatus with a psychological sense of evil and a power of suggestion that earlier practitioners of the genre lacked. Maturin is especially effective in his handling of the emotion of fear; in another of his novels, *The Fatal Revenge* (1807), he expressed his intention of founding "the interest of a romance on the passion of supernatural fear, and on that almost alone." In his handling of nameless fear he sometimes suggests to the modern reader Edgar Allan Poe, who, like many other nineteenth-century poets and novelists, admired him. But, though the terror novel can in its most sophisticated form generate considerable power and even subtlety, it remains in itself a crude form of fiction, requiring careful blending with and subordination to other elements if it is to reach the level of mature art. Mere sensationalism, however, can always count on a certain amount of popularity, and this form of fiction has never wholly died out.

If women took an active part in producing the novel of terror, they were even more active in producing a kind of novel at the other end of the emotional scale, the novel of contemporary social and domestic life in which the chief interest is the delineation of manners and the detail and intimacy with which the behavior of characters in a specific and limited social environment is described. Fanny Burney (1752–1840) had a notable success in this kind of novel with her *Evelina; or, The History of a Young Lady's Entrance into the World* (1778). *Evelina* is the story of a girl of humble education entering the world of fashion, and suffering a variety of frustrations and humiliations there before she finds her inevitable happy ending. Such a plot gives the author an opportunity for satirical observation of character and social pretension and for showing all the little fopperies, hypocrisies, snobberies, and cruelties which govern the behavior of men and women in the world. There is nothing here of the comic epic of *Tom Jones:* society is observed more intimately and more closely and the author's sense of the petty rebuffs and stings suffered by the heroine is far from comic. There is irony but not aloofness in the picture of the defects of society. There is no exaggeration or burlesque, but a careful and *committed* rendering of contemporary social behavior. In its unpretentious way, *Evelina* is a considerable achievement, a "novel of manners" firmly and brightly done. *Cecilia* (1782) is more pretentious and less impressive: the scene is crowded with characters many of whom are mere caricatures, and the conflict between passion and convention (a theme of the sentimental novel) somewhat mechanically handled in a mass of not fully integrated material.

Maria Edgeworth (1767–1849) wrote of the Irish social scene and was one of the first to treat Irish character seriously and not in the tradition of comic caricature. Though most of her novels were written with a frank didactic purpose, her best display a lively awareness of the realities of Irish social conditions and the moral and psychological problems arising out of an impinging on them. *Castle Rackrent* (1800) gives a vivid picture of the decayed Irish gentry, done with sufficient particularizing detail to make it something more than animated social history and sufficient humor and sense of character to enlist the sympathetic participation of the reader. It was Miss Edgeworth's rendering of the Irish scene that inspired Walter Scott to try to do the same for Scotland. In his General Preface to the Waverley Novels (1829), Scott recalled that he was led to remember and take up again the original fragment of *Waverley* by "the extended and well-merited fame of Miss Edgeworth, whose Irish characters have gone so far to make the English familiar with the character of their gay and kind-hearted neighbours of Ireland," and he went on to talk of her "rich humour, pathetic tenderness, and admirable tact," adding that "I felt that something might be attempted for my own country, of the same kind with that which Miss Edgeworth so fortunately achieved for Ireland." The modern reader is not likely to agree with Scott's very high estimate of Miss Edgeworth's work, but he would do well to remember, in considering Scott's own achievement, that he began partly under her influence as a novelist of manners of his own country.

The greatest of all the novelists of manners of this or any other period, and one who raised the whole genre to a new level of art, was Jane Austen (1775–1817). With no exhibitionist critical apparatus, such as Fielding's theory of the comic epic, no pretentiously announced moral purpose such as Richardson kept repeating, and indeed with no apparent awareness that she was doing more than essaying some novels in an established social mode, this unpretentious daughter of a Hampshire rector, with her quietly penetrating vision of man as a social animal, her ironic awareness of the tensions between spontaneity and convention and between the claims of personal morality and those of social and economic propriety, her polished and controlled wit, and beneath all her steady moral apprehension of the nature of human relationships, produced some of the greatest novels in English. She had begun writing at an early age, though only for the family circle. She produced as a youngster a history of England "by a Partial, Prejudiced, and Ignorant Historian," which is full of exuberant wit and burlesque. She also wrote stories in which she parodied, with ebullient humor and a fine sense of caricature, some of the literary fashions of the day. Her life, lived as it was amid English country society of neither the lowest nor the highest stratum, provided her with the opportunity of learning by heart the world of social pretension and ambition, of balls and visits and speculations about marrying and giving in marriage, of the hopes and fears of genteel people of moderate means—a world which, through her delicate and highly finished art, she turned into a microcosm of life in its social aspect.

In the daily routine of visits, shopping, sewing, gossip, and other trivial matters which are recorded with an easy liveliness in her letters, she found the raw material of her novels. The world which her books present to us is essentially an eighteenth-century world in its habits, tastes, and appearance. Jane Austen wrote just before the Industrial Revolution changed for the worse so much of the face of England, and the clean stillness of her country towns, the unspoiled beauty of her countryside with its well-kept estates and cheerful farms, provide a perfect background to her finely etched pictures of social life. There is a luminous clarity about her style as well as about the scenes she portrays. She was describing, though she did not know it, the last generation of Englishmen and Englishwomen who could face life as they faced a minuet, with cheerfulness, decorum, and determination to go through the appropriate motions with grace, elegance—and enjoyment. This is neither romanticism nor sentimentality, but shows a remarkable insight into the relation between social convention and individual temperament.

It has often been remarked that, although the Napoleonic Wars were going on throughout Jane Austen's writing career, she keeps mention of them out of her novels, in which soldiers appear only as attractions for the girls or in some similar social capacity. This is a tribute not to her narrowness but to the calm accuracy with which she saw her subject. In the days when wars were fought by small professional armies the impact of the fighting on the daily life of people living in small country towns was negligible, and it would have been unrealistic as well as artistically inappropriate for Jane Austen to have expanded her horizon to include discussion of world affairs which were not relevant to the situations she was presenting. She worked deftly and wittily, with a fine pen, and restricted her scope deliberately because her intention was microcosmic—to create a world in little, perfectly proportioned and shown in the liveliest detail, and an accurate model of the total social world of which this was only a small part.

The chronology of Jane Austen's works is somewhat obscure, for many of the novels were revised for publication a considerable time after they were first written, and it is often impossible to tell how much rewriting was involved in the revision. *Pride and Prejudice,* the second of her novels to appear, in 1813, was a rewriting of the early *First Impressions,* finished in 1797. After the rejection by the publisher of *First Impressions,* Jane Austen returned to a still earlier work, *Elinor and Marianne,* and rewrote it as *Sense and Sensibility,* the first of her works to be published, in 1811. *Northanger Abbey,* first published posthumously (together with *Persuasion* in 1818), was originally written in 1797 and 1798, and finally finished in 1803. It is thus the first written of all her published novels apart from juvenile works and fragments not published until long after her death.

Northanger Abbey is the unpretentious story of a rather ordinary girl, goodhearted and rather simple, who spends some weeks in Bath with a middle-aged couple who are friends of her family, and makes various friends and acquaintances there, including a girl whom at first she becomes very friendly with and who becomes engaged to her brother but whom she later discovers to be an unscrupulous careerist who breaks off the engagement when something better comes in sight. She also meets in Bath Henry Tilney and his sister. The former is a rich and intellectually superior young man who is attracted by the heroine's simple goodheartedness; the latter becomes the heroine's good friend. The heroine falls in love with Henry, whose father invites her to the family home, under the impression that she is a wealthy heiress who would be a good match for his son. The home is an old abbey (though with new, modern buildings), and the heroine expects to find there the atmosphere and even some of the adventures which she had learned from Mrs. Radcliffe's novels (of which she is an addict) to associate with old abbeys. She misconstrues some very ordinary circumstances as part of a Radcliffian situation and is temporarily humiliated. Henry's father, discovering that she is not an heiress after all, rudely terminates her visit, but in the end he is brought round and the hero and heroine finally marry.

The plot thus summarized sounds dull enough, but the novel is far from dull, in spite of Jane Austen's deliberate refusal to use any of the more violent contemporary novelistic devices in order to enliven it. The life of the novel comes from the combination of wit and profound sense of the meaning and interest of the events of daily life in the social world she knew so well. The irony is sometimes a little crude in comparison with what Jane Austen showed she could do in later novels, but it is always carefully poised and well directed. The tone is not mock-heroic or burlesque; a note of affectionate understanding runs together with the irony. The romantic expectations of the heroine are shown as slightly ridiculous, but not in order to emphasize the drabness of her real life. The ordinariness of real life is really the more interesting. This is at the opposite extreme from *Madame Bovary*. Catherine's dream world is easily pushed aside by the greater interest of reality—choosing a dress, visiting a friend, even enjoying a meal. And her love, though it is not the passionate love of romantic novelists, is nonetheless sensitive and true. Jane Austen understood how young people come to fall in love; she realized exactly the degree to which Nature imitates Art and the varying parts played by admiration, gratitude, and vanity. If she never shows us her lovers alone, making passionate avowals, she does indicate very clearly that she knows their state of mind.

She was assured of his affection; and that heart in return was solicited, which, perhaps, they pretty equally knew was already entirely his own; for, though Henry was now sincerely attached to her, though he felt and delighted in all the excellencies of her character and truly loved her society, I must confess that his affection originated in nothing better than gratitude, or, in other words, that a persuasion of her partiality for him had been the only cause of giving her a serious thought.

It is perhaps a little crude of Jane Austen to add: "It is a new circumstance in romance, I acknowledge, and dreadfully derogatory of an heroine's dignity; but if it be as new in common life, the credit of a wild imagination will at least be all my own." More typical of the quietly amused irony that pervades the novel is the author's comment on the gap between what Mrs. Radcliffe's novels had led Catherine to expect at Northanger Abbey and what she actually found there:

Charming as were all Mrs. Radcliffe's works, and charming even as were the works of all her imitators, it was not in them perhaps that human nature, at least in the midland counties of England, was to be looked for. Of the Alps and Pyrenees, with their pine forests and their vices, they might give a faithful delineation; and Italy, Switzerland, and the South of France, might be as fruitful in horrors as they were there represented. Catherine dared not doubt beyond her own country, and even of that, if hard pressed, would have yielded the northern and western extremities.

Of the gap between passionate feeling and the dictates of prudence and common sense Jane Austen writes with characteristically quiet matter-of-factness from behind which the irony only occasionally looks out:

As they walked home again, Mrs. Morland endeavoured to impress on her daughter's mind the happiness of having such steady well-wishers as Mr. and Mrs. Allen, and the very little consideration which the neglect or unkindness of slight acquaintance like the Tilneys ought to have with her, while she could preserve the good opinion and affection of her earliest friends. There was a great deal of good sense in all this; but there are some situations of the human mind in which good sense contradicted almost every position her mother advanced. It was upon the behaviour of these very slight acquaintance that all her previous happiness depended; and while Mrs. Morland was successfully confirming her own opinions by the justness of her own representations, Catherine was silently reflecting that *now* Henry must have arrived at Northanger; *now* he must have heard of her departure; and *now*, perhaps, they were all setting off for Hereford.

Behind this kind of writing lies not only irony directed at the difference between the mother's complacent advice and the daughter's real feelings, also a profound sense of quotidian life, of the dailiness of daily living.

Sense and Sensibility is similarly directed, on the surface at least, against a fashionable taste, this time the enthusiasm for picturesque beauty and the self-indulgent cultivation of feeling discussed earlier in this chapter. Marianne, the heroine, a lover of the picturesque and a believer in sensibility, falls sentimentally but passionately in love with a young man who eventually, for complicated reasons, jilts her; and finally she discovers a more moderate and realistic happiness with a much older man whom she had previously regarded in any other light than that of lover. Her sister Elinor, who controls her feelings throughout with more decorum and a deeper sense of the privacy of personal emotion, wins her way through various difficulties to the man she loves, and in the process acts in some respects as a foil to her younger sister. The irony in the novel is

still restricted in its object, the characterization limited to the needs
of the plot and of the ironic intentions, and the plot itself rather
awkwardly contrived. But we do find that crystal precision of style,
the beautifully poised sentences and paragraphs, the calmly dexterous marshaling of dialogue and incident, that characterize the later
novels. The character of Elinor may be somewhat wooden, that of
her lover Edward Ferrars even more so, and Mrs. Ferrars a mere
necessary obstacle to the course of true love; but Marianne is drawn
with a fine combination of affectionate sympathy and gentle mockery, Mrs. Jennings is skilfully portrayed as the apparent vulgarian
whose good nature eventually emerges as more important than her
vulgarity, John Dashwood (the girls' stepbrother, whose unmali-
cious egotism precipitates the action of the novel) is a perfect picture of a not ill-disposed young man "unless to be rather cold-
hearted, and rather selfish, is to be ill-disposed," and the relations
of these characters with each other and with other characters in the
novel are manipulated with wit and dexterity.

There are few novelists in English who can achieve so much
meaning with a simple descriptive sentence: with a few brief strokes
Jane Austen can give the reader the sense of a solidly based *social*
world, a world in which the adjustment of personal relationships is
the most interesting and significant of problems, a world in which
individuals, however sensitive or introspective, belong in the first
instance to a community pattern, whose smallest important unit is
the family and whose largest is no larger than the circle of relatives,
friends, and acquaintances within which the individual moves. That
is, of course, the world in which most middle-class people do in fact
live, and it is pointless to criticize Jane Austen for the limitations
she imposes on herself. Hers is an art of delicacy, precision, and
shrewd, ironic insight; her talent was for the exploration of those
aspects of human emotion and behavior most closely associated with
the social and economic framework that looms so large in most
people's lives. If Marianne possesses a sensibility in excess of what
is demanded or justified by the kind of world she lives in and by
the facts of human nature manifested in that world, Miss Austen
arranges for life to educate her, gently but firmly. In fact, all of
Jane Austen's heroines are thus educated by life, and the firmness
with which she sees that education through is a tribute to the unsentimental realism at the core of her art. But if she is firm, she is
neither tragic nor melodramatic (though there is, if not a tragic
element, a sense of permanent loss and of finally being satisfied with the second-best in Marianne's story); she is, rather, an
affectionately ironic observer of the relations between society and

individual personality, who expects no more from human nature than what it has to offer, and who thoroughly enjoys it even when she is most ironical at its expense. Of perhaps no other English writer save Shakespeare can it be said that she would have hated to have human beings other than she found them.

Sense and Sensibility is not a satire, and Marianne, for all the delightful absurdity of some of her remarks, is neither despised nor chastised, but allowed to work out her salvation through the impact of social reality on her own sensibility. That impact, and what follows from it, is the novel's main theme.

There is less flexibility of style in *Sense and Sensibility*, and the dialogue is often more bookish than in the later novels. This is not always a defect; for this kind of novel, depending so much on the interplay of character with character through formal discourse, requires a certain deliberateness in the dialogue, and, further, Marianne's speaking by the book is part of Jane Austen's ironical treatment of the fashion of sensibility. The function of the dialogue can be illustrated by such a simple passage as this:

"I do not attempt to deny," said she, "that I think very highly of him—that I greatly esteem him, that I like him."
Marianne here burst forth with indignation—
"Esteem him! Like him! Cold-hearted Elinor! Oh! worse than cold hearted! Ashamed of being otherwise. Use those words again and I will leave the room this moment."

Or this:

"And how does dear, dear Norland look?" cried Marianne.
"Dear, dear Norland," said Elinor, "probably looks much as it always looks at this time of year. The woods and walks thickly covered with dead leaves."
"Oh!" cried Marianne, "with what transporting sensations have I formerly seen them fall! How have I delighted, as I walked, to see them driven in showers about me by the wind! What feelings have they, the season the air altogether inspired! Now there is no one to regard them. They are seen only as a nuisance, swept hastily off, and driven as much as possible from the sight."
"It is not every one," said Elinor, "who has your passion for dead leaves."
"No; my feelings are not often shared, not often understood. But *sometimes* they are."—As she said this, she sunk into a reverie for a few moments;—but rousing herself again, "Now, Edward," said she, calling his attention to the prospect, "here is Barton valley. Look up it, and be tranquil if you can. Look at those hills! Did you ever see their equals? To the left is Barton park, amongst those woods and plantations. You may see one end of the house. And there, beneath that farthest hill, which rises with such grandeur, is our cottage."
"It is a beautiful country," he replied; "but the bottoms must be dirty in winter."

"How can you think of dirt, with such objects before you?"

"Because," replied he, smiling, "among the rest of the objects before me, I see a very dirty lane."

Willoughby, the young man who jilts Marianne, bears more than a resemblance in name to Wickham of *Pride and Prejudice*: both are engaging scoundrels who represent a constant menace in the social world in which Jane Austen's heroines live. Genteel but moneyless young ladies who depend on their good looks to secure themselves a congenial marriage, which alone can guarantee economic and social security, must always beware of equally moneyless gallants who have nothing to offer but their gallantry. Mere gallantry, in Jane Austen's novels, generally accompanies cowardice, selfishness, and general lack of moral principle. Willoughby is perhaps more convincing as a charmer than as a villain, and least convincing of all as a repentant villain, but he is just the right character to captivate the lively and generous-hearted Marianne. Those who deny Jane Austen any insight into passion should study her description of Marianne in London: Marianne's anguished waiting for Willoughby to call on her can be compared without extravagance to the moving description in Chaucer's *Troilus and Criseyde* of Troilus waiting in vain at the walls of Troy for Criseyde's return.

Pride and Prejudice, by far the most popular of all Jane Austen's novels, requires no detailed description. Jane Austen said of it that it "is rather too light, and bright, and sparkling; it wants shade," and this is perhaps the reason for its popularity. The precision and vivacity of style carry the reader through the novel with ease and spirit; there is a sparkling life about the characters and a rain-washed freshness about the scenery which combine to make this the gayest of Jane Austen's novels, in spite of deeper overtones which emerge when Charlotte Lucas agrees to marry the egregious Mr. Collins or when Lydia is discovered to have run off with Wickham with no prospect of marriage. The speed and skill with which the author moves into the story are remarkable:

It is a truth universally acknowledged, that a single man in possession of a good fortune, must be in want of a wife.

However little known the feelings or views of such a man may be on his first entering a neighbourhood, this truth is so well fixed in the minds of the surrounding families, that he is considered as the rightful property of some one or other of their daughters.

"My dear Mr. Bennet," said his lady to him one day, "have you heard that Netherfield Park is let at last?"

And so we are away, in the midst of that brilliant opening dialogue in which the characters of both speakers so satisfactorily reveal themselves. The pace never falters, and even in that middle section of the book when Bingley and company have left the neighborhood apparently for good (a section corresponding to that part of *Sense and Sensibility* in which Marianne is awaiting the return of Willoughby) the plot continues to unfold with new and arresting developments, each arising naturally out of the preceding action and leading as naturally to the conclusion. Structurally, the novel shows the highest degree of craftsmanship. We begin with the Bennet family and their interest in the new tenant of Netherfield; Jane and Mr. Bingley, Elizabeth and Darcy, come together (helped by Jane's illness) and in the process produce the appropriate revelations of character from Miss Bingley and others. The appearance of Wickham, who first claims Elizabeth's attention, diversifies the picture and prepares the way for developments which are to be so necessary to the later working out of the plot. The ball at Netherfield helps to center the action and concentrates Elizabeth's dislike of Darcy as well as providing a clue to Wickham's true character by making it clear that he avoids the ball to escape confrontation with Darcy. Up till now the characters have circled round each other in an almost ballet movement: beautiful and kindhearted Jane, witty and high-spirited Elizabeth, charming Bingley, proud Darcy, gallant Wickham, scheming Miss Bingley, not to mention foolish and garrulous Mrs. Bennet and her self-defensively offensive husband. Each reveals his character in conversation, helped out by an occasional flashing forth by the author of a brief but pungent descriptive remark.

The problem posed in what might be called the first movement of the novel is the marrying off of the elder Bennet girls. They have beauty and intelligence, but (thanks to the entail so deplored by Mrs. Bennet) inconsiderable fortune. Mrs. Bennet's desire to have them married, though her expression of that desire reveals the defects of her character in a richly comic manner, is itself both natural and laudable; for girls of negligible fortune genteelly brought up must secure their man while they may, or face a precarious shabby-genteel spinsterhood with few opportunities of personal satisfaction or social esteem. The problem as originally posed has its comic side, but the arrival of Mr. Collins (though he himself is a highly comic figure) shows it in another light.

Mr. Collins is a kind of grotesque, who takes his place in the stately ballet of social life with fantastic *gaucherie*. By his proposal to Elizabeth (again, a richly comic incident in itself) he points up another side of the marriage-seeking business: economic security can be won at too great a cost. When Elizabeth's friend Charlotte Lucas accepts Mr. Collins, we are for the first time made fully aware of some of the ugly realities underlying the stately social ballet. It is a dance on the sunlit grass, but some of the dancers at least are in earnest, and if they do not secure a permanent partner before the end of the day they will be left alone for ever on the dark and deserted lawn, or forced to find refuge in the pathless woods which surround the trimly kept grass plot. Rather than face such a fate—rather, that is, than be left with no prospect of social or economic security in an age when few means of earning an independent livelihood were open to the daughters of gentlemen—Charlotte Lucas, an intelligent girl who enjoys the friendship of such a discriminating person as Elizabeth, marries the grotesque Mr. Collins. She knows it is her last chance, and she takes it deliberately, weighing her future husband's intolerable character against the security and social position he offers. Elizabeth is shocked, but Jane Austen takes some pains to let her readers know how hopeless the choice was, and how in fact Charlotte has chosen the lesser of two evils.

Elizabeth's visit to the Collinses after their marriage gives the author her opportunity of clarifying this aspect of marriage and showing how calmly and deliberately Charlotte makes a liveable way of life out of her situation—a scene in which Jane Austen shows her underlying compassionate awareness of the ordinariness of ordinary life that both sets off and in a way enriches her sharp irony. With skillful structural economy, she uses the same episode to reintroduce Darcy in connection with Mr. Collins' patroness, Lady Catherine de Bourgh. This reintroduction, which gives Darcy an opportunity to propose to Elizabeth and be refused, marks the turning point in the relationship of these two, for the refusal is followed by Darcy's letter of explanation about Wickham, so that from this point Darcy is in the ascendant and Wickham's stock is steadily falling. It also marks the movement of Darcy away from pride to a genuine awareness of values hitherto outside his class-bound scheme of things, and a similar movement in Elizabeth away from undue dependence on her own judgment and a greater concession to the social view. For these two originally represented the two extremes, each of which must be modified if happiness is to be achieved—the extreme of putting social position and obligation before private feeling and the extreme of depending entirely on individual judgment rather than on the public or social view. Happiness is achieved by the proper combination of character and fortune. Society is kept going by its members continually compromising between the individual impression and desire on the one hand and public tradition and duty on the other. And the basis of such a view, which underlies all Jane Austen's novels, is a clearly apprehended moral vision.

Elizabeth's visit to Derbyshire with the Gardiners is neatly contrived to bring Darcy into the picture again, and in a still more favorable light, but the interruption of the visit by news of Lydia's elopement with Wickham gives the plot an effective new twist. Wickham's past is itself so tied up with that of Darcy that instead of the elopement alienating Darcy from the Bennet family (as Elizabeth fears), it gives him the opportunity of showing his love for Elizabeth by using his influence to make Wickham marry Lydia. At the same time the episode of the elopement gives us once again a glimpse of the abyss that yawns for the indiscreet or unfortunate marriage-seeker. The lot of the "fallen woman" in this kind of society is indeed hopeless, and reckless or stupid playing of one's cards might, as it almost did with Lydia, lead one to that final degradation. It is significant that the shock of Lydia's behavior forces Mr. Bennet for once out of his mood of sardonic teasing into genuine suffering and self-reproach.

The tying up of the action, with the cunning use of Lady Catherine de Bourgh's offensive intrusion into Elizabeth's affairs to produce a result exactly the reverse of what she intended, could not be more neatly done. Elizabeth and Darcy have each discovered themselves and each other in their loss of pride and prejudice, while the other characters (who, unlike these two, achieve no real development) settle back into their accustomed modes of behavior, symbolized by Mr. Bennet's remarking, after giving his consent to Elizabeth's marriage with Darcy so soon after having done the same for Jane and Bingley: "If any young men come for Mary or Kitty, send them in, for I am quite at leisure." And, a little later on: " 'I admire all my sons-in-law highly,' said he. 'Wickham, perhaps, is my favorite; but I think I shall like *your* husband quite as well as Jane's.' "

The characters of Mr. and Mrs. Bennet illustrate clearly how Jane Austen could use comic characterization to reveal a marital situation which, if fully explored, would show its tragic aspects. Mr. Bennet had been captured by a pretty face, and the resulting marriage tied him to a foolish and vulgar woman for the rest of his life. Mrs. Bennet, in this genteel world where eligible marriages are young ladies' (and their mothers') chief objectives, had succeeded in her aim, using her good looks while she had them. The result was disastrous to Mr. Bennet's character: he was forced into an unnatural isolation from his family, into virtual retirement in his study and the cultivation of a bitter amusement at his wife's folly and vulgarity. He thus, as is made clear in the latter part of the novel, in some degree abdicated his role as husband and father, with Lydia's behavior one of the results. He is shocked into momentary self-reproach in talking to Elizabeth after Lydia's escapade, but he only really lifts the mask once, in discussing with Elizabeth her engagement to Darcy. "My child, let me not have the grief of seeing *you* unable to respect your partner in life."

In the gradual unfolding of the truth about Darcy's character in *Pride and Prejudice,* the revelation of his goodness to his tenants and in general of his playing the part of the landowner who understands the social duties that ownership implies (we see this in the housekeeper's talk to Elizabeth and her aunt and uncle at Pemberley) represents a crucial stage. Jane Austen had a strong sense of class duty and a contempt for any claims for superiority based merely on noble birth or social snobbery. Lady Catherine de Bourgh is a monstrous caricature of Darcy: she represents pride without intelligence, moral sense, or understanding of the obligations conferred by rank. Jane Austen of course accepts the class structure of English society as she knew it; but she accepts it as a type of human society, in which privilege implies duty. Her view of life is both moral and hierarchical. But it is far from snobbish, if by snobbery we mean the admiration of rank or social position as such.

A more complex novel, and one in which there is more light and shade, is *Mansfield Park* (1814), in which the heroine, instead of being the vivacious and witty Elizabeth Bennet, is the kind and humble Fanny Price, brought up as a poor relation among her rich cousins. Fanny is the most passive of all Jane Austen's heroines, and the novel is one in which wit appears in the end to be entirely on the side of evil (unlike *Pride and Prejudice,* where real wit and virtue go together, at least so far as the principal characters are concerned). The wit of *Mansfield Park* is, however, in the texture of the narrative rather than in the dialogue of hero and heroine. Further, though in terms of the plot the heroine is passive, in that the decisive actions are all taken by others and her fate seems to depend on what others do, in terms of the moral pattern of the novel she is the most active. Her opinions, attitudes, reactions, provide the moral norms throughout the book, and though Fanny is not a saint or a martyr she is the most morally strong character in all Jane Austen's novels, in spite of her timidity, shyness, and lack of social brilliance. Her refusal to marry the charming Henry Crawford, who has captivated everyone else in the book, and her maintenance of this refusal in spite of well-meant pressure from those she esteems, is a negative action, but a decisive one in the working out of the whole pattern of the novel. True virtue is tolerant and gentle in behavior but utterly firm in moral decision, and sympathy rather than ironic wit is its deepest characteristic. Wit itself appears in *Mansfield Park* as morally neutral; it can operate on the side of evil as well as of good, and is one of the ways in which evil can disguise itself.

Mansfield Park employs a simple Cinderella theme and gives it new dimensions by the subtlety and complexity of its working out. Fanny is not ill-treated by her uncle and aunt, Sir Thomas and Lady Bertram, and if her cousins Maria and Julia assume that she, as a poor relation, is both socially and intellectually below them, that assumption does not cause her real suffering. Even the petty spitefulness of her Aunt Norris (one of the most brilliant portrayals of mean-spirited selfishness in English literature) is only allowed to cause Fanny minor irritation, and that is more than made up for by the understanding affection of her cousin Edmund. Sir Thomas is a good man with a lack of sympathetic imagination who tries to cover up this deficiency by pomposity of manner. We see him sometimes as a solemn bore and at other times—especially later in the novel—as a rather pathetic character whose well-meaning attempts to act the part of the dignified head of the family make him sometimes faintly ridiculous and sometimes almost tragically out of touch with reality. His behavior on his unexpected return from Antigua to find his family engaged in amateur theatricals is quite admirable—firm, just, and quite unvindictive. The modern reader who cannot see why on earth the presentation of a Kotzebue melodrama by a group of young people in a private house is immoral is of course missing the whole point that Jane Austen takes such pains to make clear. In Sir Thomas's absence, leaving his children and niece to be supervised by the vain self-importance of Mrs. Norris and the languid unimaginativeness of Lady Bertram, the whole moral atmosphere of the family degenerates, largely under the influence of Henry and Mary Crawford, the gay young brother and sister who are staying at the parsonage, and of Tom Bertram's light-headed friend Mr. Yates. Henry makes love to both the Bertram daughters, finally concentrating on Maria, who is engaged to the rich and dull Mr. Rushworth. The play they choose to perform is a sentimental and melodramatic piece about a wronged woman and her noble illegitimate son and enables various kinds of love-making to go on in the house under the excuse of rehearsing. Further, they all know that Sir Thomas would disapprove if he were at home, though most of them do not admit it to themselves, and the violence

done to his study in the interests of the domestic theater is a symbol
of this. The planning of the performance releases the worst in all
the characters. Julia sulks because her elder sister is Mr. Crawford's
favorite; Maria, engaged though she is, triumphs in her affair with
Mr. Crawford; and even the good and strong-minded Edmund is
led by his passion for Mary Crawford (though he disguises this reason from himself) into acquiescing and actually participating in a
plan which at first he violently objected to. Only Fanny sees the
truth steadily throughout the whole proceedings: not only does she
never waver in her view of the impropriety of the amateur theatricals (and the modern reader must not allow his impatience with the
word "impropriety" to blind him to the moral realities involved in
the term as Jane Austen uses it), but her position as an observer
enables her to see exactly what is going on between the various
couples and particularly to note the unscrupulous behavior of Henry
Crawford. She remains alone in possession of this knowledge until,
toward the end of the novel, Henry's running off with the now-
married Maria shows everybody his true character and vindicates
her stubborn refusal to marry a man whom everybody had persuaded her she ought to love.

What sticks in the throat of some modern critics is the character
of Henry and Mary Crawford, the gayest, wittiest, and in some respects most likable people in the book. What sudden access of
prudishness and sanctimoniousness, they cry, made Jane Austen
turn them into villains? Does not this suggest that wit and gaiety
are instruments of the devil and the life of passive resignation the
only one to be recommended? And is this not flatly in opposition
to the whole tenor of Jane Austen's work? But surely the whole
point of the Crawfords is to show that qualities of mind which can
be and often are innocent and attractive do not necessarily go with
a laudable character and that these qualities can disguise corrupt-
ness of character from all but the most discerning, just because of
their attractiveness. Only Fanny sees through them, because, like
the child in the story of the Emperor's new clothes, only she is not
misled by factors drawn from other sources than her own simple
vision. Her exclusion from the world of social frivolity in which her
cousins moved, her training in quiet and generous service, her love
for her warmhearted and high-principled cousin Edmund, and her
awareness of her own good fortune in being removed from the
poverty and confusion of her own family to life in the ordered
dignity of Mansfield Park—all this helps to preserve the integrity of
her vision. Fanny may be timid and retiring, but she is not undis-
cerning. She is no Parson Adams, simple and credulous; she turns

out in fact to be the least credulous character in the novel. She has nothing in common with the naïve gullibility of the heroes of such sentimental novels as Henry Mackenzie's *Man of Feeling*. Though she is unworldly, her calm vision teaches her to know the world better than her more worldly companions. The counterpointing of the personal and the social in this novel is done more complexly than anywhere else in Jane Austen.

Just as in *Pride and Prejudice* clues to the real character of Darcy are planted throughout the earlier part of the novel for the discerning reader to find, so (but in a much subtler manner) clues to the real character of the Crawfords are provided throughout *Mansfield Park*. For example, in talking to Edmund of the difficulties of having her harp delivered from Northampton, Mary Crawford displays a mixture of selfishness and insensitivity—insensitivity to the due agricultural work of the seasons (for which Jane Austen had a real feeling) and indifference to the fact that farmers need all their facilities for transport at harvest time:

"You would find it difficult, I dare say, just now, in the middle of a very late hay harvest, to hire a horse and cart?"

"I was astonished to find what a piece of work was made of it! To want a horse and cart in the country seemed impossible, so I told my maid to speak for one directly; and as I cannot look out of my dressing-closet without seeing one farm-yard, nor walk in the shrubbery without passing another, I thought it would be only ask and have, . . . Guess my surprise, when I found that I had been asking the most unreasonable, most impossible thing in the world, had offended all the farmers, all the labourers, all the hay in the parish. . . ."

In the course of the same conversation, Miss Crawford says: ". . . but coming down with the true London maxim, that every thing is to be got with money, I was a little embarrassed at first by the sturdy independence of your country customs." At the bottom of Miss Crawford's attitude to everything lies her view of money; nothing is valuable without lots of it (not even marriage with a man she loves) and nothing which brings lots of it can be wholly valueless. Jane Austen, by her manipulation of the action, insists again and again that London is the source of this corrupt view; it is a view bred by London society, a society out of touch with country simplicities, with the elemental rhythm of the seasons, and with the significance of the family as microcosm of human organization. Henry Crawford's basic vice is his view of sex as merely self-indulgent play: this is revealed to us quite early in the novel and steadily developed. Jane Austen's own view of sex, love, marriage, and family is part of the complex pattern in which social and individual elements in human life are correlated: this pattern is implicit in greater or less degree in all her novels. In the light of it, the serious moral defects of both the Crawfords are visible from the beginning. That they are witty and attractive and often kindhearted and generous only makes their basic moral weaknesses to be the more deplored. Certain kinds of attractiveness, even certain kinds of real goodness, can coexist with underlying moral corruption: Jane Austen was never unsophisticated enough to deny that. The unalloyed evil of melodrama was not what she was after at all. It is characteristic of the subtlety with which she treats all moral questions that the petty selfishness of Mrs. Norris is shown as by far the most repulsive vice in the novel, yet though it helps to lead to greater vices it is not itself the most dangerous or the most reprehensible of the various qualities and attitudes displayed.

It should be realized, too, that Fanny, for all her relative passivity, is clever. She is mocked by her cousins on first arriving from her humble home because she does not know certain things that they know: but she does not know them because she has not yet been taught them. In numerous little touches Jane Austen makes clear that Fanny read a great deal, had taste and discernment in literature, and was in fact positively highbrow. And she never fools herself with any kind of sentimental delusion. The brilliant interlude describing her visit to her own family in Portsmouth and showing how the continuous noise, lack of order, and semi-poverty of her original home frayed her nerves and caused her to long for the peace and order of Mansfield Park, is a deliberately antisentimental episode. With an almost Dickensian sense of colorful squalor, Jane Austen shows us what it is like to bring up a large family on a small income where the mother is indolent and the father self-indulgent. Yet this is not introduced as a psychological or sociological excursus: the Portsmouth scenes are carefully integrated into the total action of the novel; they play a part both in revealing the full nature of Fanny's character and in precipitating the final events.

The wit in *Mansfield Park* is less ebullient than in *Pride and Prejudice* and conveyed more in Jane Austen's own descriptive prose than in dialogue. The quiet opening, with its characteristic insistence on the financial position of the family in whose midst the action is set, has its own controlled irony: "About thirty years ago, Miss Maria Ward of Huntingdon, with only seven thousand pounds, had the good luck to captivate Sir Thomas Bertram, of Mansfield Park, in the county of Northampton, and to be thereby raised to the rank of a baronet's lady, with all the comforts and consequences of an handsome house and large income. All Huntingdon exclaimed on the greatness of the match, and her uncle, the lawyer, himself, allowed her to be at least three thousand pounds short of any equitable claim to it." Everybody's income is dealt with most minutely, as so often in Jane Austen's novels. The landowning and financial basis of the social order is explicitly realized. And disparity between the social position given by wealth and landed property and the qualifications provided by personal character and intelligence provides a frequent source of irony. Jane Austen accepted such disparities as inevitable in any social organization; but that did not prevent her from employing her irony on them.

Emma (1816) is a novel more acceptable to those who take *Pride and Prejudice* as the type of Jane Austen fiction. In outline it is the story of a rich and clever girl whose overconfidence in her own understanding of people and well-meaning desire to manipulate the lives of her social inferiors as well as of some of her equals involve her in a number of delusions, the destruction of which gives her some salutary shocks and helps her to achieve a greater degree of self-knowledge than she possessed before. Possessed by that self-knowledge she is at last able to see her elder sister's husband's brother Mr. Knightley as the man she truly loves, with the result that a character who has hitherto been something of a father-figure in the book (Emma's real father is a gently selfish old hypochondriac) moves by an easy transition into the role of lover and husband. Emma has not the obvious charm of Elizabeth Bennet; her self-deceptions and condescensions make her sometimes an almost comic figure; but she never entirely loses the reader's sympathy and never at all loses the author's. She is treated throughout with affectionate irony, Jane Austen's more cruel type of irony being reserved for more obvious and more culpable examples of folly and affectation, notably in the character of Mrs. Elton. Emma is never vicious, only spoiled by good fortune. As the characteristic opening explains:

Emma Woodhouse, handsome, clever, and rich, with a comfortable home and happy disposition, seemed to unite some of the best blessings of existence; and had lived nearly twenty-one years in the world with very little to distress or vex her.

The novel proceeds to set little traps for Emma's vanity and self-importance, and she falls into every one of them. She takes under her protection Harriet Smith, "the natural daughter of somebody," and decides to arrange a suitable marriage for her, which means breaking off Harriet's incipient love affair with the farmer Mr. Martin, a wholly worthy and suitable person, and trying to maneuver the vicar, Mr. Elton, into love with her. But Mr. Elton, a vain and foolish young man, misunderstands Emma's behavior and proposes to Emma herself, to her disgust and annoyance (but she fails to reflect why a suitor she wishes for her friend should be so monstrous for herself), and Mr. Elton, firmly rejected, goes off to marry a wife even more vain and silly than himself. In her second attempt to marry off Harriet, Emma becomes involved in more serious trouble, for while Emma is trying to get Harriet interested in the handsome and eligible Frank Churchill, Harriet, misunderstanding Emma's elegant hints, thinks she is referring to Mr. Knightley and obligingly falls in love with him: it is the shock of discovering this that first makes clear to Emma that she will allow no one to marry Mr. Knightley but herself. This kind of misunderstanding makes for lively comedy, but as Jane Austen handles it it is much more than the comedy of confusion and resolution. The moral pattern is carefully woven, and Emma's attempt to play God is made to involve her in a variety of situations all of which contribute in the end to her self-knowledge.

The Frank Churchill whom Emma wants to marry Harriet is attractive enough to Emma herself, and there is an interesting tension between her admiration of his vitality and wit (an admiration which observers take to be something more) and her half-realized love for Mr. Knightley, "one of the few people who could see faults in Emma Woodhouse," her adviser and monitor who does not conceal his disapproval of her schemes for Harriet. Mr. Knightley is a somewhat more human Darcy; a wealthy landowner, some seventeen years older than Emma, grave, generous, kind to his tenants, intolerant of deceit and cruelty, with none of the superficial gaiety of Frank Churchill. While Emma is scheming for Frank and Harriet to marry, Mr. Knightley imagines that she is falling in love with Frank herself. The situation is enriched with further ironies with the introduction of Jane Fairfax, niece of Miss Bates, the genteelly poor spinster daughter of a clergyman. Jane Fairfax, staying with her aunt, is conjectured by the knowing Emma to be secretly in love with one Mr. Dixon, who lives in Ireland, and soon Emma's conjecture becomes a certainty. Jane is a foil for Emma; she has no fortune, but is equally talented, and at music more talented, a fact which arouses Emma's unconscious jealousy. Emma amuses herself by hinting and speculating about Jane's relation with Mr. Dixon and joking about it with Frank. It appears that Frank and Emma are having a lot of knowing fun at Jane's expense. The fun is not wholly innocent on Emma's part; there is an element if not of spite at least of jealousy in it; and further, Jane's lack of fortune means that if she does not marry soon she will have to take a position as a governess, and the horrors and humiliations of that sort of work are made abundantly evident, notably through Mrs. Elton's insufferably patronizing offers of help in getting her a job. Emma therefore has no moral right to laugh either at Jane or at her well-meaning and garrulous aunt, a worthy but tiresome character on whom Emma vents a momentary irritation, to be castigated for her lack of generosity by Mr. Knightley. It emerges at last that the relation between Jane and Mr. Dixon which Emma has conjured up and about which she has joked so often with Frank has no basis in fact, and all the time Jane and Frank were secretly engaged. So far from being a fellow-conspirator with Frank as she imagined, Emma suddenly realizes that she is and has been his dupe. At every point Emma's wit and knowingness have involved her in humiliation, with Mr. Knightley standing by to give gentle and affectionate reproof. It is the relief of discovering that Emma was never in love with Frank (as everyone expects her to be) that precipitates his declaration. The whole plot contrivance is brilliant, and the exploration of different kinds of selfishness which the unfolding of the action makes possible, as well as the sharply ironic character sketches of such characters as the Eltons and (ironic in a different way) Miss Bates, give the novel real depth below the surface brilliance. The character of Emma's father, whose concern for other people is a way of implementing a profound selfishness, opens and closes the book; it is a masterly picture of combined gentleness and querulousness, flourishing on the kind and tyrannical assumption that what is bad for him must be bad for and therefore prohibited to others. It symbolizes the ambiguities of selfishnesses, which is one of the themes of the novel. The moral pattern is spelled out more clearly in *Emma* than in *Pride and Prejudice*, but in other respects it is a less sharply drawn novel, standing midway, with respect to subtlety and complexity, between *Pride and Prejudice* and *Mansfield Park*.

Persuasion (1818) is the most complex of all, and the least like *Pride and Prejudice* of all the other novels. Here again there is a Cinderella element in the plot: Anne Elliot, the second daughter of the vain and silly widower Sir Walter Elliot, is imposed upon and condescended to by her family, though not to a degree which makes her life really miserable. When the novel opens she is twenty-seven years old, faded and resigned, after having allowed herself eight years before to be persuaded by her friend and substitute-mother Lady Russell to give up her lover, Frederick Wentworth. Circumstances conspire to bring Wentworth, now a naval commander with some fortune, back on the scene, and after various adventures have educated each of them in the real state of their hearts they marry at last. Anne is closer to the general type of Catherine Morland and Fanny Price than to the vivacious and witty Elizabeth Bennet and Emma Woodhouse; like Fanny, she has "an elegance of mind and sweetness of character," and cheerfully allows herself to be made use of by others; she is also strong-minded when she wants to be, highly intelligent, and able to penetrate superficialities of behavior to see or at least to guess at real character. Jane Austen can therefore allow many of her characters to be seen through Anne's eyes, but she is not content to do this consistently and adds her own coldly ironic gaze at frequent intervals. There is a colder irony in *Persuasion* than in any other of Jane Austen's novels. Sir Walter Elliot is very different from the well-meaning if pompously unimaginative Sir Thomas Bertram: he is summed up in the novel's opening: "Sir Walter Elliot, of Kellynch-hall, in Somersetshire, was a man who, for his own amusement, never took up any book but the Baronetage; . . ." His main characteristic was vanity, a quality quite different (as his daughter Anne discovered) from true pride, in which he was disgustingly deficient, for he would prostrate himself before a superior title, however worthless its possessor. Nowhere in Jane Austen is her dislike of snobbery and her distinction between true and false notions of social rank made so clear. Lady Catherine de Bourgh in *Pride and Prejudice* is a comic caricature; Sir Walter is a real and thoroughly unpleasant person.

Intelligence and good will are both necessary in a character to whom Jane Austen would give her total respect, and the characters in *Persuasion* reflect a great variety of permutations and combinations of different degrees of each. Marv Musgrove, Anne's younger married sister, "though better endowed than the elder sister, . . . had not Anne's understanding or temper," and the other members of the Musgrove family reflect various dispositions all tolerable but each in different ways far from perfect. The part played in the novel by the Musgrove family illustrates different kinds of ordinariness in character; there is vanity, self-will, lack of imagination, silliness, and also kindness, simple human emotions and a contented triviality to be found among them. The quality of ordinary daily living among reasonably moneyed people in the country is admirably shown in the various scenes in which they are involved. It is almost as though Jane Austen is saying that while she follows the traditional plot pattern of having her hero and heroine marry in the end she is well aware of the unromantic nature of daily life and has no illusions about people being divided sharply into morally black and white. Even the formal villain, the scheming and unscrupulous William Elliot, Sir Walter's nephew and heir, is not a melodramatic bounder, but a man of charm and intelligence who (like the Crawfords in *Mansfield Park*) lacks fundamental principle. True married love is illustrated by Admiral and Mrs. Croft, as unromantic but as genuinely affectionate a couple as one would wish to see. *Persuasion* does not ask too much of human life, and the subdued second thoughts which lead to the hero's proposing marriage to the heroine eight years after he has been rejected is a symbol of chastened expectation. Anne "had been forced into prudence in her youth, she learned romance as she grew older," but this meant that romance was something different from what it was to other novelists.

Though *Persuasion* has the air of only moderate expectations from life this does not mean that Jane Austen is any more tolerant of vanity, folly, or selfishness. When Mrs. Musgrove, as a purely social exercise, works herself up into an emotional state about the death some years before of a sailor son, the author comments coldly:

The real circumstances of this pathetic piece of family history were, that the Musgroves had had the ill fortune of a very troublesome, hopeless son; and the good fortune to lose him before he reached his twentieth year; that he had been sent to sea, because he was stupid and unmanageable on shore; that he had been very little cared for at any time by his family, though quite as much as he deserved; seldom heard of, and scarcely at all regretted, when the intelligence of his death abroad had worked its way to Uppercross, two years before.

He had, in fact, though his sisters were now doing all they could for him by calling him "poor Richard," been nothing better than a thick-headed, unfeeling, unprofitable Dick Musgrove, who had never done any thing to entitle himself to more than the abbreviation of his name, living or dead.

The calm cruelty of this outburst seems to be the author's response to the hypocrisy of the wretched young man's surviving relatives in using his death as a means of claiming sympathy for themselves on various social occasions. It is characteristic of the "no nonsense" air about the novel. Jane Austen has hardly time to laugh at Sir Walter Elliot; his vanity makes him so absurd as to be quite despicable.

What are human emotions and what are they really worth? The novel poses this question again and again. Both Anne Elliot and Frederick Wentworth are concerned with the true state of their own feelings. What was Anne going to feel like when she met her rejected lover for the first time after eight years? It is a moment that she, and the reader, await with trepidation, but it comes and goes finally with surprising insignificance:

. . . a thousand feelings rushed on Anne, of which this was the most consoling, that it would soon be over. And it was soon over. In two minutes after Charles's preparations, the others appeared; they were in the drawing-room. Her eye half met Captain Wentworth's; a bow, a courtsey passed; she heard his voice— he talked to Mary, said all that was right; said something to the Miss Musgroves, enough to mark an easy footing: the room seemed full—full of persons and voices—but a few minutes ended it. Charles showed himself at the window, all was ready, their visitor had vowed and was gone too, suddenly resolving to walk to the end of the village with the sportsmen: the room was cleared, and Anne might finish her breakfast as she could.

It is an anticlimax, and it is meant to be: that is how things happen. It has often been noted that Jane Austen prefers to hasten over the actual moment of declaration of passion, carefully charting the emotions of the lovers up to that point, and then summarizing the climactic scene in a few words. "There they exchanged again those feelings and those promises which had once before seemed to secure every thing, but which had been followed by so many, many years of division and estrangement. There they returned again into the past, more exquisitely happy, perhaps, in their re-union, than when it had been first projected; . . ." People are not interesting in the incoherent babbling with which the articulation of passion takes place; it is a false romanticism to dwell on the actual professions of love rather than on the developments of character and action that lead up to them. This is true, at least, in the moral and psychological world in which Jane Austen lived.

Yet no novelist was ever more concerned with particularizing detail than Jane Austen. In the duties, errands, engagements, irritations, worries, and pleasures of daily domestic life her novels are able to follow the exact curve of experience, and render it with a precision that inevitably suggests, if not love, then that special relationship with one's subject that is the artist's form of love. This is far from photographic realism. The moral pattern is always strong in Jane Austen, and in *Persuasion* the gradations of character and deployment of the action are such as to create a background of moral feeling that is rich yet subdued. From the "goodness of heart and simplicity of character" of Admiral Croft through Captain Benwick's "affectionate heart: he must love everybody" to the more cultivated and discriminating intelligence and generosity of Anne Elliot, a whole map of morality is spread out, as there is also, on the other side, between the intermittent selfishness of Mary Musgrove through the selfish vanity of Sir Walter to the intelligent scheming of his nephew. The character of Lady Russell is an interesting intermediate one; she is obviously a "good" person, yet her original advice to Anne had been wrong and she is blind to the full preposterousness of Sir

Walter's character. The complexity of the moral picture is indicated by Anne's final summing up of Lady Russell's earlier behavior to Captain Wentworth:

"I have been thinking over the past, and trying impartially to judge of the right and wrong. I mean with regard to myself; and I must believe that I was right, much as I suffered from it, that I was perfectly right in being guided by the friend whom you will love better than you do now. To me, she was in the place of a parent. Do not mistake me, however. I am not saying that she did not err in her advice. It was, perhaps, one of those cases in which advice is good or bad only as the event decides; and for myself, I certainly never should, in any circumstance of tolerable similarity, give such advice. But I mean, that I was right in submitting to her, and that if I had done otherwise, I should have suffered more in continuing the engagement than I did even in giving it up, because I should have suffered in my conscience. . . ."

A heroine who can admit, after eight years of bitter regrets at having to part with a man whom she loved and who loved her, that the person who parted them may have been right after all, at least in some sense, is an uncommon sort of heroine in English fiction. But then Jane Austen is an uncommon sort of novelist, a novelist of manners with a brilliant ironic wit, an affectionate understanding of the ordinariness of human life, a mastery of plot structure, a lively and often subtle sense of character, and a moral universe within which to set and pattern all her novels. Confining herself to that limited area of contemporary English social life which she knew well, she wrote of the human comedy with profound art to produce novels unequaled in English literature for technical brilliance, ironic poise, and awareness of the differing claims of personality and society.

CHAPTER NINETEEN

Eighteenth-Century Philosophical, Historical, and Critical Prose, and Miscellaneous Writing

NEWTON HAD PROVIDED the charter for the Augustan belief in a benevolent divine order. As Pope put it,

> Nature and Nature's laws lay hid in night;
> God said, *Let Newton be!* and all was light!

Belief that the universe was ordered, both physically and morally, by a benign and sagacious planner was at the bottom of much eighteenth-century deism: the great deistic argument from design. God becomes a distant if benevolent First Cause, and morality consists in following those impulses to virtue which God implanted in man. The theory of the "moral sense"—man possesses a faculty for recognizing virtue akin to the senses—was first elaborated in England by Anthony Ashley Cooper (1671–1713), third Earl of Shaftesbury, whose *Characteristics of Men, Manners, Opinions, and Times* (1711) presented in three volumes of gentlemanly essays a view of natural morality that captivated a host of readers in the first half of the century. Shaftesbury is neither a profound thinker nor a great essayist, but his writings distil much of the spirit of the age. We have come a long way from the enthusiasms of seventeenth-century Puritan sects and the fierce concern with individual salvation found in Bunyan when we read that the nature of virtue consists "in a certain just disposition or proportionable affection of a rational creature towards the moral objects of right and wrong" or that "the fear of future punishment and hope of future reward" cannot possibly "be of the kind called good affections, such as are acknowledged the springs and sources of all actions truly good." He is equally far away from his contemporary Swift in expressing such a thought as this:

Nothing indeed can be more melancholy than the thought of living in a distracted universe, from whence many ills may be suspected, and where there is nothing good or lovely which presents itself, nothing which can satisfy in contemplation, or raise any passion besides that of contempt, hatred, or dislike. Such an opinion as this may by degrees embitter the temper, and not only make the love of virtue to be less felt, but help to impair and ruin the very principle of virtue, *viz.* natural and kind affection.

It was the very confidence with which contemporary philosophers extolled the self-regulating beauties of Nature and Reason that made the age also a great age of satire; Swift could never forgive men for not behaving according to what seemed to him and to so many of his age the strong clear light of reason.

Shaftesbury's *Letter concerning Enthusiasm* (1708) reveals a related aspect of the Augustan mood; and here he and Swift were in complete accord. But though both deprecated violent individualistic behavior in religious matters, Shaftesbury's insistence that even the most sacred matters can only be appropriately discussed by leisured gentlemen in an atmosphere of calm cheerfulness is very un-Swiftian.

In short, . . . the melancholy way of treating religion is that which, according to my apprehension, renders it so tragical, and is the occasion of its acting in reality such dismal tragedies in the world. And my motion is that, provided we treat religion with good manners, we can never use too much *good humour* or examine it with too much *freedom* and *familiarity*.

The good-humored discussion of ethics was continued by the Scotsman Francis Hutcheson (1694–1746), whose *Inquiry into the Original of our Idea of Beauty and Virtue* (1725) developed the theory of the moral sense into a neat utilitarianism ("The virtue, then, of agents, or their benevolence, is always directly as the moment of good produced in like circumstances, and inversely as their abilities: or $B = \frac{M}{A}$").

To philosophers like Shaftesbury, Nature rather than Revelation was the proper source of religion for reasonable modern men, whatever might have been necessary in earlier times for primitive people.

Nature, the general order of things in the universe (the term "nature" bore a great variety of meanings in the eighteenth century), was good, designed by a benevolent First Cause. If our individual experience led us to doubt that good, this was because we looked at the part and not the whole; the philosopher would see, with Pope,

> All discord, harmony not understood,
> All partial evil, universal good.

That there were many obviously undesirable creatures in the universe could be explained on what has been called the principle of plenitude: the Creator manifested his benevolence by creating everything that could be created, produced as great a diversity of creatures as possible, and arranged them in a "great chain of being" extending in an unbroken ladder from the crudest reptile to the angel. This view was not original with the eighteenth century—it had already had a long history in European thought when eighteenth-century philosophers invoked it to encourage optimism. Again, Pope's *Essay on Man* sums the matter up very prettily:

> Of systems possible, if 'tis confest
> That Wisdom infinite must form the best,
> Where all must full or not coherent be,
> And all that rises, rise in due degree;
> Then, in the scale of reas'ning life, 'tis plain
> There must be, somewhere, such a rank as Man: . . .

Man has his place in the chain, and his powers and limitations arise from this. The moral, of course, was acceptance of things as they are, and the political and social consequences of this were readily drawn. That things have to be as they are is not, however, the same argument as that things are as good as infinite benevolence could possibly make them, and sometimes in eighteenth-century thought what starts out as an apologia for the nature of things ends as a revelation of the inescapable horror of things. The notorious argument of Soame Jenyns in his *Free Enquiry into the Origin and Nature of Evil* (1757) was designed to demonstrate that every kind of human suffering is the natural and proper consequence of man's place in the general scheme of things; the social order among men is a proper consequence of the natural order of the universe, and each has its "just inferiority of the parts." But when Jenyns goes on to argue that "the sufferings of individuals are absolutely necessary to universal happiness" and to use the theory of the great chain of being to suggest that just as men derive pleasure from dominating, enslaving, and tormenting inferior creatures, so creatures superior to man in the chain of being intermediate between man and God might derive pleasure from deceiving, tormenting, or destroying us, the principle of "universal happiness" (already vague enough) disappears, and we are left with a possible explanation of the horror, not of the beauty, of the universe. Any argument designed to persuade men that the world we live in is the best of all possible worlds is liable to end in the pessimism it aims to prevent; for if this world is the best possible, it is a black lookout for the nature of things. So long as Jenyns is arguing that the poor and the uneducated are as happy as the rich and the educated because their ignorance and simplicity limit their wants and make them easily satisfied, his reasoning, however unconvincing, is directly aimed at increasing complacency; but when he suggests that man might well be tormented by superior creatures just as men themselves torment animals he is simply revealing the whole universe as a carefully designed torture chamber for all except the Supreme Torturer. No wonder that Dr. Johnson, who never shared the facile optimism of so many of his predecessors and contemporaries, burst into rage in his review of Jenyns' book. With a single sentence—"I am always afraid of determining on the side of envy and cruelty"—he exposed the social implications of this mode of thinking. He dismissed with scorn the comfortable doctrine that the poor are in their way just as happy as the rich. "Life must be seen, before it can be known. This author and Pope, perhaps, never saw the miseries which they imagine thus easy to be borne." As for Jenyns' notion "that as we have not only animals for food, but choose some for our diversion, the same privilege may be allowed to some beings above us, *who may deceive, torment, or destroy us, for the end, only, of their own pleasure or utility*," Johnson grimly agrees that it is a very likely surmise:

I cannot resist the temptation of contemplating this analogy, which, I think, he might have carried further, very much to the advantage of his argument. He might have shown, that these "hunters, whose game is man," have many sports analogous to our own. As we drown whelps and kittens, they amuse themselves, now and then, with sinking a ship, and stand round the fields of Blenheim, or the walls of Prague, as we encircle a cock-pit. As we shoot a bird flying, they take a man in the midst of his business and pleasure, and knock him down with an apoplexy. Some of them, perhaps, are virtuosi, and delight in the operation of an asthma, as a human philosopher in the effects of the air-pump. . . . Many a merry bout have these frolic beings at the vicissitudes of an ague, and good sport it is to see a man tumble with an epilepsy, and revive and tumble again, and all this he knows not why. As they are wiser and more powerful than we, they have more exquisite diversions; for we have no way of procuring any sport so brisk and so lasting, as the paroxysms of the gout and stone, which, undoubtedly, must make high mirth, especially if the play be a little diversified with the blunders and puzzles of the blind and deaf.

Johnson, of course, is not denouncing Providence; he is registering his often-stated belief that "human life is everywhere a state in which much is to be endured, and little to be enjoyed" and his view that no fancy rationalizations can explain away the difficulties and paradoxes of life, which only religious faith can enable one to support.

There were some interesting modifications of the popular argument from design. Bishop Joseph Butler (1692–1752) argued against deism and in defense of Christian orthodoxy in his *Analogy of Religion* (1736), in which he tried to bring men back to a belief in Revelation (which the deistic position regarded as unnecessary) by showing that the evidence of design in the created universe (evidence which no deist questioned) was as murky and indirect as biblical revelation. What Francis Bacon had called the two books of God's work and God's word revealed the same difficult handwriting. Bernard Mandeville (1670–1733) developed an even more paradoxical view. In *The Fable of the Bees* (1714) he added to an earlier essay in octosyllabic verse entitled *The Grumbling Hive: or, Knaves Turned Honest,* a prose essay which he called "An Enquiry into the Origin of Moral Virtue" to produce a double-barrelled attack on Shaftesbury's view of morality whose general tenor is summed up in his subtitle, "Private Vices, Public Benefits." The verse gives the description of a beehive in which everyone worked for his own selfish ends and practiced every kind of knavery and fraud, but the total result was a happy and prosperous society. "Thus every part was full of vice, /Yet the whole mass a paradise." At last Jove in anger decided to "rid the bawling hive of fraud." Everyone as a result became ideally honest; commercial, political, legal, and other activities languished; arts and crafts lay neglected; rapid depopulation set in:

> So few in the vast hive remain,
> The hundredth part they can't maintain
> Against the insults of numerous foes,
> Whom yet they valiantly oppose,
> Till some well-fenced retreat is found,
> And here they die or stand their ground.

They triumphed, at a cost, and the few survivors settled in a hollow tree "blest with content and honesty." The moral is that "fools only strive /To make a great an honest hive." It is Utopian nonsense to believe that a country can be strong and prosperous without great vices. The prose essay is a more elaborate argument, developing a somewhat Hobbesian view of how the notions of virtues and vices originally came into being.

It being the interest then of the very worst of them, more than any, to preach up public-spiritedness, that they might reap the fruits of the labour and self-denial of others, and at the same time indulge their own appetites with less disturbance, they agreed with the rest, to call every thing which, without regard to the public, man should commit to gratify any of his appetites, VICE; if in that action there could be observed the least prospect, that it might either be injurious to any of the society, or ever render himself less serviceable to others: and to give the name of VIRTUE to every performance, by which man, contrary to the impulse of nature, should endeavour the benefit of others, or the conquest of his own passions out of a rational ambition of being good.

The conclusion is that "the moral virtues are the political offspring which flattery begot upon pride." The real force which operates to make people behave decently is desire for praise. If it is objected "that virtue being its own reward, those who are really good have a satisfaction in their consciousness of being so, which is all the recompense they expect," Mandeville answers that we can only judge a man's performance from a knowledge of his motives, and that many actions which appear to be the result of the disinterested practice of virtue are actually due to the operation of selfishness. Thus pity is really a weakness, and "there is no merit in saving an innocent babe ready to drop into the fire . . . for to have seen it fall, and not strove to hinder it, would have caused a pain, which self-preservation compelled us to prevent." Men who really do good disinterestedly and in silence, "such men, I confess, have acquired more refined notions of virtue than those I have hitherto spoke of; yet even in these . . . we may discover no small symptoms of pride, . . ." And there are very few of them anyway. To the "too scrupulous reader" who may think this view of the origin of moral virtue offensive to Christianity, Mandeville replies

that nothing can render the unsearchable depth of the Divine Wisdom more conspicuous than that Man, whom Providence had designed for Society, should not only by his own frailties and imperfections be led into the road to temporal happiness, but likewise receive, from a seeming necessity of natural causes, a tincture of that knowledge, in which he was afterwards to be made perfect by the True Religion, to his eternal welfare.

The special use which Mandeville made of materials common to his age gives him a peculiar place among eighteenth-century moralists. Sometimes he seems to be writing with Swiftian irony, at other times he seems to be arguing with genuine complacency for the maintenance of things as they are. He is both cynic and optimist—or does his optimism conceal a deeper despair at the possibility of true virtue among men? The official optimism of the Augustan Age did

not prevent it from being one of the great ages of satire. The coexistence of both elements in Mandeville's *Fable of the Bees* gives that
work a greater interest than the author's philosophical powers or his
literary distinction would otherwise yield. He is a paradox emblem-
atic of his age.

Locke's empiricism led other English philosophers in other directions. George Berkeley (1685–1753), Bishop of Cloyne, pushed
Locke's views to their logical extreme and maintained in his *Treatise
concerning the Principles of Human Knowledge* (1710) that sensations cannot be taken as evidence of an objectively existing material
reality which "caused" them; the external world exists only insofar as
it is perceived by individuals, and the only cause of individual perceptions can be the divine mind. This was a logical development of
Locke's view of matter with its primary and secondary qualities,
for Locke's classification of primary qualities was not in itself (as
Locke seemed to believe) an explanation of matter or a proof of its
existence. Berkeley's view that sensations are their own reality and
do not represent anything external is argued with grace and clarity;
but it had no real influence on eighteenth-century thought (except
on Hume, who made his own use of it), although his criticism of
Newtonian physics, to which his view of nature as simply a set of
actual or potential perceptions led him, and the metaphysical implications of his conception of the world of sensation as constituting a
divine code revealing God's message about Himself, influenced some
of the Romantic poets. On the whole the reception of Berkeley's philosophy in his own century can be illustrated by the well-known anecdote of Dr. Johnson kicking a stone and saying, "Thus I refute
him."

The Scottish philosopher David Hume (1711–76) carried the
analysis of causation much further; our idea of cause, he urged, is
based on nothing more than previous experience of one phenomenon
being followed by another; all we really know is a succession of
events (either in the sensible world or in our minds). To infer the operation of laws of cause and effect from observed sequences or clus-
ters of events or ideas, even to infer the existence of a rational personality from groups and sequences of impressions and ideas in the
individual mind, is quite illogical. Thus Hume brought to light the
skeptical implications in the whole mainstream of European philosophy since Descartes, and his work is a watershed in European
thought. After him, progress had to be in a different direction. If for
Hume most things that people believe cannot be demonstrated by
reason, this does not mean that we must rest in complete confusion
and uncertainty. Pure reason (and therefore absolute certainty), he

argued in his *Treatise on Human Nature* (1739), is applicable only
to an investigation of the relations between ideas, as in pure logic
and pure mathematics, and if we want to understand why men believe what they do we must investigate the development of custom
and habit, for it is custom and habit rather than reason which account
for people's beliefs. Such an investigation, Hume believed, could
lead to a sound and fruitful science of human and general nature,
grounded on psychological fact. "In pretending . . . to explain the
principles of human nature, we in effect propose a complete system
of the sciences, built on a foundation almost entirely new, and the
only one upon which they can stand with any certainty." Hume developed his views on man, on ethics, on epistemology, and kindred
subjects in two volumes of essays (1741–42), *An Enquiry concerning
Human Understanding* (1748), and *An Enquiry concerning the Principles of Morals* (1751). He finds that what is morally good is simply
what is esteemed, and proceeds cheerfully to show why it is that
certain qualities have been generally esteemed—they possess some
kind of usefulness or agreeableness either personal or social. Such a
view assumes the uniformity of human nature and the acceptance of
one's own society as a fair model of human society in general—and
here Hume was very much a man of his age. There is an optimism
underlying Humean skepticism, for he believed that sympathy was
an innate human characteristic and that it accounted in large measure for the origin of morality. Indeed, a hedonistic and utilitarian
view of morals can account for the facts of the moral life only if it
assumes some degree of benevolence innate in man.

Much in Hume's arguments about morality was in apparent agreement with ideas popular in his age, such as that of the moral sense.
The whole basis of his philosophical operations was, however, radically counter to the mainstream of eighteenth-century thought;
Hume's content with skepticism about the province of reason, his
ability to move from a radically skeptical argument to a cheerful acceptance of the manners and amusements of the society of his time,
his occasional apparently amused skepticism about the implications
of his own skepticism, were attitudes not expected of a philosopher.
His sharpest attack on the beliefs of his age was his *Dialogues Concerning Natural Religion,* published posthumously in 1779, for he
never had the courage to publish the book during his lifetime. By
means of a cunningly contrived dialogue, Hume here directs a dam-
aging attack against the argument from design—the view that evidence of design in nature proves the existence of a designing God.
The irony, the dramatic liveliness, the sly way in which he makes the
most orthodox speaker play into the hands of the most skeptical,

make this book the most attractive, from the literary point of view, of all Hume's works. But its central argument is serious and has never been rebutted. Hume shows that the analogy between the universe (which is unique) and humanly designed objects in it is a false one, but even if we were to accept it and infer from the natural world the existence of a designer, such an inference would tell nothing about his attributes and might well suggest that he was a novice or a blunderer. Deism rested so heavily on the argument from design, and natural theology flourished so luxuriantly in the eighteenth century, that it is understandable that Hume should have hesitated to attack the main citadel. William Paley in his *Natural Theology* (1802) repeated the standard argument from design as though Hume had not written, and Paley's work remained popular throughout the nineteenth century.

Hume, known to his friends as *le bon David,* was a man of charm and urbanity whose skeptical views did not prevent him from leading a virtuous life. His humanity and generosity were resented by those (like the minor poet and philosopher James Beattie) who believed that only religious belief could guarantee moral behavior. He was in many ways the ideal eighteenth-century gentleman, a good-natured conservative who never for a moment believed that his revolutionary ideas about causation and human knowledge should produce any change in the status quo. There was a streak of skepticism running right through English thought from the latter part of the seventeenth century, but among most people it was covered up by calm rationalizations about the First Cause and the implications of Newtonian order. Hume exploded these rationalizations, but he went on behaving as though he had not. He at the same time typified the eighteenth century and blew up its foundations. Unlike the French *philosophes,* whom in many respects he resembled, he was not anxious to blow up anything.

In almost every way the antithesis of Hume yet also in his own way typical of his age (the same age) and a far more dominating figure in it, Samuel Johnson (1709–84) illustrates in his life and work both the changing position of the man of letters in eighteenth-century England and the operation of one of the most vigorous literary minds in English history. That he is remembered as a personality rather than as a man of letters is not entirely the result of Boswell's great biography; something is due to his extraordinary vigor of utterance. He spoke in many respects for his age, or at least for the age which was coming to an end in his lifetime; but his utterance was always unmistakably his own. Poet, critic, essayist, journalist, editor, and great literary personality, Johnson was one of the first full-dress professional men of letters in England. He graduated from Grub Street, the world of literary hacks employed by booksellers in miscellaneous writing. Grub Street, originally in Johnson's definition, a London street "much inhabited by writers of small histories, dictionaries, and temporary poems," had become by the early eighteenth century a term signifying the fate of impoverished writers who scribbled for a pittance provided by bookseller-publishers. This was an important transitional phase in the status of the English writer, between the decline of patronage and the possibility of an independent writing career with author negotiating with publisher from a position of vantage. Johnson, in moving out of Grub Street and simultaneously rejecting patronage (which he had sought in vain from Lord Chesterfield on first planning his dictionary), demonstrated how a writer could now achieve economic and social status as a result of his own literary efforts. His early years of poverty and drudgery gave him a knowledge of the seamy side of London life and an impatience with the official optimism of eighteenth-century gentlemen who were always happy to discover reasons for believing in the perfection of the status quo. Johnson had no illusions about poverty, suffering, cruelty, or any of the other dark patches of experience; "the cure for the greatest part of human miseries is not radical, but palliative," he wrote in the thirty-second number of *The Rambler*. Yet he was no reformer; the defects of the human situation he believed to be radical, and no change in political or social organization could make any difference. Johnson inserted into Goldsmith's poem, *The Traveller*, the lines

> How small of all that human hearts endure,
> That part which kings or laws can cause or cure.

His Toryism was based on a profound pessimism, and his devotion to the Church of England sprang from his conviction that Christianity *must* be true if the universe is not a meaningless horror and since (as he told Boswell) he thought "all Christians, whether Papists or Protestants, agree in the essential articles, and that their differences are trivial, and rather political than religious," he considered the order, authority, and tradition of his native Church the most proper for an Englishman. Authority and tradition, with their accompanying ritual and ranking, he believed in profoundly, but as means rather than ends; human society needed them. His pessimism about man in general, his contempt for reformers and innovators, his almost desperate conservatism in politics and religion as a bulwark against despair, went side by side with great personal charity and generosity. His public character as the Great Cham of literature, developed in his later years and revealed so brilliantly in Boswell's *Life*, reminds one of his "talking for victory" and the thundering pronouncements with which he could deliver judgment or administer a snub. But there is also the Johnson who housed and supported a number of pensioners including his blind landlady Mrs. Williams and the unsuccessful physician Robert Levet as well as the Johnson who once wrote to Mrs. Thrale: "He that sees before him to his third dinner, has a long prospect."

The range and significance of Johnson's writing is indicated by the fact that a fair amount of it has already been discussed, and many of his critical opinions quoted, in preceding chapters. His literary career in London began with miscellaneous writing for Edward Cave, publisher of *The Gentleman's Magazine*. His first important published work was his poem *London*, which appeared anonymously in 1738; its companion piece, *The Vanity of Human Wishes*, appeared with Johnson's name eleven years later (both poems are discussed in Chapter 17). In 1747, he published *The Plan of a Dictionary of the English Language*, addressed to Lord Chesterfield, who did nothing for Johnson until, once the *Dictionary* was finished and ready to be published, in 1755, he wrote two letters in praise of it in *The World*, to draw forth from Johnson his famous reply:

> Is not a patron, my Lord, one who looks with unconcern on a man struggling for life in the water, and, when he has reached ground, encumbers him with help? The notice which you have been pleased to take of my labours, had it been early, had been kind; but it has been delayed till I am indifferent, and cannot enjoy it; till I am solitary, and cannot impart it; till I am known, and do not want it. I hope it is no very cynical asperity, not to confess obligations where no benefit has been received, or to be unwilling that the public should consider me as owing that to a patron, which Providence has enabled me to do for myself.

It is while he was working on his dictionary that Johnson turned to the periodical essay—that peculiarly eighteenth-century literary form of which many examples sprang up between Steele's *Tatler*, started in 1709, and Henry Mackenzie's *Mirror* (1779) and *Lounger* (1785). Between 1750 and 1752 he produced *The Rambler*, which appeared twice weekly for 208 numbers, each number consisting of a single essay, of which Johnson wrote all but five. Though they did not have a good sale on their initial appearance, the collected volumes of 1751 and 1753 and later editions sold well and helped to establish Johnson's reputation which during his lifetime depended to a greater degree on these essays than it has since done. From April, 1758, until April, 1760, Johnson contributed a series of weekly essays entitled *The Idler* to *The Universal Chronicle*. Most of the

Rambler essays have moral themes, handled in that carefully balanced, somewhat abstract and Latinate English which at its best combines weight and wit in a wholly characteristic way. There is no great originality or profundity in Johnson's moral essays, and they do not have that almost belligerent concentration on the moment of expression which gives so much of his conversation, as reported by Boswell, its special flavor. Johnson's critical creed led him to avoid numbering the streaks of the tulip and to concentrate on truths of general application. The somber Johnsonian music is partly the result of his finding words and cadences to carry the weight of general ideas:

It is the fate of almost every passion, when it has passed the bounds which nature prescribes, to counteract its own purpose. Too much rage hinders the warrior from circumspection; and too much eagerness of profit hurts the credit of the trader. Too much ardour takes away from the lover that easiness of address with which ladies are delighted. Thus extravagance, though dictated by vanity and incited by voluptuousness, seldom procures ultimately either applause or pleasure.

It is justly considered as the greatest excellency of art, to imitate nature; but it is necessary to distinguish those parts of nature which are most proper for imitation: greater care is still required in representing life, which is so often discoloured by passion, or deformed by wickedness. If the world be promiscuously described, I cannot see of what use it can be to read the account; or why it may not be as safe to turn the eye immediately upon mankind as upon a mirror which shows all that presents itself without discrimination.

Equally dangerous and equally detestable are the cruelties often exercised in private families, under the venerable sanction of parental authority; the power which we are taught to honour from the first moments of reason; which is guarded from insult and violation by all that can impress awe upon the mind of man; and which, therefore, may wanton in cruelty without control, and trample the bounds of right with innumerable transgressions, before duty and piety will dare to seek redress, to think themselves at liberty to recur to any other means of deliverance than supplications, by which insolence is elated, and tears, by which cruelty is gratified.

The morality preached by Johnson in *The Rambler* is practical, not theoretical; he is concerned to advise his readers on how to cultivate a proper state of mind and to employ their time and their energies properly. "The folly of mis-spending time," "Disadvantages of a bad education," "Idleness an anxious and miserable state," are typical themes. The essay on the first of these contains a peculiarly choice piece of early Johnsonian prose:

It is usual for those who are advised to the attainment of any new qualification, to look upon themselves as required to change the general course of their conduct, to dismiss their business, and exclude pleasure, and to devote their days or nights to a peculiar attention. But all common degrees of excellence are attainable at a lower price; he that should steadily and resolutely assign to any science or language those interstitial vacancies which intervene in the most crowded variety of diversion or employment, would find every day new irradiations of knowledge, and discover how much more is to be hoped from frequency and perseverance, than from violent efforts and sudden desires; efforts which are soon remitted when they encounter difficulty, and desires which, if they are indulged in too often, will shake off the authority of reason, and range capriciously from one object to another.

Sounding like a refrain throughout these essays are pungent sentences on the vanity of human wishes. "The natural flights of the human mind are not from pleasure to pleasure, but from hope to hope." "It is not therefore from this world, that any ray of comfort can proceed, to cheer the gloom of the last hour." The *persona* of sage and moralist which for the most part Johnson assumed in writing these essays corresponded to something deep-seated in his own character. Yet it must be remembered that the same man who preached against idleness and misuse of time with such sonorous eloquence also remarked: "A man is seldom in the humour to unlock his book-case, set his desk in order, and betake himself to serious study; but a retentive memory will do something, and a fellow shall have a strange credit given him, if he can recollect striking passages from different books, keep the authors separate in his head, and bring his knowledge artfully into play." And late in life he maintained that "No man but a blockhead ever wrote, except for money." And he once said to Mrs. Thrale, in a moment of irritation, "If it rained knowledge I'd hold out my hand; but I would not give myself the trouble to go in quest of it." Johnson could exhibit mischievous perversity as well as moral gravity, though more often in his conversation than in his writing.

In the *Idler* essays Johnson frequently attempted a somewhat lighter touch, as in his satirical account of the critic, Dick Minim. But even this is rather labored, and we feel that Johnson is more himself when, in the concluding passage of the final essay, he gives vent to his innate melancholy in reflecting on the emotions with which one does something for the last time:

. . . there are few things not purely evil, of which we can say, without some emotion of uneasiness, *this is the last*. Those who never could agree together shed tears when mutual discontent has determined them to final separation; of a place which has been frequently visited, though without pleasure, the last look is taken with heaviness of heart; and the Idler, with all his chillness of tranquillity, is not wholly unaffected by the thought that his last essay is now before him.

The secret horror of the last is inseparable from a thinking being, whose life is limited, and to whom death is dreadful. We always make a secret comparison between a part and the whole; the termination of any period of life reminds us that life itself has likewise its termination; when we have done any thing for the last time, we involuntarily reflect that a part of the days allotted us is past, and that as more is past there is less remaining. . . .

Johnson's *Dictionary of the English Language: in which the Words are deduced from their Originals, and Illustrated in their different Significations* was not a pioneer work—Nathaniel Bailey's *Universal Etymological English Dictionary* appeared in 1721—but it was the first to attempt to stabilize the English language, "to preserve the purity and ascertain the meaning of our English idiom." This was an ambitious aim; it was to undertake singlehandedly (as a friend once pointed out to Johnson) what it took the forty members of the French Academy forty years to accomplish. Johnson's intention was not to dictate; it was to discover, define, classify, and standardize. He was concerned with good usage, which he found in writers of the late sixteenth and the seventeenth century, from whom his main examples are chosen. "So far have I been from any care to grace my pages with modern decorations, that I have studiously endeavoured to collect examples and authorities from the writers before the Restoration, whose works I regard as *the wells of English undefiled*, as the pure sources of genuine diction." It may seem paradoxical that Johnson, who accepted the view of the "reform of our numbers" in the last third of the seventeenth century and believed that his own century had finally learned how to handle language with propriety, should have turned to an earlier period for the examples and quotations with which he illustrated the meanings of words. But he believed that, so far as vocabulary and phrasing went, English had been, for almost a century, "gradually departing from its original Teutonic character, and deviating towards a Gallic structure and phraseology, from which it ought to be our endeavour to recall it, by making our ancient volumes the groundwork of style, admitting among the additions of later times only such as may supply real deficiencies, such as are readily adopted by the genius of our tongue, and incorporated easily with our native idioms." Later on in his Preface he explains that

I have fixed Sidney's work for the boundary, beyond which I make few excursions. From the authors which rose in the time of Elizabeth, a speech might be formed adequate to all the purposes of use and elegance. If the language of theology were extracted from Hooker and the translation of the Bible; the terms of natural knowledge from Bacon; the phrases of policy, war, and navigation from Raleigh; the dialect of poetry and fiction from Spenser and Sidney; and the diction of common life from Shakespeare, few ideas would be lost to mankind, for want of English words, in which they might be expressed.

Johnson's *Dictionary* did not stabilize and standardize the English language; the aim was probably misguided. But it was a remarkable work of scholarship and of classification, one of the great works of its kind in English, and the basis for numerous popular revisions. Further, it made his reputation; from the publication of the first edition in 1755 (there were several further editions in his lifetime), Johnson was a notable man of letters. But he was still under the necessity of earning his living by his pen. He wrote *Rasselas* in 1759 "to defray the expense of his mother's funeral, and pay some little debts which she had left." This somber tale of the Prince of Abyssinia leaving his native happy valley with his sister, her maid, and the sage Imlac, in order to find happiness, only to discover in the end that "human life is everywhere a state in which much is to be endured, and little to be enjoyed" and go back whence they had come, is the most complete statement of Johnson's pessimism. Using the popular form of the oriental tale, and employing a deliberately sententious prose, Johnson, often through the mouth of Imlac, recorded his verdict on human activities. Every way of life has its own tedium and its own discontents. The shepherds in their pastoral life were not only rude and ignorant but also "cankered with discontent." The happiness of solitude is equally delusive; the hermit tells them that "the life of a solitary man will be certainly miserable, but not certainly devout." And so with every way of life: discontent and ennui lie in wait for all. The most eloquent statement of this theme is Imlac's discourse on the pyramids:

. . . He that has built for use, till use is supplied, must begin to build for vanity, and extend his plan to the utmost power of human performance, that he may not be soon reduced to form another wish.

I consider this mighty structure as a monument of the insufficiency of human enjoyments. A king, whose power is unlimited, and whose treasures surmount all real and imaginary wants, is compelled to solace, by the erection of a pyramid, the satiety of dominion and tastelessness of pleasures, and to amuse the tediousness of declining life by seeing thousands labouring without end, and one stone, for no purpose, laid upon another. Whoever thou art, that, not content with a moderate condition, imaginest happiness in royal magnificence, and dreamest that command or riches can feed the appetite of novelty with perpetual gratifications, survey the pyramids, and confess thy folly!

Meanwhile, Johnson was involved with Shakespeare, an edition of whose plays he first proposed as early as 1745 in an advertisement appended to his *Miscellaneous Observations on the Tragedy of Macbeth*. The original scheme fell through, but in 1756 Johnson, by this time made famous by *The Rambler* and the *Dictionary*, published elaborate and detailed *Proposals for Printing the Dramatic Works of William Shakespeare* in which he defined his conception of an editor's duty with cogency and understanding. "The business of him that republishes an ancient book is, to correct what is corrupt, and to explain what is obscure." He gave an account of the "causes of corruption" of Shakespeare's text which influenced generations of editors, though modern scholarship has vindicated the text of the Folio from many of Johnson's charges.

[The plays] were immediately copied for the actors, and multiplied by transcript after transcript, vitiated by the blunders of the penman, or changed by the affectation of the player; perhaps enlarged to introduce a jest, or mutilated to shorten the representation; and printed at last without the concurrence of the author, without the consent of the proprietor, from compilations made by chance or by stealth out of the separate parts written for the theatre: and thus thrust into the world surreptitiously and hastily, they suffered another depravation from the ignorance and negligence of the printers, as every man who knows the state of the press in that age will readily conceive.

Such an extreme view of the corruption of Shakespeare's text puts a large burden of emendation on an editor's shoulder, a burden which earlier eighteenth-century editors from Pope to Sir Thomas Hanmer had cheerfully accepted. They, however, had emended according to their own taste and fancy; Johnson announced his intention of correcting corruptions "by a careful collation of the oldest copies," with a minimum of conjecture and the relevant variant readings given so that the reader, if he wishes, may disagree with the editor's choice. Only when the early editions are "evidently vitiated" so that collations of them would not help does "the task of critical sagacity" begin. "But nothing shall be imposed . . . without notice of the alteration." Johnson shows his awareness that often "a wrong reading has affinity to the right" and that "there is danger lest peculiarities should be mistaken for corruptions, and passages rejected as unintelligible, which a narrow mind happens not to understand." He expressed his intention of reading the books which Shakespeare read, so as to equip himself better for elucidating obscure passages, and "he hopes that, by comparing the works of Shakespeare with those of writers who lived at the same time, immediately preceded, or immediately followed him, he shall be able to ascertain his ambiguities, disentangle his intricacies, and recover the meaning of words now lost in the darkness of antiquity." No previous editor had expressed such sound editorial principles.

The edition did not appear until 1765, though the *Proposals* had stated that it would be out by Christmas 1757. It was published by subscription, and the delay caused some grumbling by those who had subscribed and some sharp lines in Charles Churchill's satirical poem *The Ghost*. However, once it appeared it took its place as a classic edition, the basis of many later editions up to the Johnson-Steevens-Reed "First Variorum" of 1803, which in turn was the basis of the "Second Variorum" of 1813, and in some degree of the Malone-Boswell "Third Variorum" of 1821. Johnson's text was not as great an improvement over that of preceding editors as his better notions of editorial procedure might have led one to expect. He was careless about collation. "I collated such copies as I could procure, and wished for more, but have not found the collectors of these rarities very communicative. Of the editions which chance or kindness put into my hands I have given an enumeration, that I may not be blamed for neglecting what I had not the power to do." He saw quite clearly, however, what the problem was. In his *Preface* he remarks of Theobald that "in his enumeration of editions, he mentions the two first folios as of high, and the third folio as of middle authority; but the truth is, that the first is equivalent to all others, and that the rest deviate from it by the printer's negligence." Johnson did not set up a fresh text, but used as his base the text of Warburton's edition of 1747, correcting it by collation with the Folio and the few Quartos which "chance or kindness" put in his way. Inevitably he took over some of Warburton's misprints, including some taken over by Warburton from Theobald. It was the *Preface* and the notes which gave Johnson's edition its immense distinction and which have preserved it as a central work of criticism.

The *Preface* opens with a tribute to Shakespeare's long-continued popularity, which Johnson considered a proper criterion of greatness. "No other test" of the greatness of literary works (i.e., "works not raised upon principles demonstrative and scientific") existed "than length of duration and continuance of esteem."

> The reverence due to writings that have long subsisted arises therefore not from any credulous confidence in the superior wisdom of past ages, or gloomy persuasion of the degeneracy of mankind, but is the consequence of acknowledged and indubitable positions, that what has been longest known has been most considered, and what is most considered is best understood.

This is not meant as a mere pragmatic acceptance of the verdict of the ages, for "nothing can please many, and please long, but just representations of general nature." Nowhere is the neoclassic position on art as imitation more cogently expressed than in this section of the *Preface*:

Shakespeare is above all writers, at least above all modern writers, the poet of nature; the poet that holds up to his readers a faithful mirror of manners and of life. His characters are not modified by the customs of particular places, unpractised by the rest of the world; by the peculiarities of studies or professions, which can operate but upon small numbers; or by the accidents of transient fashions or temporary opinions: they are the genuine progeny of common humanity, such as the world will always supply, and observation will always find.

This is the basis of Johnson's high estimate of Shakespeare. "His persons act and speak by the influence of those general passions and principles by which all minds are agitated, and the whole system of life is continued in motion." For Johnson as for so many readers and critics of his age, it was the duty of a poet to give pleasure, and the way to give pleasure to the greatest number over the longest period of time is to provide accurate pictures of general human nature. The implication is, of course, that human nature (at least civilized human nature) never really changes. So when Pope tells us that the Greek and Roman writers found out the best way of "imitating Nature" and that therefore to copy Homer is to copy Nature, he is assuming that men in Homer's day were, in those aspects of their nature which are of interest to the poet, identical with the men of his own day. Universality implies generality; Shakespeare can only appeal to every age if he refrains from emphasizing the differentiating qualities of one time and place and concentrates on what men have in common. Similarly, in *Rasselas* Johnson had put into the mouth of Imlac his view of the importance of generality: "The business of a poet," said Imlac,

is to examine, not the individual, but the species; to remark general properties and large appearances; he does not number the streaks of the tulip, or describe the different shades in the verdure of the forest. He is to exhibit in his portraits of nature such prominent and striking features as recall the original to every mind, and must neglect the minuter discriminations, which one may have remarked and another have neglected, for those characteristics which are alike obvious to vigilance and carelessness.

It is because of his knowledge of general human nature that Shakespeare is able to fill his plays "with practical axioms and domestic wisdom." If we compare him with other dramatists, Johnson continues, we see that Shakespeare does not, as so many others do, deal mainly with love and pretend that love is the major human motive and emotion. In other dramatists, "probability is violated, life is misrepresented, and language is depraved" in order to concentrate interest on the love story. "But love is only one of many passions; and as it has no great influence upon the sum of life, it has little operation in the dramas of a poet, who caught his ideas from the living world, and exhibited only what he saw before him. He knew that any other passion, as it was regular or exorbitant, was a cause of happiness or calamity." Shakespeare's plays are genuinely "the mirror of life," and from them "a hermit may estimate the transactions of the world, and a confessor predict the progress of the passions." Johnson brushes aside the stricter neoclassic notions of propriety with respect to character.

Dennis and Rymer think his Romans not sufficiently Roman; and Voltaire censures his kings as not completely royal. Dennis is offended that Menenius, a senator of Rome, should play the buffoon; and Voltaire perhaps thinks decency violated when the Danish usurper is represented as a drunkard. But Shakespeare always makes nature predominate over accident; . . . His story requires Romans or kings, but he thinks only on men.

The line of argument leads him to defend the mingling of tragic and comic scenes—a mingling condemned by strict neoclassic theory but defended by Johnson on the fundamentally neoclassic ground that imitation of general human nature demands it. Shakespeare's plays, combining comedy and tragedy, exhibit

the real state of sublunary nature, which partakes of good and evil, joy and sorrow, mingled with endless variety of proportion and innumerable modes of combination; and expressing the course of the world, in which the loss of one is the gain of another; in which, at the same time, the reveller is hasting to his wine, and the mourner burying his friend; in which the malignity of one is sometimes defeated by the frolic of another; and many mischiefs and many benefits are done and hindered without design.

Johnson is aware here that he is flouting "the rules of criticism," but confidently asserts that "there is always an appeal open from criticism to nature"—which means that he is appealing from one aspect of neoclassic theory, concerned with decorum, to another, concerned with imitation. If criticism is based on adequate principles with respect to the relation between art and nature then an appeal "from criticism to nature" is meaningless: Johnson, in making this appeal, is uncovering a possible contradiction in the critical principles of his time. If literature aims at "just representation of general nature," then any rules concerning the proper method of representation must be tested by their effectiveness as means to this end. But for Johnson the imitative function of literature went side by side with its didactic function. "The end of writing is to instruct; the end of poetry is to instruct by pleasing." It seems at times as though Johnson's point is that poetry should instruct the reader in the facts of human psychology; "it may be said that he [Shakespeare] has not only shown human nature as it acts in real exigencies, but as it would be found in trials to which it cannot be exposed." Yet Johnson also insisted that literature should instruct morally, should help to make the reader a better man. "It is always a writer's duty to make the world better." On this count he holds Shakespeare defective. "He sacrifices virtue to convenience, and is so much more careful to please than to instruct, that he seems to write without any moral purpose." Johnson objects that Shakespeare "makes no just distribution of good or evil, nor is always careful to show in the virtuous a disapprobation of the wicked; he carries his persons indifferently through right and wrong, and leaves their examples to operate by chance."

Johnson finds himself in a dilemma here, though he does not clearly recognize it as such. If a poet's duty is to represent human nature accurately and vividly and at the same time to arrange his story so that it provides moral instruction for the reader, then it must follow that human nature in itself must be edifying. Sir Philip Sidney had argued that poetry should be morally instructive, but, well aware that life as it is does not convey a moral lesson to the observer, he insisted that the poet create a new and better world. Johnson wants to have it both ways, which would be fair enough if he believed that the real world is in fact morally edifying, but he knew very well that it was not and despised those facile optimists who thought that it was. He almost comes to grips with his dilemma in a long note on *King Lear*:

A play in which the wicked prosper, and the virtuous miscarry, may doubtless be good, because it is a just representation of the common events of human life: but since all reasonable beings naturally love justice, I cannot easily be persuaded that the observation of justice makes a play worse; or that, if other excellencies are equal, the audience will not always rise better pleased from the final triumph of persecuted virtue.

But under what conditions are "other excellencies equal," and what if they are not? And are representational adequacy and moral edification two quite separate qualities, with the latter to be added if it can be done without doing violence to the former? And is the pleasure we get from "poetic justice," from seeing virtue rewarded and villainy punished, a wholly separate kind of pleasure from that of recognizing or of being instructed in the truths of human nature? Johnson, in developing the old notion that literature should both teach and delight, and in expressing both his own somberly didactic temperament and his belief that literature will survive only if it continues to give pleasure, makes his individual points with persuasive cogency but fails to explore all the implications of his views or to resolve implied contradictions.

Johnson had certain objections to Shakespeare's diction. "He is not long soft or pathetic without some idle conceit or contemptible equivocation. . . . A quibble was to him the fatal Cleopatra for which he lost the world, and was content to lose it." This objection to Shakespeare's "conceits" and in particular the aversion to puns derives from the separation of wit and judgment insisted on by Addison and first developed in England by Hobbes and Locke. This whole approach to poetic language is important in both the theory and the practice of poetry from Dryden to Johnson; its critical implications are seen most clearly in Johnson's *Lives of the Poets,* especially in his discussion of the metaphysical poets.

In discussing Shakespeare's lack of regard for the "unities" of time and place, Johnson reveals that characteristic awareness of the difference between art and life which is responsible for what has been called his "sturdy common sense." The theory that representation on the stage should confine itself to events covering a limited time (twelve or twenty-four hours) and occurring in a single place, assumed that the more closely action on the stage approximated its temporal and spatial dimensions to those of actual experience the more esthetically satisfying the action. Johnson pointed out that the action of a play is based on a set of conventions, which the audience accepts, and that it is no more difficult to accept the convention of shifting scenes or leaps in time than the convention that a particular actor "is" Julius Caesar or Alexander. "The necessity of observing the unities of time and place arises from the supposed necessity of making the drama credible." But nobody expects drama to be credible in *that* way.

The truth is, that the spectators are always in their senses, and know, from the first act to the last, that the stage is only a stage, and that the players are only players. They came to hear a certain number of lines recited with just gesture and elegant modulation. The lines relate to some action, and an action must be in some place; but the different actions that complete a story may be in places very remote from each other; and where is the absurdity of allowing that space to represent first Athens, and then Sicily, which was always known to be neither Sicily nor Athens, but a modern theatre?

If this strikes the modern reader as rather too negative an argument, making no effort to consider what the imaginative life of a play and its dramatic unity truly is, it nevertheless makes a salutary distinction between conventions and rules in drama and puts the onus on the defender of the unities to show why representation on the stage should be more confined in its handling of the dimensions of time and space than the epic or the novel. Johnson, in fact, put an end to the view of the dramatic unities as an end in themselves.

Thus Johnson's *Preface to Shakespeare* is at the same time one of the noblest monuments of English neoclassic criticism (in its expression of the theory of imitation and of general human nature) and an exposure of some of the weaknesses, contradictions, and unnecessary rigidities of some widely accepted neoclassic principles by testing their effectiveness in gauging adequacy of imitation of nature and the giving of pleasure. Its pungent style, emphatic clarity, and tendency to epigrammatic summing up of each argument, carried its ideas home with enormous force. In some respects more valuable, and of more permanent use and interest, are Johnson's notes on the individual plays. If Johnson did not adequately carry out the textual principles he so admirably enunciated, he nevertheless consistently rejected the unjustified and "improving" emendation of earlier editors and made many sound and impressive suggestions on textual matters, based on his own wide reading in Elizabethan literature. His running comments on the characters are often illuminating, and his notes on the meaning of words and phrases (in which he drew on the reading he did for his dictionary) consistently sound and helpful. His comments on both parts of *Henry IV* have helped to lead modern criticism back to a juster understanding of the moral pattern of these plays. Johnson's Shakespeare remains an edition which no later editor of Shakespeare can ignore.

Johnson's most sustained and mature critical work is to be found in his *Prefaces, Biographical and Critical, to the Works of the English Poets*, generally known as *The Lives of the Poets*, first published between 1779 and 1781 as a series of introductions to a ten-volume collection of the English poets from Cowley, Denham, Milton, and Waller at one end to Akenside and Gray at the other. The great majority of the fifty-two poets chosen by the group of publishers responsible for the enterprise came after the "reform of our numbers" for which Denham and Waller were given credit, and for the most part Johnson is dealing with men writing in a tradition he understood and employing the kind of verse for which he had an extremely accurate ear. No living poets were included. Some of those included were insignificant: who now remembers Edmund Smith, William King, John Hughes, Thomas Yalden, James Hammond, or Gilbert West? One of the longest and the most purely biographical, the "Life of Richard Savage," had been written and published much earlier (1744) as a lively and compassionate tribute to a brawling scapegrace whom he had known in his own young and miserable Grub Street days and whom in spite of everything he had loved. But the Lives of Cowley, Milton, Dryden, Addison (a poet in virtue of his long poem on the Battle of Blenheim, *The Campaign,* and his drama *Cato*), Pope, and Gray, to cite no more, gave Johnson the opportunity of developing and illustrating his view of poetry, and often of life and letters in general, with a relaxed confidence that can be matched nowhere else in his written work. He wrote these prefaces out of a full mind and after a lifetime of reflection on literature; the research he did for the biographical parts was perfunctory and even in the critical parts he depended to an astonishing degree on his remarkable memory for poetry, which often enabled him to quote freely without looking the passages up. He wrote with pleasure and gusto, and the comparatively lax way in which he undertook his duties as biographer— "To adjust the minute events of literary history is tedious and troublesome; it requires, indeed, no great force of understanding, but often depends upon inquiries which there is no opportunity of making, or is to be fetched from books and pamphlets not always at hand," he remarked in his "Life of Dryden"—is bound up with the pleasure and spontaneity with which he wrote.

Johnson had always been interested in biography; he had a curiosity about people, which was related to his view of the function of literature as the rendering of universal human experience with liveliness and originality. Poets and dramatists, as he so often maintained, write to please and survive by pleasing; the character of the writer as well as the character of the audience is therefore of interest to him, but the latter can only be discussed generally while the former can be inquired into with some particularity. Further, genius for Johnson did not consist in some highly specialized aptitude; "the true Genius," he observed in his "Life of Cowley," "is a mind of large general powers, accidentally determined in some particular direction." So a discussion of a poet's mind and character is not simply the analysis of the uniquely poetic mind and character, but discussion of the degree to which he possessed general human intellectual and imaginative powers. Poetry for him was essentially an activity rather than a series of works of art existing timelessly and anonymously. How well it can be done can best be gauged by observing the total poetic scene, and making comparisons. "In the productions of genius, nothing can be styled excellent till it has been compared with other works of the same kind," he wrote in his *Preface to Shakespeare*. "All human excellence is comparative," he wrote in a *Rambler* essay, ". . . no man performs much but in proportion to what others accomplish, or to the time and opportunities which have been allowed him." This encourages both the biographical and the comparative approach. The characteristic method of *The Lives of the Poets* is to give first the facts of a poet's life, then an account of the quality of his mind, and then a criticism of his poems. The poet is a man seeking to give pleasure by conveying general truths about experience with freshness and skill; the questions to be asked of a given poet are: what kind of a man, living in what age and circumstances, was he, and, being that sort of a man, with what degree of success did he produce works capable of giving pleasure by their truth and liveliness? Liveliness, or novelty, it should be added, was always a criterion insisted on by Johnson, as well as general truth. In his "Life of Cowley" he objected to Pope's celebrated definition of true wit as "what oft was thought but ne'er so well expressed," and added: "If by a more noble and more adequate conception that be considered as wit which is at once natural and new, that which, though not obvious, is, upon its first production, acknowledged to be just; if it be that, which he that never found it wonders how he missed; to wit of this kind the metaphysical poets have seldom risen." Here his definition is used as a means of criticizing adversely the metaphysical poets, but it is none the less central to Johnson's critical position. It is with reference to that position that he makes what critics today would regard as his greatest blunders, in his assessment of the metaphysicals and in his estimate of Milton's "Lycidas." Wit that was new without being natural he could not accept, nor could he accept conventional, "hereditary" similes and images which were handed down ready-made from one generation of poets to the next. As a result, he rejected metaphysical wit because "their thoughts are often new, but seldom natural; they are not obvious, but neither are they just; and the reader, far from wondering that he missed them, wonders more frequently by what perverseness of industry they were ever found." And he objected to the classical and pastoral imagery of "Lycidas"—"Jove and Phoebus, Neptune and Aeolus, with a long train of mythological imagery, such as a college easily supplies"—because he considered it utterly conventional and mechanical, wholly lacking in novelty.

Johnson accepted the view that English versification was permanently improved in the Age of Dryden, who "refined the language, improved the sentiments, and tuned the numbers of English poetry." He states this view emphatically in his "Life of Dryden." "The new versification, as it was called, may be considered as owing its establishment to Dryden; from whose time it is apparent that English poetry has had no tendency to relapse to its former savageness." Waller and Denham were pioneers in this movement, but "it may be doubted whether Waller and Denham could have overborne the prejudices which had long prevailed"; Dryden was the true hero of this reformation, and Johnson's ear was attuned to the music of the kind of verse it produced. As T. S. Eliot has put it, "The deafness of Johnson's ear to some kinds of melody was the necessary condition for his sharpness of sensibility to verbal beauty of another kind." He has nothing to say in his *Preface to Shakespeare* of Shakespeare's incomparable mastery of versification, and he condemns "Lycidas" in an often quoted phrase: ". . . the diction is harsh, the rhymes uncertain, and the numbers unpleasing." His ear was attuned primarily to the heroic couplet. He never fully approved of blank verse, and never fully understood the kinds of varied cadence of which that meter was capable: his own blank verse (in his rather wooden tragedy *Irene*) reads like disappointed couplets, and moves by the line rather than by the verse paragraph.

Johnson's limitations as a critic thus derive from his rather special view of what was "natural" in imagery and subject matter and from his highly specialized ear for verse. It was his insistence on the "natural" that led him to discard the whole neoclassic view of kinds and of the sort of diction and imagery appropriate to each. His method was practical and comparative, looking to see what he had before him and how it compared with other works he knew; he never simply applied rules about what was appropriate to a certain genre. When this leads him to justify Shakespeare's neglect of the dramatic unities, we applaud him, but the same method also led him to write of "Lycidas": "In this poem there is no nature, for there is no truth; there is no art, for there is nothing new. Its form is that of a pastoral, easy, vulgar, and therefore disgusting: whatever images it can supply, are long ago exhausted; and its inherent improbability always forces dissatisfaction on the mind." Johnson's insistence on both naturalness and novelty could make him grossly insensitive to certain kinds of originality that depended on a new handling of conventional material. It is in the essays on Milton and Cowley that Johnson's critical limitations are most clearly seen. He was further prejudiced against Milton on political grounds: "Milton's republicanism was, I am afraid, founded in an envious hatred of greatness, and a sullen desire of independence; in petulance impatient of control, and pride disdainful of superiority." Yet he regarded him as a very great poet, and he considered *Paradise Lost* "a poem which, considered with respect to design, may claim the first place, and with respect to performance the second, among the productions of the human mind." The view of the epic which he gives in this connection is cogent statement of the neoclassic position on the subject:

By the general consent of critics, the first praise of genius is due to the writer of an epic poem, as it requires an assemblage of all the powers which are singly sufficient for other compositions. Poetry is the art of uniting pleasure with truth, by calling imagination to the help of reason. Epic poetry undertakes to teach the most important truths by the most pleasing precepts, and therefore relates some great event in the most affecting manner. History must supply the writer with the rudiments of narration, which he must improve and exalt by a nobler art, must animate by dramatic energy, and diversify by retrospection and anticipation; morality must teach him the exact bounds, and different shades, of vice and virtue; from policy, and the practice of life, he has to learn the discriminations of character, and the tendency of the passions, either single or combined; and physiology must supply him with illustrations and images. To put these materials to poetical use, is required an imagination capable of painting nature, and realising fiction. Nor is he yet a poet till he has attained the whole extension of his language, distinguished all the delicacies of phrase, and all the colours of words, and learned to adjust their different sounds to all the varieties of metrical modulation.

In his "Life of Cowley" Johnson takes the opportunity of examining the whole metaphysical manner and finding it vitiated because it drew too heavily on what Addison (and Johnson quotes him) called "mixed wit." "The fault of Cowley, and perhaps all the writers of the metaphysical race, is that of pursuing his thoughts to their last ramifications, by which he loses the grandeur of generality; . . ." Johnson's famous definition of metaphysical wit sums up with peculiar force the view of an age of "dissociated sensibility" (as we have learned from T. S. Eliot to call it) on the poetry of an age of unified sensibility:

But wit, abstracted from its effects upon the hearer, may be more rigorously and philosophically considered as a kind of *discordia concors;* a combination of dissimilar images, or discovery of occult resemblances in things apparently unlike. Of wit, thus defined, they have more than enough. The most heterogeneous ideas are yoked by violence together; nature and art are ransacked for illustrations, comparisons, and allusions; their learning instructs and their subtlety surprises; but the reader commonly thinks his improvement dearly bought, and, though he sometimes admires, is seldom pleased.

. . . Sublimity is produced by aggregation, and littleness by dispersion. Great thoughts are always general, and consist in positions not limited by exceptions, and in descriptions not descending to minuteness. . . . Those writers who lay on the watch for novelty could have little hope of greatness; for great things cannot have escaped former observation. Their attempts were always analytic; they broke every image into fragments: and could no more represent, by their slender conceits and laboured particularities, the prospects of nature, or the scenes of life, than he who dissects a sun-beam with a prism, can exhibit the wide effulgence of a summer noon. . . .

Yet great labour, directed by great abilities, is never wholly lost: if they frequently threw away their wit upon false conceits, they likewise sometimes struck out unexpected truth: if their conceits were far-fetched, they were often worth the carriage. To write on their plan, it was at least necessary to read and think. No man could be born a metaphysical poet, nor assume the dignity of a writer, by descriptions copied from descriptions, by imitations borrowed from imitations, by traditional imagery and hereditary similes, by readiness of rhyme, and volubility of syllables.

Great poetry for Johnson required both nature and novelty; "Lycidas" had too little of the former and metaphysical poetry had too much of the latter. But in the last analysis, Johnson held that exhibitionist novelty was better than the mechanical repetition of hereditary similes.

Johnson's account of Dryden is that of a man looking back with both admiration and discrimination on the founder of the poetic age in which he himself lived. He is more sympathetic with Dryden's whole position than with Milton's and gives him the benefit of the doubt in the matter of the genuineness of his religious convictions —which he never accorded to Milton in discussing the latter's political convictions. The "Life of Pope" is sufficiently critical of aspects of Pope's character and behavior, and even in discussing the poetry, Johnson frequently pauses to take exception to something Pope had written; but the critical section is nevertheless a reasoned vindication of Pope's claims to greatness as a poet. It was a vindication because Pope's claims had already been challenged by a changing taste; but Johnson had no sympathy with a point of view such as that expressed by Joseph Warton. "After all this, it is surely superfluous to answer the question that has once been asked, whether Pope was a poet, otherwise than by asking in return, If Pope be not a poet, where is poetry to be found?" The remark comes at the end of Johnson's analysis of the poetry, and the reader is thus referred to that analysis for the real answer. He had earlier compared Pope with Dryden in a classic passage which has had a permanent effect on the history of the reputation of those two poets:

. . . The notions of Dryden were formed by comprehensive speculation, and those of Pope by minute attention. There is more dignity in the knowledge of Dryden, and more certainty in that of Pope.

Poetry was not the sole praise of either; for both excelled likewise in prose; but Pope did not borrow his prose from his predecessor. The style of Dryden is capricious and varied, that of Pope is cautious and uniform; Dryden obeys the motions of his own mind, Pope constrains his mind to his own rules of composition. Dryden is sometimes vehement and rapid; Pope is always smooth, uniform, and gentle. Dryden's page is a natural field, rising into inequalities, and diversified by the varied exuberance of abundant vegetation; Pope's is a velvet lawn, shaven by the scythe, and levelled by the roller.

Of genius, that power which constitutes a poet; that quality without which judgment is cold and knowledge is inert; that energy which collects, combines, amplifies, and animates; the superiority must, with some hestitation, be allowed to Dryden. It is not to be inferred that of this poetical vigour Pope had only a little, because Dryden had more; for every other writer since Milton must give place to Pope; and even of Dryden it must be said, that if he has brighter paragraphs, he has not better poems. Dryden's performances were always hasty, either excited by some external occasion, or extorted by domestic necessity; he composed without consideration, and published without correction. What his mind could supply at call, or gather in one excursion, was all that he sought and all that he gave. The dilatory caution of Pope enabled him to condense his sentiments, to multiply his images, and to accumulate all that study might produce, or chance might supply. If the flights of Dryden therefore are higher, Pope continues longer on the wing. If of Dryden's fire the blaze is brighter, of Pope's the heat is more regular and constant. Dryden often surpasses expectation, and Pope never falls below it. Dryden is read with frequent astonishment, and Pope with perpetual delight.

Something has been said of Johnson's view of Gray in the discussion of that poet in Chapter 17. His dislike of what he considered Gray's forced extravagance of language is on a par with his suspicion of Milton's pastoralisms and of the excesses of metaphysical wit: this was no way to combine truth and novelty. Johnson—and this is one of many ways in which he asserts his total independence of the neoclassic view—had a deep suspicion of the use of classical mythology in modern English poetry; such imagery was "hereditary" and lifeless. "The second stanza, exhibiting Mars's car and Jove's eagle, is unworthy of further notice. Criticism disdains to chase a schoolboy to his commonplaces." This reminds us of Johnson's dismissal in "Lycidas" of the "long train of mythological imagery, such as a college easily supplies." Sometimes, however, Johnson is pleased in spite of himself. "Idalia's *velvet-green* has something of cant. An epithet or metaphor drawn from Nature ennobles Art; an epithet or metaphor drawn from Art degrades Nature. Gray is too fond of words arbitrarily compounded. *Many-twinkling* was formerly censured as not analogical; we may say *many-spotted,* but scarcely *many-spotting.* This stanza, however, has something pleasing." Johnson's opinion of "The Bard" again springs from his basic position on truth and pleasure: "To select a singular event, and swell it to a giant's bulk by fabulous appendages of spectres and predictions, has little difficulty, for he that forsakes the probable may always find the marvellous. And it has little use; we are affected only as we believe; we are improved only as we find something to be imitated or declined."

But Johnson makes handsome amends to Gray in his concluding paragraph, on the "Elegy." As always, Johnson pays tribute to the verdict of readers, to the critical significance of continued popularity. (It should be realized, however, that by the phrase "the common reader" Johnson meant the ordinary, educated reader of poetry of his day; in the eighteenth century, in spite of the great and rapid growth of the reading public, literacy was still limited, education when it was acquired was more or less uniform, and expectations about poetry among readers were more or less the same. The universal literacy, or semiliteracy, which the Industrial Revolution brought in its wake, and the resulting fragmentation of the reading public into highbrows, lowbrows, and middlebrows, posed problems never envisaged by Dr. Johnson.)

In the character of his *Elegy* I rejoice to concur with the common reader; for by the common sense of readers uncorrupted with literary prejudices, after all the refinements of subtlety and the dogmatism of learning, must be finally decided all claim to poetical honours. The *Church-yard* abounds with images which find a mirror in every mind, and with sentiments to which every bosom returns an echo. The four stanzas beginning *Yet even these bones,* are to me original: I have never seen the notions in any other place; yet he that reads them here, persuades himself that he has always felt them. Had Gray written often thus, it had been vain to blame, and useless to praise him.

Thanks largely to James Boswell's *Life,* Johnson is remembered more as a great personality and a great talker than as a poet or critic. Johnson was indeed a great talker, though often a dominating one who would "talk for victory" on whatever side would help him most to discomfit his opponent. His was an age of conversation, an age in which the specialization of knowledge had not proceeded far enough to prevent intelligent men from expressing their ideas on whatever subject might be brought to their attention. Boswell—who knew Johnson only in the latter part of his life, after he was well established as the Great Cham—was adroit at arranging situations and broaching subjects that would bring forth Johnson's views on all the major topics of life and letters, and the brilliance of his *Life of Johnson* derives in considerable measure from the art with which Boswell was able to precipitate various moods in Johnson preparatory to recording what he said. The art of the *Life* is only partly an art of recording; it is also an art of stage-managing what to record.

Boswell himself is a puzzling and fascinating character. His vanity, extreme self-consciousness, sexual promiscuity, drinking habits, proneness to hero-worship, and that extraordinary narcissism which compelled him throughout his life to record his feelings and activities almost daily, represent an odd combination of qualities. He was cursed with fits of acute melancholia, worried continually about the truth of religion and the nature of the next world, tried intermittently to model himself on whatever character temporarily aroused his admiration, was both intensely proud and timidly defensive about his being a Scotsman. From the moment he marked Johnson down as a great man he wished to become intimate with, he allowed himself to be the butt of Johnson's conversation or played any role from humble seeker after truth to guide and showman if it would help to draw Johnson out and make him exhibit some truly Johnsonian aspect of himself. His greatest work is of course his *Life of Johnson*, but the journals which were discovered in such large numbers only recently are, if of much less literary interest, of great importance as psychological and social documents. His *Journal of a Tour to the Hebrides* (taken with Johnson), published in 1785, has all the qualities of the *Life*, with its carefully recorded conversations and triumphant curiosity about Johnson's reactions to different aspects of Scottish life. Johnson's own account of the Scottish journey he made with Boswell in 1773 is much more pedestrian. It was a great victory for Boswell to have brought Johnson, the professional anti-Scot, to take this arduous journey to the Highlands and Islands at the age of sixty-four, and Johnson responded to the experiences he was subjected to with that combination of wisdom, humanity, prejudice, and curiosity which Boswell knew so well how to make the most of. Boswell's own opinions were often of the shallowest; he had little literary taste and was prone to rationalize all moral questions so as to justify himself in doing what he happened to want to do at the time. But he was a showman, an impresario, an artist in arranging and recording scenes for the biographer, as well as a pathological narcissist. The discovery of the mass of autobiographical material which he wrote throughout his life has helped to shift interest from Boswell the biographer to

Boswell the diarist and psychological case. But his real claim to fame still lies in what he made of his association with Johnson. It is not his fault if the Johnson he gives us in his *Life* eclipses by its power and fascination the Johnson who wrote "The Vanity of Human Wishes," the *Preface to Shakespeare,* and the *Lives of the Poets.* Boswell's Johnson stays with us like a character in a great play or novel, but it is none the less a true Johnson. The other Johnson, the writer, shows the same personality at work, but less spectacularly and more maturely.

Of Johnson's circle, Oliver Goldsmith (1728–74) is in many ways the most attractive, though not the most profound. He came to Grub Street after an oddly adventurous career, which took him from Ireland, where he was born, to Edinburgh, Leyden, and a walking tour through Europe. From 1756 he was in London trying to make a living by literary journalism, and gradually established himself as an essayist. He contributed to a variety of periodicals, including *The Monthly Review, The Critical Review, The Weekly Magazine,* and *The British Magazine,* and published his periodical essays, *The Bee,* in eight issues in 1759, as well as bringing them out in book form in the same year. In 1759, he also brought out his *Enquiry into the Present State of Polite Learning,* a superficial study of the literary culture of his time written with characteristic ease and lucidity. He catered to the taste for compilations and surveys which developed so rapidly in the eighteenth century; his *History of England* (1764) was praised by Johnson as "telling the reader shortly all he could want to know; and written in a style that would bear frequent re-perusal," and he produced many other works of history, biography, and popular science. His work as a novelist and as a poet has been discussed previously; his main claim to fame apart from this (and apart from his plays) is as an essayist. The "Chinese Letters" which he contributed to *The Public Ledger* in 1760 and 1761, were published together in 1762 as *The Citizen of the World.* These are supposed to have been written by a visitor from China, who comments, often with ironical humor, on the English scene. The irony is neither subtle nor bitter, and the essays reveal their author's combination of gaiety and moral earnestness, personal feeling and formal wit, which sometimes suggests the familiar essay of the early nineteenth century, though it is never so exhibitionist or self-consciously subjective. In these and other essays, Goldsmith's moralizing is sometimes heavy-handed, sometimes verging on the sentimental, but their geniality, ease of movement, and what might perhaps be called their purity of tone give them a charm that is not often found in the essays of the mid-eighteenth century. In some respects Goldsmith was a glorified hack; he could turn his hand to almost anything and do an acceptable job. But though much of his writing is hack work, and nobody today is likely to want to read his *History of the Earth, and Animated Nature* or his *Survey of Experimental Philosophy, Considered in its Present State of Improvement*, he was a great prose stylist, mingling the colloquial and the formal in new proportions. He was regarded with somewhat patronizing affection in Johnson's circle, as a man possessed of an engaging simplicity and a ludicrous vanity who was also, by accident as it were, something of a literary genius. He was one of the founders of The Club, with Johnson, Joshua Reynolds, Edmund Burke, and others, and though he does not appear to have been able to hold his own conversationally in that distinguished company (he "wrote like an angel, but talked like poor Poll," as Garrick put it in his famous couplet) there was at least one occasion when he had the better of Dr. Johnson—when Johnson had expressed contempt for those who thought it difficult to make animal characters in a fable talk, and Goldsmith retorted: "This is not so easy as you seem to think; for if you were to make little fishes talk, they would talk like WHALES."

Another member of The Club (which became The Literary Club), whom Johnson particularly esteemed as a conversationalist, was Edmund Burke (1729–97), the Dublin-born political philosopher and statesman who opposed to the rising influence of Rousseau and general theorizing on the Rights of Man an organic conception of the state and a suspicion of a priori theorizing in politics which he embodied in speeches and discourses that have survived the occasions which prompted them. Burke's sense of continuity and tradition was in some respects similar to Johnson's, but it was neither so pessimistically conservative nor did its application lead to the same practical conclusions. Burke's principles—and in spite of his pragmatic wisdom and his suspicion of theory he *had* clear principles—led him to oppose the British Government's policy with respect to the American colonies, to criticize bitterly and in the greatest detail the whole conduct of the East India Company in the government of India, and to attack the French Revolution and those who supported it. This may look like inconsistency today, when political thinkers past and present are neatly labeled into Right and Left, but in fact, as Morley put it, "Burke changed his front, but he never changed his ground," and it is not difficult to trace through all his speeches and other political writings a single view of the state, of society, and of history.

Burke's first published work was *A Vindication of Natural Society* (1756), a satire on the views of Bolingbroke, aiming to prove that Bolingbroke's theoretical arguments against Christianity were fundamentally disruptive of all civil society; but, as so often happens in ironical works, its irony was missed by most contemporary readers. *A Philosophical Enquiry into the Origin of our Ideas of the Sublime and the Beautiful* followed in 1757. But he soon turned to those political and historical themes in which his real interest and genius lay. His *Thoughts on the Cause of the Present Discontents* (1770) discussed the unhappy influence of the Court faction under George III with an acute analysis of the proper relations that, in the light of British traditions and the interests of efficient government, should exist between king, ministry, Parliament, and people. It was with his speeches in favor of conciliation with the American colonies, in which he urged in vain an understanding of the historical and psychological factors involved and a policy based on their realistic appraisal, that the full force of his genius as political orator and practical statesman became apparent. (Burke was a great orator in the sense that he wrote brilliant and memorable speeches; but contemporary evidence suggests that he was not a lively public speaker.) His *Speech on American Taxation* (1774) illustrates again and again his combination of political principle with shrewd pragmatic wisdom. "I am not here going into the distinctions of rights, nor attempting to mark their boundaries. I do not enter into these metaphysical distinctions; I hate the very sound of them. Leave the Americans as they anciently stood, and these distinctions, born of our unhappy contest, will die along with it. . . . Perhaps we might wish the colonists to be persuaded that their liberty is more secure when held in trust for them by us . . . than with any part of it in their own hands. But the question is not whether their spirit deserves praise or blame—what, in the name of God, shall we do with it?" In all the American speeches and pamphlets—in the speech on taxation, in the speech he made in April, 1777, on moving his resolution for conciliation with the colonies, in his *Letter to the Sheriffs of Bristol on the Affairs of America*—Burke speaks primarily as a statesman interested in a practical solution to a specific problem, and the appeal to history and psychology, which is made often, is made in order to illustrate, explain, and push home his points. The Government talked as though they could "prosecute that spirit [of American independence] as *criminal*," and Burke replies: "I do not know the method of drawing up an indictment against a whole people." Conciliation, far from disrupting the empire, was the only way of preserving it. "Such is steadfastly my opinion of the absolute necessity of keeping up the concord of this empire by a unity of spirit, though in a diversity of operaticns, . . ." His own proposals, carefully framed both to soothe American feeling and to save British face, are scrupulously documented by precedents. He is unconcerned with vague, emotional charges. "I am charged with being an American. If warm affection towards those over whom I claim any share of authority be a crime, I am guilty of this charge." Above all, he will not have people canting about freedom without understanding the concrete implications of what they are saying:

Civil freedom, Gentlemen, is not, as many have endeavoured to persuade you, a thing that lies hid in the depth of abstruse science. It is a blessing and a benefit, not an abstract speculation; and all the just reasoning that can be upon it is of so coarse a texture as perfectly to suit the ordinary capacities of those who are to enjoy, and of those who are to defend it. Far from any resemblance to those propositions in geometry and metaphysics which admit no medium, but must be true or false in all their latitude, social and civil freedom, like all other things in common life, are variously mixed and modified, enjoyed in very different degrees, and shaped into an infinite diversity of forms, according to the temper and circumstances of every community.

Burke's almost mystical sense of the organic nature of society and the way in which institutions develop and the will of the people manifests itself lies behind his sense of outrage at the deliberate and violent break with the past represented by the French Revolution. As he wrote in *Reflections on the Revolution in France* (1790):

Our political system is placed in a just correspondence and symmetry with the order of the world, and with the mode of existence decreed to a permanent body composed of transitory parts; wherein, by the disposition of a stupendous wisdom, moulding together the great mysterious incorporation of the human race, the whole, at one time, is never old or middle-aged or young, but, in a condition of unchangeable constancy, moves on through the varied tenor of perpetual decay, fall, renovation, and progression. Thus, by preserving the method of nature in the conduct of the state, in what we improve we are never wholly new, in what we retain we are never wholly obsolete. By adhering in this manner, and on those principles, to our forefathers, we are guided, not by the superstition of antiquarians, but by the spirit of philosophic analogy. In this choice of inheritance we have given to our frame of polity the image of a relation in blood: binding up the constitution of our country with our dearest domestic ties; adopting our fundamental laws into the bosom of our family affections; keeping inseparable, and cherishing with the warmth of all their combined and mutually reflected charities, our state, our hearths, our sepulchres, and our altars.

Again and again Burke insists that political organization is the result of a complex and delicate mechanism, which cannot be changed for the better by the simple application of large general theories.

The moment you abate anything from the full rights of men each to govern himself, and suffer any artificial, positive limitation upon those rights, from that moment the whole organization of government becomes a consideration of convenience. This it is which makes the constitution of a state, and the due distribution of its powers, a matter of the most delicate and complicated skill. It requires a deep knowledge of human nature and human necessities, and of the things which facilitate or obstruct the various ends which are to be pursued by the mechanism of civil institutions.

And, most emphatically of all: "The science of constructing a commonwealth, or renovating it, or reforming it, is, like every other experimental science, not to be taught *a priori*."

The nature of man is intricate; the objects of society are of the greatest possible complexity: and therefore no simple disposition or direction of power can be suitable either to man's nature or to the quality of his affairs: When I hear the simplicity of contrivance aimed at and boasted of in any new political constitutions, I am at no loss to decide that the artificers are grossly ignorant of their trade or totally negligent of their duty.

Burke was a Whig, not a Tory, though he quarreled with his party over the French Revolution and was eventually expelled from it. He believed in progress, and was far from acquiescing in things as they were. In his speeches on India—notably the speech *On the Nabob of Arcot's Debts* (1785) and his speech in opening the impeachment of Warren Hastings (1788)—he bitterly denounced what he considered to be the cruelty, greed, and corruption of the British officials in that country. Hastings was acquitted of the charges brought against his conduct as Governor-General of Bengal, and history has supported that verdict; but Burke's zeal against Hastings was a zeal for the purification of the Indian civil service (at that time still largely managed by the East India Company) and the raising of British standards of colonial administration by a more rigid adherence to the principles of humanity and incorruptibility. He had high ideals for the British Empire, and in his Indian as in his American speeches, spoke with high moral passion about what it might be. At the end of his life he regarded his campaign for better government in India as the most important and most sustained effort of his career.

Burke's practical wisdom and his tact in knowing how far to press a principle or a precedent are often, but not always, in evidence. In his attacks on the French Revolution he was sometimes led into extreme statements about the benevolence and sense of honor of the French aristocracy. His impassioned purple passage about the French Queen is a splendid piece of rhetoric, but it is not really relevant to his argument, and the conclusion—"But the age of chivalry is gone. That of sophisters, economists and calculators has succeeded; and the glory of Europe is extinguished forever"—is unusually abstract and generalized for Burke. Tom Paine's charge that in attacking the French Revolution Burke pitied the plumage and forgot the dying bird has its element of truth. Nevertheless, if his writings against the French Revolution contain more rhetorical generalizations than are to be found elsewhere in his work, they also include some of his most memorable political utterances, such as his remark on Rousseau's theory of the social contract:

Society is, indeed, a contract. Subordinate contracts for objects of mere occasional interest may be dissolved at pleasure; but the state ought not to be considered as nothing better than a partnership agreement in a trade of pepper and coffee, calico or tobacco, or some other such low concern, to be taken up for a little temporary interest, and to be dissolved by the fancy of the parties. It is to be looked on with other reverence; because it is not a partnership in things subservient only to the gross animal existence of a temporary and perishable nature. It is a partnership in all science, a partnership in all art, a partnership in every virtue and in all perfection. As the ends of such a partnership cannot be obtained in many generations, it becomes a partnership not only between those who are living, but between those who are living, those who are dead, and those who are to be born.

Sometimes a sentence rings out which seems to have risen without his awareness from the depths of Burke's emotional being. "I do not like to see anything destroyed, any void produced in society, any ruin on the face of the land." This feeling seems to underlie much of the argument, or at least to provide much of the emotional force behind the argument, in his writings on the French Revolution. But his sharpest outbursts are against those who abuse the name of an abstract idea. "The effects of the incapacity shown by the popular leaders in all the great members of the commonwealth are to be covered with the 'all-atoning name' of Liberty. . . But what is liberty without wisdom and without virtue? It is the greatest of all possible evils; for it is folly, vice, and madness, without tuition or restraint." It should be observed, however, that "wisdom and virtue" for Burke are not qualities achieved by philosophers and saints; they reside in the people and operate through slowly and complexly developing institutions. In a brilliant speech delivered in Parliament in February, 1780, on the question of administrative reform, he indicated his view of the way in which government and people should be identified:

We have furnished to the people of England (indeed we have) some real cause of jealousy. Let us leave that sort of company which, if it does not destroy our innocence, pollutes our honour; let us free ourselves at once from everything that can increase their suspicions and inflame their just resentment; let us cast away from us, with a generous scorn, all the love-tokens and symbols that we have been vain and light enough to accept—all the bracelets, and snuff-boxes, and miniature pictures, and hair-devices, and all the other adulterous trinkets that are the pledges of our alienation and the monuments of our shame. Let us return to our legitimate home, and all jars and all quarrels will be lost in embraces. Let the commons in Parliament assembled be one and the same thing with the commons at large. The distinctions that are made to separate us are unnatural and wicked contrivances. Let us identify, let us incorporate ourselves with the people.

And in a letter on parliamentary reform in April of the same year he wrote:

I most heartily wish that the deliberate sense of the kingdom on this great subject should be known. When it is known, it *must* be prevalent. It would be dreadful indeed if there was any power in the nation capable of resisting its unanimous desire, or even the desire of any very great and decided majority of the people. The people may be deceived in their choice of an object; but I can scarcely conceive any choice they can make to be so very mischievous as the existence of any human force capable of resisting it.

Burke's democratic principles are rather different from those professed in most liberal circles today. But they are not merely traditional or just simple-minded. The full scope and depth of his political thinking can only be appreciated when a reasonably large and representative section of his work has been carefully followed through.

If Burke was not a great speaker, he was a great prose *arguer*, who could move with grace and eloquence from principle to fact and back again. His prose has the air of a man thinking as he talks, yet of one who is never in any doubt about what his guiding ideas are. He can soar into long sentences with rhythmically balanced clauses which fall seductively on the ear; he can also be short and sharp and almost epigrammatic. His combining of short and long sentences, of pithy remarks in simple language and sonorous amplifications in a more Latinized vocabulary, shows great skill. He is the greatest master in English of the rhetoric of political wisdom.

Thomas Paine (1737–1809) is in many ways Burke's antithesis. His mind is curiously abstract and generalizing; he had no trace of Burke's feeling for the organic development of social institutions and the delicately complex nature of the social organism. All problems of politics and government could for Paine be solved by bold theorizing. "In order to gain a clear and just idea of the design and end of government, let us suppose a small number of persons settled in some sequestered part of the earth, . . . In this state of natural liberty, society will be their first thought." Burke had refused to contrast nature and society, for he held that it was man's nature to be social and so human society was essentially natural. Burke also had a deep suspicion of any simple explanation of government. Paine, however, held that the simpler the better: "I draw my idea of the form of government from a principle in nature which no art can overturn, viz. that the more simple any thing is, the less liable it is to be disordered, and the easier repaired when disordered; and with this maxim in view I offer a few remarks on the so much boasted Constitution of England." A brilliant pamphleteer, an inspired journalist who responded to the new ideas about the rights of man and the new appeal to "nature" and the "original equality" of man with enthusiastic belligerence, he produced in his *Common Sense* (1776), *The Rights of Man* (1791), and *The Age of Reason* (1792–95), breezy, slapdash, and eloquent statements of the radical and rationalist position on politics and religion. His fiery support of American independence made him an American hero, but the rationalistic deism of *The Age of Reason* was too much for popular American sentiment. He had a career on both sides of the Atlantic, and played his part in both the American and the French Revolutions.

Winds from France affected more than Tom Paine. As we saw in an earlier chapter, Rousseau's view of man and nature had an influence on the sentimental English novel, and the concept of the child of nature was developed in a whole stream of fiction in the latter part of the century. This strain can be seen in Henry Brooke's novel, *The Fool of Quality* (1765–70), which combined the inspiration of Wesley and Rousseau, in *A Simple Story* (1791) and *Nature and Art* (1796) by Mrs. Inchbald, better known for her sentimental comedies, and, with more interest in a revolutionary political moral, in Thomas Holcroft's *Anna St. Ives* (1792) and his autobiographical *Hugh Trevor* (1794–97). But far more important and influential than these writers was William Godwin (1756–1836), rationalist revolutionary, whose *Enquiry into Political Justice* (1793) influenced so many of the younger poets and writers and whose novel *Caleb Williams* (1794) is one of the few successful didactic novels of its kind. Rationalist, revolutionary, optimist, the strong simple current of Godwin's thought flowed strongly in England for a time; it took disillusion with the course of the French Revolution to stem it, and even then not wholly. Paine's *Rights of Man* was a reply to Burke on the French Revolution, and Godwin's wife, Mary Wollstonecraft (1759–97), also answered Burke in her *Vindication of the Rights of Men* (1790), which even her husband considered "too contemptuous and intemperate." Her *Vindication of the Rights of Women* (1792) is her most important book, a significant contribution to the feminist movement in England. Godwin was the center of revolutionary English thought in his day. Abolish all institutions, go back to first principles and re-establish society in the light of nature and reason, and man will be innocent and happy. Such a statement of the Godwinian position is of course a gross oversimplification; but it is a position that lends itself to oversimplification. His writings appealed to all the generous and idealistic emotions of youth, and if the rise of Napoleon had not prevented the Godwinians from persisting in regarding the French Revolution as a great ideal movement back to nature and reason the consequences for English thought and politics might have been greater than they were.

This brings us into the nineteenth century. Before leaving the political writing of the eighteenth century, however, we should notice the letters of Junius, which appeared under that pseudonym in the London newspaper, *The Public Advertiser*, between 1769 and 1772. The identity of Junius has never been settled with complete certainty. Junius' letters were directed against the Duke of Grafton, then Prime Minister, his friends and associates, and the political influence of George III. Dealing with personalities as much as with ideas, Junius wrote a strong and stinging prose, treating Grafton, the Earl of Bute, the Duke of Bedford, Lord North, and others of his villains with savage contempt. For all their liveliness and vigor, the letters of Junius are too much bound up with the details of contemporary politics and personalities to arouse real interest in a later age. The prose is not artful enough to be relished for its own sake. The urgency is the urgency of personal interest and resentment rather than of cogent political argument, and we sense it rather than respond to it.

Are Mr. Crosby and Mr. Sawbridge likely to execute the extraordinary, as well as the ordinary, duties of the Lord Mayor? Will they grant you common-halls when it shall be necessary? Will they go up with remonstrances to the King? Have they firmness enough to meet the fury of a venal House of Commons? Have they fortitude enough not to shrink at imprisonment? Have they spirit enough to hazard their lives and fortunes in a contest, if it should be necessary, with a prostituted Legislature? If these questions can fairly be answered in the affirmative, your choice is made. Forgive this passionate language. I am unable to correct it. The subject comes home to us all. It is the language of my heart.

This conclusion of Letter LVIII, addressed to the Livery of London, illustrates Junius at his most eloquent and direct.

The aspect of eighteenth-century thought and culture known as the Enlightenment—the belief that human affairs can best be investigated by calm and rational inquiry, the interest in general human nature, the reduction of all philosophical problems to those that can be investigated empirically, curiosity about human motives, behavior, and institutions—was favorable to the growth of historical writing. In France, Voltaire had endeavored to emancipate history from theology on the one hand and parochialism and personal bias on the other. His *Essay on the Manners and Character of the Nations* (1764–69) was directed against Bossuet's massive and popular *Universal History* (1681), which saw the history of the world as a divinely arranged progression from Adam through Old Testament history, the birth and spread of Christianity, to the triumphal re-establishment by Charlemagne of the Roman Empire as a Christian political order. Such a view of history, which had been standard since St. Augustine, saw Palestine and Rome as the main theaters of human affairs. Voltaire sought a wider perspective and a more impartial view of the Western achievement. Bossuet ignored altogether India and China, and undervalued the civilization of non-Christian peoples in Europe such as the Arabs. For Voltaire, ancient Hebrew history was a small part of world history, and was to be investigated in the same way as everything else. And medieval Christendom was a "heap of crimes, follies, and misfortunes" compared with the more brilliant and more scientific civilization which Islam spread over the Mediterranean and elsewhere or the high achievements of the Indians and Chinese. Voltaire's secularizing of history at the same time as he enlarged its geographical scope had a permanent effect on historical writing in Europe. His view that his own age represented a height of enlightenment which previous ages, least of all the Middle Ages, could not possibly have aspired to was common enough in the Age of Reason; condemnation of the gothic and barbarous Middle Ages began in the Renaissance, as earlier chapters have shown. It was Voltaire's determined secularism together with his air of calmly rational impartiality that made his historical writings so important. And he was aware that even the steady growth of enlightenment could not be counted on: "Anyone who would have predicted to Augustus that one day the Capitol would be occupied by the priest of a religion derived from the religion of the Jews would have astonished Augustus greatly."

The connection between philosophical skepticism and historical interest is seen in Britain in David Hume, who saw history as a storehouse of facts which would help the philosopher to understand human nature much more than any a priori theorizing. "These records of wars, intrigues, factions, and revolutions, are so many collections of experiments, by which the politician or moral philosopher fixes the principles of his science." Hume's eight-volume *History of England, from the Invasion of Julius Caesar to the Revolution of 1688* (1754–

63), was not a work of original scholarship, but a fluent narrative dealing with the general sweep of events in such a way as to illustrate the
nature of historical development and the kind of motives and causes
which produce it. The style of quiet eloquence, allowing both for
flowing narrative and for calmly philosophical inquiries into causes,
consequences, and general principles, represents a considerable literary achievement.

Mid-eighteenth-century Scotland showed a special fondness for
history, particularly among the "literati," the urban men of letters
who, especially in Edinburgh, maintained at this time as lively an
intellectual life as anywhere in Europe. "This is the historical age
and we are the historical people," Hume exclaimed in a burst of
Scottish national pride. William Robertson (1721–93), another Scot,
produced his *History of Scotland during the reigns of Queen Mary
and of King James VI* in 1759, his *History of the Reign of the Emperor
Charles V* in 1769, and his *History of America* in 1777, works whose
great popularity in their day was more the result of the elegance with
which he presented his material and the clarity and control with
which he marshaled his facts than of any great historical scholarship
or philosophical penetration. "The perfect composition, the nervous
language, the well-turned periods of Dr. Robertson," wrote Gibbon
in his autobiography, "inflamed me to the ambitious hope that I might
one day tread in his footsteps: the calm philosophy, the careless inimitable beauties of his friend and rival [Hume], often forced me to
close the volume with a mixed sensation of delight and despair." Another Scot, the philosopher and economist Adam Smith (1723–90),
produced in 1776 his *Inquiry into the Nature and Causes of the
Wealth of Nations,* a reasoned inquiry into the nature of economic
activity and organization which founded the science of political
economy and had an immense influence on economic thought and
behavior throughout the nineteenth century.

Edward Gibbon (1737–94) produced his monumental *Decline and
Fall of the Roman Empire* in six volumes between 1776 and 1788.
The mind and imagination of the "enlightened" later eighteenth century worked more happily and often with more genuine art in history
than in almost any other form of writing. In Gibbon, the Enlightenment found its greatest historian, a man who was both scholar and
skeptic, interested in general principles of causation and movement
in history and at the same time capable of the liveliest dramatic writing, learned enough to be able to take into his scope a whole sweep
of Western history and philosopher enough to restrict his main theme
to one complex and developing event—the decline and fall of the
Roman Empire. From the opening chapters on the age of the Anto-

nines, where he describes the vast extent of the Empire, the resultant importance of military forces, the significance of the emperor's personality for good or ill, and then goes on to examine the forces which held the Empire together and the way its constitution had developed, to the somber conclusion where he surveys the ruins and reflects on the "four principal causes of the ruin of Rome," Gibbon is in fullest control of his material and knows exactly what he is doing. The early chapters make clear the conditions under which the Empire could be held together and the kinds of situations which might arise to remove those conditions; emphasis on the character of individual emperors is important when the individual emperor, all other constitutional machinery having been scrapped, is the sole authority; and so at each point Gibbon makes clear his awareness of the various kinds of causes which operate in history. He had no general theory of final causes, as Bossuet had, but sought for the reasons for human events in the multiple factors which make up any given state of things and which can be inquired into after the event by the conscientious historian. General conclusions about the main causes of any particular historical movement (such as the one he was dealing with) could of course be arrived at, but they represented the end, not the beginning, of the historian's effort. The general principles—such as that of the balance of power—which are openly stated in or can be inferred from the total work are both political and moral, revealing a humane and skeptical mind not unlike that of Hume.

Gibbon's attitude to religion is consistent with his whole historical approach. He had the consistency to apply to early Christianity the unfavorable view of "enthusiasm" held by so many thinkers of his age, and to assume that what was bad for one age was bad for all. Thus Christianity becomes one of the causes of the decline of Roman civilization. He explained in his autobiography:

As I believed, and as I still believe, that the propagation of the Gospel, and the triumph of the Church, are inseparably connected with the decline of the Roman monarchy, I weighed the causes and effects of the revolution, and contrasted the narratives and apologies of the Christians themselves, with the glances of candour or enmity which the Pagans have cast on the rising sects.

As for the style, again he tells us in his autobiography: "The style of an author should be the image of his mind, but the choice and command of language is the fruit of exercise. Many experiments were made before I could hit the middle tone between a dull chronicle and a rhetorical declamation: . . ." The result is a prose eloquent, balanced, and flexible; more rapid than Johnson's and graver than Addison's, capable of both descriptive splendor and dry irony.

Gibbon has told us, in a well-known passage in his autobiography, of his first determining to write on the decline and fall of the Roman Empire, when on a visit to Italy:

After a sleepless night, I trod, with a lofty step, the ruins of the Forum; each memorable spot where Romulus *stood,* or Tully spoke, or Caesar fell, was at once present to my eye; and several days of intoxication were lost or enjoyed before I could descend to a cool and minute investigation. . . . It was at Rome, on the 15th of October, 1764, as I sat musing amidst the ruins of the Capitol, while the barefooted friars were singing vespers in the Temple of Jupiter, that the idea of writing the decline and fall of the city first started to my mind.

He enlarged his scheme from the city to the empire, but the completed work retains something of the melancholy emotion with which he first determined to embark on it. Here is an enlightened eighteenth-century mind looking back over the great gap between ancient and modern civilization and documenting the nature and causes of that gap. No historical theme could have been more fascinating for a man of Gibbon's age. The scholarship of the preceding century had made available the documents; the mind of his own age supplied the method and the motive. "To say that he applied the mind of the eighteenth century to the learning of the seventeenth," comments G. M. Young, "would fix Gibbon's position exactly in the movement of European letters."

CHAPTER TWENTY

Scottish Literature from
Allan Ramsay to Walter Scott

IN CHAPTER 14 some account was given of the way in which
the growing tendency of Scottish writers to write in English, while
continuing to talk (and in a sense to "feel") in Scots, led to the disappearance of the Scots literary language and the survival of Scots only
as a series of regional dialects. The Reformation, the Union of the
Crowns in 1603, and the prestige and influence of English Elizabethan
writers, all helped in this movement. The Union of Parliaments in
1707, when the Scottish Parliament ceased to exist and Scotland
ceased to be a political entity and became only the northern part of
Great Britain, marked a further step in the assimilation of Scottish culture to English, at least in the long run; its short-run influence was in
the other direction. Frustrated in their political hopes, Scotsmen
turned to their literary past for consolation, with the result that antiquarian interest in older Scottish literature grew steadily throughout
the eighteenth century and at the same time attempts were made to
imitate and perpetuate, in however limited a way, some of the older
Scottish literary traditions. The limitations of these attempts were
determined by the cultural situation of the country. There was no
literary center; Scots law and the Church of Scotland survived the
Union of Parliaments as independent institutions quite distinct from
their English counterparts, but although each exerted a peculiar influence on eighteenth-century Scottish culture neither proved an
adequate substitute for the lost Court as a center of artistic patronage. It was inevitable that English speech and English literary forms
should be looked on as the proper medium for Scottish writers who
wished to succeed in the great world. Though there was a revival of
Scots verse, it was a dialect verse used for the most part for humorous
or sentimental purposes, in a patronizing, exhibitionist, or nostalgic

manner. Most serious poets (James Thomson, for example) turned to English, and left their country behind, often physically as well as metaphorically. And all the prose writers wrote in English. David Hume, Adam Smith, William Robertson, and other Scottish philosophers, historians, and men of letters whose work was known all over Europe, wrote in English, though their speech was often a broad Scots. David Hume was not the only eighteenth-century Scotsman to have his manuscripts carefully corrected by an English friend to make sure that all "Scotticisms" would be removed. Not that Hume lacked Scottish pride and patriotism; but it took the form of acclaiming minor Scottish poets who wrote in English and of trying to show that in the world of artistic and intellectual endeavor Scotsmen, writing in English for a European audience, could do as well as or better than citizens of any other European country—including England.

In 1706, the year before the Union of Parliaments was finally effected, James Watson, an Edinburgh printer, brought out the first of three volumes entitled *A Choice Collection of Comic and Serious Scots Poems both Ancient and Modern,* with two further volumes in 1709 and 1711. Watson saw himself as a pioneer, producing for the first time a collection of poems "in our own native Scots dialect" to rival the "collections of miscellaneous poems in our neighbouring kingdoms and states." With their mixture of poems of popular revelry, labored exercises in courtly English, macaronics, mock elegies, serious sixteenth-century Scots poems, trivial epigrams and epitaphs, poems by Drummond and Montrose, flytings, laments, and miscellaneous patriotic pieces, Watson's volumes appear at first sight to represent the casual putting together of whatever he found to his hand. Yet (except for ballads, which it lacks, and songs, which are few, and the perhaps surprising lack of anything by Sir David Lyndsay) the collection represents with a fair degree of accuracy the different kinds of material available for the development or reconstruction of the Scottish poetic tradition in the eighteenth century. The tradition of the makars was represented by Montgomerie (the Scottish Chaucerians were not to be made available until later, by Allan Ramsay); the courtly tradition in English by Drummond and Aytoun; the older popular tradition by "Christ's Kirk on the Green" and the newer by "Habbie Simson" and other pieces; the characteristic Scottish humor and Scottish violence are represented in several ways, as is the goliardic tradition as it developed in Scotland and the tradition of macaronic humor associated with it. The fact that the texts are often bad does not mean that Watson was indifferent or unscrupulous in textual matters; as his preface shows, he printed the best texts he could find, and if these were often broadsides and other examples of popular and none too conscientious printing, that at least was a tribute to the vitality of the poems so printed. The fact is that throughout the seventeenth century the line between folk poem and song and "art" poem was often obscured in Scotland; poems even by courtly poets found their way to popular singers and printers of broadsides, as well as to private collectors, and changes, corruptions, emendations, and additions were the natural result. What Watson printed represented things that were still going on in Scotland, though often not on the surface. In bringing them to the surface, he prevented them from being obscured by the new face of Scottish culture and at the same time helped to divert patriotic attention from politics to literature. Scotland became concerned about its literary past and about the possibilities of continuity with that past. It is true that that concern was soon to become mixed up with confused ideas about the vernacular and primitive poetry and the natural man, and this confusion was to make serious difficulties for Burns. But it also produced an environment which encouraged the production of certain kinds of vernacular poetry, and that was decisive for the course of eighteenth-century Scottish poetry from Ramsay to Burns.

At the same time the practice of rewriting or imitating traditional Scottish songs, and of setting new genteel English words to older Scottish airs, grew among ladies and gentlemen, and collections of such songs were popular. Lady Grizel Baillie's "Werena my heart licht, I wad dee," and Lady Wardlaw's imitation ballad, "Hardyknute" were two of the best known of these exercises in older Scottish modes. William Hamilton of Gilbertfield produced a modernized version of Blind Harry's *Wallace* (which was to fire Burns' imagination) and also, in his "Last Dying Words of Bonnie Heck," continued the "Habbie Simson" tradition. He also wrote verse epistles which he exchanged with Allan Ramsay, thus beginning a tradition of familiar verse letters in the vernacular which was to be finely exploited by Burns. It provided a medium for "occasional" poetry, a kind of verse to which the vernacular was particularly suited, for its endeavor was to capture the accent of conversation. With literary prose always English and not Scots, and the vernacular allowed in verse only for the familiar, the popular, the comic, or the mock-antique, the verse letter provided an opening wedge for those concerned with enlarging the scope of vernacular Scots verse. If the novel had been developed in Scotland by the early eighteenth century, dialogue in prose fiction might have effectively employed the spoken Scots speech of the time—that is how John Galt and Walter Scott were later to use dialogue. But lacking a tradition of colloquial prose, the eighteenth-century Scottish writer turned to the tradition of familiar Scots verse which Hamilton of Gilbertfield helped to establish.

Watson's contribution was editorial and antiquarian rather than creative, but a creative movement soon followed. Allan Ramsay (1686–1758) was concerned with both. Ramsay came to Edinburgh from his native Lanarkshire at the turn of the century, and there he developed from an obscure wigmaker's apprentice to a significant literary figure whose work set the direction for Scots poetry for the rest of the century. He was neither a great scholar nor a great poet; but he had enthusiasm, liveliness, good humor, and persistence. His activities as bookseller, antiquarian, poet, patron of the arts, member of the Easy Club (founded in 1712 by Ramsay and others for mutual improvement in conversation, that they might be "more adapted for fellowship with the politer part of mankind"), and general literary busybody, was carried on with a mixture of gusto and vulgarity peculiarly his own. His cheerful sociability helped to turn Edinburgh literary life into social channels, and it is his combination of a feeling for literature (however confused and uncertain) with a feeling for social life that was partly responsible for the association of social clubs with literary enthusiasm which soon became a feature of Edinburgh life.

In 1724 Ramsay brought out both *The Evergreen* and the first volume of *The Tea-Table Miscellany*. The former consisted mostly of poems from the Bannatyne Manuscript, an anthology of earlier Scottish poetry compiled by George Bannatyne in 1568, including much of the work of Henryson and Dunbar. It thus introduced readers to the poetry of Scotland's first Golden Age, an age when the country was vigorous both politically and culturally. Ramsay's intention was deliberately patriotic, as he makes clear in his Preface:

When these good old Bards wrote, we had not yet made use of imported trimmings upon our clothes, nor of foreign embroidery in our writings. Their poetry is the product of their own country, not pilfered and spoiled in the transportation from abroad. Their images are native, and their landskips domestic, copied from those fields and meadows we every day behold.

The Tea-Table Miscellany, which was completed in four volumes by 1737, was a mixed collection of old and new songs and ballads by authors living and dead, known and unknown. Ramsay had none of the modern scholar's respect for the original text, and often made considerable alterations in an attempt to improve or refine older work. His taste was always uncertain and his notions of refinement had the wavering exaggeration of a man of innate vulgarity, so that his alterations are on the whole to be deplored, quite apart from questions of textual accuracy. But the real point is that he made this varied collection, and presented it as living poetry. He printed songs, tragic ballads, love songs, folk songs on a great variety of themes, grave and gay, original and imitative, lively and dull, popular and genteel. It was the richest collection of its kind that had yet appeared in Scotland, and the reading public responded to it as it did not to *The Evergreen*. The disintegration of Scottish literary culture was too far advanced for the Scottish Chaucerians to be useful as an active influence on creation; but the new vernacular movement could handle at least some of the song and lyric forms represented in *The Tea-Table Miscellany*.

Ramsay's original work shows him as far from a great poet, but he was a facile versifier with certain happy flashes, and when circumstances were propitious he could turn out admirable specimens of familiar verse. The Easy Club provided him with the environment for the development of this gift; it also provided a background of patriotic sentiment against which Ramsay's nationalism flourished vigorously. A gentleman of the Augustan Age and an ardent Scottish patriot; an admirer of Pope and Gay and Matthew Prior and a devoted champion of the older Scottish makars and of the use of vernacular Scots by contemporary Scottish poets; a seeker after polish and good breeding and a vulgar little gossip whose schoolboy snicker spoils many of his poems and songs; a sentimental Jacobite and a prudent citizen who cannily absented himself from Edinburgh on the plea that he was detained in Penicuik in illness when Prince Charlie held court in Holyrood in 1745; a champion of Scottish folk song and a wrecker of scores of such songs by turning them into stilted, would-be neoclassic effusions—the dualism in Ramsay's life and character was deep-seated and corresponded to a dualism in the Scottish culture of his day. He was both proud and ashamed of Scotland.

Ramsay's best original poems are Scots poems dealing in a familiar, realistic tone with daily events; he is at his worst at his most formal. In lively verse epistles in the vernacular, in an occasional simple love lyric in the folk idiom, in translations of odes of Horace or of French fables into racy Scots, now and again in a piece of merriment or celebration which carries it off by sheer exuberance, he can be admirable: when he imitates his English contemporaries he is nearly always poor. His most popular work was his dramatic pastoral *The Gentle Shepherd,* an expansion of an earlier pastoral dialogue into a full-length verse play. Here the combination of the formal and the realistic—the stylized pastoral and actual description of contemporary

rustic life—in a somewhat Anglicized Scots does, surprisingly, succeed in bringing a certain freshness to a worn-out mode. Ramsay's
basic uncertainty of taste, which could lead him into the most
hideous vulgarities, was less of a liability in this kind of writing: the
touches of rustic realism make for freshness, not vulgarity, and the
idiom and cadence of popular speech embedded in the slow-moving
iambic lines water the aridity of a stock situation.

Ramsay's *Tea-Table Miscellany* was followed by many more collections of songs throughout the century. The interest in "primitive"
poetry which prompted the publication of Thomas Percy's *Reliques
of Ancient English Poetry* in 1765 and which later helped to determine the terms of the Ossian controversy, began earlier in Scotland
and was there mixed up with patriotic motives. Collections of songs
and ballads, with and without music, were numerous in Scotland
from *The Tea-Table Miscellany* to George Thomson's *Select Scottish
Airs* (1793). In 1726 the *Orpheus Caledonius* was published in London, containing about fifty Scots songs with the music, and similar
collections followed in Scotland, culminating in James Johnson's
Scots Musical Museum, of which the first volume appeared in 1787,
and to whose subsequent volumes Burns contributed so much. Of
the books of Scots songs without music, the most important was
David Herd's *Ancient and Modern Scots Songs*, first published in
1769, and then enlarged in a two-volume edition in 1776. Herd reprinted a fair number of pieces that had appeared in Watson and in
The Tea-Table Miscellany together with much that had not appeared
before, and he printed almost everything anonymously, without any
indication of age; but he never tampered with his material; he
printed the pieces as he found them, and he was content to let many
of the older songs appear in fragmentary form. Unlike Percy and
most other editors of his time, he had no urge to complete and improve. Herd is thus an important figure in the transmission of the
Scottish popular tradition in poetry. Scholarly, accurate, modest, he
never put his own name to his work (neither of the editions mentions
an editor), and in his preface to the two volumes of 1776, he "antici-
pated the censure of the severe, by confessing them a work of slight
importance."

The kind of interest in Scottish literature represented by Ramsay's
original and editorial work and by that of the collectors and imitators
of older Scottish songs who followed him must be seen in its true
perspective. The general cultural current was still flowing strongly
toward England, and the Edinburgh historians, philosophers, scientists, and literary critics who contributed so much to Scotland's
second Golden Age wrote in English and studiously avoided any

"Scotticisms" in their speech. In 1761, the Irishman Thomas Sheridan (father of the dramatist) delivered twelve lectures on the "correct" speaking of English at St. Paul's Episcopal Church, Edinburgh, and about three hundred of the city's most distinguished citizens attended. As late as 1788, James Beattie produced a preposterous little book entitled *Scotticisms, arranged in Alphabetical Order, designed to correct Improprieties of Speech and Writing*, while in Henry Mackenzie's periodical *The Mirror* for February 22, 1780, a writer explained why Scotsmen, writing in English they did not speak and speaking a dialect they did not write, were incapable of writing humorously in English or seriously in their native dialect:

When a Scotsman . . . writes, he does so generally in trammels. His own native original language, which he hears spoken around him, he does not make use of; but he expresses himself in a language in some respects foreign to him, and which he had acquired by study and observation. . . . Hence Scottish writers may have been prevented from attempting to write books of humour. . . . In confirmation of these remarks it may be observed, that almost the only works of humour which we have in this country, are in the *Scottish* dialect. . . . The *Gentle Shepherd*, which is full of natural and ludicrous representations of low life, is written in broad *Scotch*. . . .

Scots thus remained a vernacular, and there was no tradition of written Scots prose in the eighteenth century. Anyone who had claims to international fame in dealing with general matters of scientific or philosophic interest wrote in English for the same reason that he would have written in Latin in an earlier age. And in poetry the vernacular established itself as a vehicle only for exercises in the mock antique or for humorous or convivial or skittish or condescending verses. Ramsay's Scots-besprinkled English (or vice versa) did not represent an enlargement of the potentialities of the Scottish vernacular; still less did it recreate Scots as a full-blooded literary language. Nobody, in fact, achieved that in the eighteenth century or later: it is one of the ideals of the twentieth-century Lallans movement. But one eighteenth-century Scottish poet did achieve a Scots idiom which combined ease, weight, variety, and cunning, and which pointed the way toward the re-establishment of Scots as a literary language (though it was a way that nobody was to take). This was Robert Fergusson (1750–74), not the greatest of the eighteenth-century Scottish poets, but the only one who consistently used Scots with wholeness and centrality. Burns, the greater poet, was often less assured in his attitude toward his medium, and his enormous prestige removed any chance of Fergusson's being the dominant influence on later Scottish poetry (though Burns would have approved of such an influence: he was perfectly aware of Fergusson's claims in this regard, and called him "by far my elder Brother in the Muse"). If Fergusson had not died at the age of twenty-four, the whole future course of Scottish poetry might well have been different.

Fergusson was an Edinburgh man and an Edinburgh poet; the Scots poems he contributed in 1772 and 1773 to *Ruddiman's Weekly Magazine and Edinburgh Amusement* rendered the life of the city with warmth and color. Just as Ramsay had found encouragement and a congenial atmosphere in the Easy Club, so Fergusson found in the Cape Club a varied group of sociable Edinburgh characters who helped both to enhance his feeling for the city and to provide stimulating companionship. Together with tradesmen of all kinds and some lawyers, doctors, and other professional men, there were included among its membership painters, musicians, singers, and actors, as well as David Herd, whose enthusiasm for Scots poetry must have encouraged Fergusson to turn to the native Scots tradition. Fergusson's English poems are of little interest, but his lively and colorful Scots poems descriptive of Edinburgh life are unequaled. "The Daft Days," "The King's Birthday in Edinburgh," "Caller Oysters," "Hallow Fair," "Leith Races," "The Rising of the Session," and "The Sitting of the Session" project the life of the city in all its richness and color. Fergusson had both an eye and an ear; he had a fine sense of weather and could render the feel of a November afternoon or a spring morning in precise and sensitively chosen imagery; he had a feeling for movement and bustle and could suggest with a deftly chosen incident the dynamic quality of urban life; he responded to the social symbol, and could handle conviviality with a splendid vivacity; and he had a fine control over the Scots language which he handled with speed and relish. Like Ramsay, he was fond of the old Scots verse form in which "Habbie Simson" had been written, and it was from Fergusson and Ramsay that Burns got it. He could handle some other stanza forms with equal skill, and in "The Farmer's Ingle"—a better poem than Burns' "Cotter's Saturday Night"—he employs a slow-moving nine-line stanza with complete control. "The Farmer's Ingle" is a picture of Scottish rustic life done with sympathy and affection and wholly without sentimentality or affectation. Fergusson, who had spent holidays in his parents' Aberdeenshire and as a student at St. Andrews had explored Fife, knew the countryside as well as the city, and though he dealt with it less often, when he did so he employed the same responsiveness to sights and sounds, the same feeling for the illustrative situation or anecdote, the same firm control over the tempo of his verse, as we find in the city poems.

In his mock elegies, he carried on the "Habbie Simson" tradition and passed it on to Burns; in his verse letters he took over from Hamilton of Gilbertfield and from Ramsay and again transmitted the tradition to Burns; in his language, which was Edinburgh Scots flavored with varying amounts of his parents' Aberdeenshire, he showed Burns the way in not confining himself to a limited regional dialect; in his amused and sympathetic curiosity about his fellow men he was often more mature than Burns, though he lacked Burns' range and Burns' gift as a song writer.

Robert Burns (1759–96) brought to a brilliant close the chapter in the history of Scottish poetry that had been begun by Allan Ramsay. The son of a tenant farmer who was dogged all his life by economic misfortune, Burns approached the contemporary world of letters from below, as it were; but he was not an illiterate "Heaven-taught plowman" as the critics of his day took him to be; he had a sporadic but not negligible formal education, knew some French and had a smattering of Latin, and had read most of the important eighteenth-century English writers as well as Shakespeare, Milton, and Dryden. He was restless and ambitious from early youth, and, though his formal education had been oriented entirely toward English literature, a chapbook edition of Blind Harry's *Wallace* as modernized by Hamilton of Gilbertfield and, later, his discovery of Fergusson's Scots poems, encouraged him to write poetry in the Scottish vernacular of his native Ayrshire, or at least in a language which incorporated in varying degrees certain Scots words and expressions, most of which came from the spoken dialect of his own region and some of which came from his reading in older Scottish literature.

Early in 1783 Burns began to keep a Commonplace Book in which he entered his poems and his comments on poetry and song. "I never had the least thought or inclination of turning Poet till I got once heartily in love," he noted in April, 1783, "and then rhyme and song were, in a manner, the spontaneous language of my heart." This observation accompanied an unpretentious, lilting song-poem, written in an English tipped with Scots, but turning to pure neoclassic English in the final stanza. Shortly afterward he entered in the Commonplace Book sentimental, melodramatic, or melancholy pieces whose thought reflected the family misfortunes of the time and whose vocabulary and manner derived from minor eighteenth-century English poets. He was reading Gray, Shenstone, Thomson, *The Man of Feeling, Tristram Shandy* and Macpherson's *Ossian*, and cultivating a gloomy sensibility. But suddenly we come across a lively, swinging piece deriving from Scottish folk tradition rather than from contemporary English sentimentalism.

My father was a farmer upon the Carrick border O
And carefully he bred me, in decency and order O . . .

He added an apologetic note saying that it was "miserably deficient in versification." Meanwhile he was getting involved in local Church politics (taking the side of liberal Deism against rigid Calvinist orthodoxy) and writing Scots verses supporting the liberal side in local Church quarrels. He was also branching out in various ways. He had an affair with a servant girl on the farm which resulted in the birth of his first illegitimate child, whom he welcomed with a lively poem which was part swagger and part the expression of genuine paternal affection and delight:

Thou's welcome, wean; mishanter fa' me,   [wean: child]
    If thoughts o' thee, or yet thy mamie,   [mishanter:
    Shall ever daunton me or awe me,   misfortune]
        My bonie lady,   [daunton:
    Or if I blush when thou shalt ca' me   discourage]
    Tyta or daddie . . .

His eye was not on Gray or Shenstone here; the stanza form is one that had had a long history in Scottish—indeed, in European—poetry, and had been used by Ramsay and Fergusson, while the language is the spoken language of Ayrshire enlarged by words from southern English and others from the older Scots literary tradition. Even more purely in the Scottish literary tradition is "The Death and Dying Words of Poor Maillie," entered in the Commonplace Book in June, 1785; this is a "mock testament" put into the mouth of a dying sheep, done with shrewd ironical humor and considerable technical adroitness. Burns had by now available to him not only the Scottish folk tradition but also some at least of the traditions of Scottish "art" poetry both as they came to him through Fergusson and as he found them for himself in collections of older Scottish poetry. Though some significant areas of earlier Scottish poetry had not been made available by eighteenth-century editors, Burns was nevertheless in contact with the main tradition, and his development as a poet clearly shows how the eighteenth-century antiquarian movement fed the creative impulse.

Burns developed rapidly throughout 1784 and 1785 as an "occasional" poet who more and more turned to verse to express his emotions of love, friendship, or amusement, or his ironic contemplation of the social scene. But these were not spontaneous effusions by an almost illiterate poet. Burns was a very conscious craftsman; his entries in the Commonplace Book reveal that from the beginning of his activity as a poet he was interested in the technical problems of versification. If he never learned to distinguish emotional control from emotional self-indulgence in eighteenth-century English poetry (his critical sense remained uncertain in this area of literature), he did learn to appreciate economy, cogency, and variety in the work of Pope and others, and, most important of all, he learned from older Scots literature to handle traditional Scottish literary forms and stanza-patterns, particularly in descriptive and satirical verse, with assurance and cunning. From the oral folk tradition he learned a great deal about song rhythms and the fitting of words to music. And out of his own Ayrshire speech, his knowledge of older Scots, and his reading in standard English, he fashioned a flexible Scots-English idiom which, though hardly a literary language in the sense that Henryson's or Dunbar's language was, proved time and time again to be an effective medium for at least one man's kind of Scottish poetry.

Though he wrote poetry for his own amusement and that of his friends, Burns remained restless and dissatisfied. His farm did not prosper, and harassed by insoluble emotional and economic problems, he thought of emigrating to Jamaica. But he first wanted to show his country what he could do. In the midst of his troubles he went ahead with his plans for publishing a volume of his poems at the nearby town of Kilmarnock—*Poems Chiefly in the Scottish Dialect,* 1786. Its success was immediate and overwhelming, and Burns set out for Edinburgh to be lionized, patronized, and showered with well-meant but dangerous advice.

The Kilmarnock volume was an extraordinary mixture. It included a handful of first-rate Scots poems—"The Twa Dogs," "Scotch Drink," "The Holy Fair," "Address to the Deil," "The Death and Dying Words of Poor Maillie," "To a Mouse," "To a Louse," and some others, including a number of verse letters addressed to various friends. There were also a few Scots poems in which he was unable to sustain his inspiration or which are spoiled by a confused purpose (such as "The Vision"), and one ("Hallowe'en") which is too self-consciously rustic in its dogged descriptions of country customs and rituals and its almost exhibitionist use of archaic rural terms. There were also six gloomy and histrionic poems in English with such titles as "Despondency, an Ode" and "Man was Made to Mourn, a Dirge." There were four songs: "It was upon a Lammas night" (to the tune of "Corn rigs are bonie"); two insipid love songs in English, two Scottish tunes; and a farewell to his fellow-Freemasons of Tarbolton, Ayrshire, to the tune of "Goodnight and joy be wi' you a' " (the traditional Scottish song at parting until Burns' "Auld lang syne" replaced it), an unsuccessful combination of familiar Scots and pretentious

English. The final pages are padded out with a handful of poor epigrams and epitaphs. There were also, what to contemporary reviewers seemed the stars of the volume, "The Cotter's Saturday Night" and "To a Mountain Daisy."

"The Twa Dogs" is a cunningly wrought dialogue between a gentleman's dog and a humbler example of the species. Its immediate inspiration was probably a poem of Fergusson's, but the dialogue is in fact in an old Scottish tradition, which Burns handles with complete assurance. Caesar, the aristocratic dog, begins by pitying the life of a poor dog such as his companion, Luath, and Luath replies that poverty has its drawbacks, but there are compensations. Caesar, anxious to maintain his superiority, answers this by pointing out how contemptuously the poor are treated by the rich (a favorite theme of Burns') and gives a brief but vivid description of the insults to be endured by "poor tenant bodies" at the hands of landlords. Luath replies with a sharply etched picture of the bright side of rustic life, wholly unsentimental and quite free from the synthetic pieties of "The Cotter's Saturday Night." The real turn in the poem comes when Luath, admitting that after all the poor are often ill treated by the rich, talks about a member of Parliament giving up his time "for Britain's guid." Caesar interrupts him:

> Haith, lad, ye little ken about it;   [haith: faith]
> For Britain's guid! guid faith! I doubt it.
> Say rather, gaun as Premiers lead him,   [gaun: going]
> An' saying *aye* or *no's* they bid him:
> At operas an' plays parading,
> Mortgaging, gambling, masquerading:
> Or may be, in a frolic daft,
> To Hague or Calais taks a waft,
> To make a tour, an' tak a whirl,
> To learn *bon ton* an' see the worl'.
>
> There, at Vienna or Versailles,
> He rives his father's auld entails;
> Or by Madrid he taks the rout,
> To thrum guitars an' fecht wi' nowt;   [fecht wi' nowt:
> Or down Italian vista startles   fight with cattle]
> Whore-hunting amang groves o' myrtles: . . .
>
> For Britain's guid! for her destruction!
> Wi' dissipation, feud an' faction.

This is adroitly done. Caesar, the defender of the rich, is so anxious to display his knowledge of them to the ignorant Luath that the bitter truth about them comes from *his* mouth, not from Luath's. It is now Luath's turn to express pained surprise, and he goes on to ask demurely:

> But will ye tell me, master Caesar,
> Sure great folk's life's a life o' pleasure? . . .

In order to show how foolish Luath is in making this presumption, Caesar is led into a vivid picture of the bored and hypochondriac rich which by insensible degrees turns into a bitter denunciation of their wickedness. This is not mere abuse; it is successfully controlled satire. The tone of contempt for the amusements of the idle rich is brilliantly conveyed in such a phrase as "to thrum guitars an' fecht wi' nowt," where the homely Scots word for cattle reduces at once the ritual splendor of bullfighting to a meaningless brawl with a beast. Further, putting the dialogue into the mouths of dogs is not simply a humorous trick; the dog's-eye view of man is carefully manipulated so as to enhance the satire without in the least idealizing or sentimentalizing the dogs. They go off at the end, "rejoic'd they were na *men*, but *dogs*."

"The Twa Dogs" is not by any means Burns' greatest poem, but it is a good example of his technical competence in a traditional Scottish mode. Burns here knows exactly what he is doing; he is absorbed in his job as he writes, and does not look up at intervals to see whether Henry Mackenzie or some other member of the Edinburgh literati approve of his sentiments. In the "Epistle to Davie," on the other hand, which opens magnificently with a vivid description of the January scene in a complex traditional Scottish stanza, the poet suddenly remembers the genteel audience he is hoping for, and the poem degenerates into pretentious and exhibitionist sentimentalism.

"The Holy Fair" is one of the finest poems in the collection. Written in the old Scottish tradition of poems describing popular festivities, and adopting an old Scottish stanza form which came down to him through Fergusson (whose "Leith Races" is Burns' model here), "The Holy Fair" describes with ironic humor the goings-on at one of the great outdoor "tent preachings" that were held annually in connection with the communion service. The poet describes himself as sauntering forth on a summer Sunday morning, and meeting three young women, one of them Fun and the other two Superstition and Hypocrisy· Fun explains that she is off to Mauchline Holy Fair and asks the poet to accompany her. The tone is thus humorous rather than bitter, and Burns' Brueghelesque account of the noisy, bustling, many-colored scene, with rival preachers thundering to indifferent or drunken audiences, and drinking, roistering, love-making, and other profane activities going on all around, emphasizes the human weaknesses, follies, passions and appetites which indulge themselves at the Holy Fair. There is no moral indignation in the poem, only an ironical amusement at the thought that human nature will have its way even in the midst of Calvinist thunderings on the one hand and less orthodox "moderate" pleading for good works on the other. The concluding stanza, with its deliberate confusion of theological, biblical, and amorous imagery, sums up the meaning of the poem:

> How monie hearts this day converts
>   O' Sinners and o' Lasses!
> Their hearts o' stane gin night are gane,   [gin night: by night-
>   As saft as ony flesh is.   fall; gane: gone]
> There's some are fou o' love divine;   [fou: drunk]
>   There's some are fou o' brandy;
> An' monie jobs that day begin
>   May end in Houghmagandie, . . .   [Houghmagandie:
>   fornication]

The "Address to the Deil," drawing on the devil of folklore rather than of Calvinist theology, uses a tone of amused familiarity in order to diminish the Devil's stature from that of the terrifying father of evil to that of a mischievous practical joker; the poem is a fine example of Burns' technique of implicitly criticizing theological dogmas by translating them into the daily realities of ordinary experience. The ending is masterly:

> An' now, auld Cloots, I ken ye're thinkin,
> A certain Bardie's rantin, drinkin,   [rantin: roistering]
> Some luckless hour will send him linkin   [linkin: hurrying]
>   To your black pit;
> But, faith! he'll turn a corner jinkin,   [jinkin: dodging]
>   An' cheat you yet.
>
> But fare you weel, auld Nickie-ben!
> O wad ye tak a thought an' men'!
> Ye aiblins might—I dinna ken—   [aiblins: perhaps]
>   Still hae a stake—
> I'm wae to think upo' yon den,   [wae: sad]
>   Ev'n for your sake!

The familiar titles of "auld Cloots" and "auld Nickie-ben" successfully reduce the Devil's stature; the poet's genially penitent reference to himself includes the conventional religious reproof in a context of casual cheerfulness, and the concluding suggestion that perhaps the Devil himself might repent (again made with deliberate casualness), implicitly includes the Devil among weak and sinful humanity, the final step in his dethronement and dismissal.

Some notion of the different degrees of skill and integrity displayed by Burns in the Kilmarnock volume can be obtained by setting side by side "To a Louse," "To a Mouse," and "To a Mountain Daisy." The first is easily the best, a bright, lively, humorous poem moving adroitly toward a conclusion which is expressed with the gnomic pithiness of a country proverb. It begins with a sudden projection into the heart of the situation, as Burns addresses the louse he sees crawling on a lady's bonnet in church:

> Ha! whare ye gaun, ye crowlin ferlie!   [crowlin: crawling; ferlie: wonder]

The lady, unconscious of the "ugly, creepin, blastit wonner" crawling on the back of her bonnet, is full of airs and graces and the poet chides the louse for daring to set foot on her:

> How daur ye set your fit upon her,
> Sae fine a Lady!

The contrast between the vulgarity of the insect and the social pretentiousness of the lady is developed with humorous irony until suddenly Burns drops his pose of outraged observer and addresses the lady herself:

> O Jenny, dinna toss your head,
> An' set your beauties a' abread!   [abread: abroad]
> Ye little ken what cursed speed
>   The blastie's makin! . . .

At once, in calling her by the simple country name "Jenny," the poet has changed her from a proud beauty to an ordinary girl whom he is warning, in friendly fashion, about an accident that might happen to anybody. Her airs and graces are stripped away, but not in the least savagely; the note of amusement is still there, but it is kindly now. The lady is restored to common humanity from whom she was distinguished earlier in the poem. And the conclusion has a simple proverbial note:

> O wad some Pow'r the giftie gie us
> To see oursels as others see us!
> It wad frae monie a blunder free us
>   An' foolish notion:
> What airs in dress an' gait wad lea'e us,
>   An ev'n Devotion!

"To a Mouse," one of Burns' most charming and best known poems, nevertheless lacks the tautness and the skillful manipulation of irony and humor that we get in "To a Louse." The poet expresses his regret to the "wee, sleekit, cowrin, tim'rous beastie," on turning her up in her nest with the plough, and goes on to reflect that, just as the mouse's provision for winter has been brought to nothing by this accident, so

> The best laid schemes o' mice an' men
> Gang aft a-gley   [go often awry]

and he himself is in an even worse situation. The fellow-feeling for the little creature is spontaneous and engaging, and conveyed in a cleverly controlled verse, and the introduction of the proverbial note, as in "To a Louse," is most effective; but the emergence of self-pity at the end as the real theme seems somewhat forced, and there is a touch of attitudinizing about the poem. This attitudinizing runs right through "To a Mountain Daisy," a forced and sentimental poem in which he laments the fate of the crushed flower (also turned down with the plough) and compares it to that of a betrayed maiden. Burns was here posturing as a man of feeling. It is significant that he wrote to a friend, enclosing the poem, as follows: "I am a good deal pleased with some sentiments myself, as they are just the native querulous feelings of a heart which, as the elegantly melting Gray says, 'Melancholy has marked for her own.'" A similar fault mars "The Cotter's Saturday Night," a grave descriptive poem in Spenserian stanzas describing with pious approval an evening in the life of a Scottish peasant family. The poem is modeled on Fergusson's "The Farmer's Ingle," but Burns is more pretentious than Fergusson and displays too clearly his object of showing off the Scottish peasantry for the approval and edification of men of feeling in Edinburgh. The poem contains some admirable descriptive passages and shows considerable technical accomplishment in the handling of the stanza, but the introduction of hollow sentimentalities and rhetorical exclamations at critical moments spoils the work as a whole.

Burns selected the Kilmarnock poems with care: he was anxious to impress a genteel Edinburgh audience. In his preface he played up to contemporary sentimental views about the natural man and the noble peasant, exaggerated his lack of education, pretended to a lack of technical resources which was ridiculous in the light of the careful craftsmanship which his poetry displays, and in general acted a part. The trouble is, he was only half acting. He was uncertain enough about the genteel tradition to accept much of it at its face value, and though, to his ultimate glory, he kept returning to what his own instincts told him was the true path for him to follow, far too many of his poems are marred by a naïve and sentimental moralizing.

The real Burns is revealed in his satiric and humorous poems and in the abandonment to the moment of experience which we find celebrated in many of his best songs. Burns the song writer was hardly represented in the Kilmarnock edition; most of his songs were still unwritten, but in any case the Edinburgh literati did not consider songs as one of the higher kinds of poetry. Burns the satirist was revealed in some degree, but the greatest of his satiric poems he deliberately omitted from the Kilmarnock volume in order not to shock his genteel audience. He omitted "The Ordination," a brilliant satire on Ayrshire church politics in the same stanza as "The Holy Fair" and done with great verve and dexterity. He omitted the "Address to the Unco Guid," a somewhat pedestrian attack on Puritan hypocrisy which might have been included without offense. He omitted the amusing and skillful "Death and Doctor Hornbook" and the rollicking satire, "The Twa Herds," an early poem which Burns himself described as a "burlesque lamentation on a quarrel between two reverend Calvinists." And he omitted "Holy Willie's Prayer," the greatest of all his satiric poems and one of the great verse satires of all time. Burns is here concerned to attack the Calvinist view of predestination and of salvation by predestined grace regardless of "good works" (for, according to this view, no works of fallen man can possibly be good in God's sight), and he makes the attack by putting a prayer in the mouth of a strict Calvinist who is convinced that he is predestined to salvation by God's grace. A solemn, liturgical note is maintained throughout the poem, and the creed damns itself in the process of its expression. It opens with a calmly expressive statement of the view that man's salvation or damnation is decreed by God without any reference to man's behavior; it is the very quietness and assurance of the statement that conceals at first its preposterousness and then suddenly reveals it when we least expect it.

> O thou that in the heavens does dwell!
> Wha, as it pleases best Thysel,
> Sends ane to heaven and ten to hell,
>   A' for thy glory!
> And no for ony gude or ill
>   They've done before Thee.

> I bless and praise Thy matchless might,
> When thousands Thou has left in night,
> That I am here before Thy sight
> For gifts and grace,
> A burning and a shining light
> To a' this place.

As the poem proceeds in this stately liturgical manner, the speaker's appalling complacency and egotism, disguised, *even to the speaker himself,* as humility, are cumulatively revealed. Holy Willie is not a conscious hypocrite. When he attributes his lust to God's protective desire to remind him that, however gifted and elect, he is still a man, he is revealing the moral horrors that, for Burns, lay beneath any claim by any individual that he had inner assurance of predestined salvation. When he asks God's vengeance on his personal enemies he really believes that his will and God's cause are one. And when he asks for economic prosperity in this world in addition to his assured reward in the next, it is in order to demonstrate to the heathen that God protects and favors those whom He has elected. As the poem proceeds it becomes increasingly impossible to disentangle godliness from the most abandoned self-indulgence, and in the confusion the creed of election and predestination becomes monstrous. The poem ends in the same stately organ tones with which it began:

> But Lord, remember me and mine
> Wi' mercies temporal an' divine!
> That I for grace an' gear may shine,   [gear: wealth]
> Excell'd by nane!
> And a' the glory shall be thine!
> Amen! Amen!

Burns also omitted from the Kilmarnock volume his remarkable anarchist cantata, "The Jolly Beggars," in which he assembled a group of social outcasts and put into their mouths roaring songs of social defiance and swaggering independence. There was always a streak of pure anarchism in Burns, and here he associates it with conviviality in a characteristic way. All institutions, all conventions, anything that limits the freely chosen association of friends and lovers with one another, are here abandoned in roaring professions of antisocial independence. It is not a mature or a complex attitude, but it does touch a fundamental human drive, and "The Jolly Beggars" gives brilliant expression to man as outcast and vagabond. Complete independence of social order implies poverty, squalor, and vice, but Burns does not shrink from that. He is not romanticizing independence from society, but simply bodying it forth, motivated less by doctrinaire anarchism than by sheer high spirits.

Edinburgh unsettled Burns, and after a number of amorous and other adventures there, and several trips to other parts of Scotland, he settled at a farm in Ellisland, Dumfriesshire. At Edinburgh, too, he arranged for a new and enlarged edition of his poems, but little of significance was added to the Kilmarnock selection. Substantially, it was by the Kilmarnock poems that Burns was known in his lifetime. He found farming at Ellisland difficult, and later obtained a position as an excise officer. He had met at Edinburgh James Johnson, a keen collector of Scottish songs who was bringing out a series of volumes of songs with the music, and enlisted Burns' help in finding, editing, improving, and rewriting items for his collection. Burns was enthusiastic about the project, and soon became virtual editor of Johnson's *Scots Musical Museum*. Later, he became involved with a similar project for George Thomson, but Thomson was a more consciously genteel person than Johnson, and Burns had to fight with him continuously to prevent him from "refining" words and music and so ruining their character. He did not always succeed. The latter part of Burns' life was spent largely in assiduous collecting and writing of songs, to provide words for traditional Scottish airs and to keep Johnson and Thomson going. The only poem he wrote after his Edinburgh visit which showed a hitherto unsuspected side of his poetic genius was "Tam o' Shanter," a magnificently spirited narrative poem based on a folk legend associated with Alloway Kirk. The poem is in octosyllabic couplets, and in variations of speed and tone, in unfolding the details of the story and in creating the proper atmosphere for each part, Burns showed himself a master of a form which, unfortunately, he never attempted again.

Burns was the greatest song writer Britain has produced. In refurbishing old songs, making new ones out of fragmentary remains, using an old chorus as a foundation for a new song, and sometimes simply touching up a set of characterless old words, as well as providing entirely new words to traditional airs and dance tunes, he was of course going much beyond the editorial and improving tasks he undertook for Johnson and Thomson, and if he had not been an original poet himself, and uncannily in tune with the folk tradition, he would have been execrated by later scholars for spoiling original material with false improvements. His work as a song writer was a unique blend of the antiquarian and the creative. He took the whole body of Scottish folk song and, in a passion of enthusiasm for his native culture, brought it together, preserved it, reshaped it, gave it new life and spirit, speaking with the great anonymous voice of the Scottish people and uttering that voice with an assurance, a technical skill, and a poetic splendor that cannot be matched in the literature of any other country. And he not only rescued and preserved the words; he also took the mass of song tunes and dance tunes and saw to it that they each had words properly fitted, if necessary altering the pace and movement of a melody in order to bring out a quality that had been lost in speeding it up for dance purposes. He could sing the songs of either sex. No man has ever captured the feminine delight in prospective motherhood combined with the feminine joy in sexual surrender as Burns did in the song he wrote for Jean when she was about to bear his child:

> O wha my babie-clouts will buy,　　　[clouts: clothes]
> O wha will tent me when I cry;　　　[tent: look after]
> Wha will kiss me where I lie.
> The rantin dog, the daddie o't. . . .

Nor has any poet so powerfully and simply expressed the combination of tenderness and swagger, which is a purely male attitude toward love, as Burns did in "A Red, Red Rose." Nor has the note of male protectiveness sounded so poignantly as in the poem that Burns wrote for Jessie Lewars, the girl who helped to nurse him in his final illness: with a supreme effort of the imagination Burns as he lay dying reversed their roles and wrote, to one of Jessie's favorite old Scottish airs,

> Oh wert thou in the cauld blast,
> 　On yonder lea, on yonder lea;
> My plaidie to the angry airt,　　　[airt: direction]
> 　I'd shelter thee, I'd shelter thee: . . .

Nor has the note of remembered friendship ever been so movingly expressed as in "Auld lang syne," Burns' rewriting of an older song, which he never claimed as his own. It must always be remembered, however, that these are *songs*, and should never be judged without their tunes, for Burns thought of words and music as part of a single whole.

Burns' influence on Scottish poetry has not been happy, for he was canonized partly for the wrong reasons and had his weaknesses imitated and his great strength ignored. That was not his fault, but his posthumous misfortune. Thus modern Scottish poets have preferred to go back to Dunbar rather than back to Burns, for they object, not to Burns, but to what has become of the Burns tradition. A coyly self-conscious emphasis on sensibility as such, a cloying coziness of tone, a false sugaring over of the realities of experience with stock sentimental situations, all done in a vernacular whose main feature is the adding of diminutive endings in "-ie" to as many words as possible—this is what later generations too often made of Burns. His faults rather than his virtues were praised and imitated. This was all the easier because Burns was a rustic poet who wrote when Scotland was on the verge of the Industrial Revolution, after which the temptation to sentimentalize over an idealized country life was irresistible. Burns did not—and could not have been expected to—help Scottish literature to come to terms with the Industrial Revolution.

The imitators of Burns began in his own lifetime: some were friends with whom he exchanged verse epistles. Lady Nairne (1766–1845) continued the tradition of Jacobite songwriting which flourished in the eighteenth century and which Burns had taken up. The failure of the Jacobite rebellion of 1745 provided Scotland with a nostalgic folk emotion, and even those Scots who had no political sympathy for the political and religious position of the Stuarts found in what Burns called "sentimental Jacobitism" a mood of mournful Scottish pride which seemed to reflect the confused state of Scottish culture. But while increasingly faded Jacobite emotion continued for some time to inspire minor poets and song writers, the general influence of Burns' poems of rural life was in the unhappy direction of sentimental vulgarization. James Hogg (1770–1835), the "Ettrick Shepherd," wrote and adapted Jacobite songs and produced also a variety of rustic Scots songs that show the direction which the Burns tradition was to take. Hogg, a Border shepherd and farmer, had very much the sort of education Burns was for long popularly supposed to have had—almost nothing except the oral tradition. He was ambitious and versatile and produced a large amount of both prose and verse, much of the former consisting of stories using doctored folk material. He produced one remarkable piece of prose fiction, *The Private Memoirs and Confessions of a Justified Sinner* (1824), a powerful story of the effect of Calvinist self-righteousness and belief in predestination on an unstable character, in which he employs supernatural machinery to illustrate the movement from a certain kind of Calvinist piety to horrifying diabolism. The power and economy of the tale is in the end dissipated in crude melodrama, but it remains nevertheless a most impressive piece of work, mediating, as it were, between Burns' "Holy Willie's Prayer" and Stevenson's *Dr. Jekyll and Mr. Hyde* (which was probably influenced by it). At his best, Hogg displays a liveliness, often an exhibitionism, which might have served literature better had he had available a really usable literary and critical tradition. In his

poetry, Hogg did best with song and ballad and least well with ambitious literary forms. His "Kilmeny" is a well-known fairy piece
which, though it begins with an intriguing lilt, cannot sustain its
music or come to adequate poetic terms with its theme. Hogg
boasted to Scott that whereas Scott was king of the school of chivalry,
he himself was "king of the faery school"; and he tried hard in many
ways to justify this title. Hogg's literary character as the Ettrick Shepherd was idealized and in part created by John Wilson (who wrote
under the name of Christopher North) in the series of dialogues entitled *Noctes Ambrosianae* which appeared in *Blackwood's Magazine*.

Blackwood's was founded in 1817 as a Tory rival to Francis Jeffrey's
Edinburgh Review, founded in 1802. The final phase of Edinburgh's
Golden Age, which had begun in the mid-eighteenth century, was
as much the age of Jeffrey and the reviewers as it was the age of
Scott. The lively, if superficial, literary and political articles, squibs,
controversies, and personalities of the first three decades of the nineteenth century in Edinburgh reflected a culture as vigorous as it was
confused, but even though we may attribute a certain sentimental
and moral strain in Jeffrey's criticism to a Scottish tradition that goes
back to Francis Hutcheson, we cannot describe the last of the Edinburgh literati as concerned with Scottish literature as such or as in
any way conscious of a distinctive Scottish literary tradition. Jeffrey's
reviews, done with brilliant and sometimes aggressive assurance,
represented a major part of the literary life of Edinburgh, a minor
phase of the history of English criticism, and no definite part at all of
the history of Scottish literature or criticism, if by Scottish literature
we mean literature that is part of a Scottish tradition extending back
to the Scottish Chaucerians and beyond.

In a sense, there is no Scottish literature of any significance after
Burns, until the twentieth-century Scottish Renaissance led by Hugh
MacDiarmid. In another sense, however, we can see the vigorous intellectual and literary life of early nineteenth-century Edinburgh as
a Scottish contribution to contemporary British culture. In poetry,
the Burns tradition degenerated into the *Whistle-Binkie* tradition.
Whistle-Binkie, a Collection of Songs for the Social Circle appeared
first in 1832, and there were numerous later editions. As the Preface
to the 1853 edition states, "the songs are of different degrees of merit,"
but "it will be found that most of them express some feeling or sentiment which the heart delights to cherish." They are for the most part
humorous or sentimental, from such things as "Now let's sing how
Miss M'Wharty, /T'other evening had a party," to "O saftly sleep,
my bonnie bairn! /Rock'd on this breast o' mine" and "Behave yoursel'
before folk, /Behave yoursel' before folk, /And dinna be sae rude

to me, /As kiss me sae before folk." Street ballads, humorous recitations, mock folk poems of love or grief, a surprising number of Irish comic poems—these and other kinds of verse show the steady degeneration of the Burns tradition into a debased Music Hall tradition, with the stereotyped pawkie, couthie, canny Scot, a figure of fun even more than a national caricature. This road ended with Harry Lauder.

It was not altogether, however, a *descensus Averni*. The sketches, tales, and dialogues contributed by Christopher North and others to *Blackwood's*, while often preposterously sentimental, sometimes revealed a sense of Scottish landscape and Scottish history with a certain vigor. And later in the century, amid the host of *Whistle-Binkie* verses and mawkish tales of idealized rustic life (the "kailyard" tradition, which culminated and was partly transmogrified in Barrie), one finds occasional attempts to use a Scottish idiom and treat a Scottish theme with dignity and originality. R. L. Stevenson's Scots verses show at least some awareness of the need for emotional discipline and verbal craftsmanship.

But this is to look ahead. To return to the early nineteenth century, we find in the work of Walter Scott (1771–1832) a deep sense of Scottish history and nationhood as well as an attitude to the past and the present which derives from a peculiarly Scottish experience and colors his best novels. Scott's poems and novels belong, of course, to the history of English literature, but they belong also, if in a rather special way, to the history of Scottish literature. In some respects he was the last important Scottish writer for almost a century; in others he was the first of a new kind of Scottish writer. His life and work are both a symptom and a symbol. As a figure in English literature he is known as the author of vigorous verse narratives which reflect a romantic interest in the past and as the founder of the historical novel. But seen in the context of Scottish culture, Scott emerges as an almost antiromantic figure, torn between love of the ancient traditions of his country and a nostalgic feeling for Scotland's lost independence on the one hand and on the other a shrewd yet reluctant appreciation of belonging to the modern world of commercial progress and English ascendancy.

Scott's literary interests were first formed by Percy's *Reliques* and by the new German romanticism which had been popularized in Scotland by Henry Mackenzie. This romanticism took the form of an interest in folklore and in the supernatural; it had something in common with the Gothic excesses of Horace Walpole and others in England, but it looked more to folk literature and the ballad than Walpole and his followers did. Gottfried August Bürger's *Musenal-*

manach (1774) introduced a German narrative poetry based on folklore and ballad; it included the ballad "Lenore," which Scott translated in 1795, publishing his translation the following year together with "The Wild Huntsman," a version of Bürger's "Der wilde Jäger." His translation of Goethe's *Götz von Berlichingen* appeared in 1799. But his interest in the traditions, antiquities, and landscape of the Scottish Border country, where he had spent part of his childhood, as well as the more general interest in Scottish antiquities which characterized the legal profession (to which he belonged) in Scotland in the latter part of the eighteenth century, led him from Germany back to his own country, and in 1802–3 he published his collection of Border ballads, *The Minstrelsy of the Scottish Border*. Believing that the texts available to him represented oral corruptions of the original compositions of minstrels, Scott endeavored to restore them to what he considered would be something like their original form by conflating, emending, "regularizing," or patching. The results were sometimes powerful and impressive poems, often somewhat smoother than a genuine ballad was likely to be, and sometimes showing a sophisticated savoring of romantic detail which betrays at once the hand of the improving editor. He explained his motive in collecting and editing these ballads in two significant sentences at the end of his introduction: "By such efforts, feeble as they are, I may contribute somewhat to the history of my native country; the peculiar features of whose manners and character are daily melting and dissolving into those of her sister and ally. And, trivial as may appear such an offering, to the manes of a kingdom, once proud and independent, I hang it upon her altar with a mixture of feelings, which I shall not attempt to describe."

Scott then embarked on the writing of a series of original narrative poems—*The Lay of the Last Minstrel* (1805), *Marmion* (1808), *The Lady of the Lake* (1810), *Rokeby* (1813), and others. The first of these shows the influence in its rhythms of Coleridge's *Christabel*, but it soon settles down into a trotting octosyllabic couplet (varied occasionally with interspersed shorter lines rhyming with each other in balladmeter style) which was to represent the norm of Scott's narrative verse. Tales of love and adventure set in a feudal past and presented at a swinging pace in vigorously moving verse have their own kind of appeal, though less to modern taste than to the taste of their first readers. Scott wrote at speed, and so long as he could keep the rhymes and the verse movement going he was content. He never had much of an artistic conscience, either with his verse or with his novels, and there are many moments in even the best of these poems (which are the first three) where his laxity as a craftsman is all too evident. He is best at describing settings (the well-known opening lines of *The Lady of the Lake*, "The stag at eve had drunk his fill . . ." are a good example of this) and sometimes in presenting fierce and rapid action; he is worst in love scenes and in sentiment generally. The description of the Battle of Flodden in *Marmion* has a fine heroic vigor and at the same time conveys a sense of doom in a manner almost, but never quite, suggestive of, say, *The Battle of Maldon*. But it is rarely that we can read for long without coming across some mechanical piece of padding inserted to carry the verse on at all costs. The narratives themselves are studiedly objective, and this adds to their vigor; but Scott developed the habit of interspersing personal passages at the beginning of different sections, and the result (especially in *Marmion*) is a rather different kind of verse, discursive, reflective, often happily informal.

Though vigorous objective narrative was Scott's aim in the bulk of his verse, he had a strangely melancholy lyric strain which appears to best effect in incidental lyrics in the narrative poems and in a greater degree in the songs he introduced into his novels. Some of these show clearly the influence of ballad and folk song, and occasionally Scott achieves a note of distilled simplicity which, while owing much to his study of the ballad, owes something too to the peculiar kind of elegiac sensibility with which so many writers of the time looked at folk literature:

> Proud Masie is in the wood
> > Walking so early;
> Sweet Robin sits on the bush,
> > Singing so rarely.
>
> "Tell me, thou bonny bird,
> > When shall I marry me?"—
> "When six braw gentlemen
> > Kirkward shall carry ye."
>
> "Who makes the bridal bed,
> > Birdie, say truly?"—
> "The gray-headed sexton
> > That delves the grave duly.
>
> "The glow-worm o'er grave and stone
> > Shall light thee steady,
> The owl from the steeple sing,
> > 'Welcome, proud lady.'"

(Madge Wildfire's song in *The Heart of Midlothian*.)

The other pole of Scott's lyrical range is best shown by such a poem as "Bonny Dundee," the swinging Cavalier ballad in *Woodstock*:

> To the Lords of Convention 't was Claver'se who spoke,
> "Ere the King's crown shall fall there are crowns to be broke;
> So let each Cavalier who loves honour and me,
> Come follow the bonnet of Bonny Dundee.
>   Come fill up my cup, come fill up my can,
>   Come saddle your horses and call up your men;
>   Come ope the West Port and let me gang free,
> And it's room for the bonnets of Bonny Dundee!"

Another kind of ballad influence is shown in the ballad of *Rosabelle* (Harold's song in *The Lay of the Last Minstrel*):

> O listen, listen, ladies gay!
>   No haughty feat of arms I tell;
> Soft is the note, and sad the lay,
>   That mourns the lovely Rosabelle.
>
> —"Moor, moor the barge, ye gallant crew!
>   And, gentle lady, deign to stay!
> Rest thee in Castle Ravensheuch,
>   Nor tempt the stormy firth today. . . ."

Though the subject matter of most of Scott's poems is Scottish, and many are filled with either a heroic or an elegiac sense of Scottish history, the idiom is standard English, except for a few older Scottish words sometimes introduced to give an antique flavor. Scott was writing for an English audience, for whom Scotland was a pleasing romantic emotion rather than a country with a living culture, and this fact could not but provide a distorting or an exhibitionist element to much of Scott's treatment of the past of his country. His narrative poems, particularly the first three, enjoyed great popularity, until Byron appeared on the scene with verse tales that appealed more adroitly to the same kind of taste (a taste, very often, for histrionic heroics in narrative) and Scott quitted the field to turn to prose fiction.

The Waverley Novels, which brought Scott fame and fortune (though not sufficient fortune to prevent his rash association with grandiose printing and publishing enterprises and his expensive way of life as Laird of Abbotsford from landing him in bankruptcy), appeared anonymously, beginning with *Waverley* in 1814 and continuing with *Guy Mannering* (1815), *The Antiquary* and *Old Mortality* (1816), *Rob Roy* (1817), *The Heart of Midlothian* (1818), and *The Bride of Lammermoor* and *The Legend of Montrose* (1819). It was only after these novels, which include much of his best work, that he turned from Scottish to English and then European themes to keep his public provided with new historical fiction. *Ivanhoe* appeared in 1819, *The Monastery* and *The Abbot* in 1820, *Kenilworth* in 1821, *The Pirate* (set in Scotland again, but up in the Orkneys) in 1822, *The Fortunes of Nigel* in 1822, and many others, including *Quentin Durward* in 1823, *St. Ronan's Well* in 1824 and, the same year, the last and in many ways the most revealing of his Scottish novels, *Redgauntlet*. As a historical novelist dealing with medieval England or France or Germany or the Crusaders' Palestine, Scott showed a flair for the highly colored, picturesque incident and situation, and revealed himself a master of "tushery." There was of course more than tushery in these novels; a sense of the poetry of history, an ability to project in terms of character and action something of the life and manners of the feudal ages, can be seen in varying degrees in all these novels. But as a rule the nearer Scott comes to his own time the more complex and mature a novelist he is, and when he is dealing with the recent past of his own country he is best of all. *Ivanhoe* and *The Talisman* are colorful, somewhat theatrical, novels of rather obviously stylized "period" characters and action; the sense of deeper human implication comes through fitfully where it comes through at all. *Quentin Durward, Kenilworth,* and *The Fortunes of Nigel,* set respectively in the fifteenth, sixteenth, and seventeenth centuries, show a greater awareness of the complexities of the human situation and less disposition to be content with colorful surface action arising from histrionic attitudes of somewhat cardboard figures. Scott was never much good with love scenes, but he inherited a conception of fiction which demanded a central love interest and he conscientiously did what he could. Further, he wrote too fast, and wrote simply to entertain, with his eye on as large an audience as possible. Nevertheless, in his best novels he was (in spite of himself, it might almost be said) a serious novelist, and a great one. In dealing with picturesque aspects of the distant past, as well as on the one occasion, in *St. Ronan's Well,* when he dealt with the surface of life in his own day, Scott's imagination worked perfunctorily and did not draw on its deepest sources of inspiration. In his "Scotch novels," dealing with the recent past of his own country, he produced his best work, the novels on which his claim to greatness must rest.

The fact that these novels are concerned with Scottish history and manners is intimately bound up with the reasons for their being his best novels. Scott's attitude to life was derived from his response to the fate of his own country: it was the complex of feelings with which he contemplated the phase of Scottish history immediately preceding his own time that provided the point of view which gave life—often a predominantly tragic life—to these novels. Underlying most of these novels is a tragic sense of the inevitability of a drab but necessary progress, a sense of the impotence of the traditional kind of heroism, a passionately regretful awareness of the fact that the Good Old Cause was lost forever and the glory of Scotland must give way to her interest.

Scott's attitude to Scotland was a mixture of regret for the old days when Scotland was an independent but turbulent and distracted country, and of satisfaction at the peace, prosperity, and progress which he felt had been assured by the Union with England in 1707 and the successful establishment of the Hanoverian dynasty on the British throne. His problem, in one form or another, was the problem of every Scottish writer after Scotland ceased to have an independent culture of her own: how to reconcile his country's traditions with what appeared to be its interest. Scott was always strongly moved by everything that reminded him of Scotland's past, of the days of the country's independence and the relatively recent days when the Jacobites were appealing to that very emotion to gain support for their cause. He grew up as the Jacobite tradition was finally ebbing away, amid the first generation of Scotsmen committed once and for all to the association with England and the Hanoverian dynasty. He felt strongly that that association was inevitable and right and advantageous—he exerted himself greatly to make George IV popular in Scotland—yet there were strong emotions on the other side too, and it was these emotions that made him Tory in politics and that led him to literature and history.

This conflict within Scott gave life and passion to his Scottish novels, for it led him to construct plots and invent characters which, far from being devices in an adventure story or means to make history look picturesque, illustrated what to him was the central paradox of modern life. And that paradox admitted of the widest application, for it was an aspect of all commercial and industrial civilizations. Civilization must be paid for by the cessation of the old kind of individual heroic action. Scott welcomed civilization, but he also sighed after the old kind of individual heroic action. Scott's theme is a modification of that of Cervantes, and, specifically, *Redgauntlet* is Scott's *Don Quixote*.

Many of Scott's novels take the form of a sort of pilgrim's progress: an Englishman or a Lowland Scot goes north into the Highlands of Scotland at a time when Scottish feeling is running high, becomes involved in the passions and activities of the Scots partly by accident and partly by sympathy, and eventually extricates himself—physically altogether but emotionally not quite wholly—and returns whence he came. The character who makes the journey is the more deliberate side of Scott's character, the disinterested observer. His duty is to observe, to register the proper responses, and in the end to accept, however reluctantly, the proper solution. It is not this character but what he becomes involved in that matters: his function is merely to observe, react, and withdraw. To censure Scott for the woodenness of his heroes—characters like Edward Waverley, Francis Osbaldistone, and many others—is to misunderstand their function. They are not heroes in the ordinary sense, but symbolic observers. Their love affairs are of no significance whatsover except to indicate the nature of the observer's final withdrawal from the seductive scenes of heroic, nationalist passion. Waverley does not marry the passionate Jacobite Flora MacIvor, but the douce and colorless Rose Bradwardine; Waverley's affair with these two girls is not presented as a serious love interest, but as a symbolic indication of the nature of his final withdrawal from the heroic emotions of the past. That withdrawal is never quite one hundred per cent: Waverley does marry the daughter of a Jacobite, but of one who has given up the struggle, and Francis Osbaldistone does (we are told in an epilogue, though we are not shown how it happens) marry Di Vernon, but only after she has dissociated herself from her violently Jacobite father and after Francis himself has, for all his earlier rebellion against a life of commerce, returned to his father's business. These pilgrims into Scotland carry back something of older attitudes that must be discarded, but only as a vague and regretful sentiment. Even Rob Roy tells Francis that the wild and heroic life may be all very well for himself, but it won't do for his children—they will have to come to terms with the new world.

The Jacobite movement for Scott was not simply a picturesque historical event: it was the last attempt to restore to Scotland something of the old heroic way of life. He used it, and its aftermath, to symbolize at once the attractiveness and the futility of the old Scotland. *That* Scotland was doomed after the Union of Parliaments of 1707, and doubly doomed after the Battle of Culloden in 1746: the aftermath of 1707 is shown in *The Heart of Midlothian* and of 1746 in *Redgauntlet*. In both novels, explicitly in the latter and murmuring in an undertone in the former, there is indicated the tragic theme (for it *is* tragic) that the grand old causes are all lost causes, and the old heroic action is no longer even fatal—it is merely useless and silly. One thinks of the conclusion of Bishop Hurd's *Letters on Chivalry and Romance:* "What we have gotten by this revolution, you will say, is a great deal of good sense. What we have lost is a world of fine fabling." But to Scott it was more than a world of fine fabling that was lost; it was a world of heroic ideals, which he could not help believing should still be worth something. He knew, however, even before it was brought home to him by the failure of Constable (the publisher with whom he was financially involved) and his own subsequent bankruptcy that in the reign of George IV it was not worth much—certainly not as much as novels about it.

It is this ambivalence in Scott's approach to the history of his country—combined, of course, with certain remarkable talents—that accounts for the unique quality of his Scottish novels. He was able to take an *odi et amo* attitude to some of the most exciting crises of Scottish history. If Scott's desire to set himself up as an old-time landed gentleman in a large country estate was romantic, the activities by which he financed—or endeavored to finance—his schemes were the reverse, and there is nothing romantic in James Glen's account of Scott's financial transactions prefixed to the centenary edition of his letters. He filled Abbotsford with historical relics, but they were relics, and they gave Abbotsford something of the appearance of a museum. He thus tried to resolve the conflict in his way of life by making modern finance pay for a house filled with antiquities. This resolution could not, however, eliminate the basic ambivalence in his approach to recent Scottish history: that remained, to enrich his fiction.

The subtitle of *Waverley* is "'Tis Sixty Years Since," and the phrase is repeated many times throughout the book. It deals, that is to say, with a period which, while distant enough to have a historical interest, was not altogether out of the ken of Scott's own generation. In the preface to the first edition of *The Antiquary*, Scott wrote: "The present work completes a series of fictitious narratives, intended to illustrate the manners of Scotland at three different periods. *Waverley* embraced the age of our fathers, *Guy Mannering* that of our youth, and the *Antiquary* refers to the last years of the eighteenth century." As Scott comes closer to his own day, the possibilities for heroic action recede and the theme of the lost heir is introduced as a sort of substitute. It was with recent Scottish history that Scott was most concerned, for the conflict within himself was the result of relatively recent history. The Jacobite Rebellion of 1745 was the watershed, as it were, dividing once and for all the old from the new, and Scott therefore began his novels with a study of the relation between the two worlds at that critical time. It was not that the old Scotland had wholly disappeared, but that it was slowly yet inevitably disappearing, that upset Scott. Its disappearance is progressively more inevitable in each of the next two novels after *Waverley*.

Guy Mannering is not in the obvious sense a historical novel at all. It is a study of aspects of the Scottish situation in the days of the author's youth, where the plot is simply an excuse for bringing certain characters into relation with each other. As in *Waverley*, we have an Englishman—Colonel Mannering, who, like Edward Waverley, shares many of his creator's characteristics—coming into Scotland and surrendering to the charm of the country. Scott has to get him mixed up in the affairs of the Bertrams in order to keep him where he wants him. Round Guy Mannering move gypsies, smugglers, lairds, dominies, lawyers, and farmers, and it is to be noted that none of these characters, from Meg Merrilies to Dandie Dinmont, belongs to the new world: they are all essentially either relics of an earlier age, like the gypsies, or the kind of person who does not substantially change with the times, like that admirable farmer Dandie. These people are made to move around the Bertram family, or at least are brought into the story through some direct or indirect association with that family, and the family is decayed and impoverished. The lost heir is found and restored, and, largely through the benevolent offices of an English colonel, a Scottish landed gentleman is settled again on his ancestral acres. That is how things happen in the days of Scott's youth: no clash of arms or open conflict of two worlds, but the prophecies of gypsies, the intrigues of smugglers, the hearty activities of farmers, all set against the decay of an ancient family and all put to right in the end with the help of a gypsy, an English officer, and a Scottish lawyer. If the heroic element is less than in *Waverley*, the element of common life is greater, and the two virtues of honesty (in Dinmont) and urbanity (in Counsellor Pleydell) eventually emerge as those most worthwhile.

Counsellor Pleydell is a particularly interesting character, because he represents that combination of good sense and humanity which Scott so often thought of as mediating between extremes and enabling the new world to preserve, in a very different context, something of the high generosity of the old. Pleydell is a lawyer, essentially middle-class and respectable, but he is drawn with such sympathy that he threatens to remove most of the interest from the rather artificial main plot and share with Dandie Dinmont the reader's chief attention. If the gypsy Meg Merrilies provides something of the old-world romantic note—and she does so with great vigor and effectiveness—the lawyer and the farmer between them represent the ordinary man providing comfort for the future. The bluff courage and honesty of the farmer and the kindly intelligence of the lawyer dominate the story at the end.

Scott knew much of rural superstitions from the ballads, and he saw them as part of the ancient Scotland no less than Jacobitism or the feudal system. The gypsy prophetess Meg Merrilies is thus in a way the counterpart in this novel of Fergus MacIvor in *Waverley*. She, too, dies a violent death at the end of the book, and the stage is left to the representatives of the less spectacular virtues. The different strata of dialogue here are as clear as in the earlier novel. In the speech of Meg Merrilies—notably in her eloquent curse on the Laird of Ellangowan—Scott strikes a high note, popular yet passionate, that he had learned from the Border ballads. If one puts beside this the conversation between Counsellor Pleydell and Dandie Dinmont in Chapter 36 and compares again with that the magnificent domestic scene at the Dinmont farm of Charlies-hope in Chapter 24 (both too long for quotation here), one gets a view of the range of Scott's dialogue—from the passionate outburst of the gypsy to the humorous realism of the talk between Pleydell and Dinmont and the sympathetic domestic scene at Charlies-hope. These three passages illustrate Scott's basic equipment as a realistic "social" novelist.

The nearer to the present Scott moves, the more likely he is to present men of noble birth simply as fools. Those who think of Scott as the passionate defender of aristocratic privilege should note that the most highly born character in *Guy Mannering* is Sir Robert Hazlewood, whom Scott represents as a pompous ass, so obsessed by the dignity of his ancient lineage that he can talk of little else, and in other respects a selfish and foolish nonentity. Similarly, Sir Arthur Wardour of *The Antiquary*, equally obsessed by his noble ancestry, is shown as a gullible fool, and much less sympathetic than the antiquary himself, who, it should be noted, is of humble origin and a Whig.

The scene of *The Antiquary* is the Scotland of Scott's own day. The external plot, which is once again that of the lost heir, is, as usual, not to be taken seriously: its function is to bring the faintly drawn Englishman Lovel into Scotland and so set the appropriate characters into motion. In three successive novels Scott begins by bringing an Englishman into Scotland, by sending forth an observer to note the state of the country at the time represented by the novel's action. Lovel, of course, is no more the hero of *The Antiquary* than Christopher Sly is the hero of *The Taming of the Shrew*, and his turning out at the end to be the lost heir of Glenallan is the merest routine drawing down of the curtain. The life of the novel—and it has abundant life—centers in the Scottish characters whom the plot enables Scott to bring together, and in their reactions to each other. Jonathan Oldbuck, the antiquary (and it should be noted that there are antiquaries of one kind or another in a great many of Scott's novels), represents one kind of compromise between the old world and the new that is possible in the modern world. A descendant of German printers, a man of no family in the aristocratic sense, and a Whig in politics to boot, Oldbuck is yet fascinated by Scotland's past and spends his life in antiquarian studies. In the modern world the past becomes the preserve of the interested historian, whatever his birth or politics, while those who attempt to live in the past in any other way become, as Sir Arthur Wardour becomes, ridiculous and insufferable. Sir Arthur, continually lording it over the antiquary because of his superior birth, nevertheless knows less of Scottish history and traditions than the antiquary, and is so vain and stupid that he falls a prey to the designing arts of an impostor who swindles him out of his remaining money so that he has to be rescued through the influence of his friends. Sir Arthur is the comic counterpart of the tragic hero of *Redgauntlet:* both illustrate the impossibility of seriously living in the past after 1746. In *The Antiquary* the prevailing atmosphere is comic. This is unusual in Scott, however often he may end his novels with a formal "happy ending" so far as the superficial plot is concerned. The melodramatic Glenallan episode in this novel and the drowning of the young fisherman Steenie Mucklebackit give a sense of depth and implication to the action, but they do not alter its essential atmosphere. In this novel, too, the hero is the character who plays the dominant part—the antiquary himself, the good-humored, pedantic, self-opinionated, essentially kindly gentleman who is in many respects a latter-day version of Baron Bradwardine. Round him move Edie Ochiltree, the wandering beggar; the humble fishing family of the Mucklebackits; Caxon, the comic barber who deplores the passing of powdered wigs but takes comfort in the three yet left to him; the foreign impostor Dousterswivel; and other characters illustrative of the kind of life the east coast of Scotland (apart from the big cities) had settled down to by the end of the eighteenth century.

The plot of *The Antiquary* is even less important than that of *Guy Mannering.* It is essentially a static novel, in a sense a novel of manners, and the parts that stand out in the memory are such scenes as the gathering in the Fairport post office when the mail comes in, the antiquary holding forth at dinner or at a visit to a neighboring priory, Sir Arthur and his daughter trapped by the tide and rescued by Edie Ochiltree and Lovel, the interior of the humble fishing cottage after Steenie's drowning, and similar pictures. And as always in Scott, the novel lives by its dialogue, the magnificent pedantic monologues of Oldbuck, the racy Scots speech of Edie Ochiltree, the chattering of gossips in the post office, the naïve babbling of Caxon. No action, in these early novels of Scott, ever comes to life until somebody talks about it, whether in the sardonic tones of Andrew Fairservice, the vernacular declamations of Meg Merrilies, or the shrewd observations of Edie Ochiltree. And it is to be noticed that the dialogue is at its best when it is the speech of humble people: Scott could make them live by simply opening their mouths.

The characteristic tension of Scott's novel is only occasionally perceptible in *The Antiquary*. In *Old Mortality* it is present continuously and is in a sense the theme of the story. In this novel Scott goes back to the latter part of the seventeenth century to deal with the conflict between the desperate and embittered Covenanters and the royal armies intent on stamping out a religious disaffection which was bound up with political disagreements. Though this was an aspect of Scottish history which, in its most acute phases at least, was settled by the Revolution of 1689, it represented a type of conflict which is characteristic of much Scottish history and which Scott saw as a struggle between an exaggerated royalism and a fanatical religion. It should be said at the outset that as a historical novel in the most literal sense of the word—as an accurate picture of the state of affairs at the time—this is clearly Scott's best work. Generations of subsequent research have only confirmed the essential justice and fairness of Scott's picture of both sides.

But we do not read *Old Mortality* for its history, though we could do worse. We read it, as Scott wrote it, as a study of the kinds of mentality which faced each other in this conflict, a study of how a few extremists on each side managed, as they so often do, to split the country into warring camps with increasing bitterness on the one side and increasing cruelty on the other. Scott's interest, of course, would lie in the possibilities for compromise, in the techniques of adjustment, in the kind of character who can construct a bridge between the two factions. And just as Edward Waverley, the loyal Englishman, became involved in spite of himself on the Jacobite side in 1745, so Harry Morton, the sensible, moderate, goodhearted Scot, becomes involved in similar circumstances on the side of the Convenanters. The Fergus MacIvor of the Covenanters is the magnificently drawn fanatic, Balfour of Burley. The leader of the other side, the famous Claverhouse, "Bonnie Dundee," is introduced in person, and a convincing and powerful portrait it is. Between these extremes are all those whom varying degrees of zeal or loyalty brought into one camp or the other. The novel contains one of Scott's finest portrait galleries. On the Government side there is Claverhouse himself, his nephew Cornet Grahame, the proud Bothwell, descendant of kings, that perfect gentleman Lord Evandale, Major Bellenden, the veteran campaigner, and some minor figures. On the Covenanting side there is a whole array of clergymen, from the fanatical Macbriar to the more accommodating Poundtext, each presented with an individuality and with an insight into the motives and minds of men more profound than anything Scott had yet shown. The realistic, commonsense Cuddie Headrigg trying, in the interests of their common safety, to put a curb on the tongue of his enthusiastic Covenanting mother produces some of the finest tragi-comedy (if one may call it that) in English literature: there are many fine passages here. The pious and kindly Bessie Maclure shows the Covenanting side at its best, while the generous Lord Evandale plays the same part for the other side. It is in the gradations of the characters on either side that Scott shows his greatest insight into the causes of civil conflict. Total conviction is comparatively rare on either side, and when it is, it is either bitter and passionate, as in Balfour of Burley, or nonchalantly self-assured, as in Claverhouse.

If Scotland had not torn itself in two before the issues presented in the eighteenth century were ever thought of, the fate of the country might have been different, and Scott's study of the last of the Scottish civil wars before the Jacobite Rebellions is thus linked with his major preoccupation—the destiny of modern Scotland. If moderate men on both sides could have won, the future would have been very different. But, though there were moderate men on both sides and Scott delighted to draw them, their advice in the moments of crisis was never taken. There is no more moving passage in the novel than the description of Morton's vain attempt to make his fanatical colleagues behave sensibly before the Battle of Bothwell Brig. There is a passion behind the telling of much of this story that is very different from the predominantly sunny mood of *The Antiquary*. The extremists prevail, the Covenanting army is destroyed, and a victorious Government takes a cruel revenge on embittered and resolute opponents. This is one novel of Scott's where the moderate men do not remain at the end to point the way to the future. Morton goes into exile and can return to Scotland only after the Revolution. Lord Evandale meets his death at the hands of a desperate man. And if the leaders on both sides—the ruthless fanatic Burley and the equally ruthless but gay cavalier Claverhouse—both go to their death before the novel ends, there is no particular hope implied by their elimination.

Morton returns to marry his love, and the prudent Cuddie settles down to be a decent henpecked husband, but the life has gone out of the novel by this time. The dominating figure, Balfour of Burley, may have been an impossible fanatic, but he represented a kind of energy possessed by none of the wiser characters. Harry Morton, the observer, the man who sees something good on both sides and is roped into the Covenanting side by a series of accidents, represents the humane, intelligent liberal in a world of extremists. *Old Mortality* is a study of a society which had no place for such a character: it is essentially a tragedy, and one with a very modern ring.

If *Old Mortality* is, from one point of view, Scott's study of the earlier errors which made the later cleavage between Scotland and her past inevitable (for it is true to say that after the Covenanting wars the English saw no way but a union of the two countries to ensure the perpetual agreement of the Scots to the king chosen by England and to prevent the succession question from being a constant bugbear), *Rob Roy* is a return to his earlier theme, a study of eighteenth-century Highland grievances and their relation to Scotland's destiny. It is, in a sense, a rewriting of *Waverley* and the main theme is less baldly presented. The compromise character here is Bailie Nicol Jarvie, the Glasgow merchant who is nevertheless related to Rob Roy himself and, for all his love of peace and his commercial interests, can on occasion cross the Highland line into his cousin's country and become involved in scenes of violence in which, for a conventional citizen of Glasgow, he acquits himself very honorably.

Rob Roy represents the old heroic Scotland, while the worthy Bailie represents the new. The Union of 1707 may have been a sad thing for those who prized Scotland's independence, but to the Bailie and his like it opened up new fields for foreign trade, and brought increased wealth. "Whisht, sir!—whisht!" he cried to Andrew Fairservice when the latter complained of the Union. "It's ill-scraped tongues like yours that make mischief between neighbourhoods and nations. There's naething sae gude on this side o' time but it might have been better, and that may be said o' the Union. Nane were keener against it than the Glasgow folk, wi' their rabblings and their risings, and their mobs, as they ca' them nowadays. But it's an ill wind that blaws naebody gude—let ilka ane roose the ford as they find it.—I say, let Glasgow flourish! Whilk is judiciously and elegantly putten round the town's arms by way of byword. Now, since St. Mungo catched herrings in the Clyde, what was ever like to gar us flourish like the sugar and tobacco trade? Will anybody tell me that, and grumble at a treaty that opened us a road west-awa' yonder?" Rob Roy is courageous and sympathetic, and Helen Macgregor, his wife, is noble to the verge of melodrama, but they represent a confused and divided Highlands and are, after all,

nothing but glorified freebooters. Scott, in the person of Francis
Osbaldistone, pities their wrongs and feels for their present state,
but he knows that they and what they stand for are doomed—indeed, they admit it themselves—and throws in his lot with the prudent Bailie.

There are two pivots to this novel; one is the relations between
Francis Osbaldistone and his friends with Rob Roy and *his* friends,
and the other is Francis' relations with his uncle and cousins. It is
a mistake to regard the family complications in *Rob Roy* as mere
machinery designed to provide a reason for young Osbaldistone's
journey into Scotland; they loom much too large in the novel for
that. They represent, in fact, a statement of the theme on which the
Rob Roy scenes are a variation—the impossibility of the old life in
the new world. Francis' uncle is an old-fashioned Tory-Jacobite
squire, completely gone to seed, and his sons are either fools or villains. This is what has become of the knights of old—they are either
freebooters like Rob Roy, shabby remnants of landed gentry like Sir
Hildebrand, or complete villains like Rashleigh. Francis' father had
escaped from this environment to embrace the new world whole-
heartedly and become a prosperous London merchant. He is at one
extreme, Bailie Nicol Jarvie is the middle figure, and Rob Roy is at
the other extreme. But the pattern is more complicated than this,
for the novel contains many variations on each type of character,
so much so, in fact, that it is an illuminating and accurate picture
of Scottish types in the early eighteenth century. And through it
all runs the sense of the necessity of sacrificing heroism to prudence,
even though heroism is so much more attractive.

It is interesting to observe that Scott tends to lavish most of his
affection on the middle figures, those who manage to make themselves at home in the new world without altogether repudiating the
old. Such characters—Jonathan Oldbuck, Counsellor Pleydell, Bailie
Nicol Jarvie—are always the most lively and the most attractive in
the novels in which they occur. They represent, in one way or another, the kind of compromise which most satisfied Scott.

The Heart of Midlothian shows Scott looking at his country a
generation after the Treaty of Union and finding characters and incidents to embody his emotions about it at this stage of its history.
The main element in the plot—a girl's successful effort to save her
sister from the gallows—Scott adapted from a real incident. By link-
ing this with the equally historical Porteous Riot and its aftermath,
Scott made clear that he was not interested merely in history or
merely in character, but in the degree to which one illuminates the
other. The grim and disciplined body of conspirators that hanged

Captain Porteous were acting from motives which were in a sense patriotic and in a sense heroic—but in how unsatisfactory a sense! Were the modern representatives of the old heroic tradition to be found only among crooks, smugglers, and degenerates? Is the desperate Robertson to be the type of the modern Scottish hero? As the spotlight moves from history to psychology, from the general to the particular, from the Porteous Riot to the humble cottage of David Deans and his daughters, we begin to get the answer. And with the full development of the character of Jeanie Deans, the answer becomes clear: there *is* the possibility of heroic action in modern life—at least there was at that particular transitional stage in Scottish history—and it is not to be found in acts of lawlessness and violence, but in the unpretentious faith and courage of a humble Scots lass.

Jeanie Deans is bound up with history, and in creating her Scott is answering a historical question. The whole atmosphere which surrounds the Deans family is the result of the way the past has developed into the present. David Deans has taken part in the religious struggles of an earlier generation and he retains some of the fanaticism of the extreme Covenanter; but time has changed the grim struggles and persecutions into something little more than individual eccentricity. There are both psychological and historical purposes at work here. The heroic clash between Puritan and Cavalier, between Covenanters and their persecutors, had passed away, and in place of fanaticism and tragedy we get eccentricity and pathos. And this transition leads us right back to Scott's main preoccupation—the possibilities for heroic action in the modern world. Clearly, the kind of heroic action which developed out of politico-religious conflict was now less easy to find. There was both a gain and a loss here, and the plot of the novel illustrates this ambivalence: it ends on a note of agricultural improvement and pastoral peace, against which all spirited physical action is made to sound melodramatic and silly, but the mechanical adjustment of this conclusion, as well as the tone in which it is narrated, indicates that peace has been won at the price of some valuable quality in human action.

With the loss of her independence, Scotland was left with only her legal and ecclesiastical institutions to represent concretely Scottish individuality and nationality. The Church of Scotland and Scots law remained—as they still do—separate and different from the Church of England and English law, and, more important for Scott, these institutions became the modern descendants of the old heroic Scotland. Here again we have heroism passing into eccentricity.

Scott's fascination with the oddities of Scots law produced some of his most amusing character and richest dialogue; his Scottish novels are filled with legal chatter by lawyers and litigants; but behind it all lies the sense that the antiquarian and the pedant now trod those fields that formerly bore the shock of knights-at-arms. Scottish history was now the preserve not of men of heroic action who made it, but of antiquaries who wrote and argued about it. The absurd figure of Mr. Saddletrees gives comic expression to this idea: Scott saw the humor of the situation when a national tradition becomes a breeder of eccentrics; but the fact that Mr. Saddletrees engages in his boring discussion of half-understood law in connection with a situation whose tragic implications he never realizes, is sufficient to indicate the wry manner in which Scott noted the difference between the old and the new.

One could take up character after character and show how each is related to Scott's main concern with the impact of the past on the present and the relation of both to individual psychology. Dumbiedykes, the decayed laird, who is presented to us only after the progress of his family's decay has been carefully described, is another tattered remnant of a once heroic tradition. Instead of giving up his past in a burst of tragic violence (as does the hero of *The Bride of Lammermoor*), he clings to it, and by frugality and a rather pitiful tenacity survives to prosper in the modern world. Even the Captain of Knockdunder, introduced toward the end of the book to add vitality to the too long drawn out conclusion, stands between two worlds—that of the Highland clan system and that of modern social and economic value. This transitional situation may be a source of lively and humorous character portrayal, or it may produce pathos or even tragedy. That the same general situation can be put by Scott to so many purposes only emphasizes the central part it played in his imagination.

But the principal figure is Jeanie Deans, and she and her father and sister remain the best-drawn characters in the novel. Jeanie's character is developed, as usual in Scott's best characters, through dialogue, and the climax is in her great and spontaneous speech before the Queen, which comes near enough to formal rhetoric to be supremely effective *as* rhetoric, but is saved by the rhythms and expressions of folk speech from sounding either artificial or sentimental. The continuous juxtaposition of the unconsciously heroic and the domestic is Scott's way of building up the essential reality of Jeanie's character.

Perhaps the most impressive quality in *The Heart of Midlothian* is the ease and abundance which it continuously suggests. Scott

shared with Shakespeare the ability to project whole hosts of characters who create themselves as they talk, who illustrate typical
elements in human nature while remaining (however brief their appearance) essentially individuals. Snatches of conversation over-
heard in the streets of Edinburgh, a glimpse of a citizen in his shop
or of a servant on his way to do some errand—these frequent glances
at the teeming background of human life, out of which specific
concrete fragments of talk are selected before we turn to some new
episode or character, provide that depth and perspective which is
one of the most impressive qualities of the novel. There is a lot of
the novelist of manners about Scott, and there certainly can be no
better introduction than this novel to the life and habits of the Scottish people in and around Edinburgh in the early eighteenth century. The impact of history on individual personality and ambitions
remains the real theme; the plot, the disposition of the action, provides the former part of it, while the characterizations provide the
latter; and underlying everything is the paradox of tradition and
progress. Both are valuable, but one flourishes at the expense of
the other.

Scott's attitude to the history of his own country, and to the relation between tradition and progress, emerges most clearly in *Redgauntlet,* the novel in which he returned to a Scottish subject after
having dealt with English and European history. This is the story of
a young man who becomes involved against his will in a belated
Jacobite conspiracy some twenty years after the defeat of Prince
Charlie at Culloden. The moving spirit of the conspiracy turns out
to be the young man's own uncle (for, like so many of Scott's heroes,
young Darsie Latimer is brought up in ignorance of his true parent-
age), who kidnaps him in order that, as the long-lost heir to the
house of Redgauntlet, he may return to the ways of his ancestors and
fight for the Pretender as his father had done before him. Darsie
has no liking for the anachronistic romantic role thrust upon him in
this violent manner, and he is saved from having to undertake it by
the complete collapse of the conspiracy. As with most of Scott's Scottish novels, the story moves between two extremes. On the one hand,
there is the conscientious lawyer Saunders Fairford, his son Alan, who
is Darsie's close friend, and other characters representing respectable and professional Edinburgh. At the other extreme is Darsie's
uncle, a stern fanatical figure reminiscent of Balfour of Burley in
Old Mortality. Between the two worlds—that of respectable citizens who are completely reconciled to the new Scotland and that of
fanatical Jacobites engaged in the vain task of trying to re-create
the old—Scott places his usual assortment of mediating figures,

from the blind fiddler, Wandering Willie, to that typical compromise character, the half-Jacobite Provost Crosbie. This is the Scotland in which Scott himself grew up and in which he recognized all the signs of the final death of the old order. For most of the characters, Jacobitism is now possible only as a sentiment, not as a plan of action. But to Redgauntlet, who has dedicated his life to the restoration of the Stuarts, it is a plan of action, and the tragedy—for in one of its aspects the novel *is* a tragedy—lies in the manner of his disillusion.

In describing the last Jacobite gathering Scott relentlessly exposes the widening gap between sentimental Jacobitism and active rebellion. The group of reluctant conspirators assembled at a shabby inn on the Solway Firth, brought there, as Charles Edward himself is brought there, only by the fanatical energy of Redgauntlet, are acutely embarrassed at having their professions put to the test so many years after the last fatal attempt at rebellion. Redgauntlet himself is the only one who unites theory with practice, sentiment with action, and it is his almost desperate activity in cajoling, flattering, urging, exhorting, that keeps the group together at all. None of the others—not even Charles Edward himself—believe any more in the practicability of rebellion. The picture of the slow disintegration of the meeting, of the embarrassment of the Jacobites when faced with the problem of reconciling their fierce protestations of loyalty to the house of Stuart with the realities of their present situation, is brilliantly done. The scene is one of the finest in Scott. The two worlds are finally brought together, and the romantic one disintegrates. The most poignant moment of all occurs when, as the result of betrayal by an informer, the Hanoverian General Campbell arrives, walking unnoticed into the midst of the wrangling assembly. He has, as they all know, troops to support him, and many in the Jacobite group, in a last surge of heroic action, are prepared to die fighting to cover the retreat of him whom they regard as their legitimate king. Death in this last desperate battle, or execution as traitors, seem now the only alternatives. But these heroics prove unnecessary—worse than unnecessary, irrelevant. General Campbell calmly and politely informs them that they had better break up the party, since a gathering of people whose loyalty to the reigning house was suspect might be open to misunderstanding. Redgauntlet proudly asserts that "we are not men to be penned up like sheep for the slaughter," to which the general replies with a good-natured "Pshaw!" It takes him some time to convince them that his only objective is to persuade them to go peaceably home. There is going to be no battle. Nobody is going to be arrested or executed. They had

presumably assembled here "for a bear-bait or a cock-fight," but it
was really more sensible now for them to "return quietly home to
their own houses." All were free to go. The dialogue continues:

"What!—all?" exclaimed Sir Richard Glendale—"all, without exception?"

"ALL, without one single exception," said the General; "such are my orders.
If you accept my terms, say so, and make haste; for things may happen to interfere with his Majesty's kind purpose towards you all."

"His Majesty's kind purposes!" said the Wanderer [Charles Edward Stuart].
"Do I hear you aright, sir?"

"I speak the King's very words, from his very lips," replied the General. 'I
will,' said his Majesty, 'deserve the confidence of my subjects by reposing my
security in the fidelity of the millions who acknowledge my title—in the good
sense and prudence of the few who continue, from the errors of education, to
disown it.'—His Majesty will not even believe that the most zealous Jacobites
who yet remain can nourish a thought of exciting a civil war, which must be
fatal to their families and themselves, besides spreading bloodshed and ruin
through a peaceful land. He cannot even believe of his kinsman, that he would
engage brave and generous, though mistaken men, in an attempt which must
ruin all who have escaped former calamities; . . ."

"Is this real?" said Redgauntlet. "Can you mean this?—Am I—are all, are
any of these gentlemen at liberty, without interruption, to embark in yonder
brig . . .?"

"You, sir—all—any of the gentlemen present," said the General,—"all whom
the vessel can contain, are at liberty to embark uninterrupted by me; but I
advise none to go off who have not powerful reasons, unconnected with the
present meeting, for this will be remembered against no one."

"Then, gentlemen," said Redgauntlet, clasping his hands together as the
words burst from him, "the cause is lost for ever!"

The heroic gesture cannot survive in the face of cool, good-humored, modern common sense. The Jacobite movement dissolves
in the end because it is an unreal anachronism in the modern world.
It does not really exist except as a sentiment. The victory lies with
prudence and modernity.

Scott showed both courage and imagination in setting his novel
in a period when the Jacobite movement was dwindling down to a
trickle. Twenty years after the '45 rebellion, Jacobitism had become,
except for a tiny minority of die-hards, the merest emotional self-
indulgence. It had produced a fine crop of songs, which showed
the immense appeal of Bonnie Prince Charlie to the folk (and not
only the folk) mind and cast a fine romantic glow over the whole
doomed enterprise; but in itself it was now more a matter of literature than politics. In *Waverley*, Scott had brought his English hero
into sympathetic contact with a group of Jacobites of the '45, who
were shown in the end to be noble and heroic but at the same time

histrionic and rather silly. Now, twenty years later, the essence of the movement was symbolized by its ultimate fate. It had been a foolish anachronism all along. And though a character like Redgauntlet arouses our admiration, his melodramatic posturings (which are not defects in the novel; Scott introduced them deliberately) reveal the essential unreality of the world he lives in. Like Helen Macgregor in *Rob Roy*, he is not wholly real, and just as in the earlier novel Scott revealed this unreality by bringing the shrewd and realistic Bailie Nicol Jarvie into conversation with Helen, so in *Redgauntlet*, Scott, in one of the master strokes of the novel, brings the half-crazed Peter Peebles, with his legal jargon and his utter indifference to anything except his own needs and problems, into conversation with Redgauntlet himself. Peter's brash accosting of the fanatical Jacobite is true comedy—*critical* comedy, which both amuses and exposes.

Redgauntlet is perhaps best known to the general reader for the inset "Wandering Willie's Tale." Wandering Willie himself represents the fate of the old feudal retainer in the modern world. In the days when the Redgauntlets were feudal lairds, Willie had his function, his social position, and his economic security. Now he is a wandering beggar. The violent breakup of Scotland's long-lingering feudal pattern after the '45 was in most ways a good thing, yet it broke down that paternal relationship between master and vassal which Scott could not help sighing after, and which in some degree he tried to re-create between himself and his servants at Abbotsford. Darsie Latimer, discussing with his sister the unlikelihood of Redgauntlet's former tenants rallying to his cause at this time of day, significantly remarks: "Whatever these people may pretend, to evade your uncle's importunities, they cannot, at this time of day, think of subjecting their necks again to the feudal yoke, which was effectually broken by the Act of 1748, abolishing vassalage and hereditary jurisdictions." The relation between Wandering Willie and his master in the old days, however emotionally satisfying to contemplate, also represented a "feudal yoke." Here again the ambivalence of Scott's attitude to past and present reveals itself.

"Wandering Willie's Tale" is, of course, closely linked with the main theme of the novel. A brilliantly told story of the relation between a violent old feudal landlord and his piper and tenant, with enough of the supernatural brought in to give it the air of an old Scottish folk tale yet enough shrewd and humorous realism to make it also a *critical* piece about master-servant relations in old Scotland, it occupies a central position in the story. The piper was Wandering Willie's grandfather, and the lairds concerned were ancestors of

Darsie Latimer and his uncle Redgauntlet—Sir Robert Redgauntlet and his son. In telling the tale to Darsie (who, as the heir of the Redgauntlets is, though neither of them knows it at this stage, Wandering Willie's master if the feudal pattern is to be preserved), Willie is acting as a minstrel to his lord; yet he is but a wandering minstrel, picked up by chance by Darsie in his aimless travels. The tale involves the violence of the Scottish heroic past, but that violence is in the telling filtered through a shrewd and unromantic mind. It is also, of course, a perfect piece of storytelling in itself, a model of how to tell a tale dealing with the supernatural (allowing alternative, nonsupernatural explanations, if the reader wishes to accept them, for all but one or two details), the perfect counterpart in prose, from the point of view of technique though not of content, of Burns' "Tam o' Shanter."

The language of the tale is a racy eighteenth-century Scots. The tradition of Scots literary prose was quite dead by the eighteenth century; there had been a revival of Scots poetry, but the novel came too late to rescue Scots prose. The only way in which Scots could now be effectively used in literature was through dialogue, and Scott made the most of his opportunity here. The dialogue of his "low" characters—always so much livelier and more convincing that his formal heroes and heroines—contains some of the finest Scots of the century. "Wandering Willie's Tale," being an oral tale put into the mouth of a wandering minstrel, is told in a racy spoken Scots. It was a device to enable Scott to use more Scots in his novel than he would otherwise have found possible; it never occurred to him to endeavor to restore a literary Scots prose by a deliberate conflation of dialects and standard English (as in some degree Burns did with Scots verse) and write his novels in that idiom. When Scott speaks in his own person in the novels he uses standard English, except for an occasional "Scotticism" of which he was unaware. After all, he aimed at an English audience.

The main defect of *Redgauntlet*, as of so many of Scott's novels, even his greatest, is that he uses the conventional plot patterns available to him to provide the external structure of his story, and these plot patterns are really quite unsuitable to the kind of exploration of the relation between tradition and progress which he is carrying out. Green Mantle, for all her autobiographical overtones, is just a nuisance; the love interest is perfunctory and unnecessary, and the theme of the lost and rediscovered heir (though handled here better and more organically than anywhere else in Scott) really otiose. Even a character like Nanty Ewart, the former student of divinity who goes to the dogs after carelessly ruining a girl, comes from the

sentimental tradition of the late eighteenth century and has no business in this novel at all. And the Dickensian complications and reso-
lutions of the plot, though done with considerable adroitness, are
somewhat mechanical.

The real greatness of *Redgauntlet* lies in its dramatic investigation
through the interrelations of the appropriate characters of the validity and implications of different attitudes to Scotland's past and
present. Nowhere else is this favorite theme of Scott's presented with
such vitality and power. This vitality is felt even in the most ordinary of domestic scenes—those describing the relation of Saunders
Fairford to his son, for example, which are genuinely moving in
virtue of the fully realized treatment of dialogue and action. Between sober routine and romantic melodrama, between daily domestic and professional life and the flamboyant crisis, between living in the world as it is and living in the world of the obsessed
imagination, lies a whole gamut of attitudes and experiences. In
creating a story which runs this gamut and explores all the crucial
points on it, Scott has written a kind of historical novel very different from what the historical novel is generally taken to be. He
shows that attitudes toward history and attitudes toward the
present depend on one another, and both depend on the character
of the man who has the attitude, and that in turn depends in part
on environment which in turn is the product of history. We cannot
escape from the past, for it has created us; yet we must escape from
the past if we are to live in the real world. The antiquarian can only
write books; he cannot re-enact the past he writes about. And in a
profound sense, that for Scott was a tragic insight.

J. G. Lockhart (1794–1854), Scott's son-in-law and biographer, had
a career as a literary journalist which is in some respects symbolic
of the Scottish man of letters of the period. With John Wilson, he
made the Tory *Blackwood's Magazine* famous for its vigor and liveliness. It was here that the notorious attacks on Keats and Leigh
Hunt were launched, in the articles entitled "On the Cockney School
of Poetry." Lockhart (who wrote these and other articles anonymously and whose contributions cannot always be disentangled
from those of his colleagues) was motivated by political as well as
literary principles: the former were strongly Tory and the latter an
odd mixture of German Romanticism and English neoclassicism.
His sketches of Edinburgh life and society in *Peter's Letters to his
Kinsfolk* (1819) are full of life and color. He possessed a saturnine
wit, a cogent prose style, and an ability to direct all the force of his
mind on the question at issue. He moved to London in 1824 to become editor of another Tory magazine, the *Quarterly Review,* and the

transition showed how little he was rooted in any distinctively Scottish culture. His *Life of Scott* is, however, suffused with a sense of Scott's deep relationship with Scottish history and the Scottish countryside, and it is this which provides what might be called the emotional rhythm of the book. Lockhart at Edinburgh was deeply involved with the legal-literary professional atmosphere of that city, an atmosphere which represented perhaps the last significant aspect of Scottish national culture. But, in spite of some flashes, he was not able to make significant literary capital out of it. One can distinguish certain Scottish features in all Lockhart's work, but his country could provide no proper soil in which his talents could take root. His literary intelligence remained curiously disembodied.

A novelist who had begun writing Scottish novels of manners before the appearance of *Waverley* (though none was published until afterward) and who was later encouraged by Scott's example, was John Galt (1779–1839), whose pictures of Scottish life in small town and country (often in his native Ayrshire) show a deliberate attempt to exploit, in dialogue and situation, the humors of Scottish character. The dialogue in his best novels—*The Ayrshire Legatees* (1821), *Annals of the Parish* (1821), *The Provost* (1822), *The Entail* (1823)— is based on the spoken Scots vernacular of the region, and though Galt deliberately searched for picturesque idioms to introduce into his novels, with the result that he sometimes has the air of exhibiting Scottish provincial characters for the amusement of the English reader, he had a clear perception of the shifts in social and economic atmosphere resulting from the development of the Industrial Revolution, and his careful observation of middle-class manners and patterns of thought and feeling produces some attractive writing. Though he skirts the sentimental, he actually moves into it less often than one expects, and can be drily matter-of-fact (as in the execution scene in *The Provost*) as well as conventionally "pawky." Nevertheless, Galt seems to be in doubt as to whether he is exhibiting or seriously interpreting his characters; this is the result of the confused state of Scottish culture and the mingling of contradictory attitudes to Scotland in the country at this period. David Macbeth Moir's *Autobiography of Mansie Waugh* (1828) exploits the humors of life and character in a Scottish country town in a manner rather like Galt, but with more obviously comic intent. After that, the sentimentalizing of Scottish humor and Scottish provincial life proceeded apace, to culminate later in the century in Barrie's *Auld Licht Idylls* (1888) and *A Window in Thrums* (1889), S. R. Crockett's *The Stickit Minister* (1893), and *Beside the Bonnie Brier Bush* (1894), by "Ian Maclaren" (John Watson). This is the "kailyard school" of Scottish fiction, which flourished for generations, and against which the first real blow was struck with George Douglas Brown's *House with the Green Shutters* (1901), a grimly realistic novel of the moral squalor of life in a Scottish provincial town.

The only other nineteenth-century writer of importance who can be considered Scottish in the cast of his mind and the sources of his imagination is Robert Louis Stevenson; but the context of his literary career was almost wholly English and his work must be considered in the broader context of English literature. To all intents and purposes, serious Scottish themes were throughout the nineteenth century treated by Scottish writers, either at home or in London, in order to provide sentimental caricatures of Scottish character in works which lacked all vestige of literary integrity. It was left for the twentieth century to try and revive a genuine, self-respecting Scottish literature.